PUBLIC INTERNATIONAL LAW

PUBLIC
INTERNATIONAL
LAW

by

Branimir M. Janković

TRANSNATIONAL PUBLISHERS, INC.
Dobbs Ferry, New York

Library of Congress Cataloging in Publication Data

Janković, Branimir M.
  Public international law.

  Translation of: Medunarodno javno pravo.
  1. International law. I. Title.
JX3695.Y8J31513 1983   341   83-9155
ISBN 0-941320-16-2

Manufactured in the United States of America

FOR MY FATHER MIODRAG AND MOTHER LJUBICA

Contents

PART ONE – SUBJECTS   77

CHAPTER ONE: STATES

CHAPTER TWO: INTERNATIONAL ORGANIZATIONS

CHAPTER THREE: MAN AS A SUBJECT OF INTERNATIONAL LAW

PART TWO — LEGAL REGULATION OF INTERNATIONAL RELATIONS

CHAPTER ONE: ORGANS OF INTERNATIONAL RELATIONS

CHAPTER TWO: INTERNATIONAL ACTS

CHAPTER THREE: PEACEFUL SETTLEMENT OF DISPUTES AND THE SAFEGUARDING OF PEACE

MEANS OF A PEACEFUL SETTLEMENT OF DISPUTES

CHAPTER FOUR: INTERNATIONAL CONFLICTS

Preface

While lecturing at many universities all over the world, I became aware of the need for a text book on international law. Many of my former students, today professors of law and international relations, lawyers, statesmen and diplomats, on many occasions expressed the wish to have my text book available in the English language to be used by them both in their present occupations as well as in their future professional and research work. This book is primarily dedicated to them. Of course, it will serve all those who are interested in this legal discipline.

I wish to express my particular gratitude and appreciation to my friends, Mrs. Margot and Mr. Boško Milosavljević, who translated my work into the English language from the fifth Serbocroatian edition. Their great understanding and knowledge of both languages and their general culture will contribute to the understanding of problems and institutions of contemporary international law.

I also wish to express my sincere thanks to Mrs. Domenika Delic, translator, Mrs. Vera Los, secretary, and Mrs. Živka Stojković, librarian, my collaborators in the Center for International Studies at Belgrade, for their valuable contribution in preparing this text for publication.

Special appreciation is due Mrs. Heike Fenton, distinguished international publisher, for her assistance in publishing *Public International Law* in the English language.

I also wish to express my sincere thanks to the editor of this distinguished publishing house, Mrs. Marjorie Moore, for her efforts and attention in preparing the text for publication.

B.M.J.

Introduction

I. Concept

*Appellation — Definition — Designation of Subjects —
Sphere of Operation — Interest as the Essence of Relations
among Subjects of International Law — The Legal Nature
of International Law*

1. Appellation — International Law (law of nations, droit international, Völkerrecht, mezhdunarodnoe pravo) traces its origin back to the Roman *jus gentium,* although this term referred to a uniform national legal system which could be applied to foreigners as well as to Romans, in contrast to *jus civile,* the Roman civil law which was only applicable to Roman citizens.

Indeed, it was more proper to speak of a law of states rather than law of nations prior to the emergence of modern-day democratic states in which the people began to take an active role in directing the course of international relations. Today, the term international law is far more accurate and implies a much broader concept than law of states, which in the modern system of international law nevertheless holds an important place because of that special attribute of states known as state sovereignty. This distinction of terms was particularly justified after the Second World War, when an international rather than inter-governmental organization was created in San Francisco in 1945. It promulgated what was in effect the first international constitution, the Charter of the United Nations, which opens with the words, "We, the peoples of the United Nations . . ." rather than "We, the high contracting parties . . ."

2. Definition — Public international law regulates the relations of its subjects by means of rules of law.

As we break this definition down into its various parts, we must define the

1

subjects of international law, the subject matter of their relations, and the legal nature of the rules of this branch of law.

3. Sphere of Operation — The subjects of international law are those exercising rights and duties in international relations. This is the broadest interpretation of the definition of a subject in international law. Various writers have tried to identify the subjects of international law more closely. There are, broadly speaking, two schools of thought. The classical view is that only states are subjects in international law. According to this view, states are governed by international law, just as individuals are governed by the legal system within a state. This view is still being propounded by some theorists today, for instance by Redslob. The second school of thought is diametrically opposed to the classical theory, asserting that individuals are true subjects of law in general, and by the same token of international law. According to spokesmen for this view, a right can be exercised through a free and conscious expression of will, and only human beings are capable of this, regardless of on whose behalf they act (Duguit, Politis, Scelle).

Both these theories go to extremes. States undeniably have rights and duties, but they are not alone in this, as we shall see. International organizations may also have rights and duties. And certainly the individual is today gaining increasing rights and duties, not just because man is able to express his will freely and consciously, but because the complex international life in today's world imposes certain duties upon him — no matter what country he may belong to — and democratic developments endow him with certain rights. Similarly, peoples and states possess various means of making their will known, and undoubtedly these include legal instruments.

The rapid development of present-day international relations is responsible for the expansion of the sphere of operation of international law. Today it is more proper to speak of the *extent* of rights and duties of various subjects of international law than of the different nature of legal subjects. For this reason, Bartos, for instance, prefers to analyze the scope of modern international law rather than the legal nature of those to whom it applies. However, this does not mean that we cannot speak of the character of subjectivity in a discussion of various international subjects, which Bartos also does. In our discussion, then, we should consider not just states as subjects of international law, but should put all subjects who are vested with international rights and duties in whatever capacity under one general heading. This heading would be called *Subjects* and would include states, international organizations and individuals as possessing rights and duties under international law.

4. Interest as the Subject Matter of Relations Among the Subjects of International Law — Interest is the subject matter of relations among the subjects of public international law. The interests of a state include the possession or exploitation of territory, inland waterways, the sea, or air space, or the pursuit of its internal or foreign activities. A resource may be used in part or totally. The internal activity of a state may be a matter of no concern for other states, or it may harm or jeopardize the interests of some other state, or even the interest of the international community as a whole. The foreign activity of a state, including even its declaration of intent, may be in accordance with or contrary to the interests of another state or several states. Clashing interests, caused by a state's foreign activity or declared intention, may give rise to an international dispute, which may bring about a bilateral or multilateral conflict. However, even if there is a harmony of interests between two or more states, a dispute may arise over the ways and means of pursuing a common interest, and this dispute may even touch off an international conflict between such states. A dispute of this kind may be caused by a state's action or its failure to act.

Every international dispute or conflict is a result of clashing interests implicit in the demand by one state for the maintenance of a given situation, or for another state, several states or the international community as a whole, to satisfy its interests. Similarly, several states or the international community may make such a demand upon one state. The world community may consider itself entitled to impose the question of its own, *general interests,* upon a state or several states, and to demand that the common interest be served, which in this instance would appear as an *overriding* interest in terms of general progress or regression in the development of mankind.

A conflict of interests is factually resolved if one interest prevails over another. The resolution of conflicts of interest between two or more states may be temporary or permanent. The imposition of a demand, even if it has already been stated, revives the conflict of interests. One interest has prevailed over the other if the demand for the latter to be met is withdrawn. The same holds true if the opposing side renounces a counterdemand.

It is important how an interest is to be satisfied. There are different rules of conduct of states in their relations with one another and in the community of nations as a whole. Throughout the history of international relations, rules of conduct with a religious interest prevailed. The so-called rules of conduct of an ethical nature were very vague and comprised a multitude of contradictory interests, since the notion of morals was far from clear in relations between states. Customary or conventional rules of conduct have been in various periods of time a fairly established code of international relations. Legal rules of conduct are of a special nature. They are able to adjust two or more interests, regardless of whether it partially satisfies their proponents or leaves them completely dissatisfied.

There are two kinds of grounds for propounding the interests of an international entity. These are *legal* and *political* grounds. If a currently effective international rule is cited in arguments for or against a given demand, and if a dispute arises thereupon, the grounds for the demand are of a legal nature. The reference to any other criteria brings political considerations into play.

The distinction between political and legal grounds is technically useful, for it determines the course of action to be taken on a dispute, be it political or legal. However, to make this distinction a fundamental one would inevitably lead to a formalistic and one-sided treatment of the dispute. Any emphasis on a particular situation being at variance with a rule of law has a clear political bias. Otherwise, such a demand would be absurd. Similarly, every demand by an international entity, motivated by political considerations, must be made in some kind of form. Opportunism which lies at the root of any such demand dictates the choice of one or more forms which may seem most suitable at a given moment.

5. The Legal Nature of International Law — Although there are few today who challenge the legal nature of international law, we should nevertheless take a brief look at their arguments, for the question is still sometimes raised whether international law is a legal or quasi-legal discipline. It is not the negation of international law that is the purpose of these sceptics, since their postulates are widely divergent, but that is the most frequent upshot of their general philosophical or legal reasoning.

The notion of "might makes right" was already familiar to the Greek Sophists. In his first book, *Republic,* Plato ascribes this view to Thrasymachus. Thucydides wrote his *History of the Peloponnesian War* in the same vein. Machiavelli in one of his political tracts, and Spinoza in a theological-political pamphlet, equated law with brute force. Later these ideas were transferred to the sphere of international law. The German philosopher Lasson, influenced by Hegelian ideas on the state, felt that relations between states are governed by certain rules of law only inasmuch as they are subject to the internal laws of the state. The basic assumption for such a view is that state sovereignty is absolute, there being no other authority above it. In Lasson's opinion, it is egoism that prompts states to conclude treaties in order to coordinate their interests; however, the rules contained therein do not have a legal character but rather reflect the most common considerations of power. According to him, treaties are the products of political shrewdness compounded with political opportunism. War, according to Hegel and Lasson, is cultural selection, and war releases the so-called "absolute spirit," which is reflected in victory or defeat.

This German legal philosopher constructed his theories on Hegel's philosophy, but Gumplowicz and two others, Lundstedt and Olivecrona, arrived at similar conclusions albeit by different routes. Gumplowicz is a sociologist. His models are Darwin and Spenser. Life, according to him, consists of struggle between primitive and differentiated groups. Law is a body of rules promulgated by the public authority to maintain order in society and reflect the balance of forces among the elements constituted by a given group. Since there is no organization of sanctions, international law in his view is not law but rather a collection of those usages which states observe when they are at peace with one another. However, while Lasson holds out no future for international law, Gumplowicz does not rule out the possibility of the development of international law, since he is a believer in the historical evolution of human society.

Lundstedt and Olivecrona are what might be described as "pure" jurists. They made a thorough study of internal legal regulations, particularly systems of private law, and were disappointed at the conclusions they were forced to make, in respect both to law in general and to international law. According to Lundstedt, law is a "compact metaphysical mass burdened by fictions and fetishes." In its internal life, a state works on the principle of coercion, and the same is true of international relations. Hence it is quite impossible to speak of international law, since, according to him, there is not even any law within the frontiers of a state. The other writer, Olivecrona, has not quite given himself over to Lundstedt's complete despair, but he is not very far from it. Although he has no quarrel with the practical significance of international rules, since he cannot conceive of, say, international trade without them, he still cannot recognize international law as law, for in his opinion it lacks the effective psychological motives which are present in an organized state, i.e. the social sense of the wielders of power, who act in concert.

Without dwelling on the incorrect postulates of philosophical notions or half-baked sociology, we should note that the roots of such views of international law are dualistic and diverse. Certain theorists began to view with growing suspicion the vulnerability of international law and even wondered whether this legal science could exist at all in the absence of an international organization which could ensure sanctions for its rules, or in the presence of international political opportunism which challenges the existence of fixed basic principles of international law.

Prior to the rise of absolutism, the smallness of states in Europe ruled out the feasibility of a universal regulation of relations among states. In the era of the formation and rise of large empires, international relations were the prerogative of absolutist rulers. The European congresses of the nineteenth century, which were thought to be creating the international law of that time, were actually convened more to regulate the world interests of the great powers than to lay down any new principles. The Berlin Congress of 1878 rode roughshod over the rights of many peoples to accommodate the interests of the six great powers of the time. From a subjective standpoint, many writers, particularly German legal theorists, even up to the national socialist writers on international law, insisted on an external law of the state, denying an international

and legal character of this discipline, mainly in order to justify the political actions of their state.

Wherever this negativistic note is sounded today, it is always in conjunction with political developments (Burdean) which are often given subjective interpretations (Valine) to support or justify some modern policy of aggression,
whatever form it might take.

Not far removed from the doctrinaire theorists, who see international law
as a means of wielding power, are some less radical thinkers who dispute its
legal nature by interchanging the question of morals with that of law. It was
Hobbes who emphasized that states could not comply with non-existent rules of
law, but only with moral obligations. John Austin further elaborated the
theory of moral obligation. His influence is still being felt today in the Anglo-
Saxon world. Similar views can be found in Puchta, the Frenchman Gérard de
Rehinval, and among more recent writers in Julius Binder, for whom the meaning of international life resides in a community based on a sense of ethics from
which only ethical rules can derive. The international jurist Somlo, who was at
first a positivist in legal philosophy, later to become a neo-Kantian, put forward
the view that international law was a body of rules having no legal basis, since
they were not the result of a legal system, for there could be no legal rules without a legal order.

These last two views have misgivings about international law owing to the
absence of an international community and of sanctions. The argument that
there is no international law-making body was hard to support even when it
was first advanced, since even then there was an international comity which,
in the words of Triyol, ensured an order in human relations, and it still plays an
important role today, in the more advanced forms of legal life. Custom may be
enforced in addition to positive law and at the same time have an imperative
character. A theory gaining popularity is that the General Assembly of the
United Nations is for all practical purposes becoming a kind of international
law-making body, particularly through the system of conventions, which states
can either adhere to or reject, but not discuss. Finally, there is the matter of
sanctions. This is one of the most controversial questions in international relations and in international law. It would seem that the problem is one of the effectiveness of sanctions rather than of their absence. For sanctions do exist,
although they are not nearly as effective as internal sanctions. Measures of reciprocity, the recall of diplomatic representatives, are today coercive measures
recognized by the United Nations and serve the purpose of sanctions, although
it is still debatable whether such instruments do achieve the desired results. At
any rate, those who dispute international law today, are either ignorant of or
blind to the progress that has been made in the legal organization of the modern international community.

Certain writers lump with this view the theory that international law is imperfect, and this theory is even considered a separate doctrine by some. Although their assumptions are similar to the ones held by those who deny international law, they arrive at a different conclusion, namely the legal imperfection of international law.

It would be difficult to build a school of thought around the statement that international law is imperfect. It derives from a feature of international law that is more conspicious in it than in other legal disciplines. If we assume that every legal system has a number of gaps, and since practice is always ahead of the legal norms, and must therefore be constantly brought up to date, then the same assumption must be valid for international law. It is true that there are gaps in international law, perhaps more than in any other branch of law, but it does not make international law anomalous, especially since constant efforts are being made to fill them, although this process is slower than it would be in the internal legal system of a state. Since the number of theorists subscribing to this theory is not small, let us take a closer look at their arguments.

The forerunner of this view was Savigny, according to whom international law was subject to the existence of an international community, such as could be found in Christian Europe, which would create this law on the basis of common nationality and religious system, yet it would still lack the real bases that municipal law had. This view was in substance supported by Wilson, Zittelmann, Burkhardt, and today Lauterpacht, and even Kelsen.

Woodrow Wilson, former U.S. president and Princeton University professor, was largely influenced by Austin when he placed international law somewhere between jurisprudence and ethics, treating it as a series of written legal principles of justice and mutual respect, all deriving from the consciousness of nations. Zittelmann realizes that international law has no sanctions, which diminishes its effectiveness in the enforcement of its rules. And if reprisals or war are considered to be sanctions, then in his opinion the final outcome of such sanctions can never be known with certainty, for there is no way of telling who will ultimately benefit from mutual reprisals, let alone war. The Swiss Burkhardt does not dispute the legal nature of international law but he does not recognize it as being a positive rule of law. In his opinion, international law is indeed law, but not positive law, since the latter depends on the organization which enforces it, and an organization is a necessary prerequiste for legal validity. It is noteworthy that Burkhardt draws a distinction between the conditions for and bases of validity. Whereas an organization is a condition for validity, in his opinion the basis of validity is justice, which is conceived as something that is in accordance with reason. International law, according to this writer, is subjective and customary, devoid of an objectivity or positive import. The British jurists, H. Lauterpacht, explains these thoughts in practical and theoretical terms. According to Kelsen, a legal norm consists of two parts — material and personal. International law has the material element, but not the personal element. Kelsen illustrates this view by the following example: the third Hague Convention of 1907 provided for the declaration of war, but failed to designate the individual or state organ authorized to execute this rule of law. In one of his most recent major works, *Law of Nations,* Kelsen enlarges upon this observation by stating that the general law of nations is characterized by the principle of self-help, and that it is therefore imperfect.

These writers are either citing the imperfect nature of international law so as not to have to deny its existence altogether, or they are simply describing the present state of affairs, for there are undoubtedly still gaps in abundance in international law. But a school of thought or a theory can certainly not be built upon the basis of such reasoning, nor can it be the proper approach to the current trends and institutions in this scientific discipline, particularly since many great powers have deliberately left a number of international relations and developments unregulated in order to leave themselves a freer hand for political action. To accept their practices as a modus operandi might be tantamount to endorsing a certain political behavior by great powers, which has no basis in law.

We hold the view that *international law is a legal discipline, just as every other branch of law.* International law has its own peculiarities, especially because of the sovereignty of states, but then what legal discipline does not?

The existence of differences in the branches of law — and not even the most diehard negators of international law would deny the existence of a number of legal forms in international law — bears witness to their specific character and not to their being devoid of a legal nature.

If a given social activity takes place in an organized form, if there are institutions and rules regulating it, if there are social forces which lay down rules of conduct, then the discipline which deals with this social activity cannot be denied a legal character if it is possessed, in the broadest sense, of material and legal sources, legal elements of social organization, numerous legal institutions and rules of law. And international law certainly has all of these.

The question of the effectiveness of rules in international law and in other systems of law is properly a question of their characteristics and cannot be a reason for denying their legal character.

All branches of the law have rules which are effective or less effective. (Take constitutional law in general, for instance, where rules of law have no sanctions). The same holds true for international law. If it has more than its share of ineffective rules, it is a sign that these rules differ in practice and not that they are not binding as legal elements of a social rule. If the question of how the legislating body is raised, the answer is that there has always been some body of this kind in international relations. There has always been a law-maker in international law, whether rules of international law were established from customary law or by the U.N. General Assembly. Our consideration of international law and its specific characteristics which follows will bear out the correctness of this view.

II. Classification

Public International Law and Private International Law — General and Particular International Law in Peace and in War — Special Branches of International Law

1. Public International Law and Private International Law

— Analogous to the general division into private and public law, international law has also been divided into private and public international law. Relations between states subject to private law are regulated by private international law, while public international law deals with those relations which are governed by public law. Some writers hold that private international law is only a branch of municipal law, applied outside the country. A variant of this view holds that private international law was once part of the private law of states, but in the course of time has grown into a separate legal discipline, which is neither a part of municipal law nor a part of public international law.

Private international law is increasingly becoming a part of the system of public international law. First of all, both public international law and private international law regulate the conduct of international relations. Their disparity caused them to split, but they are not two separate laws justifying a division into two legal disciplines. Secondly, there is an increasing number of legal sources of private international law which are in common with public international law (contracts, customs). Thirdly, the rights of individuals which were previously protected by private international law are becoming rights recognized in public international law. As the sphere of operation of public international law expands, international law as a whole is taking on greater cohesiveness and scope. Fourthly, the prime concern of private international law, conflict of laws, is increasingly acquiring a political basis, which is to say a basis in public law. In determining where the two spheres overlap, states are largely motivated by their own interests. In regard to purchase and sales contracts, for instance, writers, according to Briggs, champion the law with which the contract has its closest factual link, and this, as he so rightly points out, means letting the ruling class determine what is in its best interests.

Since a distinction is still made between public and private international law, we shall confine our consideration to the customary subject matter of public international law.

2. Universal and Particular International Law — A distinction is often drawn between universal international law and particular (regional) international law.

Universal international law contains general legal rules which apply to the entire international community. In the legal systems of the colonial powers we often come across the term "universal international law of civilized nations," as contrasted with uncivilized nations — i.e. the colonies — which are governed only by the law decreed, by the metropolis, despite the fact that some colonies had advanced civilizations. This division into civilized and uncivilized nations no longer applies today, and the distinction between international law of civilized and that of other nations has been abandoned. The universal international law of civilized nations has been replaced by the legal system of the United Nations, which is becoming more nearly universal every day, since it is drawing upon the legal precedents of a large number of civilizations.

Particular law, according to this division, refers to a certain number of states, while regional law refers to a number of states in geographical proximity. Thus, for instance, American law is of a regional nature. More is now being heard about the emergence of Asian law, and most recently of the regional law of African states.

3. International Law in Peace and in War — The distinction between international law in peacetime and in wartime is classical. This distinction is avoided today, not just because some rules of peacetime international law remain in force during war, but mainly because today war can no longer be a means of enforcing some international right. The word "war" is not even present in the United Nations Charter. Rules of law contained in the Charter fall under the category of universal international law. On the other hand, it would be unreasonable to exclude war from the system of international law. Therefore, war will be discussed in the second part of this study, which deals with the legal regulation of international relations, as well as in the section on international conflicts, which should be ended by legal means, or failing this, at least mitigated by the rules of international law which pertain to armed conflicts between states. (During the Korean War, for instance, the belligerents accused each other of not abiding by the so-called "laws of war.")

4. Special Branches of International Law — The rapid development of international communications created the need for the expansion of rules of international law. Thus came into being some of the special branches of

international law, e.g. international transport law (railways, air transport, river transport, road transport, maritime transport, postal services, etc.), international criminal law, international law of medicine, international atomic law, and most recently international law on outer space. The general principles of international law continue to apply to these special branches of international law.

III. Municipal and International Law

With the development of international relations, or perhaps we should say with the growth and consolidation of the family of nations, the concept of the relationship between the internal law of states and international law has undergone a theoretical and practical evolution. The tendency for either municipal or international law, or various combinations of the two, to take precedence is still in evidence today as states seek to attain their purposes which may or may not be in the general interest.

The primacy of the municipal law of a state is due to its being a recognized system which governs the legal order within a particular country. The precedence of municipal law rests on the idea of absolute state sovereignty, whatever legal arguments may be mustered to justify it.

An opposite school of thought gives primacy to international rather than municipal law. According to this view, the international community is vested with an authority which is above the people who live in a given territory and, according to Kelsen, it is derived from the hypothesis of a "basic norm" in international law (Ursprungshypothese des Völkerrechts), or takes as its source a kind of "spiritual value," such as a sense of justice (Le Fur), a sense of right (Krabbe), or a legal consciousness (Duguit).

The increasing complexity of relations between states has prompted theoreticians to try a different approach in considering the relationship between municipal and international law.

The dualist theory holds that international law and the internal law of states are two completely separate realms. This theory was advanced by Triepel and developed by the Italian jurists Anzilotti and Cavaglieri. According to them, municipal law differs from international law in regard to their subjects — municipal law governs individuals, while international law is binding on states, and in regard to sources — in municipal law the material source is the will of the state, whereas in international law it is the collective will of states. Thus these relationships engender rules of law which are different in character. These are two legal orders which exist side by side, but which are alien to one another; each order has its own special rules of law.

In contrast, the monist doctrine considers municipal law to be law delegated by international law. In the opinion of its theorists, the two together form a single legal order. International law is thus indistinguishable from the internal law of states and is of significance only as part of the universal legal order. Various writers interpret the universal order in different ways. These differences stem from the general theoretical concept of international law as a universal legal system.

This matter is also regulated in different ways in the constitutions of modern states.

According to the 1947 French Constitution, international treaties are given a higher legal force than internal laws; their provisions may not be abrogated, changed or terminated without advance notice, which must be given through diplomatic channels (Art. 28). Furthermore, international treaties which have been ratified and promulgated do not need special statutes to ensure their application (Art. 26). Article 27 of this constitution enumerates the treaties that must be ratified by law, such as treaties on international organizations, peace treaties, trade agreements, treaties involving state finances or personal or property rights of French citizens abroad, those affecting internal French laws, as well as treaties which concern the concession, exchange or annexation of territory. Article 6 of the U.S. Constitution gives equal legal validity to the internal and international orders in the phrase "the Supreme Law of the land," which includes the Constitution, the law in accordance with it, and treaties which were made or would be made by the United States. According to British practice, international treaties and customary international law take precedence if they are not at variance with an act of Parliament or a provision of the common law. Article 10 of the Italian Constitution promulgated in 1948, states that the legal order of Italy shall be brought into accordance with the universally recognized rules of international law.

If internal law is given precedence in every instance, it ultimately means giving priority to the absolute sovereignty of states, which would lead to a one-sided realization of individual interests, possibly jeopardizing the interests of other international subjects.

Should international law then be given priority? The first question that immediately arises is which international law, since international law is not a body of timeless categories. And the fact is that international life evolves through the contention and cooperation of states, peoples, social and political movements, etc. There is no denying that in this struggle the strongest obtain privileged positions for themselves. To lose sight of this fact would mean acknowledging at certain times the most rights to the strongest states. In this *de facto* and legal situation, the smaller states are wary of demands to grant primacy to high generalized and hence undefined international law.

IV. Sources

Conception — Material Sources — Formal Sources

1. Conception — Sources in international law are understood to be the means by which rules of international law are created and their application secured. In legal theory, sources are classified as material or formal. Material sources are found in the social force which creates various legal forms. A rule of law expresses a specific social relationship which in theory is interpreted in different ways. The body of rules of law, grouped according to a common criterion, represents the formal source. According to Article 38 of the Statute of the International Court of Justice, which is an integral part of the U.N. Charter, formal sources are international conventions, international custom as evidence of general legal practice, general principles of law recognized by civilized nations, judicial decisions, and finally, the writings of jurists. The Court may also decided *ex aequo et bono,* according to its understanding of justice and right, regardless of legal regulations, if authorized to do so by the parties to a dispute. However, theorists also disagree as to the number and kind of formal sources. But let us first examine material sources.

2. Material Sources — To find the material sources of a legal discipline is to discover its nature. The views of western international law theorists on material sources can be roughly placed into two groups, and according to some writers (*e.g.* Redslob), they are called the main theories. The first group considers law in its "ideal" form, whereas the second approaches it in terms of its contractual nature. The roots of the first conception lie in the doctrine of natural law, and of the second in the positivist school, although many views on this subject have gone far beyond the basic rules of these two schools. Perhaps this division will be more clear if we quote Kant's distinction between natural and positive law, which served the majority of writers in discussing this problem. According to Kant, natural law is the law which is integrally based on *a priori* principle, whereas positive law is the result of legislative regulation.

The so-called ideal law is nothing more than a compendium of ethical precepts, which prescribe a manner of behavior. According to Redslob, it is law based on beliefs rooted in the hearts of individuals. The Anglo-Saxon theory of international law is based on such a view. Scelle draws a distinction between morals and ethics. According to him, ethics are not morals, but rather a sense of good or social evil, a distinction which is based on intuition and also the criterion of whether something is in accordance with or contrary to social solidarity.

The second doctrine is of a contractual character in that it leaves it up to states to regulate their relations in a way which is in accordance with their will. The will of states generates the rule of law which is binding on their subjects. This is the authority which adopts the legal rule, which enforces it and on which its social or international survival depends. This concept was adopted by the Permanent Court of International Justice when it expressly decreed that international law regulated relations between independent states, and that international rules, which are supplied by states, derived from the wills of those who manifested them in conventions, international customs or general principles of law.

In view of the definition given above, which introduces the element of objective interest into the concept of international law, the question arises how this conception squares up with the theories outlined earlier.

The *general interest* of the international community contains no elements of ideal law conceived from the standpoint of Christian doctrine, since the interest of individuals cannot be identified with their sense of right and wrong. A person's conscience might dictate one course of action, while his interests require something altogether different. Hence, even from a subjective standpoint, the ability to distinguish between good and evil is not identical with personal interest. There is even less likelihood that the general interest would correspond to a vague idea of "general moral principles" as propounded in much of the western literature on international law. If "general moral principles" are a collection of prospects of Christianity, such morals are not of a general nature since there are other moral concepts, of a religious and even an anti-religious character.

Hence the *general interest* is far more comprehensive, aside from the fact that its content differs from the essence of so-called "general morality." The general interest is not merely a guiding idea in the development of the international community. If the general interest were to be no more than that, perhaps in its practical realization it could bring these two elements together. However, the *general interest* is something more; it is *the result of progressive efforts in the domain of universal social aspirations.* This resultant produces new components which must be guided by experiences of the moment but must at the same time engender new forces and new ideas and new components which will all meet in a common focus. Then a picture will be discernible of whether the road that has been covered was in the direction of general progress, whether it was the most direct way, or perhaps the wrong road, wrong in the sense that it led backwards, or if it generated a force which will slow down or completely halt the progress of the international community. For this reason the general interest is not a category of determined and therefore immutable elements. It is a social force which in specific times and places requires a number of political, or legal, forms and in changed situations requires modified or completely new forms. This social force is imbued with a *dynamic* content. If the view is taken that evolution of the law is a constant and necessary part of social and, by the same token, international life, it will again be found that the general interest is a dynamic social force, as the so-called function of the legal order makes provision in its normative rules of law for their modification, so that law in general, and particularly international law, has an expressly dynamic nature.

It has been said that theorists do not agree on the number of formal legal sources. We should point out here that our foregoing discussion of sources of international law injects an important consideration in this division. This division into material and formal sources of law may be maintained from a technical standpoint. However, there is no formal source of law which can be given a practical, or even theoretical, assessment unless due consideration is given to that social force which has been responsible for the acceptance and application of a concrete formal source. Let us first take a look at the legal sources as enumerated in the Statute of the International Court of Justice.

3. Formal Sources — international treaties and international custom are the main sources of international law. An *international treaty* is a legal act by which international subjects whose wills coincide regulate their interests, with the intention of bringing about the effects provided for by principles of international law. Many treaties concluded by international subjects are not a source of international law. Often trade agreements need not affect the interests of the international community. Regulation of commercial interests may be the concern of two states alone. However, even though bilateral treaties are binding only on the two parties which have concluded them and do not represent a law for the international community, they are an expression of the interests of these states within the limits of international rules on the conclusion of treaties. They would be a kind of legal act on the basis of international law. However, if identical provisions figure in a number of bilateral treaties, then they are evidence that these legal acts have become a reflection of the international standard and thereby enter international law as a criterion of what is normal in bilateral relations under international law. In French legal literature treaties which regulate present or future situations between states are called *traités-contrats* as opposed to *traités-lois,* treaties which regulate a specific general interest by laying down rules of law. The latter would include, for instance, the Hague Conventions of 1899 and 1907, the Covenant of the League of Nations, etc. Some writers include the United Nations Charter in this type of treaty as well. By virtue of its form, the U.N. Charter certainly deserves a place among treaty laws. However, in its essence the Charter is something more; it has features of an international constitution. Even in practice, there is a tendency to apply the principles from the Charter not only to member countries, but also to countries which do not belong to the United Nations.

International custom is certainly prior to treaty law. However, the International Court of Justice is obliged first to consider and assess the provisions of the international treaty which is binding on the parties to a dispute, and only then, in the case of doubt about the meaning of the treaty or in the absence of a treaty rule, the Court may investigate and eventually quote international custom, which is necessary as evidence of a general practice accepted as law.

The regulation of interests through practice alone is called international custom. International custom is a tacitly regulated interest where international subjects are aware that such a regulation is to their advantage, and since non-compliance would be to their disadvantage they consider themselves bound to act in a certain way. However, the recognition of obligation in international law should be viewed objectively and not subjectively. It is not necessary for every subject to feel bound; it is enough if a large majority of states consider custom to be a binding rule. If a subjective criterion were to be adopted in international law, then every violator of the international order would be excused because he did not consider himself bound by the rules contained in international custom.

Usage is not the same as international custom. A *modus vivendi* is not international custom. Usage and *modus vivendi* are international practices which are used in the intercourse of countries with no sense of obligation, since the parties do not wish to bind themselves with a mandatory rule but prefer to consider the relationship temporarily regulated. This means that the application of rules of usage is an attempt to regulate the interests of two or more parties. Of course, usage, or *modus vivendi*, or similar practices, whatever they may be called, can after long use prove acceptable to the interested sides and in this way become transformed into international custom, or they may just as easily be abolished unilaterally.

The third source of international law quoted in Article 38 of the Statute is *general principles of law recognized by civilized nations*. These principles have become adopted in a large number of internal legal systems, through acceptance and not on the basis of international practice. Such principles, for instance the rule of *res judicata* on the force of court decisions, the principle that a more recent enactment automatically renders null and void the older one *(lex posterior derogat lex priori)*, that a special regulation has a stronger legal force than a general one *(lex specialis derogat legi generali)*, the principle of the court proceedings on the recusation of judges, on evidence, etc.

It is controversial in legal theory whether this source of law should be classified as international customary law or as an independent source. If general principles were international custom, then it would have been superfluous to mention them in Article 38. Indeed, many modern writers do not quote them at all as a source of international law. However, it is wrong to consider this source as custom because it became a source of international law through the practice of internal legal systems by selection from the laws of other states and not through the international practice of individual states. It can be termed a source of international law, but because of its origin it should be regarded as a subsidiary source.

The application of general principles of law recognized by civilized nations is a separate question. First of all, which "civilized nations?" Many general principles of municipal jurisprudence on the continent are not in accordance with the principles in Anglo-Saxon law, for instance. Furthermore, certain general principles of law in the legal orders of similar or identical social systems may prove to be a serious handicap on the growth of such a social or state organization when applied to another social or government system.

There is also the question of whether a total acceptance of such a defined source of law might not put a brake on dynamic international social development. Instead of promoting international law as having precedence over the sovereignty of individual states which are parties to a dispute, it might have the opposite effect. The application of principles recognized by a certain number of civilized countries, for instance on the acquisition of rights by foreigners, may put a premium on sovereignty as a means of protecting national interests. Of course, we do not mean to challenge the elaboration and application of general principles of law, which would facilitate the realization of the general interest in international relations. For the realization, or application, of these principles, it would be necessary to codify them in some way, or at least to give them a broad definition.

Just as society is constantly changing, so too are general principles of law. At one and the same time we have stable principles, those which the majority of states still recognize, and controversial principles, which conservative social forces view with suspicion, while progressive forces seek to establish them in place of the old ones. As an example we could take the concept of legitimacy and the concept of the right of nations to decide on their own form of government. Both these concepts are general principles of law of civilized nations, but until such time as the latter one gained currency there was a struggle between the two views. After 1917, the question arose whether the rule on the inviolability of private property was a generally recognized legal principle of civilized nations, or whether it was the prerogative of the state to regulate ownership according to its social theory. It was only with the Bolivian resolution in the U.N. General Assembly in 1952 that the majority of states agreed that nationalization of all means of production was a permissible legal institution of every territorial state. It had taken some 35 years for this principle to gain recognition in international law. This long period of acceptance makes this source incontestable, should it ever become controversial, and allows for the possibility of using the same source to promote either reactionary or progressive tendencies.

Judicial decisions and theory were designated in the Statute as subsidiary means for determining the rules of law, in fact, as an indirect source of law. Judicial decisions are a relative source of law, since they may, but need not, depend on the court; they may have the significance of a source for contesting parties but not for third parties. The judicial decisions of a state are binding on persons within the frontiers of the state but cannot represent a source of international law. However, the general effect of similar decisions by the internal courts of various countries should be taken as evidence of international custom. Even though the International Court of Justice can under its statutes use judicial decisions as a source of law only inasmuch as they were made in an earlier dispute between the same litigants, present-day judicial practice gives much weight to jurisprudence. Rejecting judicial decision as a direct source of law, jurisprudence gives it the force of evidence that, in concrete judgements, courts had determined the existence of a certain conception of international customary law or the general principles of international law. If one custom is mentioned and reaffirmed in several forms, then all these decisions taken together are evidence of the existence of this custom. Similarly, if one problem is settled in a certain way in many different decisions by various courts in disputes between different parties, then jurisprudence considers such judgements to be evidence of the existence of general principles of law of civilized nations, deduced from the similarity of all these decisions. Although the Statute of the International Court of Justice gives no authority for such reasoning, it is the established practice of this Court, and it is used to evade the rule on the relative effect of judicial decisions as a source of law only between contesting parties. Judicial decisions have thereby taken on the significance of an objective source and are valid not only as regards the parties to a dispute but in general as regards all subjects of international law, since the Court uses the excuse that it is not bound by such a judgement but is bound by custom and general principle, which are evidenced by reference to them in a number of decisions. This shows that jurisprudence tends to raise judgements to a higher level than prescribed by the Statute (to the level of a general source) and that there is a tendency to equate judicial decisions with customary law.

Legal theory as a source is of importance in influencing judges to accept a given norm or proposed decision. Since there are contradictory views in the writings of jurists, which undoubtedly derive from their respective *milieu* the International Court of Justice at the Hague has expressly avoided citing legal theory in making its judgements. But here, too, there is a roundabout way in which legal theory is recognized as having the force of a source of law. For the judicature, theory does not have the force of a source of law, but it is used as a means of evidence for understanding custom or determining general principles of law. The World Court often quotes the writings of a number of jurists on how a legal custom should be understood. These writers are not law-makers, but they are authoritative witnesses whose works show which rules exist and what their importance is. They are witnesses to law and not to facts. They are experts whose works are compared with the internal law of states and are consulted by the Court on what customs prevail and how they are understood in a particular community.

In a separate paragraph of Article 38 of the Statute, provision is made for a court decision *ex aequo et bono* if the contesting sides give the Court this authorization. The introduction of this possible source into the Statute is a variant on the idea of ethics in international law which we have already discussed. Sibert states that fiction should be considered a source of international law. According to him, there are two kinds of fiction, legal and political or diplomatic. Extraterritoriality is a legal fiction, while the Monroe Doctrine is a fiction having a political character. However, it is debatable whether these are fictions or legal customs of international law expressed in fictions.

Scelle cites unilateral declaration as a normal source of international law, calling it a declaration of the will of one state when it can in this way delimit its own rights as in an international treaty or agreement. In this instance, too, such a declaration may be taken as a source of law.

Unilateral declaration may be a way of regulating certain general interests; as such, even though made unilaterally, it expresses an international rule which tends to have universal application. Lenin's declarations made during the October Revolution fall under this category. Similarly, a multipartite declaration may be a source of international law, with the same purpose of regulating a general interest, such as, for instance, the Moscow Declaration on German War Crimes made public at the end of October 1943, which was taken by all members of the United Nations to be an international law and not a declaration of the policy of three governments.

The decisions of the U.N. General Assembly are of special importance as possible sources of international law, especially in view of the fact that this organ of the United Nations is largely responsible for promoting the general interest of the community of nations. In the very first years of the United Nations' existence, the question was posed, in respect to Franco's Spain, as to what force should be given to the decisions of the General Assembly. There were two main currents of opinion. One was that member countries should recognize the decisions of the General Assembly as having a general binding force, despite the fact that the Charter describes the decisions as recommendations. The other view was that the letter of the Charter should be followed, *viz.* member countries were not under a binding obligation to carry out the recommendations of this organ of the United Nations, as the recommendations did not have a legal nature.

However, according to the spirit of the Charter and its logical interpretation, it would seem that the General Assembly adopts documents possessed of legal elements in all matters pertaining to the internal functioning of the United Nations, and that these acts are generally binding and enforceable. Such acts would include, for instance, elections to all organs of the United Nations, admission to membership or suspension, the conclusion of treaties on behalf of the United Nations, particularly treaties on trusteeship, approval of the budget, the establishment of new organs, ratification of the decisions of other organs, and so forth. However, whereas the General Assembly is sovereign in deciding on matters of internal concern for the United Nations, it does not promulgate any rules of law which would be binding on member countries in their domestic or political activities outside the Organization. Efforts to promote cooperation in the political sphere, to develop and codify international law, and to promote international economic cooperation, are undertaken according to the *recommendations* of the General Assembly, which do not require the strict compliance of states but only prescribe actions which the majority expect states to adopt. Each state decides whether or not to comply with the recommendation. This means that these recommendations are of a political and moral character for all states, while they have a legal character only for the United Nations as an organization and for those states which decide to comply with the recommendation. Thus a recommendation is partly legal and partly political in nature. However, this shows the legal tendency of recommendations. In recent years the opinion has begun to prevail that recommendations which reiterate principles binding on member countries also have a legal character, since their violation would at the same time be a violation of the mandatory principles of law of the Charter. Therefore, we should draw a distinction between three types of recommendations and their three-pronged effect: recommendations for the work of the Organization itself which have a legal force; recommendations which concern the mandatory principles of the Charter, with the legal force of subsidiary sources; and recommendations for the conduct of member countries, which have a political character.

Formal sources are those from which rules may be drawn. They may be direct or indirect. Direct sources contain rules, while indirect sources give evidence of rules. Some are expected to produce effects while others only indicate a desired effect. However, they all serve the same purpose, and that is to show us the substance of international law and the directions of its further development.

V. Codification

Conception — Theoretical Codification — Development of Codification — Codification within the United Nations — Codification of the Principles of Active Peaceful Coexistence

1. Conception — The codification of international law is a collection of regional legal provisions which have been gathered and collated, according to subject, helping to regulate the general interest in the international community. Understood in this sense, codification undoubtedly promotes the progressive development of international law.

But can codification also have a negative effect on the development of this branch of law, considering that the rules of law which are being established can hardly keep pace with the rapid tempo of international life?

Prior to the creation of the United Nations, this misgiving might have been even greater, since codification was left up to individual states, particularly the great powers, much more than is possible today within the United Nations, where moral and political considerations carry far more weight than at a diplomatic conference, where the balance of power was far more important than the collection of rights and obligations contained in international law.

Codification as an international task is today within the competence of the General Assembly of the United Nations, where the great powers do not possess the instruments, e.g. the veto, to hamstring the course of this progressive international activity, even though other, political, means are still available to them in situations where their own interests call for a firm stand of one kind or another. However, it should be pointed out that this misgiving could have been removed even previously by interstate treaties which would thus revise the codified rules, again creating a new undefined legal situation, a new need for regulating the general interest. In view of the practical application of codified rules of international law, it is safe to say that their absence would have been far more detrimental to the interests of the international community as a whole than their existence. Hence we can conclude that codification has for the most part been useful.

If some codified rules promote the interests of one or more powers at the expense of another state, this fact will come to light in the course of time. Harmful consequences may be removed by a demand for revising the matter in question. It is far more dangerous to avoid the obviously necessary codification of some part of international law, as was the case with Great Britain in her bid to regulate naval warfare, or with Germany on the matter of mandatory arbitration in 1907.

2. Theoretical Codification — The idea of codifying international law was launched by philosophers and political and legal writers. The English philosopher Jeremy Bentham was one of the first to advocate the codification of international law, proposing a general codification of all branches of law and of international law in particular. The names of such experts as the Abbé Gregoire, Mille, Ferrater, Kachenovski, Petruschévetz, Field, and Fiore are all familiar in this field. International institutes have also worked on codification, such as the Institut de droit international, founded in 1873, or international professional societies, such as the International Law Association, also founded in 1873. Codification is one of the main purposes of international institutes and associations for international law.

The expert codification does not have the binding force of rules of international law; it presents the opinions of individuals or groups of experts on international law, but the force of their expertise greatly influences the work of formal codification.

3. The Development of Codification — The Vienna Congress of 1815 is considered to have pioneered the codification of international law. Its work included the Declaration against the black slave trade, principles of free navigation on international rivers, contained in Articles 108 through 116 of the Final Act, the proclamation of the permanent neutrality of Switzerland, thus designing a special kind of state, and the rules on the ranking of diplomatic representatives. In 1856, the Paris Declaration on the law of naval warfare established several principles in this sphere. The Paris Peace Treaty of the same year regulated international navigation on the Danube. In 1864, the Geneva Convention was adopted on the protection of the wounded in land warfare, and it was amended in 1868.

Work on the codification of international law picked up momentum in the second half of the nineteenth century, largely at the insistence of the great powers, which were primarily interested in laying down rules of war and armed conflicts. That is why most of the work was done on codifying international laws of war. The establishment of legal conditions helped to humanize war, and for this reason the codification of the rules of international law in this sphere was quite useful, although not as effective as it could have been.

The questions of greatest import in international relations of that time were dealt with by the first and second Hague Conferences, which sought the most suitable legal forms to solve them.

The First Hague Conference convened on May 18, 1899, and was attended by twenty-six delegates from various states. The Conference worked in three commissions. The first commission studied the question of military expenditure and limitation of armaments. The second discussed laws of war, while the third studied the problem of the peaceful settlement of disputes. The conference unanimously adopted three conventions, which were the Convention for the Pacific Settlement of International Disputes, the Convention with respect to the Laws and Customs of War on Land, and the Convention on application of the principles of the Geneva Convention on Naval Warfare of 22 August 1864. Three declarations were also adopted: one under which the signatory states renounced the firing of projectiles and explosives from balloons or other airborne machines in the event of war; the second concerning prohibition of the use of asphyxiating and poisonous gases, and the third, which prohibited the use of dum-dum bullets and similar ammunition. Several resolutions were made: on the revision of the 1864 Geneva Convention, on the rights and duties of neutral powers during wartime, on the limitation of military budgets, on the bombardment of ports and maritime centers, etc. The Convention of 29 July 1899 on the Permanent International Court of Arbitration is of particular importance. According to this convention, the arbiters were not in permanent session; instead, their names were placed on a list, and states were given the opportunity of choosing suitable persons as arbiters in a dispute.

There were forty-four states present at the Second Hague Conference, which sat in four commissions. The first studied problems of arbitration, commissions of enquiry and similar matters; the second studied ways of improving the laws and customs of warfare; the third considered the question of maritime warfare, such as the bombardment of ports, and the laws concerning warships in neutral ports; the fourth considered similar matters, such as the conversion of merchant vessels into warships, private property at sea, contraband, blockade, etc.

Thirteen conventions, one declaration and four resolutions were adopted at this conference. The conventions were on the pacific settlement of international disputes, limitation of the employment of force for the recovery of debts, on the opening of hostilities, on the rules and customs of land warfare, on the rights and duties of neutral powers and persons in land warfare, on the status of enemy merchant ships at the outbreak of hostilities, on the conversion of merchant ships into warships, on the laying of automatic submarine contact mines, on bombardment by naval forces in time of war, on application of the principles of the Geneva Convention to war on sea, on the exercise of the right of capture in war on sea, on the establishment of an international prize court and on the rights and duties of neutral powers in maritime war. The declaration concerned the prohibition of the discharge of projectiles and explosives from balloons. However, Germany, France, Italy, Russia, and indeed all the great powers with the exception of Great Britain and Austria-Hungary, refused to sign this declaration. The resolutions *(voeux)* concerned the setting up of the

Permanent Court of Arbitration, commercial and industrial relations between the belligerent states and neutral countries, the position of foreigners in respect to military service, and the future codification of the laws and customs of maritime war at the next conference, held in 1915. At the Second Hague Conference, Germany refused to agree to mandatory arbitration, since it was preparing for war. Bulgaria, Italy, Montenegro, Serbia and Turkey did not ratify the conventions. Serbia signed them, but did not ratify them, although in the wars between 1912 and 1918, Serbia stated on several occasions that it considered the Hague Conventions binding rules of international law; Serbia applied them and allowed international commissions of enquiry to determine their application in its territory during the war, at the same time accusing the central powers and their allies of not adhering to the rules of these conventions.

Pursuant to Article 7 of the Hague Convention of 18 October 1907 on the setting up of an international prize court, a maritime conference met in London on 4 December 1908, attended by eight maritime powers. At this conference a declaration was adopted on the law of maritime war, which supplemented the Declaration of 16 April 1856. This declaration regulated questions of blockade, contraband, payment of reparations, change of flag, etc.

Immediately after the First World War, the League of Nations made significant attempts to codify international law. A committee of experts was set up to deal with the matter. This committee comprised 16 members, and three questions were given top priority; nationality, territorial waters and the responsibility of states for damage to aliens. The work of this committee will go down in history as a valiant attempt by a number of experts on international law to codify certain matters and as evidence of the views of states on these matters at that time, since they made written replies to the proposals of the committee. However, practical results were not forthcoming. In 1930 a conference was convened at the Hague for the codification of international law. It met for one month. Thirty-nine states were represented, but the expected results failed to materialize. It only succeeded in codifying, and only partly at that, laws concerning citizenship. There is no doubt that the League of Nations was instrumental in achieving a partial codification of international law, since it gave the initiative for the conclusion of a number of multilateral conventions. Out of close to 5,000 registered international treaties in the League of Nations, about 700 were multilateral conventions containing many rules of international law and in an indirect way undoubtedly influenced the development of general international law. The majority of these conventions were on technical questions, particularly communications, public health and work safety, and they contained rules of law of a normative character, so that they were not only applied by the signatories, but many of them were expanded under the auspices of the United Nations, or else they have become general rules of customary law.

4. Codification by the United Nations — The United Nations Charter greatly enlarged opportunities for a broad and relatively faster codification of international law by its provisions in Article 13, paragraph 1, a), authorizing the General Assembly to promote international cooperation in the political field and to encourage "the progressive development of international law and its codification." Thus by making recommendations, the General Assembly exercises its right of codification with a certain legislative initiative; it may recommend that member countries adopt a complete draft of some codified material in international law, whereas, on the other hand, codification must be carried out on the basis of treaties adopted by member countries.

In 1947, the General Assembly passed a resolution establishing the International Law Commission as an auxiliary organ of the General Assembly charged with the task of carrying out a codification of the most important parts of international law and of promoting the progressive development of international law through its discussions and studies of these problems (Resolution 147/II). The following year a group of fifteen world renowned jurists was selected. The Commission gave fourteen out of twenty-five topics priority consideration, these being: 1. recognition of states and governments, 2. succession of states and governments, 3. immunity of a state and its property in regard to foreign judicial jurisdiction, 4. jurisdiction of courts for crimes committed outside national territory, 5. the law of the open seas, 6. law in territorial waters, 7. citizenship, including statelessness, 8. the legal status of aliens, 9. the right of asylum, 10. the law of treaties, 11. diplomatic relations and immunity, 12. consular relations and immunities, 13. state responsibility, 14. arbitration procedure. Some questions received immediate attention, *e. g.* the law of treaties, arbitral procedure and the law of the sea. Later the General Assembly directed the Commission to carry out three more tasks: to formulate the Nuremberg principles, to study the possibility of setting up an international criminal court, and to prepare a draft declaration on the rights and duties of states. At its seventh regular session, the U.N. General Assembly adopted the proposal of Yugoslavia to order a faster codification of diplomatic relations and immunities. These questions were given a thorough consideration in several studies, but practical results have been rather disappointing. The Commission, which did submit its draft, was not to blame; rather the fault lay with the tense international situation, which precluded any agreements on adopting the proposals. The Commission was criticized for not representing all legal civilizations, particularly for the very small representation of the states of Africa and Asia, which had not taken part in elaborating positive rules of public international law in the 19th and 20th centuries. To remedy the situation, the Eleventh General Assembly changed the Statute and increased the number of bers of the Commission to twenty one. Since that time the work of the Commission has become considerably more intensive.

The important acts promulgated by the United Nations, which has promoted the codification and progressive development of international law, include the Universal Declaration of Human Rights, adopted on 10 December 1948 (Resolution 217/III), the Convention on Prevention and Punishment of Crimes of Genocide adopted on 9 December 1948 (Resolution 260/III), the resolution on the duties of states in the event of an outbreak of hostilities, adopted on the basis of a proposal by the Yugoslav delegation on 17 December 1950 (Resolution 378/V), the resolution on reservations to multilateral conventions adopted on 12 January 1952 (Resolution 598/VI), the resolution on making international customary law accessible, passed in 1952 (Resolution 487/V).

Much has also been done in the progressive development and codification of international law through multilateral conventions concluded within the United Nations. We should also mention the revised general act on pacific settlement of international disputes adopted on 28 April 1949, and two conventions on diplomatic law, the convention on privileges and immunities of the United Nations, adopted on 13 February 1946, and the convention on privileges and immunities of specialized agencies on 21 November 1947.

At special diplomatic conferences, the Geneva Conventions on the Law of the Sea were adopted in 1958, the Vienna Conventions on Diplomatic Relations in 1961, and on Consular Relations in 1963, on the basis of drafts prepared by the U.N. International Law Commission.

The Geneva Conventions of 12 August 1949 are considered a milestone in codification of international law. These include the convention on treatment and repatriation of war prisoners, "for the amelioration of the condition of the wounded and sick in armed forces in the field," for the amelioration of the condition of the wounded and sick and shipwrecked in armed naval forces, and the convention on protection of civilian persons in time of war. These conventions were based on earlier Geneva conventions but had been thoroughly revised on the basis of the experiences of the new warfare of the Second World War. Writers in the field of law were the first to begin calling for the convening of a diplomatic conference to adopt new Geneva conventions. The International Red Cross initiated the promulgation of new rules on the protection of civilians in total war.

The specialized agencies of the United Nations in general have greatly facilitated codification by sifting out technical issues from political considerations. Conventions concerning labor and social insurance, passed in the form of resolutions by the International Labour Organization and becoming treaties by virtue of the accession of states, are of particular importance. Also noteworthy are a world code on public health services, detailed regulations on international postal services and telecommunications, regulations on the operation of the world network of meteorological reports, as well as a number of international rules in agriculture and nutrition. Of no less importance is the activity sponsored by UNESCO concerning international law in the realm of culture, particularly the convention on protection of cultural movements during wartime and the Geneva Convention on the universal protection of copyright.

5. Codification of the Principles of International Cooperation (Active Peaceful Coexistence) — The transformation of contemporary international law is a necessary process in the further development of complex international relations. The Charter of the United Nations inaugurated a new era in the development of these relations. A postwar order of international law was created, and its further evolution has been made possible. In the year since the San Francisco Conference of 1945, many new developments have occurred which have altered the course of international affairs. These were first of all the emergence of a number of socialist countries, the collapse of colonial empires, and the extraordinarily rapid advances of science, technology, and communications. We might place particular emphasis on the role and political influence of nonaligned countries. These have all been crucial developments, which have changed the structure and ideological persuasions of the world family of nations.

At its fifteenth session, the U.N. General Assembly adopted a resolution (1505/XV), which had been sponsored by nonaligned countries, on the further codification and progressive development of international law. The resolution noted that the present situation in the world increasingly called for a greater role of international law as a means of strengthening international peace, improving friendly relations and increasing international cooperation, for regulating disputes in a peaceable way and improving the economic and social situation in the entire world. The resolution went on to describe the state of international law, proposing measures and outlining the work plan of the International Law Commission, with the aim of promoting friendly relations and strengthening the mutual cooperation of states. Countries were invited to submit their opinion of this resolution. The memorandum of the Yugoslav government dated 28 June 1961 emphasized the significance of this resolution and the need for studying legal principles of active peaceful coexistence. "The principle of active peaceful coexistence provides a basis for the development of international relations and international law on principles leading to the strengthening of peace and cooperation between states, on principles laid down in the United Nations Charter. They were promulgated in the Charter and are contained in a number of subsequent international documents of a multipartite or bipartite character. Codification of the principle of peaceful coexistence represents a creative interpretation and elaboration of the principles of the Charter in the light of the dynamic development of international relations. It would help ensure that the course of development of international relations will truly be in accordance with the principles laid down in the Charter."

At its seventeenth session, the U.N. General Assembly decided (Resolution 1815/XVII) to undertake a consideration of principles of international law concerning friendly relations and cooperation among states in accordance with the Charter of the United Nations, with a view to their progressive development and codification, so as to secure their more effective application. The seven principles under consideration were prohibition of the threat or use of force, peaceful settlement of disputes, non-intervention in the internal affairs of states, sovereign equality, cooperation of states in accordance with the Charter of the United Nations, equal rights and self-determination of peoples, and the fulfilment in good faith of international obligations assumed in accordance with the Charter.

Selection of the principles for special legal elaboration was without a doubt a landmark in the political activity of nonaligned and socialist countries in the United Nations. A special committee was set up to make a thorough study of the principles of international law on friendly relations and cooperation of states. The word "coexistence" does not appear in the title of the Committee, as the Western countries felt that it had an exclusively political meaning, but the substituted phrase "friendly relations and cooperation among states" essentially amounts to the same thing.

The transformation of contemporary international law is also needed because of the number of negative trends that have appeared in the world: violation of existing norms of international law, gross intervention, the use or threat of force, and even open acts of aggression. Elaboration of the norms of international law from periods of past alignments of the powers, including those alignments reflected in the Charter, which must be reworked to conform to the spirit of the times, should prevent the application of double standards in the common and indivisible good of all peoples and countries.

International law and its application are not the privilege of a restricted number of states which still find the outmoded and inadequate rules of international law to their liking. The majority of independent states today took no part in adopting these rules. A large number of member countries of the United Nations were not present in San Francisco in 1945 when the Charter was adopted. This is not to say that they are opposed to the Charter, only that they would like to see it given more comprehensive and effective application. And this is just one more reason for a speedier codification of the principles of active peaceful coexistence. A recommendation to this effect was made at the Second Conference of Nonaligned Countries in Cairo in 1964, in Chapter 4 of the adopted Programme for Peace and International Cooperation.

VI. Development

Introduction — the Ancient Oriental Civilizations — Greece — Rome — Middle Ages — Rise of the Bourgeoisie — Founding Fathers of International Law — French Revolution — Nineteenth Century — Period between the Two World Wars

1. Introduction — Peoples and states have unavoidably been in contact with one another since the most ancient times. They have been motivated by highly diverse interests and ambitions in their mutual dealings. The economy and technical advances, communications and trade, civilization and culture have all had the effect of proliferating ties among states. At the same time, their interests often collide to a greater or lesser extent. These unceasing fluctuations in relations between states and peoples create the need for rules of international law in the broadest sense of the word.

2. The Ancient Oriental Civilizations — A detailed regulation of inter-governmental relations was already to be found in the ancient oriental states. The oldest known example of international law is Ramses II's treaty with the Hittite king, Hattusilis III, concluded in 1269 B.C. This treaty served as the model for all subsequent diplomatic agreements for the Eastern empires as well as for Greece and Rome. This document contains provisions on non-aggression and mutual assistance, and even has clauses specifying that this assistance includes intervention in quelling internal revolts in either state.

3. Greece — Ancient Greece and Rome elaborated a large number of forms of international law. In the Greek city state (polis), enfranchised citizens enjoyed their privileges only within the bounds of their states, while they were considered foreigners and possessed no rights outside it. The only people who could be considered citizens of a Greek city state were those whose parents had been fully enfranchised citizens of that same city state. The right of citizenship in the Greek city states was not granted to many people. Slaves and foreigners *(metoikos)* enjoyed no civil rights.

Xenelasia, which was the right to persecute foreigners, was an institution in Greece. It is thought that this law was first laid down by the legendary lawmaker Lycurgus. Foreigners were held in very low esteem in ancient Greece, but the growth of international communications, contacts between towns and particularly the flourishing of maritime trade inevitably led to an easing of legal regulations concerning foreigners. Thus a new institution, *proxenia,* evolved, which offered hospitality to foreigners provided it was reciprocated. As commerce grew, *proxenia* took on a permanent character, founded on numerous treaties concluded to this effect. The *proxenoi* were persons receiving foreigners and serving in effect as their mediators before the local authorities. They conducted diplomatic negotiations, and acted as go-betweens with local authorities on behalf of foreign deputations. Such a system of hospitality provided foreigners with only a modicum of protection, and their rights were quite limited. It was only under the battering ram of economic, military and political interests that the barriers between citizens and foreigners were gradually broken down. When two city states pursued a policy of mutual friendship, they granted each other certain concessions. Agreements were concluded on *isopoliteia,* according to which the citizens of one city state had the same public and private rights in the other city-state as the local citizens. There was mutual *isopoliteia* in the Greek states, or else it was only applied to individuals in recognition of their services. Finally, as the practice of international agreements became more widespread, a very important institution, known as *symbola,* appeared. *Symbola* were treaties on legal norms applied in various judicial proceedings initiated by citizens of different city-states concerning their commercial, credit or similar affairs, for the most part concluded between allied city-states. The idea of *arbitration,* as seen in the organization of elected courts, arose in close conjunction with the practice of *isopoliteia* and the *symbola.*

The ancient Greeks had the custom of making formal declarations of war through heralds of special envoys who were under the protection of the deities and whose persons were considered inviolable. The duties of heralds were not merely to declare war but also to conclude truces needed to bury the dead and to mediate on the exchange of prisoners of war. However, according to Xenophon, wars were often waged without a formal declaration. Attacks and enslavement of the defeated population were everyday occurrences in slave-owning Greece. Laying waste the enemy territories by fire and sword was considered an accepted means of forcing an enemy to surrender. With time the old norms of warfare were gradually replaced by new ones, as the old customs were at variance with new internationalist ways of thinking. War was declared under special conditions which regulated the conduct of the war. The killing of slaves gave way to exchange of slaves or the right to purchase them (according to Thucydides). It eventually became the practice to hand over the bodies of the dead to the enemy side for burial, for which a truce was concluded.

A number of international rules and customs trace their roots back to celebrations observed by the Greek people. War between Greek city-states was halted during the Olympic Games, and any new war in this period was considered a violation of "sacred law." Whoever violated this customary law would be punished, among other things by a large fine.

There were many attempts to regulate conflicts through treaties and agreements. The system of treaties was widely applied. Various alliances, peace and other treaties were made according to the customs of the time. Peace treaties were concluded for specific lengths of time, for a "permanent peace" is never mentioned in their treaties. The periods were usually short, but some peace treaties were made for thirty or even fifty years. The treaties were publicly displayed and then most often preserved next to the deities in the Delphic or Olympic temples.

A select court or mediator was chosen to settle disputes by mutual agreement of the contesting parties. A person of authority or even a state could act as mediator. We learn from sources that oracles or *amphyktions* were most often mediators. And so gradually the notion of a life in common entered the consciousness of the people of Greece.

Although tending towards autocracy and autonomy, the Greek city states were compelled by objective circumstances to grant concessions to the citizens of neighboring *politeis* and to adopt norms regulating their mutual relations. With the further development of Greek civilization and culture, the idea of the unification of the city states evolved, the idea of a general interest which found its expression in new forms of international law.

4. — Rome — From the very earliest times, ancient Rome had an institution similar to the Greek *proxenia,* known as *jus hospitil,* and *collegium fetiales,* similar to the Greek *amphyktioni.* These were religious alliances, concluded at the holy place of a particularly revered deity. The members of the *collegium* settled disputes between tribes and tribal federations, and they declared war and concluded peace. The collection of the most ancient legal precepts *(jus fetiale)* is one of the first instances of a collection of provisions of international law. During the time of the Roman kings, the conduct of foreign affairs was a royal prerogative. Later, this prerogative was taken over by the Senate. During the monarchic period, envoys *(legati)*, oratores, were *fetiales,* while in the time of the Republic they were chosen from the ranks of the senators. The delegations were headed by *princeps legationis,* and this title was automatically awarded to the eldest senator. Envoys were expected to report to the Senate on their mission when completed *(legationem referre).*

The senate also received foreign delegations. The protocol for friendly missions differed from those sent by belligerent countries. The deputies of unfriendly countries were not allowed into the city but were detained on the Campus Martius.

Rome acknowledged generally three categories of relations: the state of war, alliances, and so-called peaceful relations, when it was on terms of mutual tolerance of friendly relations with its neighbors.

The Romans considered that there were four justifications for war: attack on their state territory, violation of the rule of the inviolability of emissaries, defection from supreme Roman authority, and alliance with Rome's enemies.

A picture of Roman foreign affairs can be pieced together from the treaties *(foedera)* concluded with Italic and non-Italic cities. Of particular importance are those treaties which Rome concluded on the basis of so-called reciprocity and equality *(foedera aequa)* with autonomous states whose friendship was expedient for Rome, or with an opponent whom Rome could not subdue. This equality was most often illusory, since it was largely Rome which benefited from these treaties. Hence the *foedera non aequa.* Virtually all these treaties were replaced by Roman law towards the end of the Republic. Roman law was imposed upon peoples who had previously held treaties with Rome. Later, after the barbarian onslaughts, Rome was forced to conclude treaties with the barbarians. Indeed, Rome is the historical epitome of a state which was never willing to release its monopoly of world power. Even when it concluded alliances, in both the early and later centuries of its history, Rome did so in order to consolidate its position. The foreign policy of the Roman state was never interested in a balance of power.

The Romans divided states into two categories: friendly and unfriendly, or, more precisely, those which were submissive and those which resisted Roman rule and defended their integrity. Roman colonies were not extensions of the motherland, as those of the Greeks had been, but dependent territories in the service of Rome. This state, as an empire and the strongest world power, adopted certain concepts of the Greek Stoics. The strict morals prescribed by the Stoics answered the needs of the Roman state and Roman society, notwithstanding their cosmopolitan ideas. Subscribing to the basic ideas of the Greek Stoics, Cicero adapted them to the needs of the empire, elaborating the concept of universal law which must prevail in the holy Roman state, "timeless and indestructible." Somewhat later, Seneca enlarged upon this view with theories not only about the "holy state," but also about "holy society" and its organization.

5. Middle Ages — Early Christianity opposed the imperial ideas of Rome. The followers of early Christianity were against war, even in self-defense. They opposed the shedding of blood of their neighbor, whoever it might be. For this reason, they refused to serve in the Roman legions and were severely punished for it. Later, after Constantine had been converted to Christianity and began to conquer in the sign of of the cross *("in hoc signo vinces"),* Christian symbols had a martial significance for later Roman emperors. Rather than opposing war altogether, St. Augustine merely sought a definition of the circumstances under which war could be waged. In the thirteenth century, however, the medieval thinker St. Thomas Aquinas, on the basis of the teachings of St. Augustine and the twelfth-century professor Graziani at the University of Padua formulated a theory according to which the church was the steward of war and peace, the main factor authorized to decide on a state of peace or war between peoples and states.

Byzantium and the papacy followed in the tradition of Roman law, elaborating on it to meet the needs of their complex international affairs. Both the Eastern and Western empires were forced not only to wage war against the barbarian tribes that had penetrated into Europe but also to conduct foreign affairs. Often weapons were substituted by negotiations which ended in treaties. In its foreign policy, Byzantium made skilful use of the Roman maxim, *divide et impera.* It is well known that Justinian incited the Huns against the Bulgars, and the Avars against the Huns. He defeated the Vandals with the help of the Ostrogoths, and defeated the Ostrogoths in alliance with the Franks. A special office for foreign diplomacy was even created under the administration of the first minister *(magister officiorum)* later known as the "great logothete." Special court ceremonials for receiving foreign emissaries were designed to dazzle them with the power of Byzantium while cloaking its weaknesses. The reception given to emissaries included the presentation of credentials and gifts. These emissaries could conclude treaties which came into effect only after the Emperor's ratification. The principle of inviolability of emissaries was respected, and any transgressions were punished by reprisals.

The Roman concept of a single and unified world government, of an indivisible empire embodied in an invincible Rome, was carried over into the world of the Byzantine Empire. Byzantium inherited the Roman imperial mantle of world rule. The idea of universal Christianity was to hold sway from the time of the Christianized Roman Empire and Justinian until the final dissolution of the Byzantine Empire, even when it fell prey to the Ottomans. In this Christian ecumene, existing states were not equal. The Yugoslav historian G. Ostrogorski describes the hierarchy of states in the Byzantine Empire, in which Byzantium was supreme and the "legitimate vehicle of the idea of a universal kingdom." The other Christian states had their specific places in this hierarchy, determined according to their importance and standing vis-à-vis Byzantium, which was without peer. Therefore, when the Serbian ruler Dušan assumed the title of emperor, this act was not only a sign of disobedience — which Byzantium, weakened by civil war, could do nothing about — but also an act of usurpation of supreme power, which was opposed by orthodox Christianity as a whole. Dušan topped the fiction of a single ecumenic empire, injected new elements into the world view of that time, and his *Codex* introduced codified laws having an international character.

In the Middle Ages the papacy was the leading power in foreign affairs. The popes combined spiritual authority with diplomacy and skilfully used a variety of ploys, the likes of which had never been seen before by any other state. Greatly threatened by the barbarians in Italy, the popes maintained permanent envoys known as *apocrisiairies,* who enjoyed diplomatic privileges. They should be viewed as an attempt to establish the first permanent envoys (the legation as a fixed institution was established in 1455, when Milan sent its permanent diplomatic representative to Genoa), but this should not be confused with the papal nuncios *(legates)* who performed ecclesiastical and political duties.

It would be difficult to speak of foreign affairs in the age of feudalism and feudal fragmentation. There were a large number of feudal lords who ruled countries or had their suzerains in various countries, *e.g.* in France and Germany, or in Germany and Italy, while at the same time being themselves the vassals of several emperors. Countries could be inherited or given as dowries, and states were created in this way, albeit they were often very short-lived. For this reason, it was not possible to draw a distinction between state and private property or between domestic and foreign affairs. Whoever was economically strong could have his own state and his own diplomacy. As a corollary, there was a law of private warfare.

6. Rise of the Bourgeoisie — With the development of economic and political relations in feudalism and with Christianity becoming the ruling ideology, Christian political theories took shape from which we can infer the ideas on international relations and international law prevalent at this time.

Foreign affairs in this period of history largely revolved around the conflict between church and state. The struggle for supremacy, begun in the ninth century after the death of Charlemagne, governed the thinking on foreign policy. Previously, the "two swords" doctrine had prevailed — the idea of dual authority: temporal, which belonged to the ruler, and spiritual, which belonged to the church, i.e. the pope. The most prominent and, from a modern standpoint most realistic defender of the pope in the ideological struggle for supremacy was without doubt St. Thomas Aquinas. Dante, however, in his famous treatise *Monarchia,* defended the idea of a holy state. According to him, the holy state must be a monarchy, and it alone was able to ensure peace in the world. Defending this thesis, which bolstered the rulers of the German Holy Roman Empire at that time, he stated that monarchy must be independent from the authority of the church. For Dante, peace was the basic goal of mankind and could only be enforced by one man, the emperor, or just as there was one God, so there must be one monarch on earth, a "universal monarch," who would be above all other kings. He would be just, in Dante's opinion, since as ruler of the world he would no longer have any desires or ambitions.

From the 11th to the 12th centuries, political theory was largely dominated by the view that the church held precedence over the state; by the early 14th century, the idea that state authority was independent of the church began to gain ascendancy, although purely theological views were still being advocated. However, the rise of capitalism strengthened the secular state, and consequently opinion increasingly swung to the opposite viewpoint.

The growth of productive forces brought about a greater division of labor until commodity relations became widespread, powerful cities sprang up, and a new class emerged, the bourgeoisie, which was interested in a national market and particularly in the protection of this market, which only a centralized government could give them. Hence, with the cooperation of the church, the feudal monarchy was strengthened in order to safeguard commerce, which was constantly being threatened by unruly and disobedient feudal lords. The great feudal monarchies, such as France, Spain, England, and particularly the powerful Italian cities, inevitably began to compete for foreign markets. Thus the stage was set for a large number of firm international contracts and international relations.

Various alliances were necessary if military, commercial and diplomatic ascendancy was to be achieved in Europe, and they were especially necessary for the long struggle between the papacy and the Holy Roman Empire, where the stakes were world rule. Since neither the emperor nor the pope succeeded in uniting the splintered feudal countries, a new force arose, according to Marx, which promised to bring order to chaos, a royal authority as the representative of nations seeking their own national autonomy. Already arbitration had become a frequent means of settling international disagreements. There was much greater contact between governments and joint discussion of intergovernmental affairs at meetings, such as the Congress of Arras in 1435. Ideas on securing world peace also began to gain currency. In his work *De recuperatione Terre Sancte* in 1306, Pierre Dubois proposed the creation of an international court of arbitration. He envisaged three ecclesiastical and three secular judges selected to hear each international dispute. The Bohemian king, George of Podebrady, proposed the court of arbitration should have a consistorium of states.

Commercial ties established between Italian cities (Venice, Genoa, Milan and Florence) and other states brought forth a further development of international law. Lively trade, both with the East and with central and northern Europe, expanded the range of interests of the mercantile Italian cities, and these interests had to be protected in the struggle for markets both to secure supplies of raw materials and to market finished goods. A far-flung network of consular services was created which had all civil and commercial jurisdiction for the affairs of their citizens abroad, the consuls acting as representatives of the interests of their citizens and state before local authorities. There were often disputes over the apportionment of rights between local authorities and consular representatives, which provided the impetus for the elaboration of new legal forms. These new laws advanced the international law of the time, bringing the interests of countries into closer accord. International trade also spurred the development of international maritime law. The notion of contraband and reprisals evolved in this period.

The discovery of the new world and the first colonial expeditions inaugurated the historical period in which the focus of world trade shifted from the shores of the Mediterranean and Baltic seas to the states on the Atlantic ocean such as Portugal, Spain, the Netherlands, France, and England. The bourgeoisie, the new progressive social class, advocated the idea of state interest as the political principle on which the foreign policies of states should be based. The desire of various states to acquire commercial hegemony prompted the formation of leagues, and other states were forced to group against these alliances, or to defend themselves alone against the expansion of stronger states. The theory of sovereignty and ideas of political equilibrium, natural boundaries of states, the right to wage war and make peace, the freedom of the high seas and inviolability of international treaties all gained wide currency. As the large absolutist states expanded, their diplomatic services grew, finally to become permanent, with a fixed hierarchy and protocol.

Before we take up the period immediately preceding the development of contemporary international law, let us outline the basic tenets of the classics of international law.

7. Classics of International Law — When the Christian states came into contact, and conflict, with non-Christian, infidel peoples, the question of war, its legal character, *i.e.* its justification, became pressing. The Spanish and Portuguese conquests in the Americas and Indies gave rise to territorial disputes over the right to make war and the right to conquer and occupy lands. The Reformation finalized the supremacy of the state over religion, launching the well-known adage, *cuius regio eius religio.* The architects of modern international law were the first to propound the idea that states were subjects of international relations, that they had a free hand in their political activities, restricted only by rules of international law, of international law as they conceived it. The classical writers on international law varied slightly in their approaches to finding a way of regulating international relations.

Although the progenitor of international law is considered to be the Dutch jurist Hugo Grotius, no history of international law would be complete without mention of the names of earlier writers: Francisco de Vitoria (1480–1546), Domingo de Soto (1494–1560), Francisco Suarez (1548–1617), and Alberico Gentili (1552–1608).

In Vitoria's writings, which were in the spirit of medieval scholasticism, international relations were treated as a "matter of conscience," that is from the standpoint of the moral code and theological beliefs of that time. He was the first to use the term *jus inter gentes,* which, according to him, was a "number of rules which the nature of reason imposed upon peoples." Actually, Vitoria was seeking moral grounds for intercourse *inter gentes,* since the flourishing commerce of the time necessitated an end to the parochial feudal order and sought guarantees for greater freedom of intercourse among peoples, who were brought closer together by world-wide trade.

Joan Bodin, a representative of the bourgeoisie, argued in favor of armed intervention, war and the right to resort to any coercion against a sovereign who breaks the rules of international law. The purpose of such a war would be not to win peace but to see that justice was done and to ensure conditions under which there would be no violation of international law.

In the works of Domingo de Soto, the effects of war are viewed from a humanitarian standpoint. De Soto reflects the neoclassical tendency, in line with which the bourgeoisie was preparing for a period of absolute monarchy and protection of the accumulated wealth in the towns. Using scholastic methods, Francisco Suarez arrived at the conclusion that international law was at the transition point between natural and civil law. According to him, international law was neither enduring nor universal as was natural law, nor was it the law of just one state; international relations had to take their course according to the criteria contained in international law, since it derived from the common "needs of the people," and therefore the "community of nations" served as its basis. This community, of course, was organized by the Roman Catholic Church. Following the line of world catholicism, this thinker was among the first to assert that states cannot exist in isolation, and taking this idea as his starting point, Suarez drew a distinction between the concepts of state, state and international law, *i.e.* Catholic society and the law which is created by its theology. Alberico Gentili was not a Roman Catholic theologian. He had left the church and was forced to flee from the Inquisition. Under the influence of Protestantism, he shook off the strictures of scholasticism and became one of the first exponents of the historical school. He coined the famous definition of war: *Bellum est publicorum armorum justa contentio.* Gentili was among the first to exclude the waging of private wars from international law, and he laid the theoretical groundwork for the law of neutrality.

The Dutchman Hugo Grotius (1583–1643) laid down the theoretical bases of international law. His most famous work was *De jure belli ac pacis.* According to him, the law of property was the "natural law" of man, which was a dictate of reason. Living at a time of protracted wars between absolutist states, Grotius made an attempt to protect the property of the new, bourgeois class by making war subject to the rules of law. Grotius, contended that war was a fact of life which sprang from the urge for self-defense, and must be waged according to the rules of fair play, which included respect for free trade, free migration, freedom of the high seas, and inviolability of enemy property. Seeking to establish peace and order in international relations, he advocated the treaty as the basis of international law. Grotius devoted special attention to diplomatic law. He held that the rights of envoys should not be postulated on the principles of natural law, since they actually depended on the will of the people, on the customs of a given country. The emissary need not be received at a foreign court, but his rejection must be explained. An envoy is inviolable, and by virtue of this fact enjoys the right of exterritoriality. In 1608, Grotius published *Mare liberum*, in which he argues in favor of freedom of navigation on the seas, which at that time was so vital for the Dutch in their war against Spain.

Samuel Pufendorf (1632–1694) was in the vanguard of jurists who began to make a systematic study of natural law at the end of the 17th and in the early 18th century. Eight of his books make up the famous *Corpus juris naturalis*, the system of public and private law. Pufendorf's assumption was that peace, and not war, was the natural condition. Natural laws rule mankind. They are laws which correspond to the nature of society. Positive international law, in his opinion, did not exist, since its rationale was largely the natural and incontestable right of defence against an unjustified attack.

Two outstanding representatives of the school of natural law were the English jurist Zouche (1590–1660) and Bynkershoek (1683–1743). Analogous to the distinctions in private law, Zouche divided international law both in peacetime and during war into four parts: status, dominium — ownership delitum — contract, and delictum — criminal act. The author won great popularity for his definition of international law as *jus inter gentes*, although some feel that the originator of this definition was Vitoria. In his works, Zouche stressed the inequality of states and called for free trade. In socalled property law (*dominium*), the main question was occupation, especially occupation of the seas. He denied the law of tradition, taking the view that special treaties were needed for such cases. The Dutch jurist Bynkershoek, like his fellow countrymen, was particularly interested in the complex question of maritime law, notably the question of control over the seas. According to him, cannon and weaponry are what create a country's title to its coastal waters. As regards ratification of international treaties, this writer, as had Grotius, advocated the view that the rules of the mandate dictated the conclusion of an international treaty.

The German Wolff (1679–1754) and the Swiss Vattel (1714–1762) are considered by Oppenheim to be outside the natural and positivist schools. He describes them as theorists, who constructed their concepts under the direct influence of Hugo Grotius. According to Wolff, international law is the law of a specific society, *civitas maxima*, which comprises the entire human race. It promulgates laws and thus creates the legal order so necessary for a common purpose. Wolff calls this law voluntary international law. This is law which is created not only by treaties but also by the reciprocal acts of states in their mutual relations. Vattel divides international law into voluntary and necessary, the latter being law which must be observed by states in order for them to be able to live together. A number of questions attracted his attention: recipro-cal rights and duties of nations, their agreements and conventions, the settle-ment of disputes and the problem of equality of states.

8. French Revolution — Machiavelli's "political realism" found an unprecedented application in the diplomatic practice of absolute monarchies. Its practice gave birth to new ideas in the history of political theory. In the 17th century, the idea of a "league of nations" as put forward by Sully (one of Henry IV's most competent ministers) was quite typical. The "league of nations" was the practical embodiment of the theory on state interest" as the common inter-est of the existing international community. According to Sully's *Le Grand Dessein,* Europe should be divided into six hereditary monarchies, five consti-tutional monarchies and five republics. These states would be headed by a council, which would be the guardian of world peace and responsible for set-tling international disputes. The pope would be president of this republic of Christian states, while Sully's own country, France, would provide the prime minister.

The apostles of the Enlightenment in the 18th century introduced new ways of thinking about international relations and international law into polit-ical thought. Their way of thinking was based on the rejection of previous views that international relations were merely contacts between ruling monarchs. International relations were properly relations among peoples and not among those ruling them. The old notions of international relations were reflected in the foreign policies of states, particularly in dynastic wars for succession. Montesquieu, representative of the liberal aristocracy, held that every great-ness, every force and every power was relative, backing his assertion with ex-amples from history. Conquest, in his view, leads to despotism.

The radical bourgeois thinkers often criticized and mocked the relations among emperors and kings and their diplomacy. Rousseau stated that rulers were motivated in their foreign policy by greed for new possessions and in do-mestic policy by autocracy and tyranny. According to him, the right of conquest was only based on the right of might. Since war did not give the victor any right to massacre the defeated population, that nonexistent right could not be the basis for the right to make slaves of subjugated peoples.

Rousseau hoped that the abolition of absolutism would make way for a per-manent peace, which would be created by the formation of states with a Euro-pean parliament and some kind of international court. Similar notions were held in France by the Abbé de Saint-Pièrre, in England by Bentham, and in Germany by Immanuel Kant.

Saint-Pièrre believed that emperors would disappear the moment a way was found to settle all international disputes by peaceful means. Although he did not personally believe it could be put into practice, even if such a way were found, he wrote his *Projet de paix perpétuelle* in the secret hope that if "sovereigns sign a treaty of perpetual alliance," a lasting peace would come about. Jeremy Bentham was much more precise and politically more realistic. In his *Plan for a General and Permanent Peace,* he defended the idea of a European federation, which would be primarily the responsibility of England and France. He proposed first reductions in armaments, and second emancipation of dependent territories (colonies) from the great powers. His contribution to international law is outstanding, especially his efforts to have "law between states" give way to "law between nations" or "law of nations," this last term being the accepted one in English literature or international law to this day.

Whereas Abbé de Saint-Pièrre was a Christian Utopian, Bentham was a philosopher whose utilitarian views of the world included the sphere of international relations. The German philosopher Immanuel Kant, in his treatise *On Perpetual Peace* sought not only to apply his concept of ethics, but also to elaborate it in "definitive articles of perpetual peace among states." Feeling that this was inadequate, he added two important essays in which he discussed the disparity between morals and politics in respect to perpetual peace and the harmony between politics and morals according to the transcendental concept of public law.

A Königsberg professor and loyal Prussian citizen, Immanuel Kant, whom the censors prohibited from receiving any written information or commentary on the course of the French Revolution, published his work *On Perpetual Peace* in 1795. This work contains provisions in its introductory chapters which are politically naive but sincerely pacifist, as indeed are most utopias of this kind. In the second part, Kant outlined his scheme for establishing world peace. The main features of this plan include a civil constitution, a federal system of liberated states based on an alliance of peace, and, finally, international hospitality. Kant describes the Perpetual Peace as a moral norm which enjoys its greatest guarantee from the existence of a natural mechanism.

The struggle of the bourgeoisie against feudalism and absolutism reached its highest pitch in the French Revolution. The concept of the divine right of kings to rule gave way to the idea of national sovereignty, with the maxim that all nations are independent and sovereign. The French Revolution changed the course of history and injected new principles into international law. Toppling the feudal system, the revolution replaced the supremacy of the monarch with the supreme power of the people. Nationals of an independent state were no longer subjects owing allegiance to the sovereign, but citizens participating in the new, bourgeois social and political life of the country and acquiring new rights in society. They called a stop to the numerous obligations they had previously had to carry out towards the feudal lord and absolute ruler. An independent nation was considered to be equal in rights and duties with other nations; it is an international subject. Hence, the interference of one nation in the internal affairs of another nation was sharply condemned, and the aggressor state was labeled an enemy of all mankind. The principle of non-interference and the inviolability of territory evolved in this period. The annexation of Avignon and Savoy to France in 1791 was carried out by plebiscite. In practice, the principle of equality among states and the principle of stability of treaties were observed. The Declaration of Abbé Grégoire contains the phrase, "treaties between states are holy and inviolable." The idea of humanizing war was the contribution of the French Revolution. After Napolean's defeat, the question of responsibility for violating international law became topical.

9. The Nineteenth Century — The first half of the 19th century saw a struggle between diametrically opposed principles; between the principle of non-interference and interventions by the Holy Alliance; and between the principle of national self-determination and that of legitimacy. After the Russian defeat at Sevastopol in the Crimean war, the Paris Conference held in 1856 marked the end of the period of the Holy Alliance and the ascendancy of its ecclesiastical, monarchical ideology. The Conference admitted Turkey to the European Concert; the Black Sea was declared neutral, while the Dardanelles were closed to warships. The Danube was proclaimed an international river.

In the era of imperialism, dating from the end of the Franco-Prussian war, the great powers began a mighty struggle to carve up the world, and the theory of the laws of "civilized" states was launched. Having confined bourgeois democracy to a narrow circle of "civilized" nations, the bourgeois theorists derived from the principle of sovereignty the concept of the right of every state to wage war, including aggressive wars. Certain anti-democratic institutions of international law, such as treaties on colonial protectorates and particularly the right of European states to occupy the territory of future colonies (viz., the Berlin Conference of 1884–85, which decided the fate of the Congo Basin with the General Act) also gained legitimacy.

This period established the principle of nationality, the natural status of certain states and regions, protectorates, codification of the law of war and arbitration. It was in this century that international law began to be differentiated and its various branches elaborated, such as international administrative law, international criminal law (prohibition of traffic in women and children, prohibition of dissemination of pornographic literature and prohibition of piracy), and others.

From the beginning of the 19th century up until the First World War, international politics and legal theory abounded in ideas about the prevailing international relations, interpreting them in different ways — either from the standpoint of the place and role in international life of the state of which the given theorist might be a citizen, or according to the school of thought to which he belonged.

In these years, the theory of nationality was studied from every possible angle in view of the emergence and consolidation of new nation states. Mancini's definition of nationality as a natural community of people who have a single state territory and belong to the same race, with identical customs and one language, caused a storm of controversy and received many different interpretations.

Political and legal theorists give the concept of nationality and the nation as an international subject a variety of meanings, depending on their own national interests. As the range of national interests has been great indeed, there is a multitude of theories on the concept and role of nations and their mutual contacts and conflicts. The moment they pass into the international sphere, theorists on nationality start discussing national sovereignty.

Rousseau was one of the first to proclaim sovereignty to be an inalienable and indivisible right of nations. He was very often to be quoted and interpreted throughout the 19th century. According to Rousseau, sovereignty was inalienable, since only the general will was able to conduct state affairs for the purpose of which the state had been established. However, this concept of nation and nationality, in the period when national expansion had escalated into imperialism, gave rise to extreme views on exclusive nations and their absolute sovereignty. In his speeches, Fichte called upon the German people to unite, stating that his nation was chosen to lead and govern other nations. Jhering identified might with right, stating in many of his writings that law was power politics. Jurists such as Laband, Jellinek and Bergsbaum elaborated upon Jhering's theses. Theorists like Gobineau, Chamberlain and many others developed and analyzed a theory of race and consciously or not gave support to the growth of the cult of absolute sovereignty. Taking the German race as their ideal, they scorned the rights of other nations.

The racial national state, according to Nazi ideology only respects its own sovereignty. The old theories of Gobineau, Mommsen, Bismarck, Bernhardi and others, as supplied by the Nazis, best typify absolute sovereignty, which would be more accurately called ruthless sovereignty, since the term absolute sovereignty is not very descriptive. The world would suggest an absolute respect for the sovereign rights of a state, but it actually means a denial of anybody else's rights in the world community.

The standing of states vis-à-vis others was often the preoccupation of political and legal writers in the 19th century.

Theorists for the great powers made heroic efforts to explain the inequality between states and to justify the hegemony of the great powers in the conduct of international affairs. They were fond of quoting Hobbes, who had described relations among nations as being similar to relations among men *homo homini lupus.* Funk-Brentano and Sorel, basing their statements on, as they put it, real life, claimed that states were equal only in theory. Inequality, they said, arises from the internal systems of nations, from their public and private customary law, and depends on the level of their intellectual culture. Actual inequality between states entails different rankings, and normally the stronger states take precedence over the weaker ones. Whereas the British jurist Lorimer called the principle of equality of states mistaken, as was the principle of equality of people, since it was merely a legal fiction, his fellow countryman Lawrence defined the mission of the great powers in the following way: even the great powers themselves, taken *en bloc,* are very different from some kind of international gang armed with clubs. They have the function of leading and governing, from which other states greatly benefit. Their position is tolerated, for the community of nations feels the need for their authority. Lawrence concludes that it is impossible to continue defending the old doctrine on absolute equality of states before the law, since it is dead, and proposes a new doctrine in its place, the doctrine that the great powers hold precedence over other states.

Certain writers who favored the theory of political inequality were forced to revise their way of thinking around the turn of the century. The "open door" policy caused theorists, particularly in the great powers that were interested in using this political principle, to launch a new theory, the theory of "relative equality," which hinged on the assertion that the great powers were relatively equal among themselves. German writers, particularly on the eve of the First World War, claimed that states were truly equal if the right to colonize other nations was matched by the nation's ability to carry out colonization. This was the point of departure for the German writers in their political demand for a new division of the world according to actual national might, as they put it.

The "open door" policy arose also as the result of demands for factual equality among the great powers. According to Redslob, the principle of equality was thus expressed in various treaties, which adopted the maximum "open door," putting "various nations" on a par in their ambitions of economic penetration. This principle really was embraced in respect to the Congo in the General Act of 1885, concluded in Berlin and in the Saint-German Convention of 1919, on the question of Morocco at the turn of the century, in the Anglo-French treaty of 8 April 1904, in the Algeciras Convention and in Franco-German agreements of 9 Feburary 1909 and 4 November 1911. This principle was also applied in respect to Persia in the Anglo-Russian agreement of 19 August 1911. It was very much in evidence in the policy of the great powers vis-à-vis China; *viz.,* exchanges of notes between Britain and Germany on 16 October 1905, the Franco-Japanese agreement of 10 June 1907, the Anglo-Japanese alliance of 12 August 1905 and 23 July 1911, and the Nine-Power treaty signed in Washington in 1922.

In line with theoretical thinking on the relative equality of the great powers, as applied in the "open door" policy, the well-known German jurist and author of an authoritative textbook on international law, Joseph Kohler, just before the end of the First World War, devised a special right of the great powers, the right to create spheres of interest, as a right having its own theoretical and historical justification. Kohler stated that the right to create spheres of interest, as a right of possession, was an entitlement to forbid other states to take control of the region in question, but it also meant that other states were forbidden to carry out preparations for taking control; in particular they must not acquire any kind of protectorate, must not build any kind of fortification or roads, and they were to be permitted passage only if it did not conflict with the interests of the empowered state. German theory was based on the assumption that the great powers were relatively equal because they did not have control of equal amounts of territory. However, when Germany lost the war in 1918, Kohler discarded the criterion that the great powers are relatively equal "according to corresponding national might," for Germany's national might had been destroyed in the First World War, and instead submitted another criterion, that of "acquired right" (meaning Germany's) in the division of the world into spheres of influence.

10. October Revolution — The October socialist revolution in Russia was a watershed in the development of international relations and in the evolution of modern international law. The solution of the nationality question on the democratic principle of self-determination of peoples, including the right of secession and formation of an autonomous state was one of the first and perhaps greatest contributions of the Russian revolution. The Declaration of the rights of peoples of Russia, promulgated on 15 November 1917, gave equality and sovereignty to the peoples of Russia. National minorities were given guarantees of free development. One act by the Soviet government, signed by Lenin on 14 June 1918, states that "the fundamental idea of international law . . . is intercourse among equal states." On 8 November 1917, the historical Peace Decree was promulgated, which proposed that "all nations and their governments should immediately begin negotiations on a just, democratic peace," on a peace, "without annexation and contributions." This Decree declared that the government rejected secret diplomacy and expressed its firm intention to carry out all negotiations in complete openness, before the entire nation. On that same day, Lenin announced, "We have no secrets. We wish the government to be under the supervision of the public opinion of the entire country." The one-sided treaties of Tsarist Russia were declared null and void, and concessions granted Russia under the capitulations were renounced. The progressive principles established in October have become the property and tradition of democratic international law.

11. Period between the Two World Wars — In the First World War, the Allies were victorious over the Central powers. Bulgaria was the first to lay down arms on 25 September 1918, followed by Turkey, Austria-Hungary, and finally, the principal belligerent, Germany, on 11 November 1918. The Allies signed five important peace treaties with their former enemies, which between the two world wars provided the foundations for positive public international law. The Versailles Treaty was signed with Germany on 28 June 1919. Amendments, ratification and coming into force were completed on 10 January 1920. That date marked the beginning of the activity of the first international political organization in the modern sense of the word, the League of Nations, whose Covenant formed the first part of the Versailles Treaty.

International law developed between the two world wars predominantly under the influence and auspices of the League of Nations. In signing the Covenant, the members of this international organization pledged that they would not resort to war, that they would maintain "open, just and honourable relations between nations," "understanding of international law as the actual rule of conduct among governments," and that they would maintain justice and scrupulously respect "all treaty obligations in the dealings of organized peoples with one another."

The Covenant of the League of Nations suffered from many gaps, which the member countries felt should be filled. To this end, the Assembly of the League of Nations unanimously adopted in September 1924 the Geneva Protocol (abrogated in 1925) giving the definition of an aggressor. According to this protocol, an aggressor was the state which refused arbitration or, having agreed to it, failed to comply with the decision handed down and instead resorted to force to achieve its aims. Sad to say, this legal definition of an aggressor state was of very little help in stemming the aggression which was soon to break out in Asia and Europe.

Although the Locarno pacts, signed in 1925, were concluded outside the League of Nations, Le Fur considers them part of the activities of this organization, for the effect of these agreements depended on Germany's admission to the League of Nations, and accordingly they would be binding only on member countries of the League. The Locarno pacts were a milestone in international law, for they rejected war as a means of settling disputes and they proclaimed that the frontiers of a state could not be altered without its approval. On 27 August 1928, the Pact of Paris, or, as it is often called, the Kellogg-Briand Pact, formally outlawed war. The signatories of the pact pledged on behalf of their nations to condemn resort to war for settling international disputes and to renounce it as an instrument of national policy in their mutual relations, agreeing that negotiations and settlement of all disputes or conflicts which might arise among them would always be carried out only by pacific means, no matter what the nature or origin of these disputes. However, this pact only partially outlawed war, for only the signatories had renounced war. On September 26th of that same year, the Assembly of the League of Nations adopted the General Act for the Pacific Settlement of International Disputes, known as the *General Geneva Act.* According to this act, before taking recourse to arbitration and the international judiciary — at that time the Permanent Court of International Justice — states should submit to reconciliation, which in principle extended to all disputes; this was mandatory for disputes of a non-legal nature, and voluntary for legal disputes.

The League of Nations was the first central international organization. The centralization of the community of nations, in the sense of concentrating principal international activities in one place, undoubtedly dates from between the two world wars when the League of Nations started functioning. However, the emulation of the system of diplomatic conferences, particularly the system of congresses in the 19th century, exaggerated idealism as seen in the overconfidence which states had in this organization, coupled with the manipulation of the League of Nations by the great powers to promote their own political aims, the subsequent isolationist policy of the Western powers and impotence in the face of the aggressions that began to occur one after the other — all this weakened and finally destroyed the League of Nations so completely that after the Second World War the United Nations decided to regard the League of Nations simply as a Cautionary Lesson and agreed not to create any direct link between the new international organization, the United Nations, and its predecessor in Geneva.

VII. Modern Theories

Introduction — Legal Positivism — Normativism — Sociological Positivism — Methodological Criticism — Theory of Interest — Soviet Theory — Concept of Neutrality and Nonalignment

1. Introduction — The postulates of modern-day theories of international law were laid down after the First World War, when the notion of the community of nations was no longer based on a "general consciousness" or similar criteria, but more on real forms of central political international organization, at that time called the Leauge of Nations, which had some features in common with the system of congresses from the 19th century, but differed in that it was a legal form of intercourse among nations with definite rights and obligations for its members and no longer just a means for adjusting the European political balance of power.

Up until this time, all thinking on international law had moved within the ambit of natural law and the school of positivism. There were some theories which went beyond this domain and heralded future developments, some good and some bad, of international law. Such theories are still interesting today, and what is more, they are often still being modified or adapted for use by modern theorists.

International law is usually approached according to its normative principles, that is as interpreted by various authors, or else according to the problems that form the burden of their considerations. The first method may be arbitrary unless based on objective analysis of the facts, and is often colored by personal prejudices. The second method of analysis almost invariably fails to shed light on every aspect of importance, since writers as a rule dwell only on that concept which is of immediate interest to them. Hence it would seem better advised to take a completely different approach. A comparative study of present-day international relations and modern international law gives a balanced and clear picture of the close interplay between the foreign political aims and actions of states and the institutions of international law, which, when classified into specific groups and systems, form a single body of rules and principles.

This dynamic and complex interaction between politics as content, and law as a system of specific institutions, is virtually impossible to separate into its component parts, even abstractly, for the purpose of analyzing "pure" legal forms and of giving them a separate interpretation. However, this does not mean that law does not have the capability of operating on its own. In certain conditions and at certain times, law and politics blend together, to the extent which the combined political forces are able to achieve in the tightly or loosely woven network of legal institutions. The question of what direction we should take is a matter of choosing the road which will lead a given society, or the international community as a whole, either towards general progress or towards general retrogression. Finding the road sign for general progress means first establishing the criteria according to which these roads will be selected. Suitable vehicles, in this instance of a legal nature, will attract the kind of content that will advance human society on the broadest front and will ensure a permanent forward motion. It is the task of that international law which we call democratic, or progressive, to find such legal norms in the international context, and it is from this standpoint that we shall discuss some of the main currents in the theory of modern international law.

It is our belief that existing schools of thought find it difficult even to cover all the present-day aspects of international law, much less explain them in either practical or theoretical terms.

Almost up until the founding of the United Nations, international law was considered to be highly decentralized, particularly in comparison with a federal state or confederation of states. The fact that the rules of international law were binding only on legal persons, i.e. states, whereas the behavior of individuals was regulated indirectly, through the internal legal systems of states, was cited as a feature of decentralization. The indirect mandatory nature of international law was seen as a consequence of decentralization. Another consequence of decentralization was the absence of organs which would perform some kind of division of labor. The enforcement of law was also decentralized. Any international obligations that were envisaged contained only a modicum of a legal nature. International law was primitive, since it depended on self-help alone.

Today, however, centralization is one of the aspects of the law of the United Nations and a pronounced tendency in the development of international law. In international law, which has been largely molded by the legal system within the United Nations. Their points of departure are perhaps the only thing that sets them apart from the negators. According to their thesis, international law is infralegal law *(Untergesetzrecht)*, whose norms acquire validity from legislative systems, each time separately as an international treaty is concluded. This line of thought leads to the theory of legal monism, based on the primacy of state law. The problem of the existence of international law is then seen in terms of the relationship between the two categories of norms of municipal law: between those norms which govern the legal system within the frontiers of the state, and the norms in that same state which regulate its relations, in the first instance, with neighbors, and then with all other states.

The most forceful advocate of this variant is undoubtedly Georg Jellinek, who never abandoned the principle of absolute sovereignty as he sought firmer ground for ensuring a greater binding force for international law. Drawing heavily on the ideas of Jhering, Jellinek found this ground in the so-called auto-limitation of the state. In his opinion, positive law is only created by the state, whether it is enacted by the state or endorsed and thereby acknowledged by it. The state creates principles of law on the basis of its statutes, which have a legal nature if passed by a legal authority, but this authority is also legal even when limited, since according to Jellinek law is nothing other than power which is restricted by legal rules. Hence state authority in his opinion is the power which is limited by law and differs from other authorities in its sovereignty, which in fact is a legal concept. If the state is a legal subject, and if its authority has a legal nature — which at the same time means that this authority is supreme and unlimited — then in this case, according to Jellinek, no one can deprive it of a single attribute of power, unless it does so itself.

Jellinek's views have been subjected to considerable criticism in legal literature. His theory on legal and state authority and on the legal character of sovereignty gives a ruling sovereign the unlimited right to promulgate rules of law, as it is his decree which actually gives them the force of law.

Legal authority boils down to the use of force without restriction, since this theory does not tell us why or in whose interests it is to promulgate a rule as law. According to this view, any internal restriction leads to despotism. In international law, such a view is wrong, because the will of a state does not create international law. This is a theory which in fact aggressive powers would like to apply. According to some writers, international law is created by the common will of states. It should be noted from the very outset that the common will of states does not possess the authority postulated by the theory of auto-limitation, since even such a common will is not limited; it is rather expressed in terms of certain international rules, which are accepted as international law. Jellinek had to argue in defense of this view in order to defend the political system in which he lived and worked (Bismarck's Germany).

The second variant, which holds that the will of states is the basis for international law, features Triepel's famous theory known as *Vereinbarung.* Carl Binding, an expert in jurisprudence and criminal law, was the primary influence on Triepel when he elaborated his theory, which pivoted upon the differentiation between two types of treaties. One type of treaty is the result of the wills of parties whose interests are conflicting. The obligations fixed in the treaty regulate these conflicting aspirations. Such treaties are called *Vertrag* in German legal terminology. In contrast, there are also treaties known as *Vereinbarung,* in which the joint wills are so closely identified and conflicting elements so minimal that the parties virtually have a common purpose. A fusion of wills has taken place to such an extent that almost all material and psychological antagonism has virtually disappeared. On the basis of this distinction, Triepel constructed his well-known theory, which he felt had also found a formula for regulating the relationship between the internal law of states and international law. International law and municipal law are two autonomous legal systems, which have separate legal sources and separate subject matter. They exist alongside one another, neither one taking formal precedence. The source of state law is the will of the state, while in international relations the legal source is the common will of states. Any reciprocity between the two is merely the reception of legal norms. According to Triepel, state law may, but need not, adopt the norms of international law as an expression of joint wills; but if the state adopts them, it cannot decide unilaterally to reject them, except in situations in which the clause *rebus sic stantibus* can be applied.

There is no doubt that in practical terms this theory provided a good basis for the development of relations between states, and even for the development of a large portion of international treaty law. This theory is considered to have made a great contribution to the evolution of the idea of the modern international community.

As soon as it appeared, it was criticized particularly from a legal stand-point. The controversial issue was the basis on which norms would be binding on states. The big question was how an international rule, created by a treaty or agreement expressing the joint will of states, acquired a legal nature. Today this question is of prime importance and has become even more acute than several decades ago, in view of the increasingly organized forms of contemporary international life. The obligations binding on members of the United Nations have for the most part been laid down in the Charter, which takes the form of a treaty but in content has the nature of a constitution. This constitution, therefore, provides the legal basis for the obligations. According to Triepel's theory, the fate of international law is in the hands of individual states. Today, even though the Charter has been in force only a relatively short time, we could not say that the fate of international law depends solely on individual states. There is a certain international pressure on states to comply with generally accepted rules of international law, and important legal forms are being constructed which induce individual states to submit to the rules contained in international laws, above all in the progressive principles of modern international law.

This weak point in Triepel's theory was noted by the Italian internationalist Anzilotti, who accordingly put international law into a separate system that was independent of the will of states, without abandoning the platform of legal positivism. In this respect, he was greatly influenced by Kelsen, who was gaining renown at the time with his normative theories. Anzilotti found his element of "independence" in the formula *pacta sunt servanda,* which he considered an objective value, a basic norm of the legal order which stood by itself, since it could not be coherently explained from any angle nor could it theoretically have a basis in any other discipline. Today this concept in international relations is certainly important, both from a political and from a legal standpoint. Certain dependent states, for instance, are held in subjugation by the kind of international treaty which is often difficult to break, since any such action would be contrary to the principle of *pacta sunt servanda.* On the other hand, we have seen international treaties arbitrarily broken off, to the obvious detriment of law and order in international relations. The problem is where to place Anzilotti's view, or rather what weight to give to his theory. Finally, one of the key questions is whether the rule *pacta sunt servanda* can be generalized to such an extent as to become a so-called "objective" basis of international law, although its importance in international treaty law cannot be denied. Perhaps one criterion would be the possibility of providing for future developments. Thus the rule *pacta sunt servanda* would always be mandatory, except when circumstances arise which cannot be forseen at the time the treaty is concluded. However, even this criterion is open to criticism. Every party to a treaty could claim (thus shifting the blame) that the conduct of the other side caused the unforseen circumstances to arise. Of course, international life is highly complex, and undoubtedly completely new circumstances do arise which the parties to a treaty could truly never have envisaged at the time. It is unlikely that any difficulty would be posed by the fact that, according to Anzilotti's theory, only the contracting parties are competent to judge whether there has been a new development or not. However, *nemo index in re sua*. For this reason, the formula *pacta sunt servanda* cannot be an objective basis of international law; rather such a basis should be sought in the foundation of the legally organized system of the international community.

2. Legal Positivism — Positivism in international law has been under constant fire from critics, mainly because it revives the fiction of a social contract, reinstates absolute sovereignty, bolsters national individualism, and prevents the development of international law in the direction of international cooperation and internationalism. This school of thought is particularly criticized for separating international ethics from international law. A general objection which is present in virtually every attack on positivism and its variants is actually the consistently dogmatic treatment of international problems.

In his most recent textbook, Professor Sibert discusses these criticisms. Natural law as discerned by human reason has over the centuries undergone so many changes that it is difficult today to say whether a maxim belongs to natural law or whether it is contrary to human reason, according to Sibert. However, this does not mean that natural law has lost every meaning for international law; Sibert goes on to say that even today, when a judge cannot find a positive regulation to refer to, he has to take recourse to his own reason and to make a decision on the basis of common sense. There are any number of such examples in the practice of law throughout the world. The question arises, states Sibert, of what is the criterion for the application of positive law or some norm of natural law when a written law does not exist. In his view this criterion is to be found in the public order, i.e. in the body of independent rules on which order and peace for all rest. Every legal act which is contrary to public order is invalid, regardless of whether it is proclaimed within a state or in international relations.

Sibert's work is based on Fauchille's classic textbook published in five volumes between 1921 and 1925, right after the First World War, when international relations were different and an international community was taking shape that differed from the one today. This fact is important from an objective standpoint as well. The school of legal positivism considers a question or set of problems in the light of those rules of international law that are in force at the time. Hence the criterion of an order is qualified by time and space. The positivist method is of a static nature which is difficult to avoid, whatever line of legal interpretation is taken. Sibert's view, for instance, on the colonial problem is essentially no different from that of Fauchille's. The modern regime of protectorates, viewed exclusively from the standpoint of the contracted relationship between the protector and the "protected" is today without a doubt a vestige from the historical arsenal of international law. Taking this outdated approach Sibert calls legal fictions to his aid, viewing them as instruments which, along with others, create present-day international law. Certainly legal constructions are not excluded from international law, nor is there any quarrel against depending on a fiction of a legal nature. However, the system of legal concepts must be identical or else it must be based on international social, i.e. political, reality. If this groundwork does not exist, every legal fiction, i.e. hypothesis, is futile and falls in the category of that legal formalism which must be rejected both as a method and as a theory because of the results it may lead to. In our opinion, precisely this mistake is made when this school of thought is espoused, and even if the desire to modernize international law is present, as it is for Sibert, it is very difficult to make any progress, because old methodological principles are used in adjusting to new international relations. Sibert avoids, for instance, the dogmatic view on the exclusive personality of the state. However, as a result he is very ambiguous concerning the concept of states in general. In certain places in his writing, the state is seen as an immanent reality, a concept which as such is acceptable, whereas in other chapters, most often in his analyses, the author treats the state as a means for achieving an end and not as an end in itself. Following this vague principle, he does not even offer his own assessment of sovereignty, as he merely reiterates the theory of absolute sovereignty and presents modern views on this legal principle.

If, however, today we look at the relationship between the proponents of positivism and the milieu in which positivism is defended, we shall see that the static view of international law, which is expressed by positivism, is maintained in those countries which are fighting against having their status in the international community changed (Great Britain, France).

3. Normativism — The normativist view of the institutions of international law, particularly the relationship between state and international law, has been exhaustively described by the former Viennese professor now teaching in the United States, Hans Kelsen, and is known today in virtually all continents. This school of thought is famous for its original classification of laws and legal systems into categories of so-called "pure" and "independent" science, without any admixture of non-legal or especially political elements.

Law, according to Kelsen, is a system of autonomous norms which are based on a specific postulate, the "basic norm," and their fundamental characteristic is effectiveness. Law is a science and not politics. This is one of the essential assumptions on which all Kelsen's other constructions are based, particularly as regards international law, The prime function of science is to seek the truth, according to Kelsen, and therefore it must not be influenced by political interests, which motivate individuals or groups in setting up a given social order or social institutions. Politics, according to Kelsen, is the art of governing, of regulating the social behavior of people, while the purpose of science is not to rule but to explain. Science sets out to describe the world, and it is not the duty of the scientist to make value judgments. Scientific statements are judgements about reality, and they may be true or false. Axiological judgements, in his opinion, are subjective, since they are based on emotions. Reality and values are two completely separate and independent spheres. To separate politics from science means removing value judgements from scientific analyses.

This logically closed system of Kelsen's is based on an unrealistic assumption, called the "basic norm." Facts derive from this sytem of presupposed norms. Law, according to Kelsen, is a ruling norm and not a fact. Herein lies the basic methodological weakness of this school of thought, and it carries with it other misconceptions. A norm is also a fact, just as the system of norms is a system which contains facts within itself. It is the effectiveness of norms which is most often dependent on the social milieu which gives a number of norms their validity. This mistake in Hans Kelsen's basic assumption was largely made under the impression that continental law had been completely codified. The author's efforts to justify this system and the difficulties he meets with on the way are particularly in evidence when he defines the importance of customary law, which he includes in the hierarchy of his norms. Here he is adopting non-legal elements, since he himself decides which rule of conduct to raise to the level of custom, even though it does not derive form the "basic norm," and here the jurist falls into the trap of becoming a politician. This self-contradiction is particularly glaring in his views on modern international law, especially in his analysis of the present-day international organization, the United Nations.

4. Sociological Positivism — Theorists of sociological positivism took an opposite track from that taken by the exponents of legal positivism. In their opinion, the will of states is not a creator of law, because legal sources are to be found in the social needs that call into being other social and legal relationships. On the other hand, the will of state authority is of particular importance, for it affirms the existence of a social rule of conduct and this in fact is what constitutes a norm of positive law. According to the view of this positivist variant, positive law is the body of rules recognized by the authorities which regulate human relations within one or more social groups. In line with this general view, international law is composed of rules recognized by the competent government authorities, and it contains a collection of legal obligations for the subjects of this legal discipline.

This positivist variant also takes account of contemporary international relations, starting from the general view that states make up the international community and that to establish order in it is in fact to introduce legal relationships, in this instance on the basis of the social needs that exist in international relations.

Although it is more flexible than the earlier concepts of legal positivism, this theoretical conception of modern international law suffers from the absence of a dynamic criterion which, generally speaking, should take into consideration the contemporary international social background, and which should also contain a guiding principle for general social progress. In other words, the concepts we have discussed so far all aim at regulating existing relationships. *They have no elements that would guide these relations towards greater internationalization of society through democratization of the institutions of modern international law.* The method of legal positivism, whose sole aim is to bring order into the existing international system, is almost always more important to these theorists than an attempt to find a new force or new outlook which would not just foster the maintenance or improvement of present relations but change them so as to promote the creation of a new international community with a new system of international law.

Certainly we must not belittle the desires, efforts and results in practical and theoretical activity aimed at improving international relations by means of legal regulation. However, we feel that the instruments and legal forms that have been developed on the basis of contemporary methodological assumptions are particularly unsuited to bring about a change in many international institutions or to create any significant number of transitional forms, which should lead the world community towards a progressive development. In this respect, international law cannot be passive. Past methods have almost always attributed to international law a more or less passive nature. The force of legal forms is not an empty fiction if it is based on various international relations. This force should be harnessed in the service of overall world progress.

That efforts are still being made by legal writers to consolidate and improve modern international relations, which are burdened by many harmful legacies from the past, can be seen from the methods of the latest variant of sociological positivism, the theory of jurisdiction in international law. The authors of the theory of jurisdiction in public international law are Scelle and Basdevant. Cavaré adopted and elaborated upon this theory, as is immediately obvious from his system. According to Scelle, the primary function of law is to compare, delineate and restrict jurisdictions. In international law, the concept of jurisdiction, according to Cavaré, must be conceived very broadly. According to him, legal authority is that which controls legal activity. Jurisdiction is a manifestation of will, but it does not create law, since the basis of every rule of law lies in social needs. Will of course may produce certain secondary legal relationships; in a certain sense it may even promulgate a rule of law, but only within the general limitations set by social needs. Hence it can be concluded that will, although not creating law, is that which can acknowledge it. Positive law designates the organs of authority that control legal activity. It follows then that the scope of authority is restricted. Will only calls forth a legal effect and is manifested in forms which are restricted by positive law. Every act of law is an embodiment of a legal effect; hence an act of law is a prerequisite for creating any new situation or for regulating a legal situation which already exists.

The question is whether this theory from the internal law of states can be applied in international law and whether it has pretensions of being adopted in general international law or in certain parts of it, and if so, in which parts? Next, how can the application of international competences be resolved, in view of the existence of the sovereignty of states.

The key consideration in these central issues is, according to Cavaré, the fact that the concept of sovereignty is today less exclusive than it was previously and that, in this respect, there are obstacles to applying international jurisdictions in general, since "social international rules" are already being enforced by states, and they represent positive international law, which is above states and binding on them. If a large source of their competences is found in social needs, a direct source lies in positive law, which ascertains and registers these needs.

Theorists of this positivist school pay special attention to jurisprudence, which, in addition to other sources, has the main role in verifying competences and determining their scope. Generally speaking, the advocates of the theory of competences in international law hold that modern international law is an undefined collection of mixed jurisdictions. They feel that the interpretation of these competences will bring order into this sphere, while adhering to the principle of the primacy of international law, of that international system which regulates relations between states in the way described at the beginning of this chapter as the concept of sociological positivism.

The shortcoming of this school of thought is that in a way it denies general rules when it seeks to explain everything as a division of competences, i.e. the so-called right of creating the law. However, the right of creating the law is not the essence of law, but is merely a process for determining it. Another failing in this theory is the belief that will, expressed by the competent law-maker, is equivalent to the general will of society and not to that socially relative interest which at a given moment uses its force to subordinate everything to its own interests.

5. Methodological Criticism — Our principal methodological criticism of the theories discussed here is that they mainly approached all regulation by international law in a static manner as a matter concerning relations between states, in which interests are more often than not promoted according to the strength of the partners. Legal norms were constructed on the basis of threat of denying certain rights. The rules of international law were in fact usually observed, insofar as it was in the interest of a state to do so or if compliance was a lesser evil than suffering the consequences of disobeying. The creation and interpretation of the system of international legal norms was approached from the standpoint of the balance of power among the states having direct dealings with one another, which means that only those suffering prejudice were legitimately entitled to redress an injustice. A case in international law was *res inter alios acta* for third states, unless, of course, their own state interests were affected.

However, today the trend is toward a greater integration of the international community. This integration is in large part a product of modern technology, which is causing the world to shrink at an incredible rate. International trade has also been an important factor here. There is virtually no country in the world whose industry can provide for its needs from domestic raw materials alone. The interdependence of different national economies has entailed a general economic cooperation among states. The internationalization of the mode of production and exchange has brought about an international division of labor. Every day the organization of a unified world market is being perfected. Hence today the interest of third states is a generally acknowledged interest in international law. World peace is thus a universal legal concern, and not just the concern of the states directly involved, such as the parties to a dispute. Sanctions are no longer just a matter of coercion outside the law, but may also be organized legal sanctions. In this way force can be changed by an instrument of law even in the international arena, which is the most difficult environment imaginable for such a transformation. We are living at a time when qualitatively new international relations are being forged, often under the pressure of the tremendous growth in productive forces. The force of change is irresistible, and we must therefore find a new approach to the qualitatively new development in international affairs.

6. Theory of Interest — The concept of an objective interest in international law could do much to remove the mentioned shortcoming in the leading school of thought that we have been discussing. In view of the implications of such an idea, we should discuss arguments in favor of making *objective interest* a methodological basis for international law.

The sociological school is making enormous efforts to separate its theoretical constructions in international law from that rather unbending formalist platform which in many ways prevents a realistic consideration of international law, and they are doing so from the standpoint of either legal (Vauchère) or sociological (Huber) positivism.

The sociological interpretation of international processes paved the way for a subjectivist theory of international law, whose arguments are based on the fact that every rule of law is formulated on the basis of some personal interest, which in coexistence with other interests seeks its realization with the aid of legal rules. This sociological variant, the theory of *subjective interest* in international law, whose forerunner in law in general was Jhering, has been given very little consideration. Whatever attention was paid to it was either from the angle of pragmatism (Pound) or from the standpoint of subjective axiological ideas (Wengler). Both these approaches intersect at a point which should denote the advantage or disadvantage of a legally designated interest in the process of the increasing material enrichment of individuals in circumstances of exploitation.

The other concept would start from a completely opposite premise. We would begin not with subjective but rather with objective considerations, which is not to say that the first should be neglected, for after all it is for the sake of human beings that attempts are made — be they sincere or false, realistic or unrealistic — to regulate social relations. If subjective elements are not ignored, it does not mean that the points of departure are identical. An objective approach to interpreting interest in international law is essentially different from the subjectivist views of the authors we have discussed.

Jurisprudence is concerned with those interests whose realization benefits the class in power. No group organized on class lines and holding power in modern society will concern itself with satisfying the interests of individuals to the detriment of the group interest. Therefore, every fulfilment of an individual interest is nothing other than a direct or indirect reflection of the class principle, conceived as such in a given time and place. The way in which an interest is realized, directly or indirectly, is a question of the concrete legal institution, which may be suitable or unsuitable. Such an institution is suitable if it produces the desired effect, and unsuitable if it produces the opposite effect.

It should be remembered that there is also pressure from the subjugated class against the class in power. In order to maintain its position, the ruling class must often steer a course between its own and other interests, those of the class which is not in power or of a nation under colonial subjugation, despite the highly developed instruments of state coercion we have today. This pressure on the ruling class is of international significance, since the need to compromise in domestic policy casts its implications on foreign relations, just as every international event is assessed from the standpoint of domestic political interest. It is clear then that this effect is also of particular importance for international law, for in present-day conditions it should not only coordinate international interests — still a very important job — but also see to the *general interest of the international community, which should be manifested in progressive principles of international law.* Today in the United Nations the general will is being put forward as a principle in regulating international cooperation. This principle has been understood in the light of Rousseau's theory, but it is nothing other than the general interest, a term which is far more accurate in describing this concept. Therefore, it seems to us that it is becoming increasingly urgent to shift the political and legal emphasis (although this is a long process) from relations between states to relations within the organized international community, where political pressures and means for realizing individual interests, most often the interests of the strongest powers, will not be made into law, but rather political goals will be achieved on the basis of a body of rights and obligations which have been fixed on principles that we call progressive.

Wengler defines interest as an internal psychological process, a feeling of pleasure or discomfort. We do not deny that a specific state of mind, which may be pleasant or unpleasant, can be created as a reflection of a given class social interest (understood by that group at any given moment as an objective interest). In fact here, we feel, is the crux of the matter.

All social development is a tooth and nail struggle between those who wish to restrict and those who try to enlarge the sum of the interests that can be satisfied. Just how the so-called objective interest will affect the psychological state of mind of individuals is often quite irrelevent, since the socially organized force imposes the rule of law according to the concept of its social ideology which determines the criteria of so-called objective needs. Whether or not these criteria lead society to a progressive development or in the opposite direction, will be judged from the results which follow from the chosen course. The road that has been traversed should show whether the scope of realized individual interests of the members of the social community concerned has been expanded. Therefore, while the process of social development is still going on, passing psychological moods cannot be taken as a yardstick of whether such a legally determined interest has been satisfied or not, regardless of whether, as is the case with Jhering, monetary ethical elements are considered, which at first may appear egoistic or altruistic, because social consciousness may call them one thing today and something else the next day, when circumstances have changed.

Can the state interest be defined simply as a psychological notion of interest; that is, do such interests, in mathematical terms, represent a "function" of the individual interests? An affirmative answer would mean that the state is a living being which has its own psyche. Logically, then, the absence of a state psyche would imply the absence of state interest. However, this interest undoubtedly exists, even according to the subjectivist view. The absurdity of this logic when carried to this extreme was recognized by Wengler himself. According to him, the criterion according to which state interests differ from other human interests is only in the means by which it is attempted to fulfil the interests.

The interests of individuals are legally regulated by the class group which holds power. Such a group may impose upon the entire subjugated class a sum of interests which actually, in terms of objective social development, and "mathematically" speaking, are not a "function of their interests." On the other hand, it is not uncommon for the class, or the entire nation, to fight for the realization of some interests, irrespective of whether or not such a "general interest" coincides with individual interests, viewed subjectively. There are innumerable instances of lives being sacrificed for a given class, social or national purpose. Here the individual interest is lost, swallowed up by the general interest. If one objects that this loss of life is nevertheless in someone's interest, then objectively the answer is that every sacrifice is undoubtedly in the interest of a given class, state, or nation.

If the subjective line of reasoning is taken, the problem would be solved quite easily. We know what is pleasing or displeasing to every person; in other words, what is or is not in his interest. It would be easy to establish these interests and just as easy to regulate them by law. However, the problem arises because such a solution is not possible; life is a constant struggle between people, socially categorized according to the class criterion.

The product of the subjectivist view is the conception of other state interests. If the continuity of state interests is seen as priority consistently given to the interests only of individuals, which are essentially an "internal psychological process," a then inevitable corollary is the theory of psychological, political heritage, that is, the predestination of dominant racial forms, which in turn leads to the thesis of "aggressor nations." Again, if we take the subjectivist view of the theory of interest and methodologically apply it in sociology, then we are forced to subscribe wholesale to geopolitical postulates that today have largely been proven unscientific. Whichever alternative we take, the subjectivist standpoint leads us to the false conclusion that history is a repetition of the same events.

If the foreign policies of a state contain similar or, from a class aspect, identical aims at different periods in its history, this is by no means proof that there is a continuity of permanent state interests. The kindred aims of the exploiting classes which hold power may give the impression that they have identical foreign policy aims. However, the interests of various ruling classes are safeguarded in different ways; therefore, in different periods of history state interests are also different. Of course, we must not forget that within limited periods of time the legal status of a state generates a number of specific state interests, on the basis of those principles of international law on which a state is founded, exists, and develops. But because every state is undergoing some kind of development, whatever it may be, the so-called permanent interests are inevitably modified.

In the formation of international law, the concept of the general interest could be applied and explained today in the following way: in society there is a great struggle going on between conflicting interests, and it is the task of international law to achieve a balance among these interests, which is relative but necessary at the present level of development of international relations, for the sake of maintaining world peace, which is a public property and as such must be safeguarded by rules of modern international law.

7. Soviet Theory — Soviet theory of international law can roughly be divided into two periods: from the October revolution up until the Second World War, and from the end of the war to the present day. Soviet experts on international law are inclined to consider the Soviet doctrine as all of a piece throughout its development, although they do not deny the possibility of the division we have made. They are of the opinion that the task of distinguishing periods should be left to future historians of international law. However, we think that there were only slight variations in the basic understanding of international law up until the Second World War. It would be difficult to speak of any controversial concepts during this time.

After the Second World War, differences in viewpoints became evident. It seems to us that immediately after the end of the war new historical elements had to be incorporated into existing definitions of modern international law, such as the appearance of a large number of new socialistic states, the growing national consciousness of many colonial and semicolonial countries, and particularly the military, economic and political dissolution of empires, the downfall of the Axis powers and the inauguration of a new international political balance. The second phase in the development of Soviet theory of international law was the cold war and division of the world into two large blocs. This second phase has its own watershed: the change after Stalin's death, i.e. after 1955, when Khruschev's influence in foreign policy became dominant. It is probably from that time on that Soviet theory began criticizing the prevailing views of Vyshinski. For instance, Vyshinski, as Stalin's "theoretical oracle," is criticized for ignoring the role of the popular masses and the principle of coexistence, and for exaggerating the importance of the element of coercion in international law. The third phase in the development of Soviet theory was marked by Khruschev's influence in foreign policy. In all the works of this period, it is Khruschev and not Stalin who is praised. Khruschev's fall marked the beginning of the fourth period in Soviet theory of international law, while the last period can be dated from the intervention of five Warsaw Pact countries in Czechoslovakia in 1968.

The term "modern international law" can be found in the legal literature of the 19th century. However, in the opinion of Soviet authors, this term had a chronological meaning at that time and in fact formally designated the change in the international law to date. Modern international law, as applied by jurists in the 19th century, was not intended to change the social character of previous international law. And from the great October socialist revolution, the term "modern international law" began to signify a new content in this legal discipline. In the view of Soviet theorists, this new social content was the regulation of relations between states having different socioeconomic systems, on the principle of peaceful coexistence.

The concept "modern international law" has undergone an evolution in Soviet theory of international law. In the course of less than fifty years, this term has been formulated in a variety of ways and interpreted differently by leading Soviet experts. This is quite understandable in view of the development of international relations, particularly in view of the place and role of the Soviet Union in the world and the political changes within the Soviet Union itself.

As early as 1926, in a work entitled *Modern Public International Law,* Korovin described this legal science as a "collection of valid legal norms, which regulate the rights and duties of collectivities of ruling classes, who are participants in international intercourse." Several years after the appearance of Korovin's textbook, the well-known Soviet legal theorist E. Pashukanis made a critical analysis of the definition of international law as a body of norms regulating the mutual relations of states. According to his understanding, such a definition was in keeping with bourgeois ideological concepts.

According to Pashukanis, international law cannot be considered apart from politics. In the era of imperialism, international law was one of the means by which imperialist states waged a mutual struggle, dividing up territories according to the criteria we are all familiar with. That is why they talked about the international law of civilized states. When the first socialist state appeared, this balance of power fundamentaly changed, and that is why, Pashukanis goes on to say, international law has become a form of struggle between two systems, the system of capitalism and the system of socialism. Having asserted that international law is a means and form of struggle between the two systems, Pashukanis denies the existing universal international law. He elaborated this idea in a paper published two years after Professor Korovin's textbook and reprinted in his later book published in 1935. Pashukanis holds that international law is the product of the last four centuries of European history. The interests of the dynasties in the period of absolutism were interrelated and considered perpetual. That is why the international law of the time guaranteed the stability and permanence of international treaties, regardless of changes that might occur in those states. When the bourgeoisie came into power, this concept changed. Previous international treaties were proclaimed invalid and not binding on the new bourgeois states. Later the interests of the bourgeois class, Pashukanis continues, became constant, regardless of any possible changes in government. However, the time came when the proletariat seized power in their own hands, refusing to allow anything to bind them to the past. All international treaties which were not concluded by the working class through their legitimate representatives are in his opinion null and void.

From the Congress of jurists held in Moscow on 19 July 1938, Vyshinski's influence on the theory of international law held sway. The theses published in the fifth issue of the periodical *The Soviet State* in 1938, signified Vyshinski's victory, not only as the public prosecutor under whom Pashukanis was sentenced to death (he has recently been rehabilitated), but also as the legal theorist of state and international law. Previously there had been many statements to the effect that international law was the least developed of all legal disciplines and that it should be elaborated from the positions of Marxism-Stalinism. Pashukanis's conception of international law was attacked because he was thought to be an advocate of compromise between the two systems of antagonistic classes, and his idea on international law as inter-class law was particularly anathematized. In the theses of the 1938 Congress of jurists, particularly in the twelfth thesis, Pashukanis and Korovin were specifically attacked. Vyshinski's definition sums up the theses adopted by the Congress. According to him, international law is a collection of norms which regulate relations between states in the process of their conflict and cooperation, which express the will of the ruling classes of these states, and whose application is secured by coercion, individual or collective. This definition can be found in Vyshinski's well-known work, *International Law and International Organization,* published in 1949.

Soon after the Second World War, in his treatise "International Law in the Present Phase," Korovin pointed out the new developments in modern international law. He gave first place in importance to the principle of sovereignty as a legal means of defending interests, not only for the U.S.S.R., but for other people's democracies and countries fighting for their freedom and national independence. He believed that international law was now reflected in the struggle between "progressive-democratic and reactionary-imperialist aspirations."

Professor D.B. Levin designates the most important fundamental principles of international law as being the principle of maintaining peace and universal security, the principle of sovereign equality of peace-loving states, and the principle of the fulfilment of international treaties and obligations in good faith. There is no doubt that the San Francisco Charter influenced Levin in his selection of these principles as the primary ones in international law.

The textbook edited by Durdenevski and Krylov and published in 1947 by the Institute of Law of the Academy of Sciences of the U.S.S.R., repeats Vyshinski's definition word for word. That same year Kozhevnikov's textbook also appeared in which modern public international law was described as a body of historically changing rules of conduct which regulate specific political, economic and other relations between states in their conflicts and cooperation with each other. The 1955 textbook by Lisovski was still using Vyshinski's definition.

A collective textbook edited by Kozhevnikov and published in 1964, rejected Vyshinski's definition, calling it a "pernicious conception." Korovin's new definition is cited and described as "interesting." Korovin considers modern international law to be an "international code of peaceful coexistence," and as such the result of competition and struggle between the two systems — socialism and capitalism, exclusively by peaceful means. That same year saw another textbook on international law, edited by D.B. Levin and G.P. Kaliuzhnai. According to these authors, modern international law is a collection of norms which are created on the basis of international treaties among states having different social systems; they represent the harmonization of their wills and are regulated in the process of conflict and cooperation for the purpose of maintaining peace and peaceful coexistence. These norms are enforced in the case of need by the interested states, either individually or collectively. The leading principle in relations among the socialist countries put forward in this textbook is the principle of socialist internationalism; a clear distinction is thus drawn between general international law and international socialist law. The authors are at pains to point out that international socialist law does not contradict universal international law; on the contrary, it strengthens its democratic content and in this way gives it social and legal validity. This textbook also defines the content of modern international law, which contains two types of norms: progressive norms and principles universally acknowledged by mankind and present throughout the history of the development of states. The progressive principles have been formulated and applied in practice by the Soviet Union and other socialist states and are recognized by other states.

The eminent Soviet expert on international law, G.I. Tunkin, offers the definition of modern universal international law as a body of norms which are formed on the basis of international agreements, which express the consensus of the states concerned and thus relegate mutual relations in the process of conflict and cooperation, with the aim of ensuring the peaceful coexistence of the states belonging to the two systems, envisaging in cases of need the enforcement of sanctions by the interested states either individually or collectively.

What is new in Tunkin's conception is the interpretation given to various elements in the definition of modern international law. Tunkin's book follows this definition with a criticism of Vyshinski. He states that the essence of modern law is peaceful coexistence, adding that it is here that Vyshinski's definition falls down, since it was formulated at the time of the "personality cult." According to Tunkin, Vyshinski exaggerated the role of coercion in securing observance of legal norms. Without denying the importance of coercion, Tunkin points out that it is not the only means for ensuring observance of legal norms, as there is less scope for imposing sanctions in international law than there is in state law. Actually, Tunkin's basic assumption is that international law is a social phenomenon, that its basic nature is social, and that accordingly it has a corresponding role in the system of social relations. In respect to international agreements, as a consensus of wills, this consensus is mutually conditioned, and therefore consensus and reciprocity of wills are an essential characteristic of contracts between states and the means by which norms of international law are created. According to Soviet theory, the primary feature of modern international law is its division into universal and socialist, analogous to the political notion of the division of the world into two blocs. Peaceful coexistence is the political groundwork for so-called universal international law, while the principles of proletarian internationalism are the political basis for socialist international law.

The principles and norms of socialist international law are in force among socialist countries, and thus their application is limited in comparison with the valid principles and norms of universal international law. Today this is the generally accepted thesis of Soviet legal writers. What is more, the relationship between socialist and universal international law is defined in the following way: socialist principles and norms are considered to be particular norms, while the principles and norms of universal international law are general norms, which may be valid and enforceable among socialist states as well. Soviet internationalists do not deny this. In their opinion, those relations between socialist countries which are not regulated by socialist principles and norms are regulated by the principles and norms of universal international law. Just which relations are not regulated by socialist but by universal international law is not specified either in textbooks or in individual treatises in Soviet theory of international law. They do give the following examples, however: the principle of state sovereignty over airspace, the principle of freedom of the high seas, the principle of sovereignty of states in territorial waters, principles and norms of diplomatic privileges and immunities. However, these examples illustrate possibilities while not solving the problem in principle. This uncharted area in Soviet theory of international law deserves special attention, particularly because of the claim that socialist international law seeks to replace the norms and principles of modern universal international law, a view particularly insisted upon by Professor Tunkin, as one of the most authoritative Soviet experts today. However, other Soviet theorists are also influenced by this thinking when they claim that socialist international law is transforming universal international law, infusing "new blood" into old principles and rules of international law.

Socialist international law is based on a political assumption which is given categorical historical significance. This assumption is the "absence of antagonism between socialist states." According to Soviet internationalists, the absence of antagonism between socialist states is a rule in the modern development of international relations in this part of the divided world. They cite Marxist teachings that the history of exploitative societies is at the same time the history of constant wars because of the inevitable atagonisms that arise in a class society. The socialist countries have a similar and unified economic base, the system of social ownership of the means of production, a peoples government, which is characterized by the victory of the working class, a single ideology, common interests in safeguarding the achievements of the revolution and national independence from the imperialist camp, and, finally, the ultimate goal of achieving a communist society. The sum total of these socioeconomic and political interests creates an objective basis for international relations within the socialist camp.

Such an assertion prompts the question of how to explain, notwithstanding all the reasons adduced for the possible absence of antagonistic relations between non-exploiting societies in the socialist states, the appearance of disputes and conflicts between states with socialist systems. The answer is that the moment a socialist state comes into conflict with the socialist camp it ceases to be socialist. If we carry the logic of this reply a bit further, it follows that if normal relations are restored with this country, then it regains the attribute of being a socialist state. The logical implications of this conclusion suggest that the character of a socialist social and governmental system lies in its foreign policy and not in the economic and social structure of the state.

On the other hand, if we subscribe to the thesis that every country does and should take its own road to socialism, then what criterion should be used to judge the degree of its socialism? If the answer is the criterion of the socialist camp, then we contradict the thesis that each country builds its socialist society in accordance with its own special socioeconomic conditions.

Finally, we come to a basic question, and one which was undoubtedly being asked even earlier in Soviet theory of international law: how to determine the attributes of sovereignty in socialist international law in accordance with its principles and norms. The answer was given after the military intervention of five Warsaw Pact countries in Czechoslovakia in 1968. In the socialist camp states have *limited sovereignty,* as the sovereignty of a socialist state is taken to mean the right to choose concrete measures for perfecting the socialist system according to a single model, the Soviet model. Anything else is revisionism. There is just one road to socialism, and that is the Soviet road. And here we have the latest, fifth phase in the development of Soviet theory of international law.

8. The Concept of Neutrality and Nonalignment — Neutrality is
an institution of international law and a political phenomenon which has un-

dergone a marked evolution from the most ancient times up to the present. In various periods of history, neutrality has been variously interpreted, both from the standpoint of international law and from the standpoint of international political relations, in view of its historically changing role and political and legal application. Today we have such an accumulation of notions of neutrality of states that quite different concepts are confused with one another, or the reconstructed institutions of neutrality are attributed a different meaning from that of a given type of neutrality, regardless of whether this neutrality is linked to the specific legal or political status of a country or to the political doctrine adopted by states and nations in their everyday international affairs. Certainly, the different interpretations are understandable insofar as they represent different roads to the same goal. However, there are often misunderstandings or deliberate misinterpretations, both in the theory of foreign affairs and in everyday political life, or else concepts which have diverse meanings are lumped together.

Neutrality comes into effect when states in conflict decide to pursue their political and military aims by means of war. Neutrality must be as old as wars between states. The interests of those states and peoples who wish to remain aloof from a given war have brought into being the institution of neutrality, first in a political and soon after in a legal sense.

Classical neutrality actually represents a legal relationship in which parties to a conflict are obliged to respect certain rights of neutral states, just as neutral states, for their part, are obliged to refrain from or prevent certain acts in regard to the belligerents, or to tolerate certain actions from them.

The system of collective security seeks to rally as many states as possible for taking joint measures against violators of world peace. When systems of collective security were created through international organizations such as the League of Nations, the question arose whether such an institution as neutrality was justified. There were many treatises on interventional law written right after the First World War which advanced that collective security was the negation of neutrality. After the signing of the Kellogg-Briand Pact, in which for the first time war was categorically outlawed as an instrument of national policy, the controversy flared even higher, and was joined by politicians as well as experts on international law. Discussions on this subject were revived after the Second World War, or more precisely, after the adoption of the Charter of the United Nations, when a far more comprehensive system of collective security was created under the auspices of this world organization, one of whose principal purposes was "to take effective collective measures for the prevention and removal of threats to the peace, and for the suppression of acts of aggression or other breaches of the peace." Chapter VII of the Charter, as we know, outlines the procedure to be taken in case of a threat to the peace, breach of the peace or acts of aggression. It is still a moot question whether the political and legal stand of neutrality can be opted for in case of a dispute or in the case of an outbreak of hostilities.

Seventy countries were involved in the Second World War. More than forty resorted to neutrality on the eve of the war. Just six states managed to retain this status throughout, these being Switzerland, Sweden, Spain, Portugal, Afghanistan and Ireland. Even these were often forced to abandon the rules of neutrality and resort to socalled "necessary measures," which were rather a violation and misuse of their declared status than legal measures. This shows that in present-day circumstances it is very difficult, and indeed well-nigh impossible, for neutral states to exercise their rights and duties as envisaged by international law. This fact alone is enough to put the survival of the institution of neutrality in its conventional sense at stake.

The system of collective security under the United Nations Charter also seems to represent a negation of neutrality, if the letter of the Charter is strictly interpreted, as opposed to practice. The orientation of the five great powers, the permanent members of the Security Council, to manage world affairs on the principle of unanimity, is proof enough that there is no room for neutrality in the international order founded upon the United Nations Charter. In this sense writers are justified in interpreting the U.N. Charter and the will of its San Francisco drafters as meaning that there is no justification for the institution of neutrality in the system of collective security of the United Nations. There are some writers — Kelsen for instance — who defend the view that neutrality is incompatible with the U.N. Charter. International life, however, has taken another path. The institution of neutrality can find its justification, both in the legal and in the political system of the United Nations only, of course, in a different form. Other legal theorists — e.g. the Viennese professor Verdross — were quick to claim that neutrality was indeed possible on the basis of the U.N. Charter itself, aside from the fact that U.N. practice had shown the advantage for certain countries to be neutral in a war under certain circumstances. Actually, the appearance of another permanently neutral state, Austria, revived the old debate on the legal nature and role of neutral states in the contemporary international order.

The institution of neutrality has been used on several occasions since the Second World War: when the status of the free territory of Trieste was determined; mention was made of neutrality in the Geneva conventions of 1949; the example of India in the Korean war; at the Geneva conference of 1954, agreement was reached on the neutrality of Laos; in January 1951 Cambodia passed a law declaring its neutrality.

Today there are only two permanently neutral states, i.e. two examples of so-called neutrality by treaty. One country has largely retained the classical form of permanent neutrality (Switzerland), whereas the other has acquired a new form of a permanently neutral state (Austria). These are two exceptional cases to which the great powers agreed because of their specific position and role, which are not in conflict with the interests of the great powers. As for the institution of military neutrality, it is still possible today.

However, our final conclusion would be that individual or strictly regional use of the classical institution of neutrality is less and less possible in the modern world. Why is this? Because the classical concept of neutrality hinges on refusal to take an active stance in modern international relations. To take such an attitude would be tantamount to condemning one's country to passivity, which is virtually impossible because a passive state will never be left alone.

This conclusion by no means suggests a negation of neutral policy or a neutral stand on conflicts of interests between the great powers. However, this is no longer the classical institution of neutrality but an active political stance, specifically the policy of nonaligned countries vis-à-vis bloc policies, which we shall discuss presently.

After the Second World War, the international political configuration underwent a radical change.

The Second World War was waged against the Axis powers by a world democratic coalition, which was already being called the united nations even before the war ended. This was a liberation war, a war with noble and progressive aims. That is why the end of the war was more than just the victory of a group of great powers over another group of states; it was a victory of democratic ideas concerning relations between states, a victory over aggressive, hegemonistic and similar notions and aspirations. This was the victory of mankind which wanted a final peace and the best possible relations among nations. However, the unequal relations between states and between peoples persisted, and disparities in economic development in different parts of the world have only increased. Economic differences between the advanced and underdeveloped countries tend to create unequal political relations. Although the old colonial system could no longer survive and forms of colonialism had to change, the world remained divided into the industrially developed colonial metropolises and the underdeveloped, raw-material-producing countries.

The most important outcome of the Second World War was the creation of military and political alliances, or blocs, which soon embarked upon an armaments race. Their very existence exacerbated the economic division of the world; instead of the normal economic relations developing between peoples and states some parts of the world opted for autarky, and world economic growth was subordinated to narrow political considerations. Even worse, the division of the world into blocs precluded any peaceful cooperation between states and peoples with different social and governmental systems, thereby jeopardizing the independence and sovereignty of peoples and states. Finally, the existence and consolidation of the blocs provided a handy smokescreen for clamping down on domestic development in certain countries, under the pretext of an external threat. Instability reigned in the post war world, where international relations blew hot one moment and cold the next.

As the world became polarized into two blocs, a qualitatively new development occurred in international relations which had repercussions on the balance of power in the world and opened the doors to a wide-scale application of principles of peaceful coexistence between states and peoples. The emergence of new states — both in Africa and in Asia — changed the political map of the world. Their emancipation as nations and states removed many sources of unrest and threats to peace in the world. As the number of states in the international community increased, opportunities for cooperation among states on the basis of equality and equal rights expanded, and determined efforts were undertaken to narrow the economic gap between the advanced and underdeveloped countries.

The reason for standing aloof from the blocs is that they are not conducive to peace, and their existence does not make the world a safer place in which to live; bloc alignment radically restricts possibilities for international cooperation; nonalignment with blocs, both present and future, means adherence to the idea of the unity of the world, of an individual world peace. Nonalignment implies efforts to improve the world as a community, the building of a unified system of international law, based on the United Nations Charter, in short, the widest possible application of the idea of peaceful coexistence and active international cooperation.

It soon became evident that the number of countries refusing to join the blocs was large indeed. In fact, they represent the majority of mankind. These countries changed the course of international affairs, which until recently had focused on East-West relations. As the peoples of Asia and Africa gained independence and states in different continents, mainly small and medium-sized countries, began to pursue a variety of roads towards political, economic and social emancipation, foreign affairs began to move in a North-South direction, as well as along the East-West course.

The foreign policies of countries which chose not to adopt the political doctrines advocated by the blocs are called a variety of names. Sometimes the differences in terminology do not change the essence of this political idea, while at other times the different terms denote a different interpretation of the political concept of nonalignment.

The word neutralism is often heard. This is a term which can be found both in Western and in Soviet literature on international law and foreign affairs. However, the Western and Soviet writers do not necessarily have the same understanding and interpretation of this policy. In Soviet literature, the word neutralism exclusively signifies the policy of nonalignment of the Asian and African countries. In his book, *Economic and Political Problems of New Sover-*

eign States, Professor Tulpanov used the term neutralism in precisely this way. This author describes neutralism as the political position and status under international law of new sovereign states and cites the states of Africa and Asia as an example.

There are writers who see neutralism as the policy of neutrality that is only proclaimed by a unilateral declaration. These are usually experts on international law with a formalist bent. In Western literature, particularly in the United States, this term is used to disparage the policy and the doctrine of nonaligned countries. Such an attitude can be traced back to the Dulles era, particularly after a speech by Dulles given on 9 June 1956 at a college in Iowa, in which he set forth the socalled tough line towards nonaligned countries. He thus equated nonalignment with neutrality and communism. Very much under this political influence, certain American writers make their assessments of nonalignment according to the leanings of various nonaligned countries towards either of the two blocs, as for instance Lefebvre. One other American writer, Liska, says that it is quite correct to use the term neutralism, for this term implies the restricted and passive role of nonaligned countries and this, in his opinion, which is of course mistaken, is what nonalignment amounts to.

Because the term neutralism has such connotations, the writers in nonaligned countries avoid using it.

The term "positive neutrality" is most often heard in countries outside Europe. As far as we know, it means the nonalignment of uncommitted countries with existing blocs. It is in fact intended to imply nonalignment, i.e. nonmembership in existing blocs, while the adjective "positive" is used to indicate the active and progressive character both of the policy of nonalignment and, theoretically, of the concept of nonalignment. Even though this term is very seldom used in Yugoslav political writings and theory of international law, we feel that it is in keeping with the Yugoslav conception of nonalignment.

There are terms, such as the policy of noncommitment, intended to stress the impartiality of countries which adhere to the policy of nonalignment, or the term non-bloc policy. Both are essentially the same. The former is more often used in political theory in socialist countries, and to a certain extent in the West, whereas the term non-bloc policy is most often found in Yugoslav literature and in the writings of Asian and African countries, in conjunction with the term nonalignment, in order to explain the concept more fully.

Nonalignment is the term most often used today, whereas previously the word uncommitted was more often heard. Nonalignment is probably a more accurate word (nonalignment, nonaligned countries, the policy of the nonaligned). "Nonaligned" countries are accordingly those countries which do not wish to belong to either bloc, nor to any third bloc. In short, the policy of nonaligned countries is the active, independent policy of countries which have declared their adherence to such a policy.

The policy of nonalignment is based on two assumptions: first, that military and political alliances on the basis of ideological differences is a method which does not help solve latent and acute international political problems; second, the development of international institutions, in line with the bloc conception of the world's division into two parts or even several parts, causes these organizations to become even more exclusive, as can be seen in the practice of some international economic organizations.

Certainly, ideological considerations loom very large in the division of the world into blocs. The policy of nonalignment is not ideologically motivated or, more precisely, is not moulded in the image of either ideology, which, of course, does not mean the absence of any ideology at all. The policy of nonalignment is opposed to the use of ideology to divide the world into hostile blocs, because such a use, or misuse, presents a stumbling block to international cooperation. Why is this so? Because it becomes a criterion in deciding upon international cooperation.

Both blocs have insisted on an internal discipline which prevents the countries belonging to them from freely formulating and applying their own policies, particularly in foreign affairs. The objection of nonaligned countries to bloc discipline is founded in their profound conviction that every nation must decide independently on both its internal and foreign affairs. Bloc discipline, in our opinion, is nothing other than the inveterate habit of the great powers in the past, particularly in the 19th and early 20th centuries, of seeking to maintain their prestige in a given coalition. In the present circumstances, this habit must be broken, notably through the emancipation of a large number of independent states in all continents. Bloc discipline, as a political, economic and psychological method, has had a pernicious effect in many international organizations, particularly in the United Nations.

Since they are not bound to comply with the interests and discipline of the large military-political blocs, the nonaligned countries are the ones that can freely make decisions, they are able both objectively and subjectively to see the common interests of international peace and international security. For this reason, their many activities, particularly their conferences, are of great importance in the development of modern international relations.

Power, as an end and as a means, is the overriding concern of the blocs. Down through history, military and political alliances have wielded power to their own advantage. Unfortunately, they were often successful, but that was at the time of conventional armaments and when militarist thinking promoted the idea of military means as the logical extension of an aggressive foreign policy. Today, however, war as a means of conducting policy, and power politics, are untenable, not only because of the modern development of technology and civilization, but also because modern weapons promise nothing short of total annihilation. Weapons today have become so destructive that it is no longer feasible to use them, and confidence in power politics has been shaken. This fact alone has struck at the very foundations of the system of blocs and their *raison d'être*. One of the forceful moral and political factors in the breakdown of the blocs is the suspicion harbored by the people and governments within the blocs concerning power politics and policy conducted from the positions of united bloc strength. This factor, among other things, helped bring about the thaw in the cold war.

We have mentioned the decomposition of the blocs. Political terminology contains the word "depolarization," while some authors, such as Morgenthau, now use the word polycentrism instead of the previous term bicentrism. What we actually have here is a development of international relations in a period of the easing of international tensions after the long years of the cold war. Clearly, relations between the blocs have reached a dead-end, since the world balance of power struck after the Second World War has not tipped in favor of either of the two blocs. Both sides have remained neck-and-neck in the armaments race and in technically improving their weaponry. Similarly, the emergence of a number of new independent states did not help either bloc to gain a safe edge over the other. Finally, the internal factor has also hastened the dissolution of the blocs, or as some say, the depolarization of power in international relations. Neither the capitalist nor the socialist world succeeded in forging a unity which would prevail in international relations. The factors we have mentioned have not only facilitated the decomposition of the blocs but have also tended to expand the concept of nonalignment. With time there has been a re-grouping of forces in terms of their policy of peace or war rather than according to the criterion of existing social systems, i.e. criteria of an ideological nature.

We have described the concept of nonalignment in negative terms — as the rejection of bloc policy and the rejection of alignment either with blocs or with their institutions. However, a positive definition of nonalignment reveals its politically active content.

First, nonalignment is a policy based on the principles of active coexistence aimed at the peaceful settlement of all international problems and the removal of all political, economic, social and other threats to world peace and the normal international cooperation of all countries in the world, regardless of their government and social systems;

Second, nonalignment is adamantly anti-colonial and anti-imperialist;

Third, it is a policy advocating the self-determination of all nations, regardless of the sizes of their populations or territories;

Fourth, nonalignment embodies the application of the principles of equality and equal rights, regardless of race, nationality, or religion;

Fifth, nonalignment is a policy safeguarding the rights, independence and territorial integrity of every country and every nation;

Sixth, the policy of nonalignment calls for a universal and complete disarmament.

Seventh, it is a policy standing for equal rights in international economic affairs and for a balanced economic development in the world economy.

In political terminology, coexistence implies respect for different government and social systems. Some authors consider coexistence to be the existence of states side by side, and do not go into the question of their internal social content. Other authors, however, feel that the term coexistence implies not just the existence of states but the existence of different social systems side by side.

The term should be given the broadest possible interpretation in political doctrine. It seeks to describe the nature of the coexistence of different social and state systems. This adjective seeks to describe the dynamic rather than static nature of coexistence. Politically, it means that the coexistence of different social and state systems must be cultivated in the common interest. And the common interest is the active development of international cooperation for the sake of promoting the general interest. Often the phrase "active peaceful coexistence" is used to emphasize the peaceful character of the coexistence of different systems. We think that active coexistence is descriptive enough, and that the term has already acquired a definite meaning, which has been clearly and precisely formulated in Chapter IV of the "Programme for Peace and International Cooperation" adopted at the Second Conference of Heads of State or Government of Nonaligned Countries in Cairo in 1964.

Active coexistence as a policy emerged in a period when it had become absolutely necessary to oppose the doctrine of blocs, which was against the parallel existence of different social and state systems. At that time, the policy of active coexistence was virtually identical with the policy of nonalignment; the policy of uncommitted nations was the policy of opposing the blocs. Therefore, the concept of the socalled coexistence of the blocs was contrary to the policy of nonalignment. By virtue of the fact that it sought coexistence not of blocs but of peoples and countries, the policy of active coexistence coincided with the policy of nonalignment. However, active coexistence does not imply bloc nonalignment. Why is this? The purpose of active coexistence is to induce even bloc aligned countries to join in international cooperation. In this way, according to the views of Yugoslav political theory, the concept of active coexistence as a political base is broader than the concept of nonalignment, since it reaches beyond the circle of nonaligned countries.

The nonaligned countries initiated the codification of the principles of active coexistence. This codification was mentioned in the "Programme for Peace and International Cooperation" of the Cairo Conference. But why should principles which are already contained in the Charter of the United Nations and in the rules of international law be codified?

First, many provisions in the Charter call for the further elaboration not just of existing organs but also of tendencies which form the nucleus of the legal guarantees fixed in the Charter.

Second, the nature and role of the principles of active coexistence have greatly changed in the course of the evolution of international relations and international law and require up-to-date political and legal formulation, particularly the principles of prohibition of the threat or use of force, the principle of sovereign equality of states, the principle of peaceful settlement of disputes, and the principle of non-intervention.

Third, this codification is generally advocated by the nonaligned countries and other countries as well, and is suggested by the need for a more effective functioning of the organs of the United Nations.

Fourth, the codification would promote a more correct and effective implementation of valid rules of international law as politically useful instruments in the progressive development of the modern international community, primarily for removing all the harmful vestiges of the past that burden today's world and the remnants of the old colonial system, and for preventing various forms of neo-colonialism. Let us round off, then, our comparison of neutrality and nonalignment. Classical neutrality, which implies an absence of partiality according to some authors and disinterest according to others, and in our opinion, always a passive stance in respect to a conflict of third states, has shown itself to be untenable and for all practical purposes useless. Those opting for neutrality in fact were the least able to maintain this status. If some countries, and they were always very few, managed to remain neutral, it was only because they did not happen to enter into the sphere of influence of the belligerent sides. Classical neutrality as a legal concept presupposes the legality of war. The moment this legality is challenged, either through collective security, as was the case in the League of Nations, or by the outlawing of war as an instrument of national policy (the Kellogg-Briand Pact), or the outlawing of war in the sense of the U.N. Charter — classical neutrality loses its *raison d'être.* Hence the elimination of war also eliminates neutrality as its corollary.

Soon after the Second World War, the conflicting interests of the great powers, unsettled international problems left over from the war, antagonistic political, ideological and other interests of states, the division of the world into blocs, etc., all began to provoke open clashes in the period of the cold war. In this situation it looked as though neutrality was being given a second chance, both as a political and as a legal concept. However, classical neutrality was at odds with the implacable fact that nuclear and thermonuclear war would erase any distinctions between the victorious and the vanquished and that because of their totally destructive power, modern armaments had become useless as a means for settling disputes in present-day international relations.

States and peoples were left with three options: to join one of the existing blocs, to retreat into isolation, or to refuse to become a party to the existing military-political setup, while taking an active part in settling international disputes and conflicts by peaceful means. If we except the superpowers, the only acceptable option for the countries and peoples, was the policy of nonalignment. This policy also acquires certain features of neutrality from its non-bloc stance. However, this kind of positive neutrality, as it is sometimes called, is rather different. All authors who equate neutrality with nonalignment are making a mistake, no matter how they come to this conclusion. One of these is Ervick, even though he does draw a distinction between neutrality which seeks to maintain its freedom in a "hot" war, and neutralism, which largely seeks to ensure free trade in the cold war. According to the Soviet author Ganiushkin, for instance, nonalignment is only one of the basic forms of neutrality.

Today there are roughly speaking three forms of neutrality:

     a. permanent neutrality of the Swiss type, which is the only one of its kind. In view of Switzerland's exceptional international status, its special role in the capitalist world and a long, although tenuous tradition, only in that country could this type of neutrality have been maintained for such a long time.

     b. permanent neutrality of the Austrian type; so far this type of neutrality has only been tried out in that country. Austrian neutrality undoubtedly represents an advance on Swiss neutrality, particularly since Austria is a member of the United Nations. However, as Bruno Kreisky, now Austria's chancellor, pointed out, Austria only makes general statements in the United Nations concerning important international political problems. It does not take part in the conferences of uncommitted countries because, as former Austrian Chancellor Dr. Josef Klaus once stated, "We seek to maintain our freedom of movement in all directions and *vis-à-vis* all groups, including the group of uncommitted countries."

     It is quite clear that permanent neutrality of either type is completely different from the positive neutrality of the nonaligned countries. Finally, permanent neutrality is based on principles and a procedure generally recognized in international law which are not binding on nonaligned countries.

     c. Traditional neutrality is that which is declared by countries in the event of a war. The policy of positive neutrality in no way presupposes an obligation to be neutral during wartime. However, there has also been a certain evolution in this respect. Traditionally neutral countries to a certain extent accept the intent and role of positive neutrality, and often their political attitudes and concepts come close to the policy and ideas of nonaligned countries.

Nonalignment is a broader concept. Positive neutrality denotes the non-bloc policy and character of nonaligned countries, although the concept may be given a broader meaning, which would coincide with that of nonalignment. However, since the term neutrality is used, we are inclined to include in this concept that part of the so-called negative definition of nonalignment, i.e. only its non-bloc character.

Nonalignment is an international political doctrine and practice of a large number of countries which, without creating fixed organizational forms, maintain an independent attitude *vis-à-vis* military and political groups and on the basis of the principles of active coexistence insist on the maintenance of peace and the creation of all-round political, economic, social and other conditions for the progressive development of the community of all nations in the world, with equal treatment and with no discrimination.

PART ONE
SUBJECTS

Chapter One: States

I. Appearance and Disappearance of States

Conception of the State — Disappearance of States and Complete or Partial Loss of Territory — Stimson Doctrine

1. Conception of the State — In the theory of public international law, a state may come into being in one of two ways: originally or derivatively. A state is original when the social community is created in an inhabited territory where previously there had been no state. Today, virtually the entire world is divided up into dependent and independent countries. All states that are not original are of a derivative nature. This distinction is obsolete today. There is no doubt that there are still many territories in the world which are still under dispute. However, by modern technical and legal methods, the whole of our planet has been carved up into different regions which are subject to authority of some state.

Until recently it was thought the appearance and disappearance of states was a consequence of events rather than of law. They included, for example war, which most frequently brought about the creation or disintegration of a state, insurrection, and, finally, revolution. Since the 17th century, the appearance and disappearance of states has been the result of a definite policy: the principle of equilibrium has become one of the regulators of the European political map; the principle of nationality has strongly influenced the creation of new (e.g. the Balkan) states, enlargement of old ones (unifications of Germany and Italy) and the disintegration of existing states (Austria-Hungary). However, we must not lose sight of a possible legal aspect in the emergence of states.

The legal formation of states also goes back a long way in history. States came into existence by an act of division among the heirs to a throne, by an act of the sovereign, by the detachment of certain territories, or by the bestowal of land in dowry, which then became a separate state. Even in the age of parliamentary democracy, separate states came into being through an act of emancipation by the constitutional power of the state that is sovereign over certain territories and approves the transfer of sovereignty: e.g. the act of the U.S. Congress giving the Philippines independence; the decision of the Allies to make Lebanon and Syria sovereign countries; the act of the British Parliament granting independence to Iraq. Until recently, then, the derivative formation of states depended on a legal act by the previous sovereign. However, in recent times we have had cases where a state has come into existence through international legal acts, by decision of the organized international community (United Nations).

2. Disappearance of States and Complete or Partial Loss of Territory — Theoretically, a state disappears when any of the elements giving a social community the character of a state ceases to be. These elements are the territory, the people, and the organized government. It is considered that the disappearance of a state, or the loss of a part of its territory to another state, unless special exceptions have been demonstrably provided for, entails the following legal consequences:

a. *in regard to international treaties* — 1. The international treaties which had been entered into by the former state are no longer valid. 2. In collective treaties such a state ceases to be a contracting party. 3. If a state merges with another, it will be bound by the treaties of the state which it has joined. 4. When a country breaks up into two or more new states, as a rule none of them shall be considered bound by the treaties entered into by the former state.

b. *in regard to national debts* — 1. The principle usually valid in this case is *res transit cum onere suo*. The national debt is transferred from the former state or part thereof to the new or enlarged state. 2. If a state is divided up between two or more states, the debt shall be proportionately apportioned among the enlarged states. The criterion may be the size of the divided territory, the proportion of the population going with it, or economic wealth. For example, under the Berlin Treaty of 1878, Serbia, Bulgaria and Montenegro were obliged to assume a part of Turkey's national debt, proportionate to the fiscal strength of the acquired regions (Article 42 for Serbia, Article 133 for Montenegro, Article 9 for Bulgaria). Under Article 254 of the Versailles Treaty, all the states which under that treaty received part of the German territory, were bound to accept part of Germany's debt. However, there have also been cases when states refused to take up part of a debt: the United States refused in the 18th century to assume part of England's debt and Germany refused to take over part of France's national debt when it annexed Alsace.

Even when states have ceased to exist, the legal modes of their disappearance were adapted to the momentary expediencies of settling the conflicting interests. Contemporary international law is trying to deal differently with the question of the disappearance of states, which until now as a rule has been regarded as the consequence of the superior force of one state.

Territorial conquest, effected by means of force or the threat of force, cannot be recognized. In this case non-recognition is used as a legal sanction inasmuch as no recognition is granted to the exercise of sovereignty by the holder of authority in the territory in question.

The conquest of an alien territory may be made by war (military conquest), by the use or threat of force against a state which is unable to offer resistance (conquest without war, e.g. the cases of Austria in 1938 and Czechoslovakia in 1938 and 1939), or by the crushing of the victim's resistance at the very beginning (the case of Albania in 1939). Conquest may be made of only one part of the territory of an alien state (Manchoukuo in 1932, Sudeten in 1938), or may involve the entire territory in the form of annexation (Austria in 1938), creation of puppet states (Manchoukuo, Slovakia, the independent State of Croatia), or by the establishment of protectorates (Bohemian-Moravian protectorate) or personal or real unions (Albania). When a state ceases to exist, parts of its territory may be disposed of in different ways (for example, annexation of Bohemian Moravia and a simultaneous creation of a puppet state in Slovakia; the dividing up of the Yugoslav territories among Germany, Italy, Hungary, Bulgaria and Albania, together with the creation of the puppet Independent State of Croatia.

Finally, states may end their existence in controversial manners that may be variously regarded as *de jure* or *de facto.* There is to this day a dispute going on concerning the Baltic states of Lithuania, Latvia, and Estonia. The Soviet thesis is that these states disappeared as international persons by a legal act, i.e. by their request to be admitted into the U.S.S.R. after the holding of plebiscites and by the decision of the Supreme Soviet of the U.S.S.R. to admit them into the Union. The Western powers take the opposite view that these states were victims of conquest, because the plebiscites were carried out under occupation by the Red Army and under the pressure of "occupying forces." Hence the United States and Great Britain refused to recognize the extension of *de jure* Soviet dominion over this territory and consider that these states have the right to be restored.

Under international law, conquest need not be recognized by third states, nor need third states recognize the conqueror's sovereign rights over the conquered territories, even though the conquest of a state has been completed. For example, on 7 June 1941, Great Britain issued a declaration stating its refusal to recognize the partitioning of Yugoslavia or the termination of Yugoslavia's sovereignty.

There is no doubt that in recognizing the effects of conquest, states are primarily motivated by political interests and considerably less by legal principles. Yet in earlier practice the question of practical non-recognition depended on whether and to what extent the sovereignty of a country had been destroyed. Usually in the event of a complete conquest the former state was considered terminated, whereas in the cases of partial conquest, third states considered it their duty to suspend their neutrality and refuse to recognize the change in sovereignty as a result of the conquest. There have been cases where even partial conquest was recognized. However, in recent times a partial conquest, unless approved by the former sovereign, has been the motive for withholding recognition. This principle of non-recognition was expressed in the Stimson Doctrine and applied to all similar situations.

3. The Stimson Doctrine — The Stimson Doctrine dates back to the time after the occupation of Manchuria during the Sino-Japanese war, when U.S. Secretary of State Henry Stimson sent notes to the governments of Japan and China on 7 January 1932, stating that the United States did not intend to recognize any situation, treaty or agreement that would be contrary to the Kellogg-Briand Pact. This move led to a resolution by the League of Nations, adopted unanimously on 11 March 1932, which denounced any territorial change brought about by aggression. A month later, on the 3rd of April, nineteen American republics made a policy statement concerning the conflict between Paraguay and Bolivia over Chaco, to the effect that they would not recognize any conquest of alien territories or adopt any settlement not obtained through pacific means. In December 1933 the same principle was adopted in the Convention on the Rights and Duties of States at the seventh International Conference of American States. Consequently, the Stimson Doctrine was applied in several international acts and undoubtedly constitutes today a principle of contemporary international law. Langer believes that a state adopting the policy of non-recognition is expected to undertake certain measures in the domain of its internal judicial and administrative affairs. Firstly, it must revise its diplomatic and consular relations as well as international treaties and secondly, it can no longer recognize the personal status, property relationships and legal acts imposed by the aggressor. However, an analysis of international practice over the last three decades shows that the principle of non-recognition of aggressive conquests has often failed to be effective. It is sufficient to recall Hitler's aggression and the fact that his conquests were given partial or even complete recognition by certain powers. It is precisely the failures in the application of this principle that demonstrate the need for perfecting an international mechanism that, by regulating the general interest, would bring within proper bounds the lengths to which states can go in pursuing their aims. It is quite clear that international law cannot solve conflicts in that way, but it will thereby provide a number of avenues through which international social forces can more effectively implement the general interest that derives from the provisions of the United Nations Charter. Holding that aggression cannot be a means of territorial aggrandizement, the 1941 Atlantic Charter, as well as the Panamanian and Yugoslav draft declaration on the rights and duties of states, put forward the principle that it was the duty of third states not to recognize territorial enlargement achieved by conquest. The Stimson Doctrine may be said to be in the spirit of the United Nations Charter and to constitute one of the principles of present-day international law.

II. Types of States

Forms of Sovereign States — the British Commonwealth of Nations — Permanently Neutral States — the Vatican — Vassal States, Protectorates, and Autonomous Provinces — International Territories — Evolution of Non-Selfgoverning Territories — the Portuguese Colonies

1. Forms of Sovereign States — States may be simple or composite in terms of their internal legal order. If a state has an integral territory and a centralized legislative power which it shares with no other local unit, it is described as a simple state. When Sweden and Norway separated, they became simple states. In this sense a simple state is of no interest to international law. What is of interest is the composite state, for the question arises of the personality of its component parts in international law. The same is true for personal and real unions, unions of states (confederations) and federal states.

Two states which are legally subject to the same ruler represent a personal union. This type of state depends on the existence of the monarchy, and as monarchies disappear this form of state community is also becoming extinct. History has known cases of personal union between England and Hanover (1714 to 1837), or the Netherlands and Luxembourg (1815 to 1890). A personal union does not have a separate international personality under international law. It is a union under a ruler, a fact which does not affect the constitutional status of each state. Each has its own diplomatic agencies. They may conclude treaties with one another, and there have even been cases where they waged war against one another.

A real union is a composite state, composed of several states which frequently, except for foreign affairs, have complete internal autonomy. Unless regulated otherwise, states in a real union have the right to conclude international treaties which bind only the signatory state. Austria-Hungary was this type of state. For instance, Hungary alone concluded a treaty with Serbia concerning the Iron Gate gorge on the Danube. Today there is a real union between Switzerland and Liechtenstein. The Austro-Hungarian monarchy is cited in textbooks as a typical example of a real union. Austria and Hungary were two states bound together by a real union and administration. They had in common the monarch, ministries of foreign affairs, finances, army and navy and, finally, the administration of Bosnia and Hercegovina granted to them in 1878 under Article 25 of the Treaty of Berlin. It should be pointed out that in addition to their common ministries, Austria and Hungary also had their own ministries of finances and army and navy; only foreign affairs were conducted from Vienna as the joint foreign policy center.

Whereas a personal union is not an international person, because it is composed of two or more separate international subjects, and some authorities therefore do not even consider it to be a composite state, a real union is a composite state which acts in foreign affairs as an international subject having a single territory and diplomatic missions.

A state union or confederation is based on an international treaty, under which individual members of the union waive their sovereign rights only to the extent they desire. The central government has only those powers that are unanimously vested in it by the member states. Theoretically, they can leave the confederation or they can make war against one another, just as they can be neutral in a conflict involving union members and a third state. For this reason the decisions of the central government must be taken in unanimity. This circumstance is regarded as one of the drawbacks of a confederation, because unanimity implies the right of veto. There were times when certain decisions were passed in the German union by a majority of votes, but then frequently they had to be implemented by force. The situation was similar in the old Polish diet (Sejm), where the only recourse against a veto was a counterattack by the majority, or the "right of the gentry" to throw their adversaries out or cut them down with swords there and then. Until the 19th century, Switzerland with its cantons was a state union. The German Confederation also had this form of state between 1815 and 1866. The member states of a confederation continue exercising their sovereignty and thereby remain international persons. However, because it is vested with certain powers, the union stands as a special subject of international law. Confederations thus represent a case of dual international personality.

A federal state, or federation, is an international person. In this type of composite state, set up on the basis of a federal constitution, foreign affairs are dealt with by federal authorities, although member states may continue exercising their own sovereignties. This is the rule, but there are exceptions to it. On the basis of a two-thirds majority in the Senate the United States of America may enter into certain contractual relations with other states. According to Articles 8 through 10 of their constitution the Swiss cantons may conclude international agreements in the domain of trade, or for regulating state servitudes with neighboring countries and the frontier police regime. The legislative, executive and judiciary functions in a federal state are divided between the federal government and the member states. Which of these functions will be predominantly within the competence of one or the other depends on the degree of centralization. Although there are exceptions, virtually all foreign affairs and control of the armed forces fall within the federal jurisdiction. One important feature of a federal state is that each of its citizens owes double allegiance — to the federal government and to the state forming part of the Federation.

Any discussion of the international personality of the federal state must deal with the question of the so-called federal clause. Does a federal state have the right to insert this clause into its international treaties? It implies dissociation from the jurisdiction exercised by the member states of the federation, by virtue of their sovereignty. The Federal clause differs from a simple reservation in that it applies to a number of topics that may differ from one federal state to another, since not every component part of a federated state has the same sovereign rights under the federal constitution. A reservation applies to specified topics and has the same operation for each signatory state attaching it. Furthermore, the filing of a reservation means automatic restriction of the competent sovereign authority for the entire territory, which is not the case with the federal clause. It cannot be identified with the colonial clause either, because by definition the latter applies to the colonies rather than to parts of a federal state. What is essential from the standpoint of international law is whether the federated states are international persons. If only the federal state exercises international rights and duties, the federated constituents have no international personality, and the federal clause should have no place in international treaties. However, in international practice the federal clause has in fact been applied and enforced. Yugoslav writers make reference to a potential but secondary personality of the federated states (Lukic). Today the members of a federal state do have a dual international personality, and it seems that following the practice in the American continent there will be an increased acceptance of the international personality of the states making up a federation. This practice may give rise to incongruities in international intercourse and is therefore criticized in literature.

The Socialist Federal Republic of Yugoslavia is a federal state. Its federal agencies and bodies have the following competence as against foreign countries:

— to safeguard the independence and territorial integrity of Yugoslavia and to protect its sovereignty in international relations;

— to decide on war and peace;

— to safeguard the government and social order, the system of socialist self-management of socioeconomic relations, and the uniform foundations of the political system;

— to formulate the foreign policy of the S.F.R.Y. and ensure its implementation;

— to regulate the external trade and foreign exchange regime, the customs system and customs tariffs, as well as other economic transactions with foreign countries;

— to conclude, ratify and secure the enforcement of international treaties and see to the fulfilment of the international commitments of the S.F.R.Y.;

— to protect citizens of the S.F.R.Y.;

— to regulate exports and imports of goods and services and crossing of the state frontier;

— to regulate the status, residence and protection of aliens in Yugoslavia.

2. The British Commonwealth of Nations — The British Commonwealth is a composite state that is unique in the world. It is composed of the most highly diverse governmental, economic and social formations. Its empire, in addition to the United Kingdom as the metropolis, includes fully independent states, members of the United Nations, which are called dominions, such as Australia, New Zealand, India, Pakistan, Canada, and Sri Lanka. It also includes colonies in the true sense of the word and self-governing colonies and, finally, territories under permanent military occupation. This great empire, extending to virtually all five continents, is a personal union, because all its dominions are linked through their allegiance to the British monarch, but it also has features of a real union because it has certain imperial organs, such as the War Cabinet, and a joint command in the event of war. These organs, however, do not exist in peacetime. Furthermore, in a real union foreign affairs are conducted from a centre, whereas the dominions have their own diplomatic representatives, may conduct different foreign policies, have separate membership in international organizations, and even conduct separate wars. If some dominions have no missions of their own in foreign countries, the diplomatic missions of the metropolis must represent them, acting on the orders of the dominions' governments.

The relationship between the metropolis and its dominions is mainly what gives this community its special character, for the other relations are more or less the customary ones. International and Commonwealth questions of common interest are reviewed at meetings of the Commonwealth prime ministers, the British prime minister being *primus inter pares.* Formerly known as Imperial Conferences, these meetings have become much less formal in character. Their decisions are not binding, being rather of a moral and political character, but they do carry significant weight if they are unanimous. The Commonwealth Relations Office (formerly Dominions Office) in London serves to supply information and to coordinate any joint plans, in addition to its diplomatic character, because the dominions communicate with the metropolis through this office and not through the Foreign Office. Their representatives are styled high commissioners and rank as ambassadors. Finally, in each dominion there is a high commissioner sent by London, who mediates more by virtue of his personal authority than on the basis of any special powers. The Statute of Westminster, adopted at the Imperial Conference of 1931, had the nature of a constitution. It went some way in laying down the terms of reference of the Commonwealth conferences by proclaiming them to be a consultative body for the foreign political questions concerning the empire.

3. Permanently Neutral States — These states have a special status under international law. This special status is today enjoyed by Switzerland and Austria. The permanently neutral states have international guarantees in regard to the preservation of their sovereignty and integrity. If a state wishes to become permanently neutral, it must first acquire international assent in a specified international legal form.

Each permanently neutral state also assumes a number of obligations. It may not conclude treaties liable to draw it into war, but may keep an army for the defense of its neutrality. Consequently, permanent neutrality is at the same time armed neutrality. Such a state is entitled to seek guarantees for its integrity from other states. The internal and external policies of a permanently neutral state cannot be restricted unless the international legal rules regulating permanent neutrality have been violated, or unless treaty obligations impairing its status have been undertaken.

These principles of permanent neutrality under international law have mainly been derived from the experience of Switzerland which, for a long time, has been enjoying this international status (according to some authors, since the 16th century). Switzerland was proclaimed a neutral country by the great powers at the Vienna Congress of 1815. Its permanent neutrality was confirmed by the Versailles Peace Treaty. In both world wars Switzerland's status was respected.

With the creation of the League of Nations, however, a crisis arose over Switzerland's permanent neutrality. When it joined the League of Nations, Switzerland acceded to an international treaty which imposed upon it international treaty obligations of a military nature. An agreement was reached between Switzerland and the League of Nations under which Switzerland was released from the obligation of participating in military sanctions and from the duty to allow the passage of foreign troops across its territory. During World War II, Switzerland succeeded in preserving its neutrality. Today, Switzerland is not a member of the United Nations because it deems the obligations under the Charter, particularly those in Chapter VII, to be incompatible with the concept of permanent neutrality.

At the Moscow Conference in 1943, the Allies decided to reestablish a free and independent Austria and proclaimed the Anschluss carried out by Hitler's Germany on 15 March 1938 to be null and void. Under the Moscow Memorandum of 15 April 1955, the Austrian and Soviet governments agreed that Austria, in accordance with its statement at the Berlin Conference of 1954, should issue a declaration binding it to the kind of permanent neutrality enjoyed by Switzerland. After signing the State Treaty of 15 May 1955, Austria promulgated its constitutional law on neutrality, which came into force in November of the same year. Since Austria's neutrality was not provided for under the State Treaty, irrespective of its constitutional law, it was necessary to find a legal form making this neutrality an obligation under international law. The constitutional law on neutrality, although indispensable, constituted a unilateral legal act. On 23 November 1955, the Austrian government sent a special note to the states with which it maintained diplomatic relations, calling upon them to recognize its permanently neutral status, and by implication to assume the obligation of respecting it.

Switzerland is not a member of the United Nations Organization, while Austria is. This was promised in the State Treaty by the great powers that were signatories of this treaty. The controversial point is whether a permanently neutral state is permitted to be a member of an international organization which, among other things, is expected to curb aggression by undertaking collective actions in the world, so that this state might one day conceivably have to act on the behalf of one of the belligerent parties. In other words, does the U.N. Charter make any provision at all for a neutral status of its members in view of the fact that Switzerland remains outside the Organization, whereas Austria is a member, and both have the international status of a permanently neutral state?

In a lecture held in 1955 at the Faculty of Law in Sarajevo, the Viennese professor of international law A. Verdross drew a distinction between the legal and political systems of the League of Nations and the United Nations Organization. Under the Covenant of the League of Nations, member states were under the obligation of taking immediate steps against an aggressor and of actively committing themselves to one of the belligerent sides. According to the United Nations Charter, a decision of the Security Council is to be awaited, until which time every member state, including a permanently neutral state, has the right to self defense. The Security Council may undertake an action without committing the states that remain neutral. The practice of the United Nations has shown that it is possible to act in this manner. For example, neutral India mediated in the Korean conflict.

Professor Verdross has taken the proper approach to this problem. It may be objected that in the mentioned case of India the question was of a voluntary rather than permanent neutrality. However, the Geneva conventions of 12 August 1949, do contain the institution of "neutral protecting power," without stating that it can only be Switzerland. This provision may therefore be applied to several such states, and the Geneva conventions are not outside the legal system of the United Nations Organization, at least not according to the practice so far. There is another important point. The League of Nations did not seek universality, so it was rather difficult to justify Switzerland's membership. The United Nations Charter, notwithstanding certain restrictions in Article 4, undoubtedly aims to make the U.N. in due course an all-embracing global international organization. Although in form a multilateral international treaty, the Charter is essentially an international constitution which may be acceded to by the neutral states, because the word "war" does not appear in the Charter. From a legal standpoint, the permanently neutral states cannot come into the situation of becoming a belligerent side, even if the Security Council did not absolve them from participation in actions designed to curb aggression. In our opinion, by virtue of its membership a neutral state, in this case Austria, indirectly participates in the maintenance of international peace and security, for which reason it sought the status of permanently neutral state in the first place. Article 2 of the Charter guarantees respect for Austria's status, permitting no infringement of its territorial integrity and permanent neutrality. This characterizes the contemporary evolution of the institution of permanent neutrality.

4. The Vatican — There are authors who refer to the Papal State of the Vatican as a state community having a people, territory, and independent government. However, the Pope as the head of the Roman Catholic Church is granted the status of international person in view of his traditional right to conclude international treaties called concordats and to maintain diplomatic relations with other states. This in fact is a vestige of the past extending into our day, thanks to the support of those countries in which the Roman Catholic Church still has a very strong influence on political life.

The Vatican is not a state which under the present-day requirements of international law qualifies as an international legal person. First of all, five hundred members of the male sex do not constitute a nation; secondly, there is no Vatican nationality; thirdly, the size of its territory is insignificant: one square and two streets; finally, the Vatican is rightly regarded as lacking the essential legal element — general and exclusive state jurisdiction. However, all this is not regarded as an impediment to its international personality. Yugoslavia broke off relations with the Vatican in 1952 because of the latter's hostile policy, but did not challenge its international status.

On 25 June 1966, a protocol was signed between the Holy See and Yugoslavia, which regulated their relations. Under the protocol, the Yugoslav government acknowledged the Vatican's right to exercise its jurisdiction over the Roman Catholic Church and its competence in matters of an ecclesiastical and religious nature, insofar as this does not run counter to the internal system of Yugoslavia. On its part, the Vatican reaffirmed that the activity of the Roman Catholic priests in performing their pastoral duties should be exercised within a religious and church context, and that, consequently, religious and ecclesiastical functions may not be misused for purposes of a political nature. Under this protocol, the Vatican denounces any acts of political terrorism or similar criminal forms of violence no matter where they originate. At the same time it was jointly resolved to exchange semi-official representatives. The Yugoslav government sent its envoy to the Holy See in the Vatican, and the Holy See appointed its own delegate to represent it with the Yugoslav government.

5. Vassal States, Protectorates and Autonomous Provinces —

Political, economic and other kinds of dependence at an international level may take various forms. Some of the most significant for international law are vassal states, protectorates and autonomous provinces.

Vassal states have existed from the Middle Ages to the present day. Egypt, Serbia, Bulgaria, Wallachia and Moldavia were for a long time vassals of Turkey. Since the 17th century Tibet has been a vassal of China. Vassalage implies the direct subordination of one state to another, a suzerain state. It is a relationship in internal public law and as a rule was established by way of an internal legal act which enumerated all the concessions of the suzerain and frequently laid down mutual rights and obligations. Today this medieval form is regarded as an anachronism, although it can still be encountered, albeit in other forms.

During the 19th and 20th centuries, protectorates were established as a form of colonial expansion. Under international law protectorate is the legal relation between two states, one politically stronger and the other weaker, instituted under an international treaty on the basis of which the subordinated state continues to perform its international functions through the good offices of the protecting state.

In international law there is no system of rights and obligations that applies equally to all protectorates. Each was created in specific historical conditions, and this is why they differ from one another. The protecting state may retain the right of diplomatic representation, as was the case with Tunisia, for which international treaties were concluded by the French government (on behalf of the Bey). Sometimes protecting states retain the right to veto international treaties, which right was exercised by Great Britain in the Transvaal. The "protecting" state may satisfy itself with an undertaking by the subordinated state not to take any measures that would encroach upon the interests of the protector. Thus France guaranteed Monaco its territorial integrity, and in return, Monaco granted the French troops the right of passage under a treaty concluded in 1918. Protectorates may also be collective. In 1815, under the Vienna Act, a protectorate was established among what were then the great powers, Russia, Prussia, and Austria, over the small Cracow Republic. There are also protectorates that are controlled by the international community. The League of Nations was authorized to control the protectorate over Danzig. A protectorate may be disguised when a sovereign state, by means of a secret or public international treaty, surrenders certain sovereign rights concerning the independent conduct of its foreign policy. Serbia became a disguised protectorate of Austria-Hungary under a secret convention signed in 1882. Protectorates *pro futuro* have also been known in history. In 1917, Haiti pledged that if ever it were to conclude a protectorate treaty, it would do so only with the United States. In return, Haiti received a sum of one million dollars. During the Second World War, the Axis powers tried to create a number of protectorates in Europe (Albania, Slovakia, the Independent State of Croatia). Under the Atlantic Charter, these protectorates were proclaimed null and void.

Until World War II, there was no exception to the rule that the treaties on protectorates were *res inter alios acta.* Today this rule does not apply to the United Nations Organization. The treaties of protectorate over Tunisia and Morocco were a subject of lively debate in the U.N. General Assembly until these countries acquired their independence. Furthermore, the claim of exclusive jurisdiction by a protecting state cannot be regarded as justified, for it is still the rule that any war breaking out between a protecting and a protected state is not a rebellion but is rather the so-called "international war" in which the latter is entitled to claim the status of a belligerent.

Autonomous provinces are territories having internal self-rule based on the constitutional regulations of a country or on an international legal act. In the latter case, such an autonomous province is an international subject in embryonic form. Serbia became an autonomous province under the Bucharest Treaty of 1812. Under the Berlin Treaty of 1878, this status was given to Eastern Rumelia. Bosnia and Hercegovina constituted an autonomous province until their annexation in 1908, as is frequently the case with such territories. Under a treaty signed by Italy and Austria in 1946, South Tyrol received local autonomy from Italy. An autonomous province may also be proclaimed by the United National General Assembly. For example, at its fifth session the U.N. granted this status to Eritrea within the Ethiopian Federation.

6. International Territories — Territories under international control are known as mandates, trusteeship territories and nonself-governing territories. Up until World War I, the great powers had a habit of taking away a piece of territory from one state and handing it over to another state. Such was the fate, for example, of Bosnia and Hercegovina, which shifted hands at the Berlin Congress in 1878. After World War I, the Allies decided that territories which were no longer under the sovereignty of the former administering states and the colonies whose peoples were not yet able to govern themselves, should be placed in the mandate of other states, which "by reason of their resources can best undertake this responsibility and are willing to accept it," but subject to the direct supervision of the League of Nations. The mandates were classified as three types:

> *Class A.* Communities that were sufficiently developed so that they could be recognized as independent nations subject to receiving administrative advice and assistance from a mandatory, (Syria and Lebanon under France's administration; Iraq, Palestine and Transjordan under the administration of Great Britain).
> *Class B.* Territories whose peoples were less developed. Administration was carried out by the mandatories, under certain guarantees of local autonomy for the inhabitants (Cameroons and Togo under the administration of France and Great Britain; Ruanda-Urundi under the mandate of Belgium).
> *Class C.* These mandates form part of the mandatory's territory. Whereas in the case of the Class B territories the mandatories were obliged to safeguard equal treatment in regard to commerce with other countries, in Class C this obligation did not exist. (South-West Africa was taken over by the Union of South Africa; New Guinea by Australia; Samoa Island by New Zealand; Nauru Island went to Great Britain to be administered by Australia; the German colonies south of the equator went to Japan; as did the Pacific islands — the Carolines, Marshalls and Marianas). The mandatory powers administered the Class C territories at their own discretion, and they were in fact glorified colonies. Today this system no longer exists. Since World War II some territories have become independent states, while others have come under the trusteeship of the United Nations. The institution of mandate does not correspond to that from civil law. It cannot be likened to an international treaty, because it lacks the essential elements of a treaty. It is considered to be a kind of protectorate with international administration and international control. This form of pseudo-protectorate preceded the modern system of trusteeship established under the United Nations Charter.

After the Second World War, the United Nations abandoned the mandate system of the League of Nations largely under the pressure of the anti-colonial policy of many countries, clearly enunciated at the San Francisco Conference in 1945. At that time the right to self-determination, previously only a political principle, was enshrined in the U.N. Charter, and thereby became a principle of international law.

Trusteeship is a contractual relationship between interested states and the competent organs of the United Nations, concerning the following types of territories:

> a. territories previously held under mandate;
> b. territories detached from the defeated states as a result of the Second World War; and

c. territories voluntarily placed under the trusteeship system by states responsible for their administration.

A trusteeship agreement must specify the following elements: a. the terms of administration of the trusteeship territories, and b. the authority that will administer these territories. The agreements are concluded for either five or ten years; upon the expiration of this term, the U.N. General Assembly is entitled to consider the new situation and, if the people of the territory in question have reached a level of development enabling them to govern themselves, such a territory may be raised to a higher degree of autonomy or may be proclaimed an independent state. With admission to the United Nations, every such territory is automatically released from trusteeship.

During the period of trusteeship, the inhabitants of that territory have the right to submit petitions or complaints against any wrongful acts of the administering authority. Similarly, the administering authority cannot refuse to permit a United Nations enquiry on the basis of a complaint by the population of a trust territory. At the same time, the Charter enjoins the administering authority to ensure that the territory "shall play its part in the maintenance of international peace and security." Hence the Charter entitles the administering authority to organize and use local volunteer forces for the purpose of fulfilling obligations towards the Security Council, and for the purpose of local defense and maintenance of law and order in such a territory.

The U.N. Charter distinguishes between ordinary and strategic trust territories, and the functional competence of the United Nations is separated accordingly. The strategic areas are those which, owing to their geographical location or the political problems likely to arise there, are important for world peace and security, which are the concern of the United Nations. Consequently, their strategic nature is assessed not according to the interests of a member or non-member state, but according to the possibility of a threat arising to the strategic interests of the United Nations as a whole. For this reason, such areas are within the exclusive jurisdiction of the Security Council. The other territories are non-strategic, and it is the U.N. General Assembly which is competent to approve the terms of the trusteeship agreement and to revise them.

The Covenant of the League of Nations provided for international supervision and responsibility for peoples who were regarded as incapable of administering themselves. This was done only for the territories placed under the mandate system, and the colonies, as a rule, remained within the exclusive jurisdiction of the colonial powers.

The Second World War had a positive influence on the legal treatment of the colonial problem. At the international conferences which preceded the 1945 San Francisco Conference, cautious steps were taken to achieve at least a partial legal regulation of this important international issue. At the San Francisco

Conference itself, the participating states took a noted interest in the fate of the populations in those territories not included in the trusteeship system. These were territories which had not achieved any degree of autonomy and were still under the jurisdiction of certain powers. At this international conference these territories were called dependent, but in the Charter received the final nomenclature of nonself-governing territories.

Until the adoption of the United Nations Charter, colonies were regarded as territories which, at best, could become part of the national territory of the colonial power through annexation. The United Nations members which possessed colonies or nonself-governing territories, were now, under Chapter XI of the Charter, internationally responsible for their administration, which must be consonant with the principles of the Charter. Colonies, in the broadest sense of the word, no longer belonged to the exclusive competence of individual colonial powers. Now their administering authorities were bound by a number of obligations. (The distinction between a colonly and other dependent territories io moot froquontly of a formal naturo and dopondo on tho oyotom of oompo tences. This is why the word colony is used here in its broadest sense.) Most important of all, a new principle was adopted — the principle of the primacy of the interests of the indigenous populations of these territories.

According to Article 73 of the U.N. Charter, the administering authorities were called upon:

1. "to promote to the utmost, within the system of international peace and security established by the present Charter, the well-being of the inhabitants of these territories." This obligation is undoubtedly milder than that of the trusteeship authority, laid down under Article 76 of the U.N. Charter. This stems from a basic difference between the trusteeship system, which is a specific contractual relationship, and the system of administering nonself-governing territories, for which the declaration (Articles 73 and 74 of the U.N. Charter) gives only general provisions.

2. "to ensure, with due respect for the culture of the peoples concerned, their political, economic, social and educational advancement." The aim of this provision is to protect their national culture, while enabling further progress to be made.

3. to ensure "their just treatment." This provision is of a general character and corresponds to Article 23 (b) of the Covenant of the League of Nations. At any rate, it should prevent any discriminatory proceedings and should be interpreted in accordance with the aims and principles of the U.N. Charter.

4. to ensure "their protection against abuses." Although this provision is not sufficiently clear, it should be interpreted as meaning protection against abuses by the colonial administration and abuses by the local native authorities, as the latter are often under the influence of the colonial officials. In the discussion at San Francisco this phrase was taken to mean: a. protection against appropriation of land by the colonial authority; b. prohibition of forced labor; and c) prevention of any humiliation, particularly on the basis of so-called racial superiority.

5. "to develop self-government, to take due account of the political aspira-

tions of the peoples, and to assist them in the progressive development of their free political institutions, according to the particular circumstances of each territory and its peoples and their varying stages of advancement."

6. "to further international peace and security."

7. "to promote constructive measures of development."

8. "to transmit regularly to the Secretary-General for information purposes . . . statistical and other information of a technical nature relating to economic, social and educational conditions in the territories for which they are respectively responsible." The Charter calls upon the colonial powers to conduct a policy of good-neighborliness, taking due account of the interests and well-being of the rest of the world in social, economic and commercial matters. But are the colonial powers obliged to promote the development of free political institutions in the nonself-governing territories? It was pointed out that, according to Article 73 of the Charter, the colonial powers were not obliged to submit political reports to the Secretary-General. Nevertheless, even though the platform of voluntarism was adopted, and even though the U.N. Charter in the cited article does not mention political reports, the phraseology used suggests that such is indeed the duty of the states administering these territories. This interpretation is based on the aims formulated in the Charter's first chapter, particularly the principle of self-determination, which is also mentioned in Articles 1 and 55 of the Charter. The colonial problem thus came under the jurisdiction of the international community.

7. Evolution of Nonself-Governing Territories — The question of nonself-governing territories was raised at the third regular session of the U.N. General Assembly when it was found that sixty-three reports had arrived for the seventy-four territories proclaimed nonself-governing. For eleven nonself-governing territories the administering countries failed to send the required reports.

The view was quite properly taken in the General Assembly's Resolution 222/III and Resolution 334/IV that it was within the powers of the United Nations Organization to require reports on any change in the constitution or status of nonself-governing territories and that the U.N. General Assembly was competent to pass an opinion on the guiding principles which the administering countries were to observe. A Special Committee was invited to make a study of the factors which would determine when a nonself-governing territory has become capable of administering itself. The report of the Special Committee was submitted to the sixth regular session of the U.N. General Assembly. It lists eighteen such factors, and the publicity given to them was designed to put political and psychological pressure on the metropolises to extend the self-governing rights of the dependent peoples to advance them on the road to independence. On this occasion it was emphasized that these factors must not be construed as an obstacle to the acquisition of complete autonomy by these territories.

On December 14, 1960, at the fifteenth regular session of the U.N. General Assembly, the Declaration on the Granting of Independence to the Colonial Countries and Peoples was adopted without any dissenting votes under Resolution 1514/XV. This historical document is equal in significance to the Atlantic Charter, the U.N. Charter and the Universal Declaration of Human Rights. The Declaration proclaimed that, "the subjection of peoples to alien domination and exploitation constitutes a denial of the basic rights of man, is contrary to the United Nations Charter and impedes the advancement of world peace and cooperation." The Declaration called for the termination of armed action and repressive measures of any kind that were conducted and applied against nonself-governing peoples, and for the granting of full independence and protection of integrity to their national territories. Particularly significant was the Declaration's demand for the taking of immediate steps to transfer all powers to the peoples in the colonies without any conditions or reservations. At the next session of the U.N. General Assembly, a U.N. Special Committee of seventeen members was created (under Resolution 1654/XVI) with the duty of ensuring its application by way of proposals and recommendations. The Special Committee received a number of powers, authorizing it to use all the resources of the United Nations. Thus the anti-colonial states in the United Nations finally won the appointment of a qualified organ to supervise the remaining colonies. In 1961, the Belgrade Conference of nonaligned countries solemnly reaffirmed its support for the Declaration on the Granting of Independence to Colonial Countries and Peoples, and recommended on its part that colonialism should be eliminated immediately, unconditionally, completely and finally. It called upon the participating states to "make a joint effort to put an end to all forms of neo-colonialism and imperialist domination in all their aspects and manifestations." The Declaration, states the document of the Belgrade Conference, provided the most suitable legal and political basis on which the ending of colonial relationships should and can be carried out today, in full accordance with the interests of maintaining and strengthening peace among nations. Detailed proposals and recommendations can be found in the Programme for Peace and International Cooperation, adopted at the Second Conference of Nonaligned Countries held in Cairo in 1964.

III. Recognition of States and Governments

Introduction — Constitutional and Declaratory Theories — De jure and de facto Recognition of States — Conditional Recognition of States — Individual and Collective Recognition of States — Concept and Nature of the Recognition of Governments — Constitutional and Revolutionary Governments — The Torbar, Wilson, and Estrada Doctrines — De facto and de jure Governments — Conditional Recognition of Governments — Recognition of States and Governments in Yugoslav Foreign Policy

1. Introduction — Before a state can exist in an international sense, certain conditions must be met. First of all, there must be a people. Second, there must be an inhabited territory, although its size is immaterial. An organized government, independent of the government of any other state, is a third prerequisite. An anarchic community does not constitute a state. Certain authors take international recognition as the fourth condition, as in their view the recognition granted by existing states to a newly created state implies that all previously mentioned conditions have been met. International recognition would thus be confirmation that the recognized state has acquired the capacity of international subject in the family of nations.

2. Constitutive and Declaratory Theories — Is the granting of international recognition to a newly created state a prerequisite for membership in the community of nations? From the 18th century to the present day it has been a moot point in the theory of international law whether recognition by states, and particularly by governments, is required before a new state can join the international community. This question was frequently raised because in the stormy history of the European states particularly there have been frequent changes of state frontiers and the creation of new states. All this had an effect on theoretical considerations. In the course of time, two prevailing views emerged, two fundamental theories in international law known as the *constitutive* and *declaratory* theories. The constitutive theory derived from the voluntarist legal conception, which originated in the 18th century. According to this concept, the international community consisted of a number of sovereign states representing an organized entity. This community decided whether it would accept a new member into their midst or reject it. The emergence of a new state did not automatically assure it a place within the international community. Its admission was subject to the assent of each and every state. For this reason, the procedure of gaining recognition lasted a long time. If the international community, in other words the great powers, decide to accord recognition to a new state, then the latter acquires both rights and obligations. The new state has the right to expect other states to respect its independence and, on this basis, the right to establish political and other relations with other states. It is the duty of a newly created state to recognize the existing international order and its legislation. Recognition is therefore a formal act acknowledging a new state its legal existence in regard to the other already recognized international persons, and hence this recognition has a constitutive character.

The declaratory theory, according to Chatelain, is based on the "collective phenomenon of international solidarity" rather than on the system of state particularism, like the constitutive theory. This theory considers that a new state coming into existence in any way whatever (either by separation, as was the case with Belgium in 1831, or by the creation of a new national state), automatically acquires the rights inherent in an international person. Louis le Fur believes that this theory was first elaborated by the Scottish writer Lorrimer, and, according to him, the recognition of a state is a kind of birth certificate of the state in question. Provided all the mentioned elements are present, the state exists under international law. If one of the elements is missing, such a community is not an international person. Consequently, it is not established by recognition; only an acknowledgement is made that a state has been created and exists.

We believe this concept to be essentially correct. The fact remains, however, that a newly created state (and even new governments) are extremely anxious to be recognized by other states, particularly the great powers. Consequently, individual recognitions are accorded through the central international organization, the United Nations, of which more will be said later.

Today the declaratory theory is predominant in international law and diplomatic practice, although views widely differ. The American republics concluded a convention in Montevideo in 1933, in which the declaratory view of recognition was given precedence. The same formulation of recognition was accepted in the Bogota Charter, passed in 1948. Ricardo Alfaro, the Panamanian delegate to the second part of the first session of the United Nations General Assembly, submitted a draft declaration on the rights and duties of states, in whose articles 2 and 3 the same thought was elaborated. The Panamanian draft declaration was to serve as the basis for the formulation of a new draft declaration by the International Law Commission. However, the Commission omitted the reference to recognition from its draft. The Yugoslav draft declaration of the rights and duties of states contained a clearly declaratory principle, with an original provision in regard to the creation of national states on the basis of the principle of self-determination.

3. The Nature of Recognition of States — What is the nature of recognition; is it an act of a political or legal character? Kelsen says that in traditional theory there is a certain amount of vagueness in the matter of recognition. The reason for theoretical inconsistencies and impracticability is the failure to distinguish between the political and legal acts of recognition. The American legal writer, Jessup, holds that the ambiguity is caused by the fact that some writers see recognition as a purely political act, while others emphasize only its legal character. Brown, however, is inclined to see recognition as solely a diplomatic or political act. Whereas Jessup only makes a passing reference to the matter in his book, *Contemporary International Law,* Kelsen and Brown argue their statements, the former with powerful logic, the latter with a number of examples from diplomatic practice.

According to Kelsen, political recognition is an act of volition by a state, and it may be unilateral or bilateral. If recognition has been granted unilaterally, such recognition constitutes a bare statement and, according to Kelsen, has no legal effect. If, on the other hand, such an act has been made at the volition of the two sides, it is then a treaty with known legal effects. A unilateral declaration of recognition is important but only politically. A legal act of recognition, according to Kelsen, differs totally from the political act. International law determines the conditions under which a state may be admitted into the international community and provides for a procedure to decide whether or not a certain social community is a state in the meaning of international law. According to Brown, recognition is nothing other than a "voluntary, free, political, diplomatic function," which is within the competence of every free government. Referring always to governments rather than to states, and working on the assumption that international law is founded on the free consent of peoples, Brown concludes that recognition has only a diplomatic function and therefore no specific legal effects.

It seems to us that to accept Brown's standpoint is to sanction the principle of might makes right in an unequal international political struggle. To reduce these rights to political powers means to depart from the basic principles of international law which regulate relations among states for the purpose of maintaining international order. At first sight Kelsen's argument appears logical and correct. The absence of an organized supra-national international community does seem to require a distinction of acts of recognition into legal and political, because there are independent, sovereign states on the one hand and a need for coexistence of these states on the other. Yet it is precisely the absence, in a legal sense, of an organized supra-national international community that prevents the distinction between strictly political and strictly legal acts. Decentralization of international law, as seen in the transfer of competences from a still undefined organized international community to individual governments, deprives a legal act of its strictly legal aspect and introduces an unmistakable element of political expediency. The biggest problem might not even be the absence of a truly organized international community but at least from the legal standpoint, the absence of a generally accepted procedure that would be strictly observed by the already existing states. It is quite clear that this is again closely related to the problem of international organization, which brings us back to square one, strongly suggesting that Kelsen's division is an abstract theoretical construction, hardly acceptable in the present international context. Finally, by following this line of reasoning, we cannot accept Brown's platform either, for reasons that have already been adduced.

It is obvious that in granting individual recognition states are motivated by their own political interests, and that recognition is basically a political act. However, this motivation becomes irrelevant the moment recognition has been given, because recognition as a declaration is a legal fact. The declaration once made binds the state to respect the obligation it has assumed. A contrary proceeding creates insecurity in international relations; therefore, the concept that unilateral recognition is only a political act might have effects that could threaten the independence and integrity of the recognized state. It is, therefore, highly doubtful whether legal recognition might be described as a right to non-intervention, and political recognition as the establishment of diplomatic, economic, communications and other relations. It would not be proper or opportune to leave these relations without a legal effect. The solution must certainly lie in the binding nature of every recognition granted and in the right of a state to be recognized through the United Nations.

4. *De Jure* and *De Facto* Recognition of States

— There is a pronounced tendency in contemporary international law not to distinguish any more between *de jure* and *de facto* recognition of a state. It is now held that a *de facto* recognition is granted to the government of a newly created state if, albeit independent and wielding effective power in its territory, it fails to offer sufficient guarantees in regard to its good will or ability to fulfil the obligations imposed by the states that have granted recognition. Thus a *de facto* recognition was given to the states that were created following World War I, e.g. Lithuania and Latvia, which were previously part of imperial Russia. The rule is that this type of recognition is provisional and can be withdrawn at any time, without any legal consequences, if the state granting it has not seen the conditions that may have been set fulfilled, or if the expectations as to the permanence of the newly created situation fail to materialize.

Kelsen, abiding by his division of recognition into political and legal acts, considers that a distinction between *de jure* and *de facto* recognition is without any legal significance. If this distinction is made, in connection with the political act of recognition, says Kelsen, then such an act does not establish any legal obligation. However, according to this author the mentioned distinction may, also be applied to the legal act of recognition, but with one limitation: that the so-called *de facto* recognition is also a *de jure* recognition because it constitutes a legal act. But such a division immediately becomes meaningless because, according to him, what matters is the division between legal and political acts and not between *de facto* and *de jure* acts.

Scelle is also opposed in principle to this division, believing that any recognition is definitive, i.e. *de jure,* because it lasts for as long as the competence that is being recognized. The provisional, *de facto* recognition, is merely conditional recognition which is a political expedient and therefore devoid of legal basis. According to Scelle, either a *de facto,* or a *de jure* authority may be recognized, but the recognition itself is always *de jure* because it recognizes a competence, i.e. a legal authority.

There is a justified tendency in contemporary international law to remove the distinction between *de facto* and *de jure* recognition. Both Kelsen and Scelle, as representatives of two opposing schools of thought, explain why such a division is baseless from the standpoint of their general legal constructions. Furthermore, this division today, particularly for young national states that are coming out of colonial slavery or tutelage, is not acceptable, and may even be harmful, because practical *de facto* recognition was most frequently given as a prelude to political bargaining. Furthermore, in an established *de facto* situation there is no legal relationship. Therefore the objection by theoreticians that diplomatic practice has introduced this term which does not belong in international law is quite justified. However, as long as diplomatic practice uses it, legal theory must take due account of the division and recognize the possibility of withdrawing a *de facto* recognition, particularly if the evolution of political events does not justify the permanence of the newly created situation (for example, some provisionally created states may be planning a union, to be decided upon at a future conference whose decision would be competent for a *de jure* recognition).

5. Conditional Recognition of States — The prevailing opinion today is that recognition cannot be granted subject to conditions; in other words, it is irrevocable. Recognition is either given or withheld, states the letter of March 8, 1950, addressed to the Security Council chairman by the United Nations Secretary-General. According to other authors, it has an unconditional and compulsory character in regard to the community which has acquired the characteristics of a state. According to Article 1, paragraph 2, of the Yugoslav draft declaration on the rights and duties of states, recognition is unconditional and irrevocable. The underlying principle is that the act of recognition must not contain any conditions. As regards the right to withhold recognition, even today there are many who believe that this right should continue figuring in international law. The reason most frequently given is the loss of national independence. If a state should lose its independence, the states which had granted it recognition would then be entitled to withdraw their recognition. However, because of a danger of political string-pulling by the great powers, which most frequently adduce this argument, an irrevocable recognition is in the interest of the smaller states and is in line with democratic international law. A conditional recognition is a lever in the hands of the great powers, which they can use to impose on a newly created state certain obligations before the latter is capable of assuming such obligations under a treaty. Conditional recognition of a newly created state most frequently amounts to blackmail, because the conditions put forward are usually those that a new state would not be expected to accept voluntarily. For this reason not only legal doctrine but also the political struggle for the democratization of the world are opposed to conditional recognition. However, international law does take into account *reasonable conditions.* Reasonable conditions are that a new state must abide by the general principles of international law; for example, a state created on the principle of self-determination of peoples must not subjugate other peoples who may cite the same principle and may have fulfilled the requirements for the setting up of an independent state. An example of reasonable and conditional recognition was that given to Pakistan by Afghanistan, which made its recognition conditional upon the return of the Afghan territories taken away by force by Great Britain, and whose annexation was never agreed to by Afghanistan. Consequently, Pakistan could not claim greater rights in regard to these territories than Great Britain had. But what international law today must take care to assure as regards conditional recognition, is that non-fulfilment of conditions should not give title to a withdrawal of recognition, but only the right to appeal to the international organization to settle the dispute.

As regards the withdrawal of recognition, Bartoš is of the opinion that reservation of such a right can have no effect because it would be contrary to present-day international law as embodied in the Charter: through recognition a state receives its political independence and the right to a guarantee of territorial integrity. If the right to revoke recognition were to be exercised, the independence of the state in question would be threatened, and this would be tantamount to an act of aggression. Even if the state were not a member of the United Nations, it would be entitled to protection and recourse to the U.N. Security Council. If the state has lost its independence on some other grounds, then there is no question of withdrawing recognition; recognition ceases to be valid because the geographic division of the world has been altered. We therefore believe that any reservations about granting recognition challenge the principle of self-determination of peoples as the principal factor in the further creation of states.

6. Individual and Collective Recognition of States — In present-day practice there are two types of procedure for recognizing new states: individual and collective. States recognize a newly created state, refuse to grant it recognition, or refrain from having to declare themselves, in the belief that it is one of their rights in the international community inherent in the principle of the sovereignty of states. There is a tendency today for the act of granting or withholding recognition to have an increasingly legal character, but it is still of a political nature, particularly in regard to procedure, and states are not inclined to give up this "right." Of course, as the international community becomes better organized, the question of individual recognition will be transferred to the central international organization.

During the 19th century several systems of granting recognition were practiced. Napoleon I enforced the system of creating states in Europe by means of decisions of the French government, and this system functioned for as long as the French domination lasted. The Vienna Congress revised Napoleon's scheme and introduced the system of collective recognition, in the belief that the recognition of states depended on the collective consensus of the then great powers. Complementary to the Vienna Congress system was the principle for legitimacy, as enforced in the practice of the Holy Alliance, without whose recognition no new states could be formed. Although territorial changes did take place, they were subject to the recognition or tolerance of the "European concert." An attempt by Russia, through a peace treaty with Turkey (the Peace of San Stefano of 1878), to create new states in the Balkans fell through owing to the opposition of the European great powers, which revised the San Stefano Peace Treaty at the Berlin Congress (1878), and decided on the fate of the Balkan peoples. This system was carried over into the 20th century (for example, the conferences of ambassadors in London in 1913 and 1919). Another definitive recognition of new states in Europe following World War I was made by the victorious great powers (Supreme Council of Allied and Associated Powers), and their arrangements were made part of the Paris Peace Treaty 1919-1920. This system appears to have been continued in the League of Nations. The Council of the League of Nations, in which the great powers sat, seems to have pursued the same practice, albeit with the participation of the small nations represented in the Assembly. It was concluded that by means of a multilateral international treaty, such as, according to certain authors, the Covenant of the League of Nations, states could transfer their competence to recognize other states to the organs of the international community. The situation thus came about where a new state could become a member of the League of Nations and gain international recognition even though some power might have withheld recognition or voted against admission, which might mean against the recognition of the candidate state. The problem of collective recognition started becoming complicated in the very first international organization, which devoted much attention to this question. The Permanent Mandates Commission of the League of Nations adopted in 1931 a list of conditions which must be met before a mandated territory could be freed of the mandatory administration and recognized as a state. As we can see, it was already the intention in the League of Nations to transform collective recognition into a series of stages through which a prospective international subject must go. It seems that the idea was to make the act of collective recognition as difficult as possible, but then the entire issue was again placed on the political terrain, where, through political methods, conditions may be imposed and compromises reached through political concessions.

The international organization may grant recognition in three ways: *through admission,* by *receiving credentials,* and *by passing resolutions.* The acceptance of credentials gives recognition to the representatives of a new government; the passing of a resolution may be the means of deciding to create a new state, and at the same time of giving collective recognition; a new state may acquire international recognition as the result of being admitted to the world organization.

It is assumed that every newly created state wishes to become a member of the United Nations; in addition, there is the principle of universality, which, although it has some exceptions, represents a cornerstone of the United Nations. However, the question of admission is not so simple. Whereas in the Covenant of the League of Nations admission of new members, as an exception to the principle of unanimity, was made by a two-thirds majority, admission to the United Nations is made by decision of the U.N. General Assembly, also by a two-thirds majority, but on the recommendation of the Security Council, which is a necessary prerequisite for admission and for which unanimity is demanded of all of its five permanent members. The question is both a legal and a political one. Admission to United Nations membership is open to a state if, pursuant to Article 4 of the Charter, it meets the following conditions: that it is a state; that it is peace-loving; that it assumes the obligations envisaged under the U.N. Charter; that it is capable of fulfilling these obligations and intends to do so.

There was a great deal of discussion over what the criterion for the "peace-loving" nature of states might be, and whether a new state may be admitted to United Nations membership on the basis of Article 4, para. 2, of the U.N. Charter by decision of the General Assembly, if the Security Council did not recommend its admission, either because the candidate state failed to receive the necessary majority or because one of the permanent members voted against it. The International Court of Justice ruled that the Security Council's recommendation was indispensable. Thus the possibility still remains that one of the big powers can veto the admission of a state for political reasons.

If admission is understood also to imply the collective recognition of a new state, then, according to the present practice and interpretation of the U.N. Charter by the International Court of Justice, collective recognition under the aegis of the United Nations is in the last resort a political issue, which is subject to the satisfaction of certain requirements under Article 4 of the U.N. Charter.

If we analyze those requirements, we find that recognition by the United Nations means more than the recognition of statehood demanded in international relations for the simple reason that admission confers upon the new state rights and obligations on the basis of universal international law, as well as the rights and duties of a United Nations member on the basis of the Charter. However, member states are under the obligation to communicate with a new member only within the limits of the rights and duties envisaged by the Charter, but in no case are they obliged to establish diplomatic and other relations outside the United Nations. However, if a new state is not admitted to the United Nations, it does not thereby lose the character of a state, which means that statehood is indispensable for admission to membership but does not automatically entail membership.

According to Quincy Wright, recognition by the United Nations usually constitutes general recognition and has an objective effect. However, the foregoing suggests the contrary. According to the provisions of the U.N. Charter and the practice in the United Nations, recognition of states by this organization does not have a general character but is narrowly limited to the relationship determined by the rights and duties which members of the United Nations must abide by. This may not be in agreement with the general intention of the U.N. Charter, but it seems to be defective at least on this point. As proof for this claim, reference is made to the attitude of the Arab states which sit in the United Nations together with Israel but do not *de jure* recognize its existence as a state, and say so at all times.

International recognition is today still a discretionary prerogative for individual states. The tendency of modern international law is to transfer the competence of recognizing states to the international organization, where the emergence of new states would be discussed at public sessions rather than in the cabinets of foreign ministries, where individual interests rule supreme. At present there is a parallelism in regard to the procedure of recognition. Competent to grant recognition are states and in a certain sense the international organization. This undoubtedly causes a vagueness in international relations and a confusion in international law, particularly since the international organization is still only empowered to grant a limited recognition which does not have a universal character. For this reason it is indispensable to transfer the competence of granting a full recognition of new states to the United Nations.

7. Concept and Nature of Recognition of Governments — Recognition of governments is not the same as recognition of states. These, as a rule, are two independent procedures by which existing states and governments, guided by their own immediate or indirect interests, formally acknowledge a newly-created state or newly-formed government. This distinction has its justification in terms of present-day practice, as often the existence of a state is recognized, while its government is denied the right to lawfully administer or represent it.

The granting of recognition to a new government is virtually always a political matter, and as policies change so new international legal institutions are devised. They have now accumulated to such an extent that it is virtually impossible to put them in any order. There are authors, such as Jessup, who believe that if a distinction were to be drawn between the establishment of diplomatic relations and the granting of recognition, if political considerations were to be separated from legal ones, there would be no ambiguity, and in many ways national courts of justice would find it easier to assess whether and how a change of government has influenced the legal validity of a transaction. However, as we have already pointed out, it is difficult to separate what is legal from what is political. Therefore, another criterion has been taken: namely, whether a new government holds power firmly in its hands, whether it implements its authority effectively, whether it is capable of controlling the territory of its state. This criterion has a practical significance. Nowadays people want the criterion to be the "will of the people" expressed in a convincing manner. In fact, every government should be the result of a freely expressed will. The tendency of contemporary international law is to remedy or at least palliate the fact that until now recognition has been linked with political intervention in the affairs of the country in question.

At various times in history different rationalizations have been made for *intervention*. During the ascendancy of the Roman Catholic Church in Europe, legal government was that which had been blessed by God through his delegate, the Pope of Rome. At the time of the Holy Alliance, each non-recognition of a new government was a crude intervention by the members of the Alliance. Such was the nature of the Russian intervention which suppressed the Hungarian uprising in 1849. If we look at the contemporary international picture, we find that new governments are anxious to gain recognition from other governments as soon as possible, particularly from the governments of the great powers, because, according to their international law, the withholding of recognition denies them the "privileges" that are enjoyed by a recognized government. They are also anxious to obtain recognition as soon as possible in order to have some kind of legitimacy in opposing the political pressures that are often very strong in the period before recognition is gained.

8. Constitutional and Revolutionary Governments. — A distinction is drawn in international law between constitutional and revolutionary governments. It is considered that a government may come into power in one of two ways: either by constitutional or by revolutionary methods. The revolutionary way may be bloodless, but for the majority of authors the criterion is whether the continuity of power has been broken or maintained.

If the change of government has been effected in accordance with the constitution in force, other states are usually notified of the change; they acknowledge the notification or congratulate the head of government or prime minister, possibly also the minister of foreign affairs, and this is considered a formal recognition. Recognition given in this manner is not only a matter of courtesy but also has a legal character. There are writers who believe that if third states do not respond, they accept the change as a normal phenomenon that produces its own legal effect. Any challenge of it would be tantamount to unauthorized intervention in the internal affairs of the said state and to an attempt to change the constitutional order by force, thus flying in the face of the constitutional procedure that produced the change of government in accordance with the legal system. However, if a new government has been formed as a result of revolutionary activity, then the newly created political situation is assessed, political interests weighed, and any possible benefits studied. Customarily an act of recognition in these circumstances is regarded as discretionary, usually in the broadest sense of the word. In Latin America concern over this question, inspired the Torbar, Wilson, and Estrada doctrines.

9. The Torbar, Wilson, and Estrada Doctrines — Frequent changes of government in Latin America prompted the foreign minister of Ecuador, Dr. Torbar, to say that the American republics, for the sake of their good name and reputation, as well as out of humanitarian and altruistic considerations, should indirectly intervene in internal dissensions among the republics on the continent. Such intervention might consist at least in a non-recognition of *de facto* revolutionary governments which came into power in an unconstitutional manner. This caused the states of Central America to sign a treaty on 29 December 1907, undertaking to withhold recognition from any government that assumes power in a forcible way. The same doctrine was proclaimed by U.S. President Wilson in 1913, following the changes of governments in Mexico and Nicaragua. Clearly these changes prejudiced the interests of the United States, which was moved to vest its interest with the trappings of an international legal principle. The Wilson Doctrine was sanctioned in an international treaty concluded by the American states in 1923.

In contrast to these "legitimist" doctrines, on 30 September 1930, Mexican Minister of Foreign Affairs Estrada sent a directive to his diplomatic representatives abroad stating that Mexico had been considerably harmed by the earlier international practice of recognition and that, consequently, "the Mexican government reserves the right to maintain or abrogate its diplomatic agencies as suits the interests of the Mexican government, irrespective of any change of government." The notion that recognition of governments is a blatant intervention in the internal affairs of another country, prejudicing the reputation of a sovereign state, is known in modern international law as the Estrada Doctrine.

10. *De Facto* and *De Jure* Governments — In theory, and even more frequently in practice, the distinction is made between *de facto* and *de jure* governments. The difference between them is that a *de facto* government is considered to be only the holder and not the repository of power, whereas a *de jure* government is, as a rule, both, although there are cases when a distinction is made between a government which holds power (*de facto* government) and the government which is the legal titulary (*de jure* government). In such cases we have parallelism of governments: for example, a government in exile and a revolutionary government which actually exercises power or has been put in power by the occupying force.

During the Second World War the United Nations took the line that the governments in exile were not only legal but also the expression of the people's will, whereas the governments created by the occupying forces, the quisling governments, were the antipode of democratic governments and the product of enemy pressures. In this case the recognition of the legitimate government is in principle progressive, for otherwise the occupying force would be recognized the right to transfer sovereignty onto puppet governments. However, if the government at home has been created by the will of the people, the situation is different.

11. Conditional Recognition of Governments — When the distinction between *de facto* and *de jure* recognition is made, either in theory or in practice, it usually follows that recognition may be either conditional or unconditional. *De facto* recognition is provisional, and it can be withdrawn at any time if the conditions have not been met.

Those textbooks of international law that reflect the vital interests of a great power, list the precise legal consequences which follow non-recognition. They constitute the legal safeguards of the interests of those states which favor the practical application of the constitutive theory. According to them, recognition gives a state the ability: a. to establish diplomatic relations; b. to conclude international treaties; if treaties were concluded previously with the state granting recognition, these then automatically come into effect; c. to appear before the courts of the states granting recognition; d. to enjoy immunity from the jurisdiction of the courts of the states granting recognition; e. to seek and receive property which is under the jurisdiction of the aforementioned states; f. if recognition is retroactive, to prevent the courts of justice of the states giving recognition from testing the validity of the legislative and executive acts of the government in the past as well as in the future.

Oppenheim rejects the argument that this distinction has no legal effects and quotes the example where Great Britain gave *de facto* recognition to the Italian administration over Ethiopia, considering that Italy was not entitled to consider Ethiopia as a part of its state. But what are the rights of the agents of a *de facto* recognized government? According to the practice of Great Britain, which Oppenheim does not dispute, no diplomatic intercourse is established if the agents of such a government would have to be accorded diplomatic immunity, which means that *de facto* recognition is designed to permit the realization of the political and economic interests of the governments granting recognition. Scelle arrives at almost the same conclusion, although from a different point of departure. According to him, governments have their international competences and are international subjects only because they are the administrators of their own states. According to Scelle, the international community has only to verify whether the investiture is constitutional; if so, international investiture follows automatically and recognition must be given. In this case it is said that international law has been sanctioned by internal law. Scelle concludes that the emergence of *de facto* governments (revolutionary governments) is a phenomenon of the internal and at the same time of the international legal system. Furthermore, in his opinion, if a government is irregular from the standpoint of the internal legal order, it may be valid from an international standpoint because it is better than no government at all, i.e. anarchy. If legal investiture were to be sought, then, says Scelle in answer to the champions of legal formalism, none of the present-day governments could justify its legitimacy. Consequently, from the substantive as well as from the formal legal viewpoint, any idea of wholly or partially adopting the Wilson or Tobar doctrines is not only harmful from the political standpoint but is also legally untenable.

Scelle's view is justified inasmuch as it points out the contradiction between real life and the principle of legitimacy. No government in the world would be legitimate if changes of governments were strictly to be made by constitutional methods. Continuity has been broken everywhere. It was particularly broken at the times when early constitutional governments were created. However, Scelle's theory also points out that non-constitutional governments can eventually become internationally rehabilitated. The recognition of such a government would amount to a kind of pardon. Its legality, at least in relation to the recognizing state, commences with the fact of recognition, and the government receiving it is prohibited from returning to illegality after recognition. Legality begins with recognition, which means, according to Scelle, that recognition entitles the recognized government to legally exist and exercise those competences which it would have to perform if it had been created legally. Some writers liken this kind of recognition to the acquiescence of a neighbor that the possession of a thing should entitle the holder to become its owner, whereby the holder would claim this recognition to be a settlement which has the power of a court adjudication, so that, if challenged at any future date, he could object to the recognition being questioned again.

12. Recognition of States and Governments in Yugoslav International Practice — Serbia was collectively and *de jure* recognized at the Berlin Congress of 1878. The recognition was conditional, subject to certain obligations imposed on Serbia. These included freedom of religion for all faiths and nondiscrimination against citizens on the grounds of religion as regards the right of taking residence, exercising political rights and entering public service; Serbia's participation in establishing a railway connection between Vienna and Istanbul, as well as Serbia's obligation to accept Hungary's mandate over Iron Gate affairs. Before its recognition became definitive, Serbia had to ratify, and submit ratification instruments for, only those parts of the Berlin Treaty which were applicable to it, which means that it was not a party to the treaty but only the beneficiary of a stipulation benefiting a third party. The question of recognizing a Serbian government came up following the assassination of King Aleksandar Obrenović and the assumption of the throne by King Petar Karadjordević in 1903. Great Britain refused to recognize the new government and broke off diplomatic relations with it. The breach lasted until 1906, when Serbia assumed the obligation to remove from the royal court and from the army the chief organizers of the conspiracy.

Prior to the Berlin Congress of 1878, Montenegro had been individually recognized by only some countries, such as France. At the Berlin Congress it was collectively recognized, but subject to various conditions, the principal being general freedom of religion, as for Serbia, restrictions on the right to a fleet, the right of Austria to police Montenegrin waters. After the unification of Montenegro and Serbia in 1918, Italy long hesitated before recognizing this fact, continuing to recognize the Montenegrin government in exile in Gaetta. This government was dissolved by Italy only after territorial questions with Yugoslavia had been settled.

The Kingdom of Serbs, Croats and Slovenes was recognized collectively by the Supreme Allied Council only in May 1919. Italy made this recognition subject to a separate treaty on delimitation (Treaty of Rapallo). The general recognition was made conditional on the obligation of the new state to assume part of the Austo-Hungarian debt, to recognize the right of legal protection for minorities, and in regard to international obligations to consider itself the continuation of Serbia.

There was a parallelism of governments during World War II. The Allies for a long time (until 1944) recognized the royal government in exile as the *de jure* goverment, and maintained diplomatic relations with it; at the same time they acknowledged the National Committee of National Liberation as the *de facto* government, having recognized it as a war ally (as from December 1944). The parallelism was ended following an agreement between the two governments and their fusion pursuant to the Tito-Šubašić agreement. This government was collectively recognized at the Yalta Conference, subject to certain conditions, the main ones being creation of a provisional parliament composed of the members of the Anti-Fascist Council of National Liberation of Yugoslavia (AVNOJ) and the former deputies who had not been compromised during the war, and subject to the submission of AVNOJ legislative acts for confirmation to the constitutent assembly. The recognition of the Republic and the new government of Tito came following recognition by individual countries from November 1945 to May 1946.

IV. Basic Rights and Duties of States

Declaration of Rights and Duties of States — Theory of Fundamental Rights and Duties of States — Sovereignty — Equality of States — Right of Selfdefense — Rights of International Intercourse — Right to Respect

1. Declaration of Rights and Duties of States — The need for states to adopt an international document defining their rights and duties is not of recent origin. Since the middle of the 18th century theoreticians have tried to lay down legal rules governing international relations. The increasingly close-knit international life, which has become more complicated in recent decades in view of the rapid growth of technology, has demonstrated the justifiability of these theoretical efforts. However, it is not only the theoreticians who are trying to determine the limits of the rights and duties of states. The regulation of this part of international law invades the political activity of states. The problem is preeminently of a political nature, yet it should not be permitted to remain solely within the sphere of politics. The rights and duties of states have a political content, but they cannot be outside a legal framework. The acceptance of such an international document would certainly not alter the flow of international life, but at least some criteria on the behavior of states within the international community would have been established. Many of the political principles guiding mutual relations would thus receive the form of legal principles, bringing more stability into international intercourse and more order into international law, and this, viewed historically, would be a major achievement.

Already at the San Francisco Conference in 1945, a demand was made for the adoption of a declaration on the rights and duties of states, which would have a binding force, similar to the declarations adopted in 1943 at the Moscow Conference. Some states proposed that the declaration should be made part of the U.N. Charter. The great powers held the view that no further progress could be made in regulating this question within the Charter. They claimed that any attempt to insert the declaration into the U.N. Charter would make the universal adoption of the Charter more difficult. Because of the disparity of interests of the great powers and because of the search for a compromise among them, many of the legal rules governing the duties of members — of which more later on — were worded so as to make possible a variety of interpretations. Soon the Panamanian delegation came up with its own draft declaration on the basis of a 1916 project by the American Institute for International Law, adding certain modern principles, particularly those which were first solemnly proclaimed by the Anti-Hitlerite Coalition during the Second World War. Following a U.N. General Assembly resolution the Panamanian draft was sent to the Committee for the Progressive Development of International Law, and in 1947 this draft was presented to the International Law Commission. At the fourth session of the U.N. General Assembly, the Commission submitted its own draft declaration, having struck out of the Panamanian text a number of important rights of states, such as the right to recognition, the right to existence, the abolition of the so-called "international standard for aliens," etc. At the same session, the Yugoslav delegation submitted a new draft declaration, more comprehensive than the one presented by the Commission. Based on contemporary positive law, the Yugoslav proposal constituted the most complete project to date for the regulation of what is probably one of the most important parts of international law. Unfortunately, because of the negative attitude taken by the big powers, the question of the declaration figured on the agenda of several regular sessions of the U.N. General Assembly and a vote on it was always postponed.

Two important theoretical questions arise here, as was noted by Kelsen. The first question is what, legally, should a declaration of the rights and duties of states represent, i.e. should it be drafted from the standpoint of *de lege lata* or *de lege ferenda*. If the U.N. Charter represents universal international law — which Kelsen does not agree with, claiming that it is only a treaty concluded by the members of the United Nations Organization — then the declaration, according to him, must adhere to the provisions of the U.N. Charter, but in fact the text of the declaration — Kelsen had the Commission's draft in mind — goes beyond the rules of the U.N. Charter. If the U.N. Charter does not have this character, then the declaration should adhere to the universal international law that is in force and that does not recognize all the principles contained in the U.N. Charter. Kelsen looks at the problem from his own standpoint of legal positivism. The question can also be asked whether an international act which purports to regulate the rights and duties of states must contain only those provisions which have been adopted and ratified in international conventions or should go beyond the adopted solutions.

First of all, a definite stand should be taken vis-à-vis the U.N. Charter: viz., is it part of universal international law or does it only regulate the relations among the United Nations Organization members by treaty? In our opinion, the U.N. Charter without a doubt constitutes part of universal international law, as the reflection of its progress. The fact that international law has been partly decentralized is confirmed in the U.N. Charter itself. From the standpoint of internal legal systems, international law has some major lacunae, but this fact should act as a spur to work on perfecting the system of norms of international law. This does not mean that the number of legal sources of international law should be expanded and increased *ad infinitum*. Yet new multilateral international acts, as well as the statutes of international organizations, should always constitute a step forward in the development of this legal discipline. Actually the U.N. Charter itself, in Article 13, exhorts the U.N. members to work on the codification and progressive development of the existing rules of international law, so that a declaration of universal character — even if it went beyond the Charter, while remaining within the limits of present international law — would not be contrary to the U.N. Charter but would be a step forward, not only in the development of this subject but also in the performance of its tasks by one of the principal organs of the United Nations.

The other question is that of separating rights from duties. According to Kelsen, reference should only be made to duties, because they take precedence over rights, and rights are merely the obverse of duties. The right to independence is the correlate of duty not to intervene, and for this reason it is superfluous for this right to be specifically mentioned in the declaration.

It is extremely difficult in law, both technically and substantively, to separate rights from duties. Just as every right is the reflection of a duty, it might also be said that every duty is correlated to some right: the right to recognition implies the duty of other states to recognize; or, each state has the duty to respect the sovereign quality of other states; at the same time, each state has a right to demand to be treated as sovereignly equal. Or, each state has the duty to maintain peaceful relations with other states; conversely, such a state has the duty to demand of other states not to treat it in an unfriendly manner. The separation of rights from duties is extremely difficult, perhaps even impossible, but in the long run probably unnecessary.

2. The Theory of Fundamental Rights and Duties of States —

The concept of the existence of fundamental rights of states derives from the theoreticians of natural law. Drawing a parallel between the existence and role of states and the existence and role of man in life, the upholders of this concept believe that the basic rights of states are their natural rights, without which a state could not exist, just as a man exercises rights acquired by nature. On the basis of natural law concepts of the rights of states, various systems of international law have been devised (Vattel, Heffter, Rivier, Pradier-Fodere, etc.). As a rule, their basic postulate is the fundamental right of a state to self-preservation, from which all other rights are derived (e.g. Rivier).

The positivist legal school, mostly the French theoreticians of this school, base themselves on the division between basic or absolute rights, which do not depend on the will of the states, i.e. on which the international legal order is based, and inferred or treaty rights, which are the results of their will (Sieber).

It is difficult to establish the number of basic rights and duties of states, because the states have not yet agreed either on how they should be worded or in what order of importance they should be ranked. Although they cannot be entirely denied, it is up to the states to decide whether and to what extent they would be restricted in practice. They have not been fixed for all time, but in various historical periods there has been a general consensus on the basic rights and duties of states. In our opinion, today they are set forth in the United Nations Charter. The declaration which was to be passed by the United Nations was in fact a recognition of the need to formulate them more precisely. We hold the fundamental rights and duties of states to be sovereignty and equality of states, the right of self defense, of international intercourse and respect for their own identity.

3. Sovereignty — Sovereignty is the right of a state to freedom from foreign intervention in its internal affairs. It is an assortment of fundamental interests of a state, which in the contemporary world should not be contrary to the general interest. For this reason sovereignty today should be embodied in the rights which appertain to states as members of the international community.

Two factors have influenced the shaping of the concept of sovereignty. The first was the desire to consolidate feudal fiefdoms, and the second factor, of an external character, was opposition to Papal omnipotence and the Holy Roman Empire. The principle of sovereignty was held to mean the supreme authority of the state, the ascendancy of the state interest in a feudal, absolutist state, and in the policy of its monarch. The idea of sovereignty originated when there appeared a growing opposition to feudal anarchy and to interference in the affairs of other states. The rulers of those times fought for their unlimited, sovereign authority, within their states as well as ouside their borders. In this struggle to supersede the feudal, retrogressive system and create a new social order, the idea of state sovereignty influenced the creation of large centralized states, and in this respect the struggle had a progressive significance. Although at first historically progressive, absolutism, because of its narrow political aims and general conditions, was based on an unlimited autocracy and brute force. It is in the ideology of absolutism that we find the roots of the theory of absolute sovereignty.

The concept of sovereignty was radically changed during the bourgeois revolutions. The bourgeois classes, identifying themselves with the people, put forward the idea of popular sovereignty and the principle of the equality of states, the national principle, prohibiting particularly foreign intervention in the internal life of a state. This new content in the concept of sovereignty undoubtedly gave force and direction to the progressive historical development and ideology of that time. Freedom and equality of individuals evolved into a general demand for independence and equality of states. Sovereignty emerged as a legal embodiment of these demands. However, as large industrial states came into being and began to vie with one another to gain control in the world, the theory of the rights of "civilized" states gained popularity. From the principle of sovereignty the theoreticians of that time developed the idea of the right of making war, including wars of aggression.

Is it possible, at the present level of development of international cooperation, to deny the sovereignty of states? To deny sovereignty as the supreme authority of a state is to favor an alien authority. To challenge another state's sovereignty is to threaten the international community, which today frequently views any encroachment on the rights of its members as a threat to itself. If the authority of a member of the international community is to be restricted in some way, it can only be done on the basis of a general interest enshrined in the U.N. Charter, as the constitution of the international community, because sovereignty today is the aggregate of the rights possessed by states as members of the organized international community.

As we view contemporary international relations and the international rules in force, we become aware of a trend for the strengthening of international communities. The development of technology and civilization demands an ever closer economic cooperation. Political isolation in any shape or form has an adverse effect on the interests of the isolated state. Any restriction of education and culture tends to lower their levels. For this reason there is an increasing economic, political, cultural and other international intercourse, which, naturally, must also be legally regulated. When dealing with international issues today we must take into account the rights stemming from the sovereignty of states as members of the international community. The threat to the sovereignty of a state and to its sovereign equality may come from different quarters and in different forms: by one or by several states undertaking, prohibiting, or permitting actions of a political or legal nature, directly or indirectly.

The most frequent encroachments against sovereignty or sovereign equality today take the form of tendencies and undertakings to establish control over the sovereign acts of another state. The means usually employed include demands in the nature of an ultimatum aiming at bringing a state into a subordinated position, demands for a privileged status for diplomatic personnel, threats of an official character in diplomatic correspondence as well as in official statements, and, finally, hostile propaganda, which is most frequently made through the press, radio and television. Indirect means are used with the aim of weakening the nation and the government in the defense of the sovereignty of their state, of concealing aggressive plans and of preparing one's own nation for aggressive action. Maneuvers along the borders with hostile intent have become a classical form of war preparations which is still practised today. However, in view of the risks involved, demonstrative movements of armed forces along the border or on several border points are more frequent. Border incidents are today less frequent and happen only sporadically, but in the strategy of military pressure, they are a tactical means of implementing a determined war policy. Most incidents result from an aggressive political move or are designed to cause a certain political effect.

The system of international economic relations and communications promotes the economic and political progress of a country. The economic blockade which follows a unilateral repeal and breaking off of international economic treaties is designed to crush the economic and thereby also the political independence of a state.

Failure to undertake certain measures, binding in terms of international law, may threaten both the sovereignty of another state and the community of nations itself. For example, the absence of frontier demarcation posts is frequently a source of border conflicts. Non-implementation of voluntarily undertaken obligations, under an international multilateral act may be harmful to its other signatories.

The sovereignty of a state may be threatened both by action and by the failure to act. For example, the absence of a service to regulate water systems may cause large-scale floods on another state's territory.

No state can permit a national minority to become a fifth column, but discriminatory acts against national minorities, because of their national difference, are a violation of international law. Similarly, acts against foreigners settled in the territory of a state, in violation of the rules governing the legal position of aliens, may have the same character and constitute an infringement of basic human rights, whose observance is binding according to the present-day international legal system. Such acts would be, for example, the refusal to allow repatriation, the forcing of citizenship upon a foreigner, prevention of contacts with diplomatic agents, etc.

The problem of sovereignty is arising today in all its acuteness. Very often sovereignty is invoked if there is a desire to avoid an obligation or international cooperation. The small states usually cite their sovereignty as an argument against the privileged position of large states, for these privileges enable the big states to influence the internal affairs of the small states and thus violate their sovereignty. The large states claim sovereignty in order to prevent intervention by small states in their spheres of interest, particularly in order to defend their empires, proclaiming their policy vis-à-vis the peoples under their administration to be a matter entirely within their domestic jurisdiction, and, consequently, a question which could only be raised by infringing upon their sovereignty.

The sovereignty of a state means today its independence from external intervention. This is the supreme authority inherent in every independent state, limited only by the universally adopted and currently valid rules of international law. This supreme power extends within the borders of the national territory and is usually described as territorial sovereignty, or territorial jurisdiction of states. However, since an alien resident in a state cannot be regarded as being outside the law and outside the protection of his national state, international law, in addition to *territorial jurisdiction,* also acknowledges *personal jurisdiction.* The concepts of both jurisdictions have the same validity, although in contemporary international law territorial jurisdiction is increasingly gaining in importance.

Both the personal and territorial jurisdictions have three common forms: jurisdiction of a state may be exclusive and this is what the states mostly insist upon; it may be competitive; it may be parallel with the jurisdiction of another state, as in the case of piracy on the high seas; and it may be restricted, if a state has renounced some of its sovereign rights under an international act.

Despite a strong tendency toward centralization of international life and thereby of international law, mainly through universal international organizations and similar institutions, there is on the other hand an opposite tendency, in view of the fact that various activities, which a few decades ago were not under the competence of states, are now being concentrated in the hands of the state administrations. A number of states operate planned management in many sectors, particularly in the spheres of the economy, finances, education, culture and others. In following this road, these states are highly interested in and highly sensitive about their national sovereignty.

What is there to restrict the territorial jurisdiction of states from the standpoint of international rights? With the application of the principle of reciprocity international law has made provision for immunity from territorial jurisdiction, as well as for a certain number of restrictions in the interest of maintaining international order.

International law has ensured complete personal protection for permanent diplomatic envoys and exempted them from the jurisdiction of domestic civil and criminal courts, as well as from taxation in the states in which they exercise their diplomatic mission. Although not diplomatic envoys in the proper sense of the word, consuls also enjoy immunity, although to a somewhat lesser extent than the diplomatic representatives. The immunity of a consul applies to the exercise of all those acts that are within his terms of reference. His archives and correspondence are inviolable. According to international customary law, immunity is also granted to warships and to a certain extent to merchant ships in foreign ports and in foreign waters. On the other hand, especially on the basis of international customary law, a state may renounce its immunity. Immunity from local jurisdiction is also observed with ships in distress and those which "innocently" cross the territorial waters of another state.

Restrictions on territorial jurisdiction are usually made through international treaties. Frequently international trade agreements contain clauses designed to establish a uniform procedure, and they tend to restrict territorial jurisdiction. There may also be a functional restriction of this jurisdiction. States refuse extradition of political offenders, except when this question is regulated by bilateral or multilateral treaties. In the preamble to the Statute of the International Labour Organization it is stated that "if a state fails to adopt humane conditions of work, there arises an impediment to other nations wishing to improve those conditions in their own countries." Thus the initiative of this international organization and its right of supervision can influence a state to improve labor conditions in its territory. Article 2, para. 7 of the United Nations Charter states that no provision of the Charter, and consequently no other decision by any organ of the United Nations, excepting the decisions of the U.N. Security Council on international intervention under Chapter VII, may be construed as authorizing the U.N. to intervene in matters that fall within the *domestic jurisdiction* of any state.

The concept of exclusive, domestic jurisdiction was introduced into international law after World War I, when the Covenant of the League of Nations was drafted and when the terms of reference were laid down for the Council of the League of Nations and the Permanent International Court of Justice. Previously this notion had been current in certain formulas used in arbitration agreements, such as "vital interests," "honour of a state," "sovereignty," "independence," etc. Fearing that a unanimously passed decision in the Council or the Assembly might prejudice U.S. interests, the Americans proposed that this important term be inserted in the basic text of the first international organization of its kind. They did so in the fear that questions of immigration, racial discrimination, customs tariffs and others might be discussed before this international forum and resolved in their country's disfavor. Similar motivations moved the British to adopt, with some alterations, the proposed American solution.

In the Dumbarton Oaks proposals for the establishment of a universal international organization, the term "domestic jurisdiction" was used only in reference to an exception from the provisions relating to the peaceful settlement of disputes. However, in San Francisco in 1945, the provision on domestic jurisdiction of states was inserted in the chapter setting forth the basic principles of the United Nations organization. This provision today is cited both by those who seek in it a guarantee for national sovereignty and by those who demand international intervention. The definition of domestic jurisdiction has been a bone of contention between the champions of the two schools of thought. The upholders of the so-called universalist thesis believe that any matter regulated by any international rule whatever removes that matter from national jurisdiction. Conversely, every state that is compelled to defend its sovereign rights seeks to prove that the subject of dispute lies within its domestic jurisdiction. There have been serious dissensions on this score in almost all the domains of political and social life. The question arises whether the observance of human rights in a state is a matter of its domestic jurisdiction or if it is implementation of a goal of the United Nations and, consequently, a question falling within international jurisdiction. The question of treatment for national minorities — for example the status of Indians in South Africa — resulted in an open conflict between the United Nations and the government of the Union of South Africa. The improvement of living standards of the inhabitants of all states is one of the goals of the United Nations.

Typically, whenever this question is raised the implicated state claims its domestic jurisdiction, but when the same question concerns another state, it regards it as an international problem. These contradictions are becoming more serious every day. Many states uphold the principle of international cooperation as long as it serves their purposes, but if they are called to account for their actions they claim the principle of national sovereignty or of domestic jurisdiction.

Obviously, this question is open to debate at the moment, and only time will bring these two opposing tendencies into harmony, but it can be said already that the question of domestic jurisdiction has priority in most states and that international jurisdiction is not presupposed, rather its grounds in each *concrete case* must be proved by referring to a voluntaryily adopted *international text.* More will be said later about the application of domestic jurisdiction in the United Nations.

4. Equality of States – In the theory of international law, states are equal, irrespective of the size of their territory, number of inhabitants or level of civilization. States are equal in international intercourse, and, according to this principle, whenever a dispute arises within the international organization, each state has a right to equal treatment.

The adoption of international regulations is not the same as the promulgation of a law within the borders of a state. The adoption of compulsory rules in the international sense is a matter of the sovereign will of a state, and no other state can force it to obey in this respect. Similarly, equality among states is seen in the generally accepted maxim *par in parem non habet imperium,* meaning that no state has a right of jurisdiction over another state. According to Article 35 of the Statute of the International Court of Justice, no circumstances may place parties to a dispute in an unequal position before the court. These are the effects of the *legal equality* of the independent states, which again are the result of the freedom which states enjoy in a legal and independent exercise of their functions, and no outside control may force them to a contrary conduct of domestic and external affairs.

No rights of a state may be restricted without its assent.

The question of equality of states was openly raised by the Latin American republics at the Second Hague Conference of 1907. On this occasion the great powers, faced with the arguments of the small states that sovereignty implies equality, tried to find a way out by dividing the principle of equality into legal equality, which they do not deny to the small states, and *political equality,* which, according to them, cannot exist because of the unequal responsibility of states throughout history. French jurists came out with the principle, elaborated particularly by Fauchille, that there is no violation of the principle of equality if he who is expected to perform a function also receives the competence to decide on certain problems on behalf of the community, whereas this right was unnecessary to those who do not decide about it. The French doctrine tried to shift the entire question onto a quasi-democratic terrain, pointing out that the voter has not the same rights as the members of the legislative body, because the voters end their function with the elections. An increased responsibility, according to this opinion, requires greater competences, which basically means inequality.

Independent states cannot be forced to accept outside control. In this respect international law has provided sovereign states with a number of guarantees. However, frequently between states there are relations of superiority and inferiority, which not only have psychological effects, but, owing to different economic and political capabilities, affect many basic interests of the small nations. Legal equality is frequently insufficient to protect their basic interests, either because a given legal system is constructed to favor the interests of some large states, or because the legal norms cannot be changed on account of the different positions and might of some of the great powers. But if, for example, negotiations take the form of bargaining, the demands of the great powers having special positions carry a certain weight but in no way represent a right on the basis of which the stronger powers may act. If a small state also needs to make use of, say, an international organization, it may be ready to make certain concessions to the great powers. This, however, does not mean that demands which have been accepted and acquire a certain compulsory force resulted from the principle of equality of independent states.

In Yalta on 6 February 1945, the United States made a proposal to the U.S.S.R. and Great Britain, in whose third paragraph it gave the view of the U.S. government regarding the voting procedure in the new organization. "The people of the United States," stated this paragraph, "considers it to be of primordial importance to safeguard equality for all the members of the United Nations." In the proposals for the establishment of a universal international organization that were adopted in Dumbarton Oaks in 1944, Chapter II provides for the United Nations Organization to be founded on the principle of "sovereign equality of all peace-loving states." At the United Nations Conference in San Francisco, under Article 2 of the Charter, the United Nations Organization was finally founded on the principle of the sovereign equality of all its members.

The characterisitics of the notion of *sovereign equality* were given at the founding conference of the United Nations by the First Committee, in its report to the First Commission. This part of the report was approved by the Conference at its plenary session and, according to it, the concept of sovereign equality contains the following elements:

    1. states are juridically equal;
    2. each state enjoys the rights inherent in full sovereignty;
    3. the personality of a state must be respected in regard to its territorial integrity as well as in regard to its political independence;
    4. a state should fulfil in good faith its international obligations and duties toward the international order.

Therefore, states are sovereign, and for this reason they have the same rights as members of the international community. Each state, irrespective of its origin, size or system of government, has the same right to regulate its own internal affairs and generally to administer its own policies within the framework of international law. States have the duty to observe and apply international legal rules, particularly in regulating international disputes.

The trend now is to define more closely the elements of the sovereign equality of states. According to the U.N. Declaration on Principles of International Law Concerning Friendly Relations and Cooperation among States, sovereign equality includes the following elements:

    a. states are juridically equal;
    b. each state enjoys the rights inherent in full sovereignty;
    c. each state has the duty to respect the personality of other states;
    d. the territorial integrity and political independence of the state are inviolable;
    e. each state has the right freely to choose and develop its political, social, economic and cultural systems;
    f. each state has the duty to comply fully and in good faith with its international obligations and to live in peace with other states.

The principle of sovereign equality forbids states to intervene directly or indirectly, for any reason whatever, in the internal or external affairs of another state. In the words of the U.N. Declaration, "armed intervention, and all other forms of interference or attempted threats against the personality of the State or against its political, economic and cultural elements are in violation of international law."

5. The Right to Defense — The right to defense has until recently been a basic and unquestionable right of every state. According to the older writers of international law, it derived from the right of self-preservation, and it was considered that a state not only had a right to undertake measures for its own security — which even today is not denied to states — but also to start hostilities (preventive war) if it anticipated being attacked (e.g. Martens, Rivier), which is prohibited today. Such action by a state, according to the rules of present-day international law, constitutes an act of aggression, a criminal act against international law.

Today self-defense is permitted to states. They can defend themselves against hostile activity by foreigners. In this event, however, the state must de fend itself by legal methods in a regular court hearing in which the legal protection of the defendants would be assured.

The United Nations Charter provides for the right of a state to self-defense. The state has a right to individual and collective self-defense (Article 51 of the U.N. Charter) in the event of an armed attack, but only until such time as the U.N. Security Council has taken the measures necessary for the maintenance of international peace and security. At the same time, the state or states which availed themselves of their right to self-defense have the duty of immediately informing the Security Council on the measures undertaken. These measures must not run counter to the powers and obligations conferred upon the Security Council by the United Nations Charter.

At the proposal of the Yugoslav delegation, the U.N. General Assembly at its fifth regular session adopted a resolution on "the duties of states in the event of an outbreak of hostilities," which permits the application of the principles laid down in Article 51 of the U.N. Charter. This resolution created the legal machinery for identifying the aggressor.

According to the rules contained in the resolution, the states involved in a conflict must immediately declare their willingness, within twenty-four hours of the outbreak of hostilities, to order a cease-fire and withdraw their armed forces from the territory or the territorial waters of the other state. At midnight of the same day, it or they must effectively cease firing and start withdrawing their armed forces to the starting positions, so that within forty-eight hours from the moment of the cease-fire they complete their withdrawal. It is the duty of such a state to notify the U.N. Secretary-General about the outbreak of hostilities and to invite the competent organs of the United Nations to send a peace observation commission to the area where the hostilities broke out. The responsibility for the violation of peace, according to the resolution, is borne by the state which failed to observe this procedure.

6. The Right to International Intercourse — States have a right to international intercourse, which means that it is left to their own free will to independently establish and regulate their international relations in a manner which is not contrary to the principles and generally accepted rules of international law. These are relations in the broadest sense of the word. They may be diplomatic, economic, cultural, or others.

States have not only the right but also the duty to engage in international intercourse. The duty of states to enter into international cooperation has been provided for under the U.N. Charter. The forms which international intercourse or international cooperation will take will depend on agreements between the states themselves.

Efforts are being made to define the rights and duties of states more closely in regard to international intercourse. The U.N. Declaration on Principles of International Law Concerning Friendly Relations and Cooperation among States affirms that, "States have the duty to cooperate with one another, irrespective of the differences in their political, economic and social systems, in the various spheres of international relations, in order to maintain international peace and security and to promote international economic stability and progress, the general welfare of nations and international cooperation free from discrimination based on such differences.

To this end:

> "a. States shall cooperate with other States in the maintenance of international peace and security;
> "b. States shall cooperate in the promotion of universal respect for, and observance of, human rights and fundamental freedoms for all, and in the elimination of all forms of racial discrimination and all forms of religious intolerance;
> "c. States shall conduct their international relations in the economic, social, cultural, technical and trade fields in accordance with the principles of sovereign equality and non-intervention;
> "d. States Members of the United Nations have the duty to take joint and separate action in cooperation with the United Nations in accordance with the relevant provisions of the Charter."

In the text on the principles of cooperation on which agreement was reached at the Third Session of the Special Committee, there is special reference to the duty of states to cooperate in the economic, social and cultural fields, as well as in the field of science and technology and in the promotion of international cultural and educational progress.

Particularly important is the provision in the mentioned text that, "states should cooperate in the promotion of economic growth throughout the world, especially that of the developing countries."

7. The Right to Respect — International law protects the good name and reputation of each state. It is a violation to offend a foreign state or its diplomatic representatives by way of statements, inscriptions, through the press, publications, radio or television, irrespective of whether it is done directly or indirectly. (In this manner international law protects the integrity of states, as detailed in Article 9 of the Yugoslav draft declaration on the rights and duties of states. It reads: "Each state has the duty to maintain peaceful relations with other states and to prevent any activity which might be designed to foment hatred against other peoples, to offend their honor and to violate the dignity of other states."

In addition to diplomatic agents, international law also protects the emblem and the flag of a foreign state. To insult and desecrate them constitutes a violation of one of the basic rights of states. This respect is manifested in the generally established ceremonial (protocol, addresses, honor guard). The rules of protocol are designed to prevent any offense to the prestige and honor of a foreign state.

As a rule, the dignity of a foreign state is protected by domestic legislation. According to Article 175 of Yugoslav criminal law, the good name of a foreign state is protected, and under Article 176, the honor and good name of the head of the foreign state and diplomatic representatives are also protected.

V. Abuse of Rights in International Law

The question of the abuse of rights is now regaining much of the interest for modern writers that it once had as one of the leading legal institutions, according to Josserand, of Roman law. Today, owing to the increasing centralization of the international community, international law is in the stage of an accelerated development with a tendency of a further elaboration of international legal norms.

Before World War I, the legal theory ruling in international law generally took the view that a state is not responsible to another state for any harm caused it as a result of the exercise of one of its rights. *Neminem laedit qui jure suo utitur.* Thus, for example, the right to self-preservation paved the way for the right to preventive war. If any reference was made to the possibility of the abuse of rights, it was done more from the political aspect. The authors of the then existing systems of international law were not inclined to transpose this already well-known legal institution into what was then rather inter-state than international law, because it was believed that a state availing itself of a right within the law could not be answerable for any damage caused by its exercise.

Between the two world wars, a tendency appeared in literature to transfer the institution of abuse of a right into international law. The question cropped up in connection with an increasingly broad and flexible conception of sovereignty. The theoretical possibility of limiting state sovereignty was related to the question of prohibiting the abuse of rights by states. This institution is a subject of considerable study in the international legal literature at the present time. What is more, as the number of entities subject to international law increases, the tendency for its application also increases. The abuse of a right can occur not only in direct international relations, but may also take place within the international organization, when a member state, exercising an acknowledged right, violates the rights of other members or of the organization as a whole. By the same token there exists the possibility that the organization might, in respect of one of its members, abuse some of the rights, legally bestowed upon it by all its members, on the basis of a collective international treaty which in its essence may be of a constitutional character. This is how we envisage the possibility for the international organization to overstep its competence. Finally, following the growing tendency to consider individuals as subjects of international law, it is correctly supposed that this legal institution will in future be systematically elaborated (e.g. Rollin).

Before an attempt is made to consider the prohibition of the abuse of rights in international law, we must first look at the concept of the right that is likely to be abused. When we speak of a certain right in the internal legal system, what we mean is a determined and legally fixed right which contains certain elements. Is this also the case in international law? The answer certainly depends on our general attitude towards international law. Whatever theoretical standpoint is taken, inevitably the conclusion is reached that a good deal of international relations are regulated by means of the most general principles of international law. It may be so because this legal matter has not yet been regulated, but may also be because the collective law-maker wanted it so for the purpose of an easier exercise of international relations. Whatever consequences might arise, due to lacunae or a deliberately vague legal approach, the fact remains that in regard to system, contemporary international law is still far from the codified continental law, although it is being developed all the time. This undeniable fact makes a general definition of the concept of abuse of a right in international law more difficult, because, obviously, we must first know the elements of the right that may be abused. If these elements are undefined, it is extremely difficult to prohibit the abuse of a right. If there is no possibility of a legal qualification, then there can be no legal prohibition. The majority of the present-day systems of international law accept the category of the *fundamental* rights and duties of states, often deliberately avoiding a systematic elaboration of this part of international law. It is being debated whether the well-established basic rights, such as the independence of states, are in fact a right or an attribute of a state. Oppenheim and Lauterpacht, for example, believe that independence is an attribute of a state as an international person and not its right. The difficulty in determining the elements of the concept of the right of states as the principal subjects of international law is noted by Kiss, and he finds a solution in the application of the theory of competence. Without engaging in a detailed analysis of this controversial question, this author devotes his entire monograph to cases relating to the abuse of the competences of states, which means those rights that incontestably constitute a state's jurisdiction. In this case, Kiss reduces the problem to a conflict of competences in regard to state territory, air space, performance of public services, personal jurisdiction of states, and the application of state competences in international trade. The appearance of this institution in the system of rights of international organizations is mentioned by this author only on one page.

In international relations, generally as regards the jurisdiction of a state in its own territory, the abuse of a right can certainly happen. It can be identified in the manner proposed by Kiss, namely, by first establishing whether the state exercising a certain right is competent to do so. But theoretically a doubt arises if one first tries to draw a distinction between a right and a competence. Furthermore, the separation of the notion of competence from that of the application of competence is still not clear in international law. When a distinction is made between rights and competences, there inevitably arises a theoretical dispute between the individualistic and solidary legal conceptions. The problem is whose right is protected in a conflict between two subjective rights, in this case the rights of states, protected under international law. Will the right being exercised be protected, thus preventing the protection of the threatened right, or will the opposite course be taken? Whichever way this question is approached from the standpoint of the assessment of subjective rights, someone's subjective right has to be restricted. This is one of the shortcomings of the individualistic conception. The advantage of this conception may be seen in the necessity of determining the scope of freedoms of the legal subjects. If a person, in this case a state, does not have a number of unconditional rights, then there is no legal security for the subjects in question. Solidarity, on the other hand, has the "social interest" at heart, and therefore this conception has for its criterion not an injured subjective right but the social injury caused by the exercise of a certain subjective right.

The above-mentioned conceptions are designed to safeguard the international legal system. The jurist M. Ago, stated in his lectures at the Hague Academy of International Law that it is difficult to relate the prohibition of the abuse of a right to the international legal system, because states are very jealous of their subjective rights.

The same situation exists today. Although trends toward international cooperation are strengthening, states are still inclined not to transfer their sovereignty to the international community. If we take into account the present level of development of international relations, it is difficult to opt just for the first or for the second conception. The individualistic conception cannot be entirely accepted because then the possibility of prohibition of the abuse of a right would be excluded, which today would not be desirable either from the legal or still less from the political standpoint, particularly if we have in view the interests of the small countries. On the other hand, we cannot lose sight of the pronounced desire of states for the preservation of their sovereign rights particularly on the part of those states which do not have very large material means for the defense of their independence. The solidary conception, as attractive as it might appear, must for this last reason be revised, although it cannot be entirely neglected. If states do not have in mind the overriding interest of the international community, then the interests of the physically weaker subjects are threatened, apart from the fact that the acceptance of the individualistic thesis would bring about consequences which would weaken rather than strengthen the forces of the organized international community. In this community, through the system of a number of international organizations, international relations are maintained within the bounds of a certain number of rights and obligations, where it is undoubtedly easier to prohibit the abuse of a right, and present encroachments by the "international authority" on the subjective rights of the member states.

Having in mind some actual disputes, Sieber laid down a few general conditions by which he determined whether a legal right had become abused. According to him, the rights involved are those that are no longer of any use to their holder or whose use is contrary to the public interest. Similarly, according to Sieber, a right has been abused if its application has gone beyond what had been agreed upon, or if a certain right has been exercised crudely and without any benefit to its holder and thus has no deeper justification. As an example he cites the expulsion of aliens without a special reason. The elements quoted by Sieber are of a general nature. They can be claimed by all the parties to a dispute in virtually every case. Thus the problem is reduced to the question of selecting one or another method of legal interpretation. The judge in such a dispute would have no criterion to help him bring a verdict. For this reason, in all probability, Kiss's emphasis on the prohibition of encroachments on the competences of states rather than the abuse of their rights can be of practical use because it is often easier to establish the competence and then the right than try to establish the right first. However, the question immediately arises of distinguishing between an established competence and its real application. In the Boffolo dispute, for instance, the arbiter stated that one should never lose sight of the extremely big difference between the state's right to exercise authority and of its actual legal exercise. According to Kiss, the overstepping of competence generally occurs if the action of a state encroaches upon the competence of another state, or the injury suffered by another state is considerably greater than the advantage which the former state would have by this action. However, the author himself admits the deficiency of these conditions and the difficulty of applying them universally. Thus the theory of competence is here only partly useful. It certainly helps to establish the jurisdiction of the state, and hence also any overstepping of its authority, although difficulties remain in distinguishing between these two legal concepts. However, as soon as one steps out of the area of direct international relations onto the terrain of international intercourse through international organizations, the problem becomes so complicated that the theory of competence cannot help much in explaining and regulating the complex international relations, nor, for example, the abuse of the right of veto by the permanent members of the U.N. Security Council.

In literature dealing with international law, one can find the notion that legal grounds for the prohibition of an abused right lie in justice. Yet the question is now what is one to take as an objective criterion for justice. The notion of justice in the Anglo-Saxon terminology is not the same as on the continent. Likewise, some of the European legal systems would be hard put to fit in some elements of justice. Finally, it is extremely seldom in the history of international justice that parties agreed for a court to adjudicate a dispute *ex aequo*. In the practice of the Permanent Court of International Justice there were no cases where the parties asked for an adjudication *ex aequo et bono*.

Is then the prohibition of the abuse of a right in international law a general principle of international law? Certain authors give an affirmative reply, claiming that it stems from the structure of the international legal system rather than from the desire for an artificial transplantation from one legal system into another. Thus the prohibition of the abuse of a right would be a general principle, not only by virtue of its origin but also by virtue of its function. In international law the prohibition of the abuse of a right becomes a general principle. Today, it is not yet so, although it is already finding its application. The difficulties are the following: a. incompleteness and imperfection of the norms of international law; b. absence of international judiciary organs which would authoritatively assess an abuse of a right, and particularly the overstepping of "international authority," whatever its character might have been. As the international community develops and strengthens, this principle will increasingly find expression.

VI. State Territory

Concept of State Territory — State Frontiers — Airspace and Outer Space — International Rivers — Danube — The Sea — Straits — Interoceanic Canals

1. Concept of State Territory — State territory is the space circumscribed by the state frontiers. It covers both land area and airspace, together with the coastal seas. In this space the state exercises its jurisdiction over the persons residing there as well as over the things belonging to it. The exercise of authority in this territory is in its exclusive jurisdiction and is only limited by the rules of international law, in the sense that every state authority must take into account the immunities recognized by international law. The state may not, by action or omission, permit its territory to be used to the detriment of the rights of another state.

In a state territory there may be dual power, the authority of the federal state and of the federal units, just as it is possible to encounter simultaneously operating two sovereign powers in the latter case the joint government is called a condominium or co-imperium. In contrast to condominium, there have been cases in history that a state retained sovereignty over its own territory while conceding the exercise of its sovereign rights to another state. This was done for example with Bosnia and Hercegovina in 1878 at the Berlin Congress.

Spheres of interest do not constitute a part of a state territory. These are areas in which powers, usually the big powers, exercise to a greater or lesser extent their political, economic, or other influence, on the basis of a treaty or agreement.

State territory is protected under international law. Threats against or violation of territorial integrity results, according to the U.N. Charter, in the application of collective action.

The territory of the Socialist Federal Republic of Yugoslavia is a single entity and is composed of the territories of the socialist republics.

2. State Frontiers — State frontiers are the barriers which separate and join state territories. They extend along their length between two states, as well as above the boundary line into the airspace, as far up as the artifacts of human technology can reach. At the same time, they extend deep down underground, by a vertical projection of the frontier line. Boundaries between states must be agreed upon in an international treaty or in the acts of collective recognition. If they have been determined by way of a treaty, it is usually a bilateral or multilateral peace treaty. In the absence of an international act, the principle of effective occupation is applied. Thus in the case of a dispute in Latin America, consideration is taken of that boundary line which in 1810 separated the administrative units of Spain and Portugal. This is the so-called principle *"uti possidetis* 1810." Bartos believes that an adjudication by the International Court of Justice or an arbitration tribunal can also provide legal grounds for the drawing of frontiers, provided the parties involved have given authorization to the court.

The drawing of frontiers, according to European practice, is as a rule done in three states: the first stage is the adoption of an international act which includes delimitation, and this is most frequently a peace treaty; the second stage is the field work of an international frontier commission, which usually has the power to move the border referred to in the international act by not more than half a kilometer and may transfer from one to the other side of the border settlements having not more than 500 inhabitants; the third stage consists in the placing of frontier posts.

If the frontier runs along a river, its geometrical median is taken to be the boundary. The drawing of the boundary along the mid-channel (Thalweg) has been abandoned because it was shown that in the course of time rivers may change their channels.

3. Airspace and Outer Space — The development of aeronautics has caused the need for regulation of international aeronautical traffic. In legal theory there are two criteria for the regulation of this question. The first is a strict respect for state supremacy and the exclusive right of a state to use and control air traffic. This conception, which is based on the theory of absolute sovereignty, was justified on the grounds of state security. The other criterion was based on the comparison between aerial navigation and navigation on the open seas. The great aerial space, according to this criterion, cannot be within the jurisdiction of a state, just as it is not in the case of the open seas. The champion of this concept is the well-known French internationalist Fauchille.

Already at the Hague Conferences, the question of the launching of projectiles from balloons and other airships was considered. After the First World War, the first air navigation convention was adopted, the so-called Paris Convention of 13 October 1919. It was then that the first international organization for air traffic was set up. According to this convention, states have exclusive sovereignty over the airspace above their territory, subject to the servitude of innocent passage which was also regulated in favor of state sovereignty. Under the Paris Convention, the International Air Navigation Commission was established, known as CINA (Commission internationale de la navigation aerienne).

During World War II (in 1944), an international conference was held in

Chicago, attended by fifty countries. The conference adopted four international conventions: the Convention on International Civil Aviation, the International Air Services Transit Agreement, the International Air Transport Agreement, and the Interim Agreement on International Civil Aviation.

The Chicago conventions adopted the sovereignty of states as their basic principle, subject to considerable limitations imposed by the so-called "five freedoms." These were:

1. the right of innocent passage over state territories, without landing;
2. the right to land for nontraffic purposes, for refueling;
3. the right to discharge in a foreign country traffic (passengers, mail and cargo) coming from the home country;
4. the right to take on traffic (passengers, mail and cargo) for the territory of that state;
5. the right to take on passengers, mail and cargo destined for the territory of any other contracting state and putting down passengers, mail and cargo coming from any such territory.

The first convention contains only the first "freedom," the second contains the first two, and the third the other three. They do not make up a legal whole, and thus states may adopt one freedom, the first two or all five of them. Under the third convention, the first four may be adopted, while excluding the fifth one.

Under the Chicago Convention on International Civil Aviation, each state is acknowledged to have complete and exclusive sovereignty over the airspace above its territory. The aircraft belong to the state in which they are registered. The registration of one aircraft in several countries is not allowed, but the registration may be transfered from one state to another. The aircraft which are used in international air navigation must bear the proper marks of nationality and registration. The states are obliged to supply details on registration and ownership of the aircraft registered there. It should be pointed out that the Convention on International Civil Aviation applies only to civil and not to government-owned aircraft. The latter includes military, customs and police aircraft. It is clearly stated in the convention that no government-owned aircraft of a signatory state may fly over the territory of another state or land upon it unless it has obtained permission under a separate agreement.

States as a rule reserve for themselves the right of *cabotage*. For this reason, every signatory state is entitled to refuse to issue a permit to take on passengers, mail or cargo for transport, against payment or on the basis of a lease agreement from one place to another in its territory. The signatory states undertook not to conclude agreements granting exclusive privileges of this kind to another state or air navigation companies of other states.

As a result of the Convention, a new international organization, the International Civil Aviation Organization was founded. The members of this international organization are the states which have ratified the Chicago Convention on International Civil Aviation.

It was in accordance with the Chicago conventions and the international legal standards that Yugoslavia's air navigation act of 1965 was adopted. According to this act, an aircraft coming from abroad or flying abroad may enter or exit from Yugoslavia's airspace only through certain frontier corridors. These corridors are established by the Federal Secretary for Transportation and Communications in agreement with the Federal Secretary for National Defense and the Federal Secretary for Internal Affairs. All foreign aircraft may fly within Yugoslavia's airspace only with permission, unless otherwise arranged by international agreements. A foreign military aircraft receiving such a permission must follow the regime stipulated by international regulations and customs.

The flights of the Wright brothers and Bleriot soon gave rise to international legal problems, which generlaly consisted in establishing the sovereign rights of states and the legal status of the aircraft. The aircraft of that day had the purpose of transporting passengers and cargo from one end of the world to the other.

Since 4 December 1967, our planet has been circled by artificial satellites, first Soviet and soon afterwards American. Other countries are also making similar attempts. These are no longer the conventional airships. They are not means of transporting passengers and cargo by air. How can their flights be regulated? How can the good that they bring be promoted, and how are we to prevent the harm that they might inflict? Can conventional legal concepts be of use in building a new international order far above the heads of the human beings on this planet?

Classical theory takes as its starting point the concept of sovereignty and in fact the first articles of all conventions to date: The Paris Convention of 1919, the Havana Convention of 1928, and the Chicago Convention of 1944. The followers of this theory tried to establish the limits of the space that can be considered sovereign, i.e. the point at which a state no longer has sovereignty over its airspace. Some see the problem in terms of altitude and even suggest figures, while others draw analogies with the sovereignty of states over the sea and try to draw boundaries in the air similar to those between territorial waters, the protective zone, and the high seas.

The fact is, however, that aircraft, as stated in article 3 of the Chicago Convention, are vehicles which remain airborne thanks to the reaction of air. The satellites and missiles move along different principles. Besides they can also operate outside the air and atmosphere.

Experts in civil law are rather inclined to look at these new phenomena as "objects." If an object is not subject to sovereignty, it is *res nullius.* If such an object moves through a space which belongs to no one, then during this motion, such an object moves through its own space. On the basis of this reasoning, if such objects and subjects should encounter a planet where there is no authority that performs some acts of government, then this planet is in the control of whoever first takes effective possession of it. Another school of thought, which has far more adherents, is of the opinion that in such a case, this object would be in common ownership, *res communis omnium.*

Most likely both are wrong if they take the "object" known in civil law and project it into a future legal regime of boundless outer space. As it is in most cases wrong to equate civil law concepts with those of public law, the same goes for international law. The public law notions of territory are certainly not the same as the civil law concepts of things, ownership and possession.

If we agree with the critics of the classical theory, it does not mean that we have theoretical and practical solutions for the international legal problem of outer space. Jurists are still trying to solve this question, but with not much success. There have undoubtedly been impressive technical successes in space exploration. How this conquest will proceed and what obstacles it will encounter are still difficult to foresee. Even the official international legal doctrines have not been standardized. Specialists in international law in both the U.S.S.R. and the U.S.A. change their view in accordance with technical breakthroughs and their own national security considerations. At first the Soviets championed the theory of national sovereignty in airspace and outer space. Soon afterwards, Professor Korovin rejected the conception of national sovereignty, describing it as an "unscientific geocentrism" and a return from Copernicus to Ptolemy. Cooper was first an opponent of national sovereignty in outer space, but later on insisted on a so-called protective national zone in airspace and outer space.

Notwithstanding the technical prerequisities, which may but need not necessarily be realized and on which present outer space law is being built, we can conclude that outer space today does not belong to any of the contemporary states. The limitless reaches of outer space must remain accessible to all the states on our planet, on condition of an exclusively peaceful use based on the legal system of the United Nations.

To this effect, the Treaty on Principles Governing the Activities of States in the Exploration and Use of Outer Space was concluded and opened for signature simultaneously in London, Moscow, and Washington on 27 January 1967. According to the provisions of this treaty, and in terms of the principle of the freedom of research and use of the cosmos, outer space and celestial bodies may not be appropriated by any state or states. Beginning with a resolution of the U.N. General Assembly (1721/XVI), to the Declaration and later the Treaty on Principles Governing the Activities of States in the Exploration and Use of Outer Space, the basic idea remains the same: outer space, including the moon and other celestial bodies, could not be an object of national conquest. Exploration and use of outer space, including the moon and other celestial bodies, was to be carried out for the general benefit and in the interest of all states. In effect, outer space was thus proclaimed to be *res communis*. However, there still remains the unresolved question of the boundary between airspace, in which states enjoy sovereign rights, and outer space, in which they do not.

4. International Rivers — Rivers are integral parts of a state territory. If a river does not flow beyond the borders of a state, it has a national character and is then not of special significance for international law. If it flows through the territory of two or more countries or forms the boundary between them and in addition is navigable and directly or indirectly flows into the sea, it may have an international character.

Naturally, in addition to the above there is also the legal requirement that a river be proclaimed international by an international act, adopted by the interested states. Therefore, the first condition for a river to be international is that it should not come under the territorial supremacy of one state only but of at least two states. Rivers forming frontiers may also be of international significance. Secondly, there is the general requirement of navigability, significant from the standpoint of international practice because as a rule rivers become international from the point at which they become navigable (e.g. the Danube from Ulm). However, even non-navigable rivers may be of international interest, but then we have a case not of the internationalization of navigation for a large number of states — a case of an international river in the proper sense of the word — but of exploitation of the river by the riparian states, as is the case in Yugoslavia with the Mura and the Drava. The third condition is the direct or indirect linking of an international river with the high seas. This reflects the view that international rivers are the natural extensions of the high seas. This requirement also has a practical significance, for without it, it would be difficult to justify the free passage of the ships of non-riparian countries over such international rivers. Finally, a river becomes international — having met all the above-mentioned geographic and economic conditions — if an international act has also been passed, as a rule an international treaty, on the basis of which a river is proclaimed to be international.

By its decision of 16 November 1792, the French Revolutionary government was the first to put forward the principle of free navigation on international rivers. It proclaimed this international principle because of its interest in the navigation on the Scheldt and the Meuse.

In the final act of the Vienna Conference of 9 June 1815, the then great powers put forward the general principle of the freedom of navigation on navigable rivers which flow through several countries. They undertook to regulate under a general agreement everything concerning navigation upon these rivers. In Article 109 of the final act, it was stated that navigation along the entire course of the river was entirely free and that no discrimination could be made in regard to trade upon it. Similarly, the great powers also agreed in this document on a uniform system of the exercise of rights along the entire length of the river. It was also established that every riparian state should maintain the barge-towing paths running through its territory as well as carry out works on the river bed in its territory to remove any obstacles to navigation.

During the 19th Century, a number of rivers were proclaimed international. For example, in Europe: the Danube, the Elbe, the Scheldt, the Meuse, the Oder, the Rhine, the Vistula, the Weser; in the Americas: the Amazon and River Plate; in Africa: the Congo and the Niger.

5. The Danube — The Danube was proclaimed an international river at the Paris Congress in 1856. The international treaty concluded on this occasion provided that the principles regulating river navigation on the Danube should be the same as those that were proclaimed in the final act of the Vienna Congress. The signatories of the Treaty of Paris agreed that this provision on the Danube should form part of European public law and assumed guarantees in this respect.

Under the Treaty of Paris, two commissions were formed: the European and the Riparian Commissions. The European Commission was made up of representatives of all the states that had signed the Treaty of Paris. The competence of this Commission applied to the delta portion of the Danube between its mouth and Isaccea. Its mandate was to be two years, during which period it was expected to complete all the necessary works in order to make the Danube delta navigable for large and small ships. The Riparian Commission was made up of the riparian states. It included the delegates of Austria-Hungary, Turkey, Bavaria, and Württemberg. As Serbia, Wallachia and Moldavia were non-sovereign states, they were only able to send their commissioners to this Commission, with the right of discussion but without the right to vote.

The Riparian Commission soon lost its raison d'être, as the act on navigation that it was expected to draft two years later could not come into force because of the categorical opposition by the British and French delegates. After this failure, the Riparian Commission was no longer able to hold its meetings.

The European Commission, which was provisionally set up for a period of two years only, remained in force for 100 years. Its mandate was extended several times. At first these extensions were justified by the engineering work which had to be continued for the sake of normal navigation along the Danube. A gathering held in Paris in 1858 decided to prolong the European Commission until 1866. The mandate was again extended to 1871, in which year a conference was held in London where it was again decided not to abolish the European Commission but to allow it to continue its work until 1883.

In 1878 at the Berlin Congress, the so-called "Danube question" was also raised. Under Article 57 of the Treaty of Berlin, Austria-Hungary was given the task of regulating the passage through the Iron Gate. Under this international treaty, the jurisdiction of the European Commission was extended up to Galati. In Article 52 of the Berlin Treaty the participating powers agreed that the Danube should be neutral from the Iron Gate to its mouth.

The London Conference in 1883 extended the European Commission's mandate for twenty-one years until 1904 and at the same time decided that the mandate should be automatically extended. Thus the European Commission became a permanent international institution in which the great powers of the day concentrated their power. According to Engelhardt, it became a state within a state, or, as Renault put it, a "small state" with legislative and executive functions and with judiciary powers, because it was able to impose penalties for any infringements against its provisions. According to some authors, it was in a true sense an international legal person, since it had the right to raise international loans, to fly its own flag and to have its own ships. The members of the European Commission were accorded diplomatic immunity.

After the First World War, an international conference was held in Paris at which, on 23 July 1921, the Danube statute was passed for the purpose of ensuring in a definitive manner free navigation on the Danube. On this occasion, free navigation was proclaimed for ships of all flags, and rules on the method of ship inspection were adopted so that the riparian states could not impede free navigation by enforcing their own laws. Two commissions continued in existence: the International Danube Commission, which had jurisdiction from Ulm to Braila, and the European Commission, which administered the portion from Braila to the sea. The creation of a single Danube Commission was not in the interest of the great powers that had been victorious in the First World War, because the participation of the riparian states in the work of a single body would allow them a certain measure of control over the mouth of the Danube, where as a rule the interested great powers had full power.

Until the Paris Congress Russia had dominated the Danube, but after its Crimean defeat, predominance on the Danube went to Austria-Hungary. After the First World War, Great Britain and France controlled Danube navigation thanks to their big capital. As Hitler's Germany strengthened, it soon gained an overwhelming influence on the river. In September 1940, an international conference was held in Vienna, which passed new rules and formed a new body, called the Danube River Council, with its headquarters in Bratislava. In this international body profascist governments were represented, so that Germany was assured complete control in the Council.

On 12 December 1946, the Allied governments of the United States, Great Britain, the U.S.S.R., and France agreed that six months after the peace treaties with Romania, Bulgaria and Hungary came into effect, a conference should be called to adopt a convention on the regime of navigation on the Danube. This conference was finally held on 30 June 1948 in Belgrade.

The Belgrade Conference was held in a period of sharp international tension between the East and the West. The Western great powers claimed acquired rights on the Danube and asserted they could not be denied them by the riparian states. Their representatives declared they would not be bound by the decisions of the conference, even if they were passed by a majority of votes. The riparian states rejected the theory of acquired rights, which they said did not represent a universal international principle. They argued that they themselves at certain times had renounced their town rights. The Danubian states further argued that the Danube Statute of 1921 was no longer in force and that, consequently, they could not recognize the so-called acquired rights of the Western great powers. Finally, on 18 August 1948, the riparian states adopted a convention on the regime of navigation on the Danube; the Western great powers walked out of the Belgrade Conference and to this day have not recognized this convention.

The Belgrade Convention proclaimed the sovereign rights and equality of the riparian states on this international river. It abrogated almost 100-year-old privileges of the great powers, whose territories were not contiguous with the Danube. While the Versailles system acknowledged the international character of the tributaries and canals of the Danube, free navigation was only recognized in the navigable part of the Danube from Ulm to the Black Sea, through the Sulina Canal. Navigation on the Danube was proclaimed to be "free and open for the nationals, vessels of commerce, and goods of all states, on a footing of equality in regard to port and navigation charges and conditions for merchant shipping."

According to the Belgrade Convention, ships plying the Danube, provided they observe the regulations of the riparian states, are entitled to enter the ports, to load and unload cargoes, to take on and discharge passengers and to take on stocks of fuel, foodstuffs, and other requisites. *Cabotage* was permitted only if it was in accordance with the national regulations of the Danubian state concerned.

Particularly significant was the creation of a single Danube Commission. The formation of an international body on the Danube is in accordance with the principles laid down in the final act of the Vienna Congress in 1815 and in the Treaty of Paris of 1856.

The Danube Commission is composed of representatives of the Danubian countries. Each of these countries is entitled to one representative. The convention fixed the terms of reference of the Commission, which was to see to the execution of its provisions, to the elaboration of general plans, to the carrying out of public works in the interest of navigation, to provision of advice in regard to the execution of these works and to various technical services, etc. The Commission cannot, however, without the consent of the state in whose territory the public works are to be carried out, take decisions concerning the general plan of large-scale works. The riparian states have the right of veto.

The Commission has a secretariat which enjoys the status of a legal personality, in conformity with the legislation of the state in which its headquarters are located. Personnel are entitled to freedom of movement on the river and in the port. The headquarters of the Commission, i.e. its offices, archives and documents, are inviolable. The Commission has the right to its own seal and its own flag.

Any dispute over the application and interpretation of the convention will be settled in the first instance through direct diplomatic negotiations. If it is not settled, a conciliation commission would be set up, whose decision is final and binding on the parties to the dispute. According to Bartos, this commission has the functions and rights of an international court of arbitration.

The first meeting of the Danube Commission was held on 11 November 1949 in Galati. The first few meetings of the Commission were dominated by attempts by the largest powers on the Danube to use this international body, which was supposed to work on the basis of the principle of equality of all members, to further their own political ends. The Soviet Union acquired the authorization from the Danube states within its orbit to give the secretary of the Commission, who was a Russian, powers exceeding those envisaged in the convention. The Yugoslav delegation protested against the predominance of the secretary in the Danube Commission, demanding an amendment to the provisions which allowed so large a concentration of power in the hands of the secretary. The Yugoslav proposal for a change in the rules of procedure of the Commission to reduce the power of the secretary was only adopted at the ninth session in 1953 in Galati. Under the changed rules, decisions in the Commission are taken collectively, on a footing of equality.

In 1963, Yugoslavia and Romania concluded an agreement on the construction and exploitation of the Iron Gage hydroelectric and navigational system on the Danube. This agreement was supplemented by a number of additional conventions regulating rights and defining duties in the joint utilization of this international river for hydroelectric purposes, on the basis of respect for the principle of sovereignty and equality of the two riparian states.

6. The Sea — In public international law, the sea is divided into several zones. These are internal waters, the territorial sea, the contiguous zone, the epicontinental zone and the high seas. According to some writers, internal waters and the territorial sea make up a belt which is called the coastal sea. The Yugoslav Law on Coastal Waters recognizes this division.

Internal waters are that portion of the ocean surface over which the coastal state exercises exclusive jurisdiction. These waters are not a coherent section of the ocean surface but consist of a number of parts, such as harbors, ports, anchorages, bays, the mouths of rivers and inland seas.

There is still no yardstick for measuring the limits of internal waters. The lack of any rules was noted in the famous Anglo-Norwegian fishing dispute, adjudicated by the International Court of Justice. The Hague Conference for Codification of International Law of 1930 heard a variety of proposals on how to set the limits on internal waters, ranging from six to twenty miles. The Conference did not agree with any of these. Thus it was still left to the discretion of the coastal states to determine the extent of their internal waters. Three components, however, are considered to enter into the decision on delimiting internal waters: adjacency to the coast, the economic needs of the coastal state, and traditional exercise of jurisdiction over these waters. The major part of Yugoslav coastal waters is internal sea, whose boundaries are defined in the 1965 Law on Coastal Waters, the Contiguous Zone and the Epicontinental Belt of Yugoslavia.

Coastal states enjoy full sovereignty over their internal waters. All traffic by foreign vessels in internal waters, including ports, is subject to the permission and control of the national authorities.

The Yugoslav Law on Coastal Waters regulates navigation in internal and territorial Yugoslav waters for foreign merchant vessels and warships (Articles 2–11).

A foreign merchant ship is allowed entry into Yugoslav coastal waters, into harbors which have been opened to international maritime shipping, as a rule by the most direct and customary route. A foreign nuclear-powered merchant vessel requesting entry must in addition supply the appropriate documents attesting to the safety of the nuclear plant as a safeguard against any possible nuclear accidents.

Passage through Yugoslav internal waters is prohibited to foreign warships, foreign fishing vessels and foreign public vessels. (Foreign public vessels are the vessels owned or used by a foreign government, which are not warships, but serve exclusively for non-commercial purposes of that state). In exceptional cases, the competent government body may approve such passage (the Federal Executive Council or a body empowered by it). The rule is that a foreign warship may stay no longer than ten days in Yugoslav internal waters, and no more than three ships of the same state may be in the internal waters at the same time. If one of these ships, because of circumstances outside its control or an accident at sea, is forced to take refuge in Yugoslav national waters, the provisions on entry in this Law will, of course, not apply.

The right of *cabotage* (transport of goods and passengers between Yugoslav ports) is exclusively enjoyed by Yugoslav vessels.

According to some authors, e.g. contemporary French writers such as Rousseau and Delbez, the *territorial sea* is that part of the sea located between internal waters and the high seas. Although all definitions of territorial waters are necessarily imprecise, because the breadth of this zone has not been determined, this particular definition is vague, for there may be other zones between the territorial waters and the high seas, such as the contiguous zone and the epicontinental belt. Hence a more precise definition would describe territorial waters as a belt of the sea which extends the length of the coast of a state. However, there still remains the question of the breadth, or extent, of territorial waters. This question has long raised storms of controversy in international law.

Bartolus thought that the sovereign jurisdiction of a state extended out to sea for a distance which could be covered in two days of sailing — about 100 Italian miles. In Hugo Grotius's time and indeed up until the present century the prevailing view was that territorial waters extended as far as the range of a cannonball fired from the shore. Modern technology has made this criterion outdated. The above-mentioned conference on codification of international law in 1930 did not succeed in arriving at a decision in regard to the extent of territorial waters. On the basis of his personal experience as one of the judges in the International Court of Justice at the Hague, especially in the Anglo-Norwegian fishing dispute, and after a theoretical consideration of the question in a monograph entitled "Teritorijalno more" ("The Territorial Sea"), Milovan Zoričić concludes that the legal situation today in regard to fixing the extent of territorial waters is that the coastal state alone is competent to determine the breadth of its territorial sea. However, in doing so it must adhere to the principles of international law. In his opinion, such a state must act *bona fide,* i.e. it must take only that breadth of the sea which is necessary for its security and for ensuring the means of subsistence for its population. Other states may raise objections if they have good reason to do so. However, Zoričić feels that mere protests, as in the case of Great Britain, are not effective. The coastal state bears full responsibility if the courts decide that its delineation of territorial waters was illegal.

The 1958 Geneva Convention on the Territorial Sea and the Contiguous Zone contains principles for determining the boundaries of territorial waters (Articles 3–13). Normally, the breadth of the territorial sea is measured from the low-water mark on the shore as drawn on charts which have been officially recognized by the coastal state. Coastal states must mark this line on the charts and, by printing the charts, make them available to all interested parties.

Artificial base lines may be drawn to connect specified low-tide points along the coast by straight lines, along parts of heavily-indented coast and where there are many close-lying off-shore islands. Of course, a state will not use the system of straight base lines if it thereby separates the territorial waters of another state from the open sea.

According to the Yugoslav Law on Coastal Waters, the Contiguous Zone and the Epicontinental Belt, territorial waters are a marginal belt extending *ten nautical miles* from the base line out towards the open sea.

The legal status of the territorial sea has two basic features: the sovereignty of the coastal state, and the international right of foreign vessels to innocent passage.

The sovereignty of the coastal state implies its legislative authority, i.e. the full enforcement of its legal regulations; its jurisdiction over the regulation of navigation in the maritime belt; its police and judicial jurisdiction; sanitary and customs control; the exclusive right of exploitation of resources under the sea and the exclusive right of *cabotage.*

Foreign vessels have the right of inoffensive passage through the territorial waters of one or more states, provided this passage is not prejudicial to any right or interest of the coastal state. This limitation on the sovereignty of a littoral state is the primary distinction between the legal position of the territorial sea and that of national waters. During passage through the territorial sea of another state, merchant ships may come under the authority of the coastal state if it considers that any of its rights or interests have been challenged. The authorities of the coastal state may carry out an inquiry or make arrests on such a foreign vessel if it is lying in the territorial waters of that state or has come out of the state's internal waters. State vessels, i.e. foreign non-commercial ships, are under the authority of the state whose flag they fly, but they must comply with the rules of the harbor police. Foreign warships also have the right of innocent passage. A coastal state may lay down the conditions under which these vessels may pass through its territorial waters. In the interest of security, it may interdict passage through certain portions of its territorial waters. Submarines are prohibited from submerging in the territorial waters of other states. They are allowed passage if they proceed along the surface in this maritime belt.

The right of inoffensive passage has been regulated by the Geneva Convention on the Territorial Sea and the Contiguous Zone adopted in 1958 (Articles 14–23). The vessels of all states, regardless of whether they are ships from maritime countries or not, have the right of passage through the territorial waters of other countries. Passage implies navigation through the territorial sea for the purpose of passing through these waters without entering into national waters, or for the purpose of leaving national waters bound for the high seas. Passage, according to this convention, is inoffensive as long as it does not disturb the peace, order or security of the coastal state and must be performed in compliance with the provisions of this convention and in accordance with other rules of international law. Submarines, according to this convention, must fly their flag as well as cruise on the surface.

Foreign vessels which are in inoffensive passage through the territorial sea of another state must comply with the laws and rules imposed by the coastal state, in accordance with this convention and other rules of international law.

The coastal states have the duty:

   a. not to hinder innocent passage through their territorial sea;
   b. to inform vessels of all known hazards endangering navigation in its territorial waters;

Coastal states have the right:

   a. to take measures in their territorial waters to prevent any passage which is not inoffensive;
   b. to undertake necessary measures to prevent any violation of conditions under which these vessels are allowed entry into their internal waters;
   c. in specific zones of its territorial waters to temporarily suspend the right of inoffensive passage by foreign vessels if this interruption is necessitated for security reasons. This interruption comes into force only after it has been properly made public.

According to the 1958 Geneva Convention (Article 19), the criminal jurisdiction of a coastal state may not be enforced over a foreign vessel passing through territorial waters for the purpose of arresting a suspect or of carrying out an investigation following a criminal act performed on board the vessel during its passage, except:

   a. if the effects of the crime extend to the coastal state;
   b. if the violation is of such a nature as to disturb the public order of the country and the order in its territorial sea;
   c. if the captain of the vessel or consul of the state whose flag the vessel carries has sought the assistance of local authorities;
   d. if these measures are necessary to prevent prohibited traffic in narcotic drugs.

The convention does not prejudice the right of the coastal state to take all measures envisaged by its legislation to make arrests or carry out an investigation on a foreign vessel which is passing through territorial seas after leaving national waters. Hence the Yugoslav Law on Coastal Waters, the Contiguous Zone and Eipcontinental Belt allows for the possibility of pursuing a ship belonging to a foreign state. The pursuit of a vessel at sea will be discussed in more detail below.

The coastal states have always sought to extend their jurisdiction farther out to sea. In recent times, territorial waters have been enlarged by a new belt, called the *protective zone* or *contiguous zone,* which is that part of the open sea stretching along the length of the territorial waters of the coastal state, and within this zone the state may protect certain clearly specified interests of a police, sanitary, or navigational nature.

The 1958 Geneva Convention on the Territorial Sea and the Contiguous Zone cites the customs, revenue and sanitary rights of states in this zone. Yugoslav law conforms to the provisions of this convention. A coastal state may also consider the contiguous zone to be a fishing reserve for its nationals. Although the breadth of this zone has also not been precisely defined, a 12 mile limit is customarily recognized. The Geneva Convention also adopted the 12 mile limit. According to the 1965 Yugoslav Law on Coastal Waters, the breadth of the protection zone is two nautical miles, measuring from the outer limit of the territorial waters in the direction of the high seas.

Recently, some maritime states have been pressing for yet another zone, in which they would have certain prerogatives (e.g. the United States, Great Britain, Argentina, Mexico, Pakistan and Honduras). The mainland does not stop at the verge of the sea. The seashore does not drop sharply into the sea but extends outwards under the water for various distances. This extension of the mainland under the sea is called the *continental shelf.* Its length and angle of slope depend on the configuration of the land. That part of the sea which includes the continental shelf and the seabed and which ends with the territorial sea is known as the *epicontinental belt.* Coastal states are demanding full sovereignty or at least control and jurisdiction (for example the United States) over that part of the sea in order to exploit the resources of the shelf. The breadth of the epicontinental belt has not been determined. The United States, for instance, holds that the breadth of this belt in the Bering Sea, along the coast of Alaska, extends from 20 to 250 miles before the high seas begin.

The 1958 Geneva Convention on the Continental Shelf defines this belt as including the seabed and subsoil thereof but outside territorial waters to a depth of 200 meters. The 200 meters depth limit can be exceeded if the natural resources can still be exploited. The convention also considers the seabed and the subsoil of the surrounding islands to be covered by the definition of the continental shelf.

The provisions on the epicontinental belt in the Yugoslav Law have been brought into conformity with this convention. Yugoslavia exercises its sovereign rights in regard to the exploitation of resources in the epicontinental belt, which comprises the subsoil beyond the outer limits of the territorial sea to a depth of 200 meters or beyond, to a depth where exploitation of the natural resources of the subsoil is still possible.

Because the high seas are contiguous with the territorial sea, it will be discussed, even though it does not form a part of state territory.

The *high seas* are the enormous expanse of water which extends beyond the national waters and the territorial sea. On the high seas, the following rules are observed: freedom of navigation, freedom of fisheries, freedom to lay underwater cables and pipelines, and freedom of passage in the airspace above.

States only may use the high seas. If a vessel wishes to navigate on the high seas, it must be registered with a state, which then assumes responsibility for the registered vessel; the vessel must have a name, permission for navigation, and must fly the flag of the state to which it belongs. A vessel which plies the high seas comes under dual jurisdiction: under the jurisdiction of the state whose flag it flies and under international jurisdiction. The vessel is subject to the laws of the state to which it belongs. However, on the basis of certain international treaties (for instance, the Convention on the Abolition of the Slave Trade), warships have the right to intercept any vessel which they have reason to suspect, in order to check its identity and to prevent the perpetration of an international crime. Warships at sea enjoy complete immunity from the jurisdiction of states whose flag they are not flying.

In accordance with the 1958 Geneva conventions on the law of the sea, the Yugoslav Law on Coastal Waters, the Contiguous Zone and Epicontinental Belt envisages the contingency of pursuit of a foreign vessel if a competent Yugoslav organ has good reason to suspect that a foreign ship, one of its boats, or a boat working together with it, has violated the Yugoslav law or other Yugoslav regulations. Pursuit is legal if it begins when the ship, or boat, is still within the coastal waters or in the contiguous zone and if the vessel does not halt when ordered to do so by visual or audible signals from a distance from which the signal could be received. If the foreign ship, or boat, being pursued is located in the contiguous zone, the pursuit may only be carried out for violations of customs, revenue and sanitary regulations and regulations on border crossing. Can pursuit be continued into the high seas? It may, if it is begun within the coastal or contiguous zones, but only for the above-mentioned reasons, and it may be continued on the high seas until the suspect ship or boat enters the territorial waters of its own or of a third state. Only Yugoslav warships or military aircraft or other vessels and aircraft authorized for the purpose may carry out pursuit.

Every vessel must have documents attesting to its legality. The ship's papers include a certificate of registry in the case of a merchant ship; a sea letter authorizing a captain to exercise command over the vessel in the case of a warship; a muster roll containing information on the identity and nationality of members of the crew; a passenger list; the log book, in which the ship's captain records the details of the voyage, with information on origin of goods, the names of the shippers and consignees; bills of lading for the goods being shipped, and the charter party, which is a duplicate of the contract on hiring the vessel.

Every state has the right to punish pirates on the high seas, regardless of the nationality of their vessel and crew. A pirate vessel is a vessel which engages in unauthorized acts of violence against persons or goods. By perpetrating these acts, such a vessel loses its statehood and thereby forfeits the right to be protected by a state.

The 1958 Geneva Convention on the High Seas (Article 15) lists the following criminal acts as acts of piracy:

> a. any unauthorized act of violence, retention or depredation carried out for personal gain by the crew or passengers of a private vessel or private aircraft, in the high seas, against another vessel or aircraft or against persons or goods on them or against vessels or aircraft, persons or goods in a place which is not under the jurisdiction of any state;
>
> b. every voluntary participatory act in using a vessel or aircraft when persons performing such acts are aware of the facts which give that vessel or aircraft the character of a pirate vessel or aircraft;
>
> c. every action intended to incite to the performance of acts enumerated in the above two paragraphs, or every action undertaken to facilitate the performance of these acts.

Slavery is prohibited. Under Article 13 of this convention, every state has the duty to prevent and punish the transport of slaves. Every slave who seeks refuge on any vessel shall become free.

An important provision in the Convention on the High Seas makes it possible for landlocked states to enjoy freedom of the seas. Through joint agreements, in accordance with international conventions and on the basis of reciprocity, landlocked states are allowed free passage through the territory of other states, and their ships are given the same treatment as the ships of the coastal states. All states, both maritime and landlocked, are thereby enabled to exercise an equal right to free navigation on the high seas.

The freedom of fisheries, i.e. of exploitation of flora and fauna in the high seas, is permitted. In exercising this right, states may not usurp a part of the high seas, because the sea is not *res nullius,* which can be occupied, but *res communie omnium,* accessible to the vessels of all states.

The Geneva Conference of 1958 also adopted the Convention on Fishing and Conservation of the Living Resources of the High Seas, under which the nationals of all states have the right to fish in the high seas in accordance with the provisions of this convention. The conservation of the "living resources" of the sea should be viewed as a body of measures which will consistently give the best possible yields of these resources, so that available quantities of sea products, food and others will be ensured to the greatest possible measure.

Measures for conservation of these "living resources" are primarily intended to provide populations with food.

7. Straits — A strait is a natural sea link between two open seas. The major world straits include the Bosporus and the Dardanelles, the Sound and the Great and Little Belts which link the North Sea and Baltic Sea, the Straits of Gibraltar between the Mediterranean and the Atlantic Ocean, the Bering Straits between the Atlantic and Pacific Oceans, the Corfu Channel, etc. The status of the various straits is regulated by international conventions. Navigation through straits which link two seas is free, even though this passage may be narrow enough to be considered territorial waters. Free passage through straits is based on the principle of free navigation on the high seas, because straits are considered an extension of the high seas. Maritime states exercise sovereign jurisdiction over this part of the sea, but they do so in conformity with the rules of international law, i.e. they must permit the innocent passage of all vessels, including warships, in peacetime, of course. The littoral states may pass regulations governing the passage of foreign vessels, but they may not interdict passage. In the Corfu Channel dispute between Great Britain and Albania, the International Court of Justice invoked this rule, stating that warships have the right of passage through straits which link two parts of the high seas, in this instance the Mediterranean and Adriatic Sea, even without the prior permission of the coastal state, if this passage is inoffensive. This rule was endorsed in the 1958 Geneva Convention on the Territorial Sea and the Contiguous Zone, which states that the inoffensive passage of foreign vessels may not be hindered in straits used for international navigation between one portion of the high seas and another portion of the high seas or the territorial sea of a foreign state.

8. Interoceanic Canals — Interoceanic canals are artifically constructed waterways between two seas which have been built to shorten sea routes and increase the safety of navigation. The most important interoceanic canals are the Suez Canal, the Panama Canal, and the Kiel Canal.

The legal regime for interoceanic canals cannot be analogous to that for straits. The construction of a canal through the territory of a state does not mean that it loses sovereignty over that part of its territory, no matter whose resources are used to build the canal.

In principle, navigation on canals is equated with navigation in internal waters. The regime of navigation through interoceanic canals is usually determined by international conventions. If such conventions to do not exist, and if a canal has become an international waterway in practice, then free navigation on this canal becomes a servitude of the state in question. The right of navigation through such a canal is safeguarded by international customary law.

9. State Servitudes — State servitudes in international law are the undertaking of a state to refrain from performing certain acts in its territory which are within its competence or to tolerate the performance of certain acts on its territory by a foreign state. This obligation of a state derives either from general rules of international law (e.g., navigation on international rivers), or from treaties (e.g. the right of transporting goods over foreign territory).

The servitudes which derive from general rules of international law are called "natural" by some authors, harking back to the idealistic view that law is divided into natural and positive law and thus rules of law are natural or conventional. Freedom of navigation on international rivers is not a natural right but rather has evolved from a specific economic necessity which became paramount at the time of the rapid rise of capitalism in the early 19th century. It was then that this freedom became a general principle of international law and served as the basis for subsequent servitudes. Thus servitudes in international law were imposed by the economic requirements of states.

If state servitudes facilitate international cooperation, above all the mutual international economic development of states, they are a positive instrument of international law. If, however, servitudes are forced upon another state or are used as a means of political pressure in the broadest sense of the word, and thus threaten the sovereignty of a state, then they are negative. It follows, then, that the nature of the function of this instrument of international law depends on its source and use. For this reason, this institution cannot simply be translated from internal, private law into international law. Servitude in private law involves property, whereas in international law it gives not the right to an absolute exercise of authority but only the right to a peaceful use, which must always be strictly interpreted.

The rapid growth of international transportation and communications is causing a corresponding proliferation in the kinds of state servitudes. Standard servitudes may be considered the free zones in a port or beside a railway station. Yugoslavia had a free zone in Salonika on the basis of a convention of 10 May 1923, and other supplementary acts. Standard servitudes also include the erection of plant facilities in foreign territory, for instance, the building of power plants; the right to lay railway tracks with the right of exterritoriality, such as, for instance, the East Manchurian Railway; finally, we should mention various fishing concessions in foreign waters.

In practice there are various types of servitudes of a military nature. They may be imposed for the purpose of demilitarizing certain regions, as a prohibition of the building of military fortifications, as is often specified in peace treaties, but may also be imposed by other international acts; for instance, on the stationing of foreign troops. These types of servitudes greatly restrict the exercise of a state's sovereign rights when it must tolerate the presence of foreign troops in its territory.

VII. Responsibility of States

Concept— Types of Responsibility— Consequences of Liability — Individual Criminal Liability

1. Concept — Responsibility in law is a special legal situation created by an injury to the right of another or to property which is protected by valid legislation. There is a similar situation in international law, although the analogy is not complete. Theoreticians largely agree that responsibility must be established in international law as well. If the absolute sovereignty of states were to be insisted upon, then the question of responsibility could not arise, and the result would be anarchy in international relations.

Responsibility in international law, generally speaking, arises from the fact of a delinquency, i.e. an injury of a right or property of another state. It is controversial if the injury of an abstract interest of a state can provide legal grounds for a complaint. There is no dispute over the existence of responsibility if damages are of a material nature. Whether or not moral damage constitutes legal grounds for complaint finds legal theory divided, with perhaps the scales tilting in favor of the opinion that moral prejudice cannot constitute a legal basis for responsibility in international relations at their present stage, but that it may be grounds for a dispute which can be adjudicated.

Damages may arise from individual acts, a contracted relationship, criminal activity, the public action of a government or its officials and, according to some authors, from the improper functioning of public and state services. At any rate, responsibility of states may be invoked from the standpoint of international law in the following instances: a. in international private relationships, b. in relations between states and individuals, and c. in relations between states as well as between states and other international collective entities.

2. Types of Responsibility — The state as an international person may bear *political responsibility* (for instance, an aggressor state may be disarmed); it may bear *civil responsibility* (for instance, by paying reparations for damage caused by war). However, the state may not be held *criminally liable* from the standpoint of international law.

Attempts by Pella and Salanha to have the criminal liability of states recognized in legal theory have not succeeded. This liability has always been seen in terms of political responsibility, over which there is not dispute.

The state as an international person cannot be held criminally liable, because there is no criminal responsibility without guilt, and the state as a whole, that is to say the entire populace of a state, cannot be placed in the dock, for such an act would imply the possibility of deliberate or negligent actions by an entire nation. Such a view is only a short step away from racist ideas about the responsibility and guilt of peoples (inferior races), against whom collective sanctions may be enforced.

A state may not be brought to court, nor may a criminal proceeding be instituted against it. The state cannot, for instance, question witnesses or testify in its own defence. The state may bear the consequences for its actions or for its policy (e.g. a fascist state). However, in this case, the consequences arise as the result of a political struggle and not as the result of a judicial proceedings and verdict.

Groups or organizations as juristic persons may be held criminally responsible within the frontiers of a state, but the state may not be held criminally responsible as a juristic person. The Nuremburg trials showed that criminal responsibility was borne only by such juristic persons as the leadership of the Nazi party, the Gestapo, the SS and SA troops, the cabinet of the Reich, the General Headquarters and High Command. However, in the Nuremberg judgment, criminal responsibility was defined in terms of individual responsibility. The Nuremburg judgment states that as the criminal responsibility of the members of an organization or group is determined by such an organization or group being of a criminal nature, the definition should exclude persons who did not know about the criminal purposes and acts of the organization and persons who were appointed to them by the state; formal membership alone in an organization is not sufficient for determining liability.

Even if membership in an organization automatically carried criminal liability with it, these juristic persons could still not be likened to the state as a juristic person. Members of a group or organization are very similar to participants in a criminal conspiracy, because they all have criminal purposes in common. They have voluntarily condoned such purposes by accepting the programme of joint action. Being a member of a nation involves more than applying for membership. Finally, there is no organization, nor is one possible today, which could pronounce itself on the jointly expressed "criminal" will of a people.

International criminal responsibility is nontransferable. Physical persons are responsible for any criminal acts they perform on behalf of the state, but not because criminal responsibility can be transferred from the state to an individual. It is nontransferable.

There is also the view that acts which the state has not performed are of no significance for international law (Strupp). This assumption implies, for instance, that administrators or government officials cannot be held criminally responsible for violating an international treaty if they did not take part in concluding the treaty. According to proponents of this view, responsibility would logically be borne by the state as a personality and not by those who felt that it was not in the state interest to observe an international treaty in whose conclusion they did not participate.

A *distinction should be drawn between the subject of a relationship regulated by international law and the subject of an attack on such a relationship.* The former is a subject who establishes a certain relationship in international law and the latter is a subject who has not established this relationship but who threatens or assails it. If administrators or government officials have not taken part in concluding an international treaty, they are not thereby entitled to violate such a treaty unilaterally. In this case as well, *responsibility cannot be transferred to the state;* the responsibility is rather borne by those who threaten or attack a relationship established in international law. Therefore, we always speak of the criminal responsibility of individuals and not of states.

There can be no talk of responsibility for constitutional and administrative acts in the domestic legal order of a state. The problem is to what extent such responsibility can be posited in international law. The direct responsibility of constitutional and legislative organs is contrary to the concept of sovereignty according to certain legal experts, whereas others are of the opinion that constitutional and legislative acts are subordinated to international law and that they must not contain provisions which would not be in conformity with the international order. Scelle states that municipal law often involves potential rather than direct responsibility. Today it is generally agreed that if anything in a constitution law runs counter to the purposes and principles of the U.N. Charter, the state bears responsibility for its constitutional and legislative actions.

According to many authors of international law, the state has a great and virtually undisputed responsibility for its administrative acts, i.e. for the actions of executive organs, particularly in regard to non-observance of treaty obligations, the abuse of various formalities, illegal arrests, detention or expulsion of aliens, negligence in regard to protecting diplomatic representatives, etc.

In the age of imperialism, the question of responsibility of a state for non-payment of contracted debts was very controversial. Like all other contracts, those of a financial nature must be observed and implemented. Today, however, in no circumstances can this principle be inferred to involve the responsibility of an entire population and justify resort to armed force as a coercive measure. In 1882, the British and French navies bombarded Alexandria, and British troops landed in Egypt to exact payment of a debt. In 1884, Patras was bombarded, and Greece was forced to submit to international control over its finances. Serbia did not meet with a kinder fate in 1892 when it was forced to create the Autonomous Monopoly Authority and hand it over to foreign control for payment of foreign debts. In the year 1902, Italy, Germany and Great Britain bombarded Venezuela for the same reasons. Incidents such as these have given rise to the emergence of several doctrines.

The Argentinian foreign minister Luis M. Drago criticized the actions of foreign powers in Venezuela and put forward his thesis of the financial sovereignty of the state. According to this thesis (the *Drago Doctrine*), a state may not recover its debt from another state by means of force.

The *Porter Doctrine* qualifies the above doctrine, stipulating that force may be used only if the debtor state does not agree to adjudication by a court of arbitration. An exception is made in the case of foreign citizens. A state has the right to demand protection of the concrete interests of its citizens in foreign territory (the *Calvo Doctrine*). In 1953 the International Court of Justice handed down the decision that no state may arbitrarily deprive foreign citizens of their acquired rights without just compensation. Every confiscation, expropriation or nationalization of foreign property should be followed by compensation.

Insofar as responsibility of national courts for their acts is concerned, the principle of the independence of national courts and their invoking of the right of *res judicata* cannot be a reason for non-observance of the international rights and duties of a state.

Violations of international law by national courts may occur in the following cases:

>   a. if a rule of law has been interpreted or applied which directly conflicts with a rule of international law;
>   b. if an international obligation of a state is breached or nullified by a judicial decision;
>   c. if court proceedings are denied (déni de justice) or if an obviously unfair decision is handed down to the detriment of the interests of a foreign state or its citizens.

The international responsibility of states can thus be summed up in three points:

>   1. the state bears direct responsibility for acts which are attributable to the state administration as a whole, and in these cases a complaint is made against the state. It is left to the municipal law of the accused state to deal with the individuals who were directly responsible. Today it is the rule that in the event of any kind of violation, the actions of individuals are recognized as a fact, but the state is held accountable.
>   2. the state is required to enforce sanctions against the individuals held liable in its territory; the complaint is made against the state as the embodiment of authority, which must give redress by instituting proceedings, and not against the state as the responsible collective unit. In these cases, the state bears direct responsibility if it fails to carry out sanctions.
>   3. a state is responsible for the functioning of its agencies and for any lack of the proper organization within its territory. The International Court of Justice awarded damages to Great Britain because the Albanian government had

not performed its duty of keeping its territorial waters free of mines and did not publish information that mines had been laid, even though there was no proof of any active participation by the Albanian government in laying the mines. Every state bears the risk for objective violations of international law in its territory.

Whereas the first two types of responsibility are unlimited and are considered to be natural, for they involve a delict, the extent of the third type of responsibility is still controversial. At the 1930 Hague Conference, the large capital exporting countries did not succeed in imposing their view that the territorial state bore unlimited and absolute responsibility for any injury to the interests of aliens in its territory as a result of inadequate and ineffective protection.

In the Albanian-British dispute, the International Court of Justice at the Hague limited this responsibility to negligence, of which a state could be accused and which constitutes neglect of the regular duty of a territorial state. Hence negligence rather than any risk borne by a state was the key consideration. This reasoning was also followed by the U.N. General Assembly after the assassination of Count Bernadotte. The Israeli government agreed to pay damages to the United Nations because of the inefficiency of its security service, which allowed an Israeli citizen to carry out the assassination attempt. Thus international law recognized a quasi-delict responsibility.

3. The Consequences of Liability— The liability of a state may entail the following forms of redress:

> a. reparation of a moral or political character, which may be in the form of a statement of regret, a solemn apology, a ceremonial salute to the flag of a foreign state, a ceremonial funeral with a commemoration, the erection of a momument, a promise that the event will never happen again, and so forth. This manner of making reparation must be public.
> b. reparation by way of compensation for damages. Damages may be compensated in two ways: either by a return to the previous state (*restitutio in integrum*) as if the injury had never occurred, as called for in one of the judgments of the Permanent Court of International Justice (in a dispute over a factory in Hortzov), by payment of a given sum of money, or in the form of some other compensation.

Kelsen remarks that it is very questionable whether general international law envisages the duty of compensation, as there is no procedure in international law to define the substance of this duty. According to him, it is even doubtful if a state that has suffered an injury is obliged to try to reach an accommodation with the state responsible for the injury. Finally, this writer draws the conclusion that the obligation to remedy an injustice done to another state is a duty rather than a sanction. However, under Article 36, item d, of the Statute of the International Court of Justice, the Court is authorized to determine "the nature or extent of the reparation to be made for the breach of an international obligation;" hence a specified procedure in international law does exist for determining the substance of the duty to make reparation. This procedure is not restricted to the International Court of Justice, for according to Article 95 of the U.N. Charter states may take their disputes to other tribunals. Consequently, compensation for damages today is not a duty, but one of the sanctions expressly provided for in international law.

It is true that responsibility, be it civil or criminal, collective or individual, contractual or delict, is always of a repressive nature. Hence, if a right of a state has been injured that is protected by generally accepted rules of international law, and if the perpetrator of this deed (regardless of whether it is the state as a collective entity, government officials as individuals or simply individuals) is forced to pay damages by the decision of a competent court (be it the International Court of Justice, a court of arbitration, or some international criminal tribunal), such compensation for damages would constitute a sanction of modern international law.

4. Individual Criminal Liability — Article 227 of the Versailles Peace Treaty represents an attempt in the history of international law to give a legal definition to the personal responsibility of government bodies and even heads of state. On the basis of this article, the former German Kaiser Wilhelm II, together with a group of other war criminals, should have been tried "for a supreme offence against international morality and the sanctity of treaties." However, the Netherlands did not extradite him. The prevailing opinion among jurists was that there were no legal grounds on which the Netherlands would have to extradite Wilhelm II, because it had not signed the Versailles treaty and could invoke the rule on extradition of persons accused of political and military crimes. Such was the doctrine at the outbreak of the Second World War. The Nazi and fascist armies, and indeed civilians, committed a horrendous number of unprecented war crimes from the very outset of the war. This fact prompted the Allies at their Moscow Conference held from 19 to 30 October 1943, to adopt the Declaration of German Atrocities with mandatory legal force. This document envisaged the punishment of all German officers and men as well as the members of the Nazi party who had a hand in these atrocities or who were responsible for them. They were to be tried and punished in the countries where the crimes were committed. Those German war criminals whose crimes were not connected with a specific geographical location would be punished under a joint decision of the Allied governments.

The decision of the Potsdam Conference, held from 17 July to 2 August 1945, reaffirmed the principles of individual international criminal liability in items 4 and 5, in the part concerning the political principles that would be followed in dealing with Germany in the initial period of control. On 8 August 1945, the so-called London Agreement was signed by representatives of the governments of the United States, France, Great Britain and the U.S.S.R., for the purpose of prosecuting and punishing the major war criminals of the European Axis. On 20 December, the Control Council for Germany promulgated law no. 10 concerning the punishment of persons responsible for war crimes, crimes against the peace and crimes against humanity. The London Agreement included an annexed Charter for the creation of an international military tribunal. This Charter specified the composition of the tribunal, its terms of reference and general principles, established the commission for investigation and prosecution of major war criminals, and provided guarantees for the rights of the accused and rules on the conduct of the proceedings and the reaching of decisions.

According to Article 6 of the Charter, there was to be individual responsibility for the following categories of crimes:

> 1. Crimes against the peace, which comprise the following groups of criminal acts: a. the planning, preparation, launching or waging of an aggressive war; b. a war violating international treaties, agreements or guarantees; c. participation in a joint plan or conspiracy to carry out any of the above-mentioned acts.
> 2. War crimes which involve violations of a. laws of war and b. customs of war. A list of criminal acts against these international provisions is provided by the Charter, with the note that the list is not exhaustive. The following categories of criminal deeds are included: a. the killing, mistreatment or abduction for forced labor or any other purpose of the civilian population of occupied territory or to occupied territory; b. the killing or mistreatment of prisoners of war or persons at sea; c. the killing of hostages; d. the plundering of public or private property; e. deliberate razing of cities, towns or villages, and destruction unwarranted by military necessity.
> 3. Crimes against humanity, which include the following criminal acts: a. murder; b. extermination; c. enslavement; d. deportation; e. other inhuman acts performed against any civilian population prior to or during war; f. persecution on political, racial or religious grounds in the perpetration of or in connection with any crime which falls within the jurisdiction of the tribunal, regardless of whether the laws of the country where the crimes were committed were violated or not.

The U.N. General Assembly in a resolution passed on 11 December 1956, endorsed the principle of international law recognized by the Charter of the Nuremberg tribunal and the judgment of this tribunal, and charged the Commission for the Codification of International Law, which had been created on that same day, with formulating these principles and with preparing a Draft Code of Offenses against the Peace and Security of Mankind.

The International Law Commission, as authorized by the General Assembly, decided upon eleven principles to be enunciated in the Code, alongside an enumeration of criminal acts. According to the report of the Commission, every perpetrator of a criminal act categorized as a crime against international law is responsible for that act and must be punished according to international law, regardless of whether the municipal law of his state regards such a deed as criminal or not. The mere fact that internal law does not punish such a deed is no reason for the perpetrator to be freed of criminal liability under international law. It is expressly stated that not even the position of head of state or of a responsible government official is a defense which would free such persons of their responsibility according to international law. As a logical consequence of these principles, the report goes on to say, if someone receives orders from his government or a superior and these orders lead directly to a crime, by the same token he must also bear responsibility. According to international law, not only the person committing a criminal act is criminally responsible and liable to punishment; the person who allows such an act to be performed is also criminally liable. Under international law, complicity in crimes is also a criminal act.

The question of punishment is still unresolved. At the Nuremberg trial, the following punishments were meted out: death by hanging, life imprisonment, and imprisonment for terms ranging from ten to twenty years. So far as territorial jurisdiction is concerned, for the time being the majority of jurists feel that the principle contained in the Moscow Declaration should be maintained: viz., that the courts of the countries in which crimes are committed are competent to try those responsible for criminal acts under international law. If the crimes have no particular geographical location, or if they have been committed in more than one country, an international tribunal should be set up to try such cases.

Some serious problems were encountered in the formulation of the Nuremberg Principles. One of the first was the question of the universal validity of these principles: i.e., were these principles binding only upon those states which had signed the London Agreement and Charter or were they also valid for other states? Any doubt cast on the validity of these principles, either from a political or from a legal standpoint, would be damaging both to the prestige and to the interests of the United Nations and, even worse, would throw a shadow on the basic principles of modern international law. Indeed, the Nuremberg trial would then be open to revision, and all the progress achieved so far in advancing the organized international community would be undone. These legal principles were general principles of democratic international law at the time they were adopted at the Nuremberg trials, and in a unanimous resolution of the General Assembly these principles were deemed "general principles of international law," a source of international law, and thus of a universal character.

The question of individual responsibility of a person who, in following the orders of his government or superior, commits criminal acts or acts conducive to a crime under international law is still a subject of debate, both in the International Law Commission and in legal theory. The report of the International Law Commission contained the qualification that such responsibility exists if the person following orders had the possibility of a "moral choice." The Nuremberg tribunal took the stand in principle that an order given to a soldier to kill or torture in violation of international laws of war has never been considered to be a justification for such a deed. The tribunal adopted the view that following orders might be considered in mitigation of punishment in a legal sense, to be decided upon by the competent court, but that it was not a reason for freeing the perpetrator of international criminal liability, as was demanded by the defense at the Nuremberg trials.

Everything that has been said about the Nuremberg principles holds true for the principles on which the international military tribunal in Tokyo was organized to try the major war criminals in the Far East.

The new rule of international law which was introduced at these trials was that states could not shield individuals from liability for international delicts by their positive legal regulations. This principle was not restricted to war crimes alone. It was endorsed in another collective convention aspiring to universality, the Convention on the Prevention and Punishment of the Crime of Genocide. It was similarly maintained in this case that the crime of genocide could not be committed without the connivance or at least tolerance of the territorial state and that the position of head of state or responsible government official did not provide immunity from international responsibility.

Nevertheless, the question of international sanctions against individual perpetrators of international crimes was not definitvely settled. Who is competent to try the persons committing these crimes has remained controversial. If the competent courts of territorial states are to have jurisdiction, the possibilities for abuse and evasion of the rules of international law are numerous. However, there is no general international jurisdiction for criminal cases. To remedy this situation, a recommendation has been submitted to the General Assembly for the setting up of an international criminal tribunal to which states would be obliged to turn over for trial persons accused of such crimes, either according to the Nuremberg Principles or pursuant to a multilateral convention, such as the Convention on Genocide, irrespective of citizenship and official position. On the other hand, states are unwilling to adopt this principle because it could give the accusing state an opportunity to interfere in the internal affairs of the accused state. Even though responsibility of this type is recognized in principle and in theory, i.e. as borne by the individual, it is still politically controversial whether the jurisdiction of such a tribunal could be accepted.

Chapter Two: International Organizations

I. Introduction: International Congresses and Diplomatic Conferences

Principle of a Balance of Power — Decisions at International Congresses and Diplomatic Conferences — Supremacy of the Great Powers — Political and Legal Nature — Transformation of International Congresses and Diplomatic Conferences — Role and Importance of International Congresses and Diplomatic Conferences Today

1. The Principle of a Balance of Power — Since the Peace of Westphalia, European diplomacy has been guided by the principle of a balance of power in Europe. The great powers strove to establish a balance of power by aggressive means, such as offensive alliances and wars of aggression, or by other means, such as, for instance, the British policy of "splendid isolation." Plans to establish or shift political equilibrium, or indeed attempts to alter it or even upset it completely, were sanctioned at international congresses or at the diplomatic conferences which usually followed the important international congresses and put into effect the political principles established at the preceding congress. The plan sponsored by Henry IV, and later supported by Richelieu, to weaken the Habsburgs and tilt the political balance of power in Europe to France's side, was finally consummated in the 1648 Peace of Westphalia, after almost four years of negotiations, at the congresses held in Osnabrück and Münster (in Westphalia). The 1815 Congress of Vienna tried to establish an order in Europe based on the political system that had existed prior to the Napoleonic wars. The 1856 Paris Congress provided an opportunity, made possible by the Russian defeat at Sevastopol, for the great powers of that time to regulate the relations and thereby secure a period of peace for Europe. The Berlin Congress of 1878 was convened, under the auspices of Bismarck's united Germany, for virtually the same reason. Bismarck himself said that if he was wasting his valuable time at the Congress in the summer heat, it was for the sake of preventing a conflict between the great powers. After the First World War, the Allied powers struck the foundations for the so-called "peace under the Versailles terms" at the Conference of Paris in 1919. Some writers link this conference with the Washington Conference of 1922 and describe the period of peace between the two world wars as the epoch of the Versailles-Washington system. The world balance of power (for the world wars gave the question of political equilibrium global dimensions) for the post-World War II period was worked out at diplomatic conferences while the war was still in progress.

Almost all legal authorities, from Vattel to Funk-Brentano and Sorel, consider congresses to be the best means for restoring peace after large-scale wars, because all the diverse interests affecting the maintenance of peace, i.e. a given balance of power, can be voiced there. Diplomatic conferences are held as a rule in times of an established balance of power with the purpose of either regulating or changing it, depending on the political aims of the initiating states.

Balance of power implies a certain system of international relations, which, under the impact of various political interests, is always in danger of being upset to such an extent that resort to armed force seems the only possible solution. When international political, economic, military and other antagonisms in the different political power blocs reach such a pitch that war seems inevitable, and if the great powers are not yet prepared to take such a step, then they resort to international political meetings in order to devise legal and political ways of maintaining or adjusting the prevailing balance of power. We need not look farther back in diplomatic history for an example than the Munich Conference of 1938. However, if powers with opposing political views feel strong enough not to have to make concessions, diplomatic conferences seldom take place, even if extensive preparatory meetings have been held to draw up the agenda of the conference, as was the case with the conference of deputy foreign ministers in Paris in 1951. As a further example, Napoleon III's intentions to bring about a "European conference," as he put it, were doomed to failure, because, among other things, Austria did not want to be a party to talks discussing its rights in Italy, and Russia was adamantly opposed to any discussion of Poland.

In the desire to maintain a given balance of power, governments mooted the idea of periodical conferences which would become a permanent European institution to regulate all disputes between states and nations. The Holy Alliance treaty of 1815 contained provisions on the political principles which were to be adhered to by the signatory states. However, the system of periodic conferences which was inaugurated in 1815 broke down after only four congresses (the Congresses of Aix-la-Chapelle in 1818, of Troppau in 1820, of Laibach in 1821, and of Verona in 1822). These congresses had all been convened for the purpose of organizing interventions to preserve the status quo. However, the internal divisions within the Holy Alliance prevented the creation of a "European institution" for maintaining peace in Europe. Austrian Chancellor Metternich feared revolution, but he was just as wary of Russian Tsar Alexander, in whom he had very little confidence. Frederick William III of Prussia also feared revolution but was even more afraid of the Russian Tsar, the French King and any eventual alliance between them. Tsar Alexander had always been ready to put down any attempt at revolution, but he was suspicious of Metternich, of Frederick William III, and of the French King. England's economic development made it take a cautious and soon thereafter negative attitude towards the Holy Alliance, as was evident at the Congress of Aix-la-Chapelle in 1818. Great Britain supported the national liberation struggle of the Spanish colonies and Greece, because the new nation states would need English capital and English goods. This is why British policy, no matter how ideologically opposed to revolutionary movements, could not go along with the reactionary politics of the Holy Alliance.

International congresses were also accompanied by special kinds of diplomatic conferences, such as, for instance, the conferences of ambassadors held after the Peace Conference of 1919 at the end of the First World War; although called a "conference," it had all the earmarks of a congress in international law. The conferences of foreign ministers of the five great powers, convened after the Berlin Conference of 1945, are a similar example.

The international congress down through history has also been used as a means of political leverage. In 1791 Leopold II and Catherine II openly threatened France they would convene a congress to decree the future form of the government in France unless it put a stop to the revolution. Leopold II and Austrian Chancellor Kaunitz produced exhaustive arguments on the right of intervention by monarchical states in the internal affairs of France, in which "a contagious revolutionary spirit" was spreading. It would seem, then, that the threat to convene a congress served as a political ultimatum in the foreign relations of past centuries, the assumption being that the congress would pass decisions which would be disadvantageous for the state in question.

2. Decisions at International Congresses and Diplomatic Conferences — Decisions at international congresses and diplomatic conferences are as a rule made unanimously, which means that any state can veto a proposed decision. The right to reject a decision at an international congress or diplomatic conference is legally based upon one of the basic international precepts — the principle of the sovereignty of states. States are sovereign if they are independent from any internal or outside authority of another state. Hence sovereign states can decide whether or not they intend to carry out a decision adopted in an international body, such as an international congress or diplomatic conference. The principle of unanimity is thus based on that of sovereignty. However, the principle of equality of all states before the law also serves as a regulating device in the intercourse of sovereign states. The right of a state to accept or not to accept a binding decision of an international assembly also derives from its equality with other states. This principle was publicly invoked at the Berlin Congress of 1878 by Count Shuvalov, who declared that decisions should be passed not by majority vote but by the unanimous consent of all participants. Bismarck echoed this sentiment by stating that the minority at the congress is not obliged to concur with the opinion of the majority.

Unanimous decisions are not always easy to achieve. Many preliminary negotiations are often needed in direct contacts between the plenipotentiaries or heads of state, tsars, kings, chancellors, or ministers of foreign affairs, so that nations can come to terms by making mutual concessions. If disputes arose during sessions, particularly the plenary sessions, separate talks and discussions would have to be held so that some prior agreement could be reached. At the Berlin Congress, for instance, Bismarck as the initiator of the congress, presided, drew up the agenda of meetings, and summed up the questions to be discussed on any given day. If, during the debate, any disagreement arose, Bismarck adjourned the meeting, and the disputed matters were referred to diplomatic channels for settlement through direct contacts. Most frequently the great powers preferred to come to a private understanding prior to reaching an agreement. After the parties came to terms, the matter was returned to the regular meeting for unanimous decision. As a rule this was the procedure followed when the great powers were interested in achieving unanimity on the vital matters for which the international gathering had been convened. Since countries had the sovereign right to accept or reject the proposed solutions, the discussions had to be conducted with care, caution, a great deal of patience, and sometimes even threats. The Berlin Congress of 1878 was similar to the earlier Vienna Congress of 1815, when decisions were made not at the regular meetings but at informal get-togethers between the plenipotentiaries of the great powers. As Castlereagh reported later, the great powers had agreed that the working caucus should consist of not more than six leading powers. This indicates that the unanimously adopted decisions were largely the result of the agreement and will of the great powers or of compromise solutions in their joint interest. Gersic quotes Barnaert and Maartens who refer to this typical feature of congresses in their theoretical works. According to Gersic, Banaert, and Maartens the great powers try to preclude any debate in the general sessions and want to make it a practice for general sessions to be convened solely for the purpose of endorsing the conclusions the great power plenepotentiaries see fit to report to the congress. This is then viewed as unanimous decision by the entire congress, if no plenepotentiary attaches a reservation or lodges a protest.

The principle of unanimity was as a rule honored, with regard to major issues, at all congresses and conferences, beginning with the congresses in

Münster and Osnabrück up to the First World War, although there were proposals — heard as early as the Second Hague Conference in 1907 — that the rule of majority vote should be accepted alongside the principle of unanimity. The chairman of the Second Hague Conference announced that the basic principle of every international conference was the principle of unanimity, but that questions of secondary importance should be passed by majority vote. The future allies of the First World War, faced with a Germany which was already openly preparing for war, were inclined to supplant the principle of unanimity with the rule of majority vote, so that they could arrive at decisions in their own interest. To this end Sir Edward Frey proposed that the third Hague Conference (which was never held because of the war) should adopt the majority vote as the basic principle in adopting decisions. An important precedent was set at the Second Hague Conference when certain amendments were adopted by majority vote, first in the commission and later at the plenary sessions. Unanimity was demanded only in the vote on the definitive draft of the final document, and it was considered that abstention did not preclude the adoption of a unanimous decision; if the explicit right of veto had not been availed of, then a decision had the effect of a unanimously adopted decision, whether there were any abstentions in the voting or not. The two professors of international law who were present, the Swiss Huber and the German Korn, noted another interesting aspect of voting at the Second Hague Conference, which they call "quasi-unanimity." They reported that minorities which voted against certain provisions in the commissions and even at the plenary sessions allowed them to be inserted in the final act of the conference.

As a rule, however, voting at international conferences and congresses followed the principle of unanimity, which is actually a rule of customary law in international law. This principle was applied at many congresses and conferences in the nineteenth century and later, for instance, at the Algeciras Conference in 1906. At the Geneva Conference in 1864, convened for the purpose of ameliorating the condition of the wounded and sick in the battlefield, General Dufour, head of the Swiss delegation and president of the conference, made it clear that decisions adopted by majority vote would not have a binding force. In Paris in 1919, Lord Robert Cecil said that by the nature of things every decision should be unanimously adopted. In an advisory opinion of the case of Mosul, the Permanent Court of International Justice called the principle of unanimity "natural" and "indispensable."

The great powers which have the main say at conferences and congresses are not always inclined to act according to this principle. At the Geneva Conference in 1868 it was decided that a question may be opened for discussion by a majority vote, and this rule was also given a prominent place on the question of procedure at the second Hague Conference in 1907. At the Peace Conference in Paris in 1946, recommendations were voted by a two-thirds majority. It would seem that the great powers ignore the principle of unanimity if they manage to secure their main goals in some other way (e.g., if participants at the conference are members of a coalition or of a political entente). If such is not the case, they return to the principle of unanimity, which would seem to be a useful tool for safeguarding sovereign rights. At the Berlin Congress in 1878, Bismarck declared that the minority would not submit to the will of the majority, but when the Turkish delegate (following instructions from his government) refused to agree to the occupation of Bosnia and Hercegovina by Austria-Hungary, Bismarck replied that he hoped the Turkish delegation would receive new instructions.

Announcement that a settlement has been agreed on unanimously by the great powers is a psychological weapon aimed at disarming the lesser powers. The great powers are formally bound to support the decision and to do nothing that might change it. Hence the small powers have very slim chances of success if they adhere to their original demands, and as a result they become demoralized. The small powers are expected not to stand in the way of a solution which was so hard won, for the sake of peace in general or to save a good idea. They are expected to sacrifice their demands for the cause of peace and international cooperation. If these appeals fail, then the small power is threatened with measures of a coercive nature. The decision of the London Conference on Albania in 1913 is a good example of these methods. The great powers agreed to inform their Balkan allies about their decision to reserve a part of the territory taken from Turkey for the establishment of an independent Albanian state. They called upon Greece, Serbia, and Montenegro to accede to this decision. The opposition of Serbia and Montenegro brought a new decision to authorize Austria-Hungary, Italy, Great Britain and France to take military measures to force them to evacuate the territories which had been assigned to the future independent Albania. Thus these two Balkan states, pitted against the great powers and abandoned by Russia, which claimed that it was not prepared to go to war at that moment, had to accept the London decision, although under protest.

3. Supremacy of the Great Powers

3. Supremacy of the Great Powers — The supremacy of the great powers at international congresses and diplomatic conferences is reflected in the system of representation of participant states and in the manner of voting, which must be seen in the light of the system of representation to be fully understood.

States are represented at a congress or conference according to the method by which individual interests are coordinated in order to arrive at certain common, objective interests. For the level of development of the international community at that time, the Hague conferences had quite a democratic character; the first Hague Conference in 1899 was attended by representatives from 26 states — twenty European countries, two American and four Asian states. This was the first time, as Lapradelle points out, for states from three continents to come together at an international conference.

Although the First Hague Peace Conference was not formally an "open conference," as only the states invited by the organizer (the Queen of the Netherlands) could attend, its spirit was democratic, for all recognized sovereign states with which the European community had intercourse on an equal footing were invited. It was up to them whether or not they would take up the invitation, because since the Peace of Westphalia it has been the rule that only the states interested in the subject matter to be discussed by a conference were invited to attend.

The Second Hague Conference held in 1907 was attended by many more states. Of the 48 states invited, 44 sent delegates. The Paris Peace Conference in 1919 was attended by 27 representatives of various states, but there was one important difference: some were designated the representatives of powers having a "general interest" in all matters, while others were representatives of powers with "limited interests." The two groups had different rights. The latter only had the right to be heard and to participate in the work of the commissions, with the exception of the territorial commission. The difference between the two was actually of a legal nature, considering that peace treaties come into force when they are ratified by the principal powers and the defeated states. The Paris Conference was also attended by states with even fewer rights, i.e. those which had broken off relations with the defeated state or which had been neutral in the war but which had claims on the defeated power that they asked the principal Allied and Associated powers to uphold (e.g. Denmark's request for the return of Schleswig-Holstein). These second two groups could send representatives to the conference, but they only had the right to submit memorandums. In this way, the conference not only lost its democratic character but departed completely from the principle of the equality of states before the law. Justification was found in the formula that the right to decide on peace is directly proportionate to the efforts and sacrifices made to achieve victory.

Twenty-one states were invited to the Peace Conference in Paris in 1946. No distinctions were drawn between the participating delegates, but then only those states had been invited which had played an important role in the military defeat of the Axis powers.

The participants at this conference did not all have equal rights. By the decision of the convening states, i.e. the four great Allied powers, the difference between the great powers and other participants was clear. The great powers only consulted the other participants on the text of the peace treaty. They reserved the right to decide on the final wording of the peace treaties, but took into consideration the recommendations adopted by a two-thirds majority. These peace treaties came into force when they were ratified by the great powers and the defeated powers, regardless of the positions taken by the other directly interested powers. These treaties even contain the threat that any dissatisfied lesser victorious power would forfeit the gains which were recognized in the treaties if it did not ratify them. This clause was first and foremost intended as a warning to Yugoslavia that it could not retain the new territory allotted to it if it did not ratify the peace treaty with Italy. This is one of the reasons Yugoslavia signed and ratified the peace treaty, even though it was not wholly in agreement with it. Although there was greater freedom for expression of views than at the 1919 Paris Conference, the principle of equality was openly flouted.

Special congresses and conferences are those attended by the great powers alone. As a rule, international issues are settled primarily from the standpoint of their interests, no matter what form their decisions might take. Such was the case at the congresses of the so-called "Quintuple Alliance" at Aix-la-Chapelle (1818), Troppau (1820), Laibach (1821), and Verona (1822). Although at times of a somewhat different nature, in form they were very similar to the conferences held during the Second World War between the Big Three. The Council of Foreign Ministers of the five great powers, which was created in 1945 at the Potsdam Conference, was intended to continue the work of the Big Three by meeting periodically to draft peace treaties with Italy, Romania, Bulgaria, Hungary, and Finland, to submit them to the United Nations and to propose settlements of the territorial questions at the end of the war in Europe. The Council was supposed to draw up a peace treaty with Germany which would be accepted by the future German government. The Council was to be composed of representatives of those states which had signed the conditions of capitulation imposed on an enemy state.

There was considerable discussion about both the practical and the theoretical aspects of the decision of the Big Three and the Council of Foreign Ministers. The states which did not participate at these conferences argued that their decisions were not binding on them if they had not expressly agreed to them. France, which had not taken part in the decisions of the Big Three, was a vehement proponent of this argument. However, for all practical purposes, both France and China as lesser Allied powers were compelled to invoke these decisions, because they involved certain rights. In this manner, the great powers unofficially acted as legislators of international law in a given period. The legal conviction in Europe and America is that this arrogation of authority should be subjected to the institution of *negotiorum gestor*. In the conditions of the Second World War, rapid decisions had to be made, and often there was the further consideration of maintaining war secrets. The Big Three, as organizers of the efforts of the United Nations, had to make decisions on the best deployment of these efforts. In doing so they took care to note that they were acting on behalf of the United Nations, meaning the Anti-Hitlerite Coalition. They reminded their allies that everything they did was on their behalf and gave them an account of their actions. At Dumbarton Oaks the United Nations had adopted the main lines of these decisions and accordingly ratified the actions of their self-styled plenipotentiaries. Thus all these decisions, although accepted unofficially, bound all the participants in the Anti-Hitlerite Coalition. The principle of sovereignty and equality before the law was not followed; rather sovereignty was expressed in accession to the coalition, and legal equality was ensured by the fact that the plenipotentiaries acted on everyone's behalf. It would follow, then, that these were conferences of the plenipotentiaries of all the nations represented in the United Nations, and that the decisions came into force when conditions were met for the will of the collective plenipotentiary to be expressed.

Although today powers are not classified as they were at the Paris Conference in 1919, the form is still maintained of convening conferences of the great powers alone, with the justification that they are "directly interested" in all world problems. The great powers often add the promise that other interested countries will also be invited to participate, but only from time to time and in connection with specific issues.

4. Political and Legal Nature — In earlier times, international congresses were meetings of the heads or representatives of states, who met as a rule at the end of a period of hostilities in order, as Scelle puts it, to establish a provisional international authority for effecting constitutional changes, by customary law or by treaty, in the international community as a whole or in part. This *de facto* international authority, whose work was also carried out in a series of subsequent diplomatic conferences controlled a number of very diverse functions, from the normative (constitutional and legislative) and judicial, in regard to settling disputes, to the executive and administrative.

Today there is no terminological difference between international congresses and diplomatic conferences. The notion of the international congress as a meeting of rulers, of the highest state representatives or their delegates is disappearing. The 1919 Peace Conference in Paris and the meetings of the Big Three during the Second World War were congresses in the classical sense but are called conferences.

Diplomatic conferences are still convened from time to time for two purposes: to adjust the international balance of power and achieve international peace and security, or, even more often, to serve as the supreme policy-making organ for a large number of international organizations. A new form of diplomatic conference is now being practiced; it has a much more precise procedure, so that in terms of the *composition of delegates* it continues to have a diplomatic character but in its *functions* it has become separated, generally speaking, into international conferences in the form of assemblies of various international organizations which adopt decisions of a normative character, and international conferences in the form of councils which have an institutional character, usually with executive and administrative competences.

5. Transformation of International Congresses and Diplomatic Conferences — It is increasingly the practice today at international conferences, no matter what their composition or function, to adopt decisions by majority vote. The introduction of this voting procedure has been facilitated by the fact that international conferences today are most often convened with a highly specialized agenda. The interests of states are indeed dealt with there, but these are not always vital interests, as questions directly affecting their independence would be. At the conference of the specialized agencies of the United Nations, for instance, motions are carried by an ordinary or qualified majority on all the important points. Padirac states that with the adoption of this practice, "the evolution begun at the end of the nineteenth century has been completed." What he wants to say is that the democratic principle of the majority vote has finally been endorsed in many international organizations. It is a fact that there is no principle of unanimity in voting procedures at the conferences of the specialized agencies. However, as their name implies, these international agencies are specialized for a specific technical area. National policies are not involved in these agencies to such an extent that the sovereignty of a country might be at stake. If its sovereignty were to be threatened, a state could withdraw from the entire organization. If no provision has been made for withdrawal, states have the right to seek protection of their so-called "domestic jurisdiction" (Article 2, para. 7 of the U.N. Charter), as, for instance, at conferences of organs of the United Nations at which, with the exception of the Security Council, all decisions are made by majority vote.

6. The Role and Importance of International Congresses and Diplomatic Conferences Today — Prior to the Second World War, international conferences primarily served the great powers for establishment of a new political balance of power, and, by the same token for the definition of principles and rules of international law which are in force at a given moment. The political purpose for which such international meetings were convened determined the choice of voting procedure for adoption of decisions.

Today, international congresses have lost their old importance in foreign affairs and in international law. Congresses have become international meetings of non-governmental organizations or of private, professional and scientific organizations. Their earlier functions have been taken over by international conferences of a constitutional character, at which rules are adopted to serve as the political and legal building blocks of the future international community. Diplomatic conferences of an expressly political character are still convened, and, as we have seen, they have not lost many of the attributes and acteristics of the international gatherings of the nineteenth century. However, today there is also a notable tendency for the holding of many conferences which are still diplomatic in their composition, but are of an institutional character in their functions and terms of reference. These are the international conferences of the organs of many international organizations, whose competences are increasingly specialized and whose procedure is much more elaborate.

II. Antecedents and the League of Nations

1. Antecedents — The idea of organizing the family of nations goes far back in time. The ancient Greek philosophers and historians (Polybius, Plato, Aristotle) propounded ideas about a league of states (the Greek League). In the Middle Ages, the power struggle between the emperor and the pope was commented upon by writers and thinkers of that period. Defenders of the papacy advocated an organization of the papal state on a federal basis, to include all Roman Catholic rulers. In the fourteenth century Pierre Dubois put forward the idea of the creation of a federal Christian republic under the administration of a joint council. Dante even proposed a world federation under the rule of a single monarch, to whom all would owe allegiance. George of Podebrady, King of Bohemia in the fifteenth century, also had ideas about how to secure peace in Europe. The Duc de Sully, minister of French King Henri IV, wrote his famous plan for the organization of Europe, in which he advocated a territorial division which, by establishing a balance of power, would ensure peace in the Europe of that day. Later in 1713, St. Pierre propounded the need for a defensive alliance of states which would join forces to defend themselves from all enemies outside this alliance.

2. The League of Nations — During the First World War, Allied leaders encouraged their nations to keep up the war effort and to achieve victory no matter what the cost. Their reward and that of future generations, it was said, would be a secure postwar peace, which would be safeguarded mainly by an international organization already known as the League of Nations.

The war came to an end. The masses began putting pressure on their governments through the press, numerous national societies for the League of Nations, British labor organizations (upon whose initiative the International Labour Organization was created) and socialist parties to fulfil their promise. Although many leading world statesmen felt that the future international organization for the preservation of world peace was a utopia — the view held, for instance, by Clemenceau and Lloyd George — there were politicians who made all-out efforts on behalf of the League, hoping thereby to win political support in their own countries. U.S. President Woodrow Wilson drafted the famous Fourteen Points calling for the formation of "a general association of nations . . . affording mutual guarantees of political independence and territorial integrity to great and small states alike." However, during Wilson's absence from the United States while he was attending the Paris Peace Conference, which began on 18 January 1919, domestic opposition to Wilson's activities to create the League of Nations increased, and the United States did not become a member of the League of Nations. Later the absence of the United States was viewed as one of the main reasons for the weakness of this organization.

The organs of the League of Nations were its Assembly and Council. They were assisted by a permanent Secretariat. Subsequently, the Permanent Court of International Justice was set up as, according to some writers, the judicial organ of the League. The Assembly was composed of the members of the League, each member state having three delegates but only one vote. The Assembly was authorized to deal with any question within the terms of reference of the League or concerning world peace (Article 2, para. 3 of the Covenant). The Council was made up of representatives of the principal Allied and Associated Powers and representatives of four other League members to be elected by the Assembly whenever it saw fit (Article 4, para. 1 of the Covenant). There was no division of jurisdiction between these two organs. The Council was also authorized to consider any question concerned with the activities of the League or concerned with peace in the world (Article 4, para. 4 of the Covenant). Decisions were adopted by unanimous vote. Questions of procedure were decided upon by a majority of votes. The Covenant provided for limitations on armaments, for the procedure to be followed in the event of a dispute and for the method of investigating disputes in the Council or Assembly. The possibility of enforcing sanctions was also provided for (Article 16 of the Covenant).

Despite a tendency for the League to be given greater powers, thus changing its legal nature, it was, according to one of its architects, D. Hunter Miller, like a permanent international conference. He even called the League of Nations a consultative organ of states. In 1923, Lord Cecil declared that the League was the group of governments composing it and nothing more.

The League of Nations was created or rather conceived as an international political and legal mechanism which, by responding to world public opinion, was also to be a means of regulating the European balance of power. While the French policy was to concentrate on guarantees and sanctions, the British policy was to pursue national aims at diplomatic conferences, which helped the British government maintain the friendship it needed among the victor states and bring the Allies closer to Germany in order to forestall any French hegemony. The Council of the League, which might also have served as an instrument for such a policy, was not in fact used as such. Great Britain was particularly fond of diplomatic conferences. From January 1920 to January 1923, over forty conferences of representatives of the chief Allied states were held. Up to 1925, every conference in which Germany took part was preceded by inter-Allied or Anglo-French negotiations. These preliminary talks were held to secure a united front against the German delegation. The British policy was to seek as many conferences as possible at which the French hegemony created by the Versailles system was gradually undermined. Against this political background, the great powers that held permanent seats in the Council of the League of Nations could not pursue their political action within it on a broad international scale; they were hindered by the presence of nonpermanent members of the Council and the possibility of unwarranted political interference (a political and psychological reason) or of their veto (a political and legal reason). Consequently, the great powers shunned this organ of the League of Nations (and especially the Assembly, where the number of members was far greater) and moved to the more promising terrain of direct diplomatic channels and diplomatic conferences.

Japan's aggression which was carried out with impunity in 1933 encouraged German imperialism. Germany, which had entered the League of Nations in 1923, failed in its demand to rearm like all other states and in 1933 left the League of Nations under the pretext of a national revolt against the inequities of the Versailles Treaty, drawing millions of disillusioned Germans into the counter-revolution which was to set off one of the most savage wars in history. The League of Nations was not able to make the many decisions needed at the time, because one veto would have been enough to prevent them from being put into effect. The policy of non-interference by the great powers weakened the already shaky legal and political system of the Geneva institution to such an extent that when after 1938 one nation after another began to fall into the slavery of fascism, the League of Nations was nowhere to be heard.

The setup of the League of Nations and the results which it produced proved to be unsatisfactory. The League of Nations was not able to gain the authority it needed to be able to prevent conflicts and to safeguard world peace. The founders of the League conceived of this international organization as a centre of international political life. The experience gained in international conferences was applied in the League of Nations. However, the great powers bypassed the League and reverted to the practice of diplomatic conferences, thereby avoiding the application of the basic principles provided for in the Covenant.

III. Creation of the United Nations Organization

The leading powers in the Anti-Hitlerite Coalition, the United States, the U.S.S.R., and Great Britain, began in mid-1941 to hold lively discussions both concerning questions of military strategy and concerning the outlook for the postwar world, world peace and its future. Their numerous conferences were characterized by unanimous decisions, particularly on matters of a military and political nature relating to the war, and on matters concerning the political ordering of international relations in Europe and Asia.

The Atlantic Charter, signed by Roosevelt and Churchill on August 14, 1941, speaks of a future broad and permanent system of general security. At the Moscow Conference held from 19 to 30 October 1943, it was envisaged that all other peace-loving large and small powers would become part of this system. It was at this conference that mention was first made of a future international organization which would operate on the principle of the sovereign equality of states and the principle of universality for all peace-loving states. In 1944, representatives of the U.S.S.R., United States, Great Britain, and China held a series of meetings in Washington at the Dumbarton Oaks estate, which gave the conference its name. The purpose for these meetings was to work out proposals for the creation of a universal international organization – the United Nations. The Dumbarton Oaks conference adopted a draft of the future Charter, which served as the basic working document later at San Francisco in 1945. The Statute of the International Court of Justice is an integral part of the United Nations Charter. The Charter together with the Statute was ratified by Yugoslavia by the promulgation of a Law on the United Nations Charter published in the *Official Gazette* on September 11, 1945. Yugoslavia is one of the founding members of the United Nations.

IV. The United Nations Charter

Purposes and Principles of the U.N. Charter — Political and Legal Nature of the United Nations Organization — Revision of the Charter — De facto Revision of the Charter

1. Introduction – The United Nations Organization is a subject of international law. In the territory of each of its members it enjoys the legal capacity necessary for the exercise of its functions and the fulfilment of its purposes. For this reason, it has special privileges and immunities for its representatives and officials (Articles 104 and 105 of the Charter).

The United Nations Organization is a juristic person, and in this capacity it may conclude treaties, acquire and transfer property and appear before courts (Article 1 of the Convention on the Privileges and Immunities of the United Nations, February 13, 1946). In 1946, the General Assembly passed a resolution on the flag of the United Nations. Yugoslav laws protect this capacity of the United Nations. Any violation of the dignity of the Organization or the honor and dignity of its representatives is punishable by imprisonment from three months to three years, according to Articles 175 and 176 of the Yugoslav criminal code.

2. Purposes and Principles of the U.N. Charter — The Charter outlines four main purposes of the United Nations. These are: first, to maintain international peace and security; second, to promote friendly relations among nations; third, to achieve international cooperation and, fourth, to make the United Nations a centre for harmonizing the actions of nations in the attainment of their common ends.

The following principles are laid down for the achievement of these goals:

> *The principle of sovereign equality of states.* Although this principle is not consistently implemented in all the U.N. organs (e.g. not in the Security Council), it has become not only the practice of this organization but a general principle of modern international law. The section of the Charter dealing with the basic rights and duties of states speaks of this principle.
> *The principle of fulfilment of obligations in good faith.* The obligations referred to here are those set forth in the Charter.

The draft prepared at Dumbarton Oaks states in Chapter II that all members of the Organization are obliged, in order to ensure their rights and benefits resulting from membership in the Organization, to fulfil the obligations assumed by them in accordance with the present Charter. At the proposal of the Colombian delegate in San Francisco in 1945, it was added that all members of the Organization shall fulfil their obligations "in good faith." In the opinion of the delegate from Panama, who is defended in literature by Kelsen, this phrase is superfluous at this place in the Charter. In the practice of the United Nations it has been controversial as to what the concept of fulfilment of obligations in good faith implies. Some member states view the fulfilling of obligations "in good faith" as a logical interpretation of actions, while others see it as meaning fulfilment to the best of their abilities under given circumstances. The South American states tried to demonstrate that they were not able to comply with recommendations to minimize relations with Franco's Spain because of their special relationship and the obligations they had assumed earlier towards Spain. Other states were of the opinion that the fulfilment of obligations in good faith referred only to those obligations which had been expressly assumed by a state. Third states asserted that decisions which had been taken over their negative vote were not binding on them (the arguments used by the Arab states in regard to Israel) and that they were not obliged to comply with them. Finally, even the measure of aiding and abetting an action may be criticized as not being "in good faith." States which are accused of not having acted in good faith claim their sovereignty precludes any judgment on their policy by another state. The phrase "in good faith," consequently, does not have the same meaning in international law as it has in civil law, because there is no model of the state acting in good faith which would be analogous to the *bonus pater familias* in everyday life. The extent of good faith depends on specific political assessments and circumstances. Although in international relations the definition of the concept of sovereignty has not often been unanimously agreed upon, this principle as enshrined in the Charter helps promote morality in the international intercourse fostered within the United Nations. The moral standards being promoted are those that are valued by world public opinion and that represent codes of behavior for achieving the purposes laid down in the Charter. In the course of time, public opinion will form a legal norm.

The principle of settling international disputes by peaceful means. War is banned as a means for settling international disputes. In the event of a threat to peace, a breach of peace and aggression, the United Nations is authorized to act pursuant to Chapter VII of the Charter and to the procedure prescribed there. The preceding chapter, Chapter VI, specifies the machinery and means for a peaceful settlement of all disputes. This chapter elaborates the principle laid down in Article 2 of the Charter and will be discussed in more detail below. One of the implications of this principle is the obligation to refrain from the threat or use of force.

The principle of the political independence of states and their territorial integrity. This principle protects the sovereign rights of member states in their mutual relations. Political independence refers to the internal life and foreign affairs of the member states, restricted solely by the rules of international law. The protection of territorial integrity is what inspired the adoption of the Stimson Doctrine which has already been discussed.

The principle of domestic (exclusive) jurisdiction of member states. This principle prohibits the United Nations from interfering in the internal affairs of any state. An exception is made in the case of the application of enforcement measures as provided for in Chapter VII of the Charter. The domestic jurisdiction of states has already been discussed in general terms.

Four theses on the application of this principle have evolved over the years in the United Nations:

The first thesis, put forward by the Republic of South Africa, is that the United Nations, i.e. the General Assembly, has absolutely no authorization to consider matters and that, therefore, it has no right to adopt recommendations on them.

The second thesis is the same as the above with the difference that it considers the General Assembly authorized to adopt recommendations in cases of violations of the principle of non-discrimination.

The third thesis draws a distinction between inquiry into a dispute and the formulation of recommendations. Fact-finding should be permissible but not the adoption of recommendations.

The fourth thesis gives this principle its broadest interpretation: the organs of the United Nations are authorized both to carry out inquiries and to make recommendations in all cases.

The thesis supported by the Republic of South Africa is unacceptable, for if it were to be applied it would hamstring this international organization. Direct interference in the internal affairs of a member state is prohibited in the United Nations. The United Nations merely urge the government of a member state (e.g. the government of the Republic of South Africa) to carry out the obligations it has already assumed by the act of signing and ratifying the U.N. Charter. This is not a matter of interfering but a question of compliance with recommendations based on the Charter itself, specifically Article 1, para. 3 and Articles 55 and 56 which, among other things, explicitly call for the United Nations to create conditions for economic and social progress and development and, in this context, for universal respect for and observance of human rights and fundamental freedoms for all, "without distinction as to race, sex, language or religion." These provisions are without a doubt general rules. But the Charter also contains provisions that were not meant to remain a dead letter or empty words. Under Article 10 of the Charter one of the principal U.N. organs is designated the task of implementing the obligations voluntarily undertaken by members, which have thereby become their duty. In addition to Article 10, the Charter contains other provisions which unmistakably show that the question of, for instance, racial discrimination is within the jurisdiction of the United Nations. We may cite Article 13, para. 1, item b, and Articles 60 and 62, which testify to the carefully delineated jurisdiction of the United Nations in this matter.

To draw a line between the competence to inquire into a situation, into the charges brought by one state against another, and the competence to make recommendations would mean turning the principal organ of the United Nations, the General Assembly, into a fact-finding commission.

The right of member states to invoke domestic jurisdiction should remain a general principle of the United Nations in all cases, except for those which call for the compulsory enforcement of the principles set forth in the Charter. Specifically, the application of encorcement measures must be decided upon in the democratic process that is undoubtedly a feature of the United Nations, although the role of reactionary forces in this development should not be disregarded. It could not, in all fairness, be stated that this principle was poorly formulated at the San Francisco Conference, when it was acknowledged that it was still undergoing its evolution; but, in retrospect we might have wished for a closer definition in political and legal terms. Advances in technology and the growth of productive forces will undoubtedly tend to enlarge the competences of the organs of the international community, although today it is difficult to imagine the disappearance of such an important legal and political instrument in the organized international community as domestic jurisdiction. Most likely this concept will undergo certain modifications rather than be abandoned altogether.

3. The Political and Legal Nature of the United Nations Organization — The Charter of the United Nations represents a political and legal compromise among the states signing and ratifying it.

The political compromise was of a dual nature. This was an agreement between the great powers, the future permanent members of the Security Council, on the one hand, and between the great powers and other states on the other. This agreement is embodied in Article 27 of the Charter and is known as the Yalta Formula. In practical terms, this formula means that the five great powers can place a veto on matters which are not considered procedural. This right of the great powers derives from their special status in the Security Council, and the broad jurisdiction of this organ allows them to have the main say on questions of vital importance both in terms of international peace and world security and in connection with the functioning of the organization itself. On the other hand, the other medium-size and small states did acquiesce in San Francisco in 1945 to the privileged position of the five great powers in the Security Council. Just as it would not have been possible to create the United Nations Organization without the participation of these great powers, it would also not have been possible to create it without the agreement of the medium-sized and small states. Hence they were given the right to bring matters to the attention of the Security Council, to state their opinions, and to demand a decision.

The political system of the United Nations, which was created above all for the maintenance of international peace and security, was based on the idea of a world balance of power after the Second World War and on the principle of universality. This political concept has had an influence on the legal character of the United Nations. The U.N. could not have taken the form of a standing diplomatic conference, for such a form would be unsuitable for the effective maintenance of postwar international peace; nor could the Organization have a supranational character, because the small powers, which were very jealous of their sovereign rights in 1945, would not have agreed to hand over the attributes of their sovereignty to the international community which was then just

taking shape. Nor were the great powers in favor of a supranational world organization, except insofar as it might help to strengthen their oligarchic system,
attempts at which were opposed by the majority of states. For all these reasons,
the United Nations was finally created as an *association of sovereign states.*

4. Revision of the Charter — Chapter XVIII, which consists of Articles 108 and 109, provides for amendments to the Charter and two procedures for review of the Charter. The procedure for making amendments is
envisaged in Article 108; paragraphs 1 and 2 of Article 109 describe a special procedure for reviewing the Charter, and paragraph 3 provides for an
automatic review.

Amendments to the Charter as adopted on 26 July 1945, in San Francisco
come into force for all member countries under the following conditions:
a. when they have been adopted by a vote of two-thirds of the members of the
General Assembly; b. when they have been ratified by two-thirds of the members; c. when they have been ratified by all the permanent members of the Security Council; d. after ratification is carried out by all member countries "in
accordance with their respective constitutional processes."

The special procedure allows for the convening of a General Conference to
review the original text of the Charter: a. the date and place of the conference
are to be fixed by a two-thirds vote of the members of the General Assembly
and by the vote of any nine members of the Security Council; b. every member
of the United Nations may have only one vote at the conference; c. the amendments to the Charter recommended by a two-thirds majority at the Conference
will come into force when they are ratified by two-thirds of the members of the
United Nations; d. the amendments must be approved by all the permanent
members of the Security Council e. ratification must be carried out in accordance with the constitutional processes of the member states.

Under the automatic procedure: a. if the Conference for review of the
Charter is not held before the tenth annual session of the General Assembly, a
proposal to call such a conference will be placed on the agenda of that session of
the General Assembly; b. the conference will be held pursuant to a decision by
the General Assembly adopted by the customary majority. This decision must
be based on a recommendation by the Security Council adopted by any seven
members; c. all amendments must be ratified by all the permanent members of
the Security Council.

The method of proposing amendments and initiating a review of the Charter under Chapter XVIII has three aspects, depending on the kind of procedure
used.

To initiate the procedure for amending the Charter, all that is necessary is
to place the matter on the agenda of the General Assembly; a proposal to this
effect should be submitted to the Secretary-General, who will then pass it on to

member states of the Organization sixty days before the opening of the regular session, as required by Article 12 of the internal rules of procedure of the General Assembly. As every matter proposed for the agenda should be supported if possible by a memorandum giving the necessary explanations, by basic documentation or a draft resolution — as provided for under Article 20 of the rules of procedure — the same holds true in this case.

The special procedure for instituting a review of the Charter requires a two-thirds majority decision by the General Assembly and recommendations by any nine members of the Security Council.

The manner of initiating the procedure reveals an important aspect of the compromise on which the U.N. Charter is based. States may present motions both to amend the Charter and to institute the special procedure for review of the Charter. If there is only one amendment to be considered, the procedure is simple. It is the same as the procedure followed whenever a state desires to bring a matter to the attention of the members of the Organization. However, if there are several amendments aiming at changing the directions of development of the Organization or altering its internal operation, then the procedure is much more complicated. A two-thirds majority decision by the General Assembly is needed, with the proviso of a prior recommendation of the Security Council adopted by nine members.

The principle of equality of states is thereby not endangered. The great powers made sure of safeguarding their interests not through the system of initiating a procedure but rather in the phase of ratifying adopted amendments. The very fact that the five great powers must ratify the amendments before they can come into effect acts as a psychological deterrent for the other member countries from any attempt to revise the Charter if one great power (permanent member of the Security Council) is against such a change. The same holds true for the automatic procedure of review. The great powers have retained the right to make the final decision when the amendments are ratified.

The automatic review of the Charter was a compromise between the large and small powers in San Francisco. As a way of offsetting the right of veto enjoyed by the five great powers and of truly providing for the convening of a general conference for review of the Charter — because it was hard to imagine even then that all the qualified powers would agree to renounce any of their rights recognized in the Charter — it was decided that a proposal for a general conference should be automatically entered on the agenda of the tenth regular session of the General Assembly. The concession was minimal, because any great power which is a permanent member of the Security Council can prevent changes in the original text by refusing to ratify the amendments.

The automatic possibility of reviewing the Charter in ten years' time after the adoption of the Charter might have made the Charter look like a compromise intended to last only ten years. The special procedure for convening a general conference provides that every member at the conference will have one vote. Hence, it will have the features of an international conference at which the same rules of procedure would be applied as for all the international conferences of the United Nations. This fact, however, is not obvious from Article 109, para. 3 of the Charter. The General Assembly, according to the envisaged procedure, is only authorized to decide whether or not the conference will be held. This means that it was intended to be an ordinary conference (in para. 3 of Article 109 it is not called "general") of a diplomatic nature, which has the right to decide on its own rules of procedure. This fact raises an important point. If the conference for review of the Charter provided for in the automatic procedure has only a diplomatic character, then it is irrelevant to link para. 3 with para. 2 of Article 109 and, in this way, deduce that the permanent members of the Security Council have the right to place a veto on the amendments adopted at such a conference. At the conference of a diplomatic character envisaged for the automatic procedure in Chapter XVIII of the Charter, the right to place a veto is enjoyed by all members in attendance with full voting rights, as at virtually all diplomatic conferences, and not just during ratification of the adopted amendments. Then not just the permanent members of the Security Council but all member states with voting rights attending the conference have this prerogative, although it need not mean that they will prevent the adoption of a decision, as in the Security Council pursuant to Article 27.

Even though the choice of procedure for review of the Charter was for the most part politically motivated — as seen in the policy of the victorious powers in the Second World War, the future permanent members of the Security Council — from the legal standpoint, this procedure may have been made complicated with an eye to preserving the stability of this basic legal document of the United Nations. The absence of a system of supranational norms in the Charter, which can be understood and condoned, but the simultaneous desire for a more permanent relationship between member states, and, above all, the expressed willingness of the permanent members of the Security Council to take unanimous action — and the mutual concessions they made to arrive at a jointly expressed will in the provisions of the Charter — all these considerations influenced the creation of the dual legal character of the U.N. Charter. In 1945 it would not have been possible to envisage machinery facilitating the procedure for a future review of the Charter. What is more, because of the political atmosphere at San Francisco in 1945, any such proposals were foredoomed. Later, however, the so-called *de facto* revision of the Charter made in practice transformed the rigid text into more flexible forms more appropriate for the new international circumstances. The primary concern was to preserve and implement the basic principles which have served as the underpinnings of peace since the Second World War. Peace in the world is the most precious possession of contemporary mankind, and it must be protected by present-day international law. One of the most important instruments of international law is undoubtedly the United Nations Charter.

So far, only Articles 23, 27, 61 and 109 of the Charter have been altered to enlarge the Security Council and Economic and Social Council, in consequence of the substantial increase in the number of states having membership in the United Nations.

5. *De Facto* Revision of the Charter — Every legal text may be interpreted more broadly than ever intended by its authors. Sometimes a rule of law may even be applied in a way quite the opposite to that envisaged by those who had adopted it. In justification of such an application of rules of law, the legal text is said to have been given a broad interpretation. Although some hold the view that the broad interpretation of a law which is not based on the will of the drafter has a negative effect on its stability, nevertheless, a broad interpretation has an important advantage because a given legal text can thus be adapted to the constantly changing conditions of everyday life. Finally, broad interpretations may cause a legal text to be changed by way of custom without necessarily requiring a formal amendment. If a given broad interpretation becomes legitimized in a resolution, then there has been a *de facto* revision.

A *de facto* revision of the Charter may be made in a number of ways (so far as the practice of the United Nations is concerned); through usage which is not objected to by other member states; by a declaration of a group of member states which have a special status and right within the United Nations; by the creation of subsidiary organs on which some of the competences of the principal organs are devolved; by a resolution containing recommendations on the conduct of members outside the Organization. These recommendations are of a moral and political nature and represent a view which the majority hopes will be adopted by all states. The Charter is also amended in practice by collective declarations which contain a specific programme of future work of the Organization, and by resolutions, which, although in the form of recommendations, impose mandatory compliance on member states voting for them. A *de facto* revision of the Charter may also be made by tacit agreement *(via facti)* not to enforce some of its provisions.

V. Membership

Original and Other Members — Admission to Membership — Expulsion — Status of Non-Members

1. Original and Other Members — The original members of the United Nations are those states which took part in the United Nations Conference on International Organization in San Francisco, or which signed the Declaration of the United Nations on 1 January 1942, and which signed and ratified the Charter. Although there are two kinds of member states: those who were original members and those who joined the United Nations subsequently, there is no legal distinction made between them, and they have the same rights and duties.

2. Admission to Membership — One of the primary purposes of the United Nations is to make every state in the world a member. This purpose was enunciated by the Allies before the end of the Second World War, when it was agreed that the future international organization should have a universal charter. However, the international conditions at the end of the war and in its aftermath called for certain restrictions, which were set forth in Article 4 of the Charter. To become a member of the United Nations, a country must be an independent state which is not under the authority of any other state; it must be peace-loving; it must accept the obligations of the Charter, and it must be able and willing to carry out these obligations. The General Assembly decides on the admission of new states to the United Nations upon the recommendation of the Security Council with the concurrence of all the permanent members of this organ.

Under the Security Council Resolution of 17 May 1946, and the amendment of 24 July 1946, a Special Committee in which every member of the Security Council is represented was set up to consider applications. A state wishing to become a member of the United Nations must submit an application to the Secretary-General which has to contain a formal statement to the effect that the state accepts the obligations of the Charter. The Secretary-General forwards the application to the Security Council, which submits it to its Committee. The task of the Committee is to consider the application and give its report to the Security Council. The Committee's report should be submitted to the Security Council thirty-five days before the regular session of the General Assembly, and the Security Council should make its recommendation to the General Assembly twenty-five days in advance; if a special session of the General Assembly is called, then the recommendation should be made fourteen days before the opening of this session.

The drafters of the Charter built in a mechanism which allows all other states which did not take part in the war on the side of the Axis to enter the world organization. However, this legal mechanism is so constructed as to provide an opportunity for the Axis states also to become members at some future time. Of course, the great powers must agree that the state in question has become peace-loving and that it fulfils the above-mentioned conditions. The gradual implementation of the principle of universality was thus provided for, and today the United Nations has 150 member states.

3. Expulsion — Upon the unanimous recommendation of the Security Council, a state which has violated the principles of the Charter may be expelled from the Organization. This provision provides for an exception to the principle of universality. Why was this exception made?

The sanction in international law is still of an ambiguous character; there are many kinds of sanctions, and they are not always enforced as quickly as within the national penal system of a country. But the sanction is indispensable. If there were no sanctions in one form or another, there could hardly be any rules of law in international life. For this reason, the Charter provides for sanctions against recalcitrant member states. Perhaps we could say the threat of sanctions, for the actual enforcement which requires a unanimous recommendation to the General Assembly by all five great powers in the Security Council, is difficult to achieve.

There is a growing demand for excision of the provision which provides for expulsion of members from the United Nations, because today it is considered more important to achieve universality than to resort to the threat of such a sanction, particularly in view of the fact that Article 5 of the Charter, which provides for suspension from membership, has never once been invoked.

A member of the United Nations should not be exposed to the possibility of being expelled from the Organization, although we are in favor of suspension as a form of sanction. It is in the interest of the Organization for all its members to be under its control. A member which does not comply with or which violates the provisions and principles of the Organization may be liable to other sanctions, even including the enforcement measures provided for by the Charter, which can be supplemented and improved upon. We feel that making it legally possible to expel a member would be contrary to the universality to which the United Nations should continue to aspire. The threat of a curtailment of rights and the possibility of isolation from virtually the entire international community, as embodied in the United Nations, will keep member states together. On the other hand, if a member cannot be expelled but may withdraw of its own free will, the Organization will not be weakened, because its influence will still be felt by the former member state. That is to say, the former member cannot evade its obligations by withdrawing from the Organization, nor does it acquire the freedom to act contrary to the principles and rules of international law.

On January 20, 1965, Indonesia sent a letter to the United Nations announcing its decision to resign its membership "at this stage and under the present circumstances." Indonesia soon returned to the fold, but in any case the United Nations never confirmed the Indonesian note, nor did it take an official stand on the withdrawal of one of its members, although a debate on this matter was initiated at the proposal of Italy. Indonesia's readmission cut short the debate on the legal and political consequences of withdrawal from membership in the United Nations, and the Italian note sent to the Secretary-General on 13 May 1965, was no longer relevant.

4. The Status of Non-Members — What is the status of non-member states according to the Charter?

Under para. 6 of Article 2 of the Charter, the United Nations requires states which are not members of the Organization to observe its principles "so far as may be necessary for the maintenance of international peace and security." For this reason, states which are not members are given certain rights under the Charter. Under Article 11, para. 2, and Article 35, para. 2, a state which does not belong to the United Nations may bring any dispute to which it is a party to the attention of the Security Council or the General Assembly, of course, "if it accepts in advance, for the purposes of the dispute, the obligations of pacific settlement provided in the present Charter." Similarly, according to Article 32 of the Charter, such a state as a party to a dispute will be invited to participate in the discussion concerning the dispute; this state has no vote, and its participation is subject to the conditions determined by the Security Council. In this manner, the provisions of the Charter from Article 31 through Article 42, can be enforced. Similarly, the International Court of Justice can give an advisory opinion to non-member states on any legal question put before it by the General Assembly or Security Council.

All the above-mentioned provisions may directly concern non-member states. However, such states may also be affected indirectly by some other articles. Furthermore, many states which are not members of the United Nations have become members of its specialized agencies and thus indirectly are affected by Articles 55 to 60 and Articles 61 to 72.

Finally, a non-member state may become a party to the statute of the principal judicial organ of the United Nations if it agrees to the specific conditions set by the General Assembly upon the recommendation of the Security Council.

Hence the provisions of the Charter may have either a direct or an indirect effect on states which are not members of the United Nations.

Commentators on the Charter, L.M. Goodrich and E.I. Hambro, consider it to be controversial whether an international instrument such as the Charter can impose legal obligations on states which have not acceded to it. They involve the traditional doctrine that treaties are not binding on third states, while admitting that it too is open to debate.

If a non-member state has become a member of one of the U.N. inter-governmental organizations which under an agreement with the Economic and Social Council has acquired the status of a specialized agency, that state has automatically become bound by the principles according to which this specialized international organization operates. If, however, a non-member state wishes to become a contracting party to the Statute of the International Court of Justice, and for this reason accepts the specific conditions laid down by the General Assembly upon the recommendation of the Security Council, then it has expressly accepted the obligations arising from this voluntarily assumed treaty relationship; naturally only so far as one organ of the United Nations is concorned, in this instance the main judicial body.

There is certainly room for debate over the nature of the obligations binding on non-member states in matters concerning international peace and security, i.e. in the case of the enforcement of Article 2, para. 6, of the Charter. If it is assumed that the United Nations is an association of independent states, then it is logical that third states cannot legally be bound by an international treaty. However, the Charter is a treaty in form, but its content gives it a constitutional nature. States have come together as independent units in order to maintain their independence and to safeguard international peace. At the same time, the Organization cannot intervene in the domestic jurisdiction of its members, under Article 2, para. 7, with the exception of enforcement measures provided for in Chapter VII. This means that for occasions involving a threat to or breach of the peace, or an act of aggression, the United Nations has created a specific legal order which is to be enforced for all states, regardless of whether or not they are members of the United Nations. In this respect the Charter is essentially of a constitutional character. It has imposed rules to be universally enforced in the sphere of the maintenance of international peace and security, thereby ensuring member states legal security and equality by giving them the opportunity to bring all disputes to which they are a party to the attention of the General Assembly and Security Council; and, when the disputes are discussed, the states must be invited to take part.

Of course, generally speaking, the status of non-members is not the same as that of members in this area either, because the right to bring disputes to the attention of the mentioned U.N. organs can be exercised only for *disputes* to which the former are a party, but they do not have the same right in regard to *situations* in which they may also be interested. A dispute is considered to be an international conflict brought to the attention of the competent U.N. organ in which the respective parties have been recognized and as such have formulated their accusations or counter-accusations in a formal complaint. A situation is a political state of affairs on some part of the globe which threatens to jeopardize peace, but in which the parties have not yet come forward to undertake litigation. This means that a non-member state would not have the right to bring its interests in a situation of political tension in some part of the world to the attention of the competent principal U.N. organs. Therefore non-member states are not authorized to take any action concerning an "international situation" as described in the Charter. Whereas under Article 35, para. 1, every state which is a member of the United Nations may bring any dispute or situation to the attention of the Security Council or General Assembly.

VI. Organs

The Dumbarton Oaks proposals envisaged only four principal organs of the United Nations: the General Assembly, the Security Council, the Secretariat and the International Court of Justice. The San Francisco Conference of 1945 considered demands for the establishment of two more main organs: the Economic and Social Council and the Trusteeship Council. Thus the Charter provides for six principal organs of the United Nations. We shall discuss the International Court of Justice separately.

Unlike the League of Nations, whose Covenant gave the Council and Assembly joint jurisdiction over important matters (e.g. in regard to the question of world peace), the organs of the United Nations have divided up their competences. According to the Charter, the General Assembly has *general jurisdiction*. It is authorized to consider any question within the scope of the Charter or any matter relating to the powers and functions of any organ. The other organs have special competences but do not enjoy the right described above.

The Charter provides for the possibility of creating *subsidiary* organs. The General Assembly may set up such organs to carry out its tasks, as may the Security Council. The Economic and Social Council is authorized to create commissions for economic and social affairs and for the promotion of human rights and fundamental liberties for all, or for the implementation of some other tasks which are within its competence.

Subsidiary organs may be permanent if they are to perform specific types of jobs all the time. The rules of procedure of the General Assembly envisage two standing committees: the Advisory Committee on Administrative and Budgetary Questions (nine members) and the Committee on Contributions (ten members). The Assembly may set up other standing committees as necessary (for example, the Committee for Investments, with three members). The International Law Commission, first comprising fifteen members and later expanded to twenty-five members, and the Peace Observation Commission of fourteen members are also permanent subsidiary organs of the Assembly.

The Assembly as a whole (at its plenary session) or its main committees may set up *ad hoc committees* for specific purposes. Examples of these are the U.N. Conciliation Commission for Palestine and the Collective Measures Committee. These *ad hoc* committees may be set up for a specific period of time, in which case they have a provisional character. For instance, in November 1947 an *ad hoc* committee called the Little Assembly was created for a trial period of one year.

VII. The United Nations General Assembly

Composition — Sessions — Organization — Functions and Powers — Voting — Legal Nature

1. Composition — The U.N. General Assembly is made up of all the members of the United Nations. It is the only organ in which all the member states are represented.

A member state in the General Assembly may not have more than five delegates and five alternates who represent their country in the Assembly with the consent of the head of the delegation. Each delegation may have a number of counsellors, experts, and other auxiliary officials, in the number that it deems to be necessary.

2. Sessions — The U.N. General Assembly meets in regular and special sessions. The beginning of the regular session is fixed for the third Tuesday in September of each year. At the beginning of each session, and at the proposal of the General Committee, the U.N. General Assembly fixes the day when the session will be closed. The General Assembly meets at U.N. headquarters or in another place if it should so decide. The General Assembly may also hold special sessions. These can be convened by the Secretary-General at the request of the Security Council or of a majority of members, in which case it must meet not later than fifteen days after the request was made. Following a General Assembly resolution (No. 337/V), an emergency special session may be called within twenty-four hours of a request sent to the Secretary-General.

3. Organization — For each of its sessions, the General Assembly elects a president and vice-presidents. The General Assembly conducts its proceedings in plenary sessions and the main committees. These are the First Committee for political and security questions, whose work load is shared by the Special Political Committee; the Second Committee, which deals with economic and financial questions; the Third Committee for social, humanitarian and cultural questions; the Fourth Committee, which deals with trusteeship matters, including nonself-governing territories; the Fifth Committee handling administrative and budgetary questions, and the Sixth Committee for legal matters. Procedural committees handle organizational questions and supervise the smooth running of the Assembly's work. There are two committees of this kind: the General Committee, which is composed of fifteen members, including the president and vice-presidents of the Assembly and the seven chairmen of the Main Committees; the second is the Credentials Committee, which is composed of nine members.

4. Functions and Powers — The General Assembly is authorized to discuss all questions and matters within the scope of the U.N. Charter or relating to any organ of the United Nations Organization. Exception is made for the cases when the Security Council considers a given dispute or situation. In such an event the General Assembly cannot make recommendations in connection with this dispute or situation unless specifically requested to do so by the Security Council. For this reason the Secretary-General, subject to approval by the Security Council, has the duty to inform the General Assembly at each of its sessions about the issues on the Security Council's agenda which affect international peace and security. Generally speaking, however, the General Assembly is competent to consider any matter relating to the maintenance of international peace and security. These questions notably include the problem of regulating armaments. In this respect the General Assembly may make recommendations to the member states and to the Security Council. These questions can be raised in the General Assembly by any member of the United Nations or by the Security Council, or even by non-member states, under the conditions prescribed by the U.N. Charter. The General Assembly itself can also draw the attention of the Security Council to a situation threatening international peace and security. If any newly arising situations threaten international peace and security, harm the general well-being, or upset friendly relations among nations, the General Assembly is authorized to recommend concrete measures to ameliorate them. Even though the General Assembly has a general jurisdiction, it still does not mean, according to the text of the U.N.

Charter, that the Security Council is subordinated to the General Assembly, because the resolutions and recommendations of the Security Council are not subject to confirmation by the General Assembly. However, recent practice has shown that in the event of any failure in the functioning of the Security Council, the General Assembly may take over the function of this organ for the purpose of maintaining international peace and security. The Security Council has not thereby become a subordinated organ *(via facti)*, but, in the event that an organ fails to do something for which it was competent or becomes incapable of performing its functions, then the United Nations is authorized, as the *negotiorum gestor,* to take over the functions of that organ and transfer them to another organ (from the Security Council to the General Assembly) for the purpose of implementing the principles contained in the Preamble and Article 2 of the U.N. Charter.

The General Assembly is specifically authorized to initiate studies and make recommendations to promote a. international political cooperation; b. the development of international law and its codification; c. international collaboration in economic, social cultural, educational and health fields; d. the realization of human rights and fundamental freedoms for all, irrespective of race, sex, language, or religion. The General Assembly is not only empowered to make recommendations in this sense but is also responsible for the implementation of these tasks.

The General Assembly receives and considers annual and other reports sent by all the main and other organs of the U.N. and considers and approves the budget and all the financial and budgetary agreements with the specialized agencies for the purpose of making recommendations to these organizations.

5. Voting — The principle of the equality of states is implemented in the General Assembly by the rule that each member state has a specified number of delegates and only one vote. The principle of unanimity — absolute, or combined with majority rule — is not applied in the General Assembly. The system in use there is majority voting: a simple majority of the members present and voting or a two-thirds majority for "major questions" as determined by the U.N. Charter. A two-thirds majority vote is required for: recommendations in connection with the maintenance of international peace and security; election of nonpermanent members to the Security Council; election of members to the Economic and Social Council; election of some members to the Trusteeship Council; admission of members to the United Nations; rescission of the rights and privileges conferred by membership; expulsion of members; and questions concerning trusteeship and budgets.

6. Legal Nature — What is the legal nature of the U.N. General Assembly? Is this organ, in terms of the British and Scandinavian legal doctrine, a parliament of the United Nations? In this case the General Assembly would have sovereign prerogatives. On the one hand, it is the supreme organ in the constitutional structure of the United Nations Organization. All the members of other organizations, excepting the permanent members of the Security Council, are elected. It is the General Assembly which does the electing. On the other hand, it does not have the character of a supranational authority, because it does not have the general powers to promulgate acts of government. Holding the view that the General Assembly has the character of a parliament, the former Secretary-General of the U.N. Trygve Lie, attempted to restrict the jurisdiction of the General Assembly, asking that it should only deliberate and lay down principles, while the rest of the work should be left to the Secretariat and other organs, as is done in the parliaments in the West. However, the general Assembly is made up not of members belonging to various political parties, but of sovereign states. Such a method would be directly prejudicial to the interests of the states in the minority and might threaten their sovereign rights. This action by Trygve Lie, supported by the delegates of Great Britain and the Scandinavian states, failed. The General Assembly's rules of procedure could not be revised at the expense of the freedom of expression of the member states, because the General Assembly is the very place for states to express their will and formulate their interests, which means that it is the seat of world public opinion.

The General Assembly is not just a diplomatic conference, because, firstly, these meet periodically, whereas the General Assembly holds sessions regularly; secondly, each diplomatic conference establishes its own procedure for each session, while the General Assembly has a definite procedure laid down by the U.N. Charter and its own rules of procedure; thirdly, as a rule the conferences adopt the principle of unanimity, while the General Assembly applies the system of simple and qualified majority. It is only according to the composition of its delegates that the General Assembly resembles a diplomatic conference. The delegates receive instructions from their governments and uphold their political lines. In short, the General Assembly has the nature of a permanent diplomatic conference in terms of its composition, and in terms of its functions it has the character of the principal organ of an international organization taking the form of association of sovereign states.

VIII. The Security Council

*Composition — Function and Powers — Voting and Proce-
dure — Right of Veto*

1. Composition — The Security Council is composed of fifteen members, including five permanent members (China, France, the U.S.S.R., the United Kingdom and the United States) and ten non-permanent members which are elected by the General Assembly for two-year terms. According to the U.N. Charter, when non-permanent members are elected, special account should be taken of the candidate state's contribution to international peace and security and to the realization of other goals of the United Nations, as well as of a balanced geographical representation. A non-permanent member whose term has run out may not be immediately re-elected.

In contrast to the other main bodies, the Security Council must be able to convene sessions at all times. For this reason, each member state keeps a permanent delegate at U.N. headquarters. Security Council meetings may be held outside U.N. headquarters if its work should thereby be facilitated.

A state which is not a member of the Security Council but has an interest in a dispute before the Council can participate in its consideration but without the right to vote. Even a state which is not a member of the United Nations, when it is party to a dispute being considered by the Council, must be invited to participate in the discussion, but again without the right to vote. The Security Council is authorized to lay down the conditions under which a non-member state may participate in considering a dispute to which it is a party. It lays down those conditions which it believes are just in the given case.

2. Function and Powers — The United Nations has entrusted the Security Council, as one of its main organs, with the "principal responsibility for the maintenance of international peace and security." The Security Council acts on behalf of the United Nations in accordance with the purposes and principles contained in the U.N. Charter. Special powers are conferred on the Council to bring about a peaceful settlement of disputes, to undertake proceedings in the event of any threats to or violations of the peace, or acts of aggression, to assist in the regional settlement of disputes and to regulate international trusteeship.

The members of the United Nations expressly undertook (Article 25 of the U.N. Charter) to accept and carry out the decisions adopted by the Security Council in accordance with the Charter.

The Security Council submits annual and special reports to the General Assembly.

3. Voting and Procedure — Each member of the Security Council has one vote, and decisions on questions of procedure are passed by the affirmative votes of any nine members, irrespective of whether they are permanent or non-permanent members of the Council. On all questions other than those of procedure, i.e. on all matters of a substantive nature, decisions are taken by the affirmative votes of nine members, including the concurring votes of the permanent members of the Security Council. If the decisions concern a peaceful settlement of disputes or promotion of a peaceable settlement of local disputes, a party to the dispute must abstain from voting, following the principle *nemo judex in re sua*.

Article 27 of the U.N. Charter, which provides for the system of voting in the Security Council, has entrenched the authority of the five great powers, permanent members of the Security Council. They have ensured for themselves full control in taking decisions. This authority not only applies to matters affecting their own security, but it is an *inhibitive authority,* which can prevent any decisions from being passed and put into effect, regardless of whether their interest is direct or indirect.

The origin of this power should be explained. The three leading Allied powers — the United States, Great Britain and the U.S.S.R. — during World War II decided to create immediately upon its termination an international organization to be responsible for peace and security in the world; this body would not be an extension of the former League of Nations but both its organization and effectiveness would be a completely new international instrument through which Allied relations would continue developing and would generally set the tone for postwar world politics. The dissensions which broke out — some sporadically owing to different policies on some questions (division of Germany, Poland, etc.), and others more sustained (e.g. the opening of a second front) — made it clear to the Allies that there would be a struggle in the foreign political field after the war in which their interests as great powers had to be safeguarded. As victory drew nearer, their desire to safeguard their own interests and indeed their ambitions to expand their foreign activities increased. In a political situation such as this, attempts were made to find a political and legal mechanism within the framework of the future international organization that would serve their common struggle and the political prospects offered to them still during the war. On many questions agreement was reached relatively quickly. However, the problem of voting in the principal organ of the future United Nations Organization responsible for the maintenance of world peace and security could not be resolved at the preliminary conference in Dumbarton Oaks held between 21 August and 7 October 1944, at which the future U.N.

Charter was drafted. This difficult question was, therefore, soon placed on the agenda of the Crimea Conference held at Yalta from 4 to 11 February 1945, which was attended by Roosevelt, Stalin, and Churchill. At this conference, the Big Three had to find a political and legal formula which would, firstly, prevent a future conflict among the the three powers, secondly, protect their interests in the international strategical struggle, and, thirdly, permit small powers to be heard by the great powers (according to the U.N. Charter, these are China, France, the U.S.S.R., the United Kingdom and the United States), when they believe one of their rights has been violated.

After long discussions an agreement was finally reached. All three powers accepted the American proposal that on all substantive decisions in the Security Council the great powers had to reach unanimity and had to win over two nonpermanent members with no right of veto, which, in their opinion, would not be difficult to do. Otherwise, a decision could not come into force, because one negative vote by a qualified great power is sufficient to prevent the proposed decision, even though it may have enjoyed the support of all the other, permanent as well as nonpermanent members. On questions of procedure in the Security Council, the required majority was formerly seven but now, after the adoption of amendments to the Charter, it is nine members, irrespective of whether the decisions are voted by the permanent members or the other states. An exception is made if one of the states is a party to the dispute before the Council. When a peaceful settlement of an international dispute is involved and when the Security Council wants to promote a pacific settlement of local conflicts, the interested party must then abstain from voting.

The Yalta Formula, adopted in San Francisco in 1945 as the famous Article 27 of the U.N. Charter, was designed by the great powers, first, to legally prevent any of the Allied powers from being outvoted by entitling each of them to a veto on any decisions relative to a threat to the peace, violation of the high seas or an act of aggression, and second, to allow each great power to conduct a wide-ranging international political activity and safeguard its interest, because it can veto any decision which is not in conformity with its policy.

This voting system made Great Britain happy, because in view of the numerous nations having different statuses within its empire, it saw in the right of veto a means of preventing anyone from interfering with its imperial interests. The United States, which proposed the Yalta Formula, believed that any other solution would not be very kindly accepted by its Senate. The U.S.S.R. agreed with this formula, which not only made its own sphere of interest safe, preventing any foreign intervention, but also enabled it to become involved in all world problems. For this reason, the Soviet Union was strongly against denying the right of veto to a great power, even if it were a party to a dispute under consideration.

Just as it was impossible to create the United Nations Organization without the great powers, it could also not have been realized without the consent of the medium and small states. This fact was particularly clear to the Western powers, which insisted that small powers must be given the possibility of at least raising an issue and pronouncing themselves if they think that the decision they want to see is denied because it is contrary to the joint interests of the permanent members of the Security Council. The U.S.S.R. tried hard to extend the veto to the sphere of pacific settlement of international disputes. Because of this Soviet insistence, the San Francisco Conference came to a halt. President Truman sent Harry Hopkins to try and persuade Stalin to back down, and the U.S.S.R. eventually did after having ensured two extra votes for itself (the Soviet republics of the Ukraine and Byelorussia were also recognized as original members). Gromyko subsequently asked for these two Soviet republics to become permanent members of the Security Council, as France and China, in addition to the three great powers (the United States, Great Britain and the U.S.S.R.), were also accepted as permanent members. Because of general opposition, this Soviet demand was not adopted.

Thus the great powers based not only their postwar cooperation but indeed the survival of the United Nations on the assumption of consensus among them as a condition for peace in the world. The right of veto, which one could use against the other, was to be the lever to move them to arrive at an understanding.

In view of the sensitivity of the small nations as regards the principle of sovereign equality, the great powers conceived the idea of safeguarding their privileged position by reaching a previous agreement, creating an actual inequality which they would often cover up by invoking legal equality or technical reasons. Thus the great powers had a secret gentlemen's agreement in regard to the application of the U.N. Charter which is known only by some disclosures, e.g. the obligation of the U.S. and Great Britain to support the U.S.S.R.'s candidate for non-permanent member of the Security Council.

4. The Right of Veto — The concepts which justify the status of the great powers in the Security Council and their special right of veto have evolved to such an extent today that they constitute a theory of a special right which must be reckoned with by modern international law. In our opinion, this theory is rather a political justification of a special right than a legal theory for a political concept based on the status of another state, for the simple reason that the status of the great powers as permanent members of the Security Council and their right of veto are not based on the guiding principle of the United Nations, the principle of sovereign equality of states, but rather on the rule of international political expediency. This opinion of ours should not be construed as an attempt to deny the reasonableness of this rule, which imposed itself as a necessity at the given level of development of international relations in the organized community of nations. On the other hand, the right of veto cannot be justified from the standpoint of the progressive principles of modern international law; in this case, from the standpoint of the sovereign equality of states.

The main upholders of this theory are the Soviet theoreticians of international law, without exception. In the legal literature of the great Western powers, this theory is politically unpopular and is not readily supported, although it is invoked in all the speeches of their officials in the United Nations whenever they have had to defend their status and their right of veto in the Security Council. This was best shown in the Legal Committee at the eighth regular session of the U.N. General Assembly.

The main premises underlying this concept are, first, that the right of veto forces the great powers, permanent members of the Security Council, to pass consensual decisions concerning international peace and security. According to Kozhevnikov, "the Second World War has given the Big Three the leading role in conducting contemporary international policy; they were given this leading role neither accidentally nor arbitrarily, as was the case earlier in the capitalist world; it is based on the fact that these three great powers bore the main brunt of the war." Because of this "historical merit" and because of their responsibility for future peace they are the leading forces in world politics.

This viewpoint was elaborated in even greater detail by Levin. He believes that the great powers could ensure peace and observance of the norms of international law by acting in concordance as participants in an international organization and by having permanent seats in the organ which bears the primary responsibility for realizing the goals of the Organization (Article 24 of the Charter). However, the creation of the United Nations Organization in no way precludes disagreements and conflicts of interest between these states. What guarantees are there that some great powers which are permanent members of the Council will not try to turn the United Nations into an instrument of a bloc of states created within the organization, which would be used to impose the will of these states on other states? The guarantee, according to Levin, is found in the principle of unanimity of the permanent members of the Security Council. Lacharière arrives at a similar conclusion, albeit by another route. In his opinion, a consensus of the great powers is the goal of the modern international political community, and the rationale for such a goal is the need for political homogeneity in the modern-day international society. Legal counsel for the French delegation in the Legal Committee for many years and professor of international law, Charles Chaumont systematically enlarged upon Lacharière's thought in a series of lectures held in 1954–55. In his opinion, the principle of unanimity is a "technical necessity" for the effective regulation of international relations. There is no other legal mechanism which could regulate relations between the great powers so well as the right to veto.

The right of veto is appropriate for the present political order obtaining in the contemporary international community, composed as it is of the most diverse political, social and economic systems. Furthermore, as it was pointed out in the Legal Committee in 1953, the creation of the United Nations was made possible by the cooperation of all states, under the auspices of the great powers during the Second World War. The members of the United Nations have preserved their sovereignty, and the great powers, which are in a special situation and enjoy special powers in the world, have certain rights, which indeed are compatible with certain duties, and one of these rights is the right of veto. Thus the right of veto is the corollary of a specific duty.

Second, the voting procedure in the Security Council is, in the opinion of the Legal Committee, in complete accordance with international law. It was stated on one occasion in the Legal Committee that the most important principle in the Charter was the sovereign equality of states, large and small, and that this principle prevents any state from imposing its will upon another state or group of states. The conclusion was drawn that the veto was a guarantee against duress. According to the Four-Power Statement of 7 June 1945, the principle of unanimity requires the unanimous agreement of five permanent members, on the one hand, and the consent of two non-permanent members, on the other. This means that if nine out of ten nonpermanent members of the Security Council do not share the view of the five permanent members, they may also use the veto.

Third, the right of veto arises from the political and legal nature of the United Nations Organization. In an international organization such as the United Nations, the interests of minority groups should be protected by means which are not used in a national parliament. This is to say that majority rule cannot be applied in the Security Council. In 1946, Korovin wrote the following: "As we know, there are presently 51 states enrolled in the United Nations Organization, so that 26 states would constitute a majority. There are 21 republics in Central and South America. Therefore, if it were to happen that all the Latin American republics took a joint stand with the support of five Arab states, they would obtain a majority in the United Nations and could impose their will on the rest of mankind. Such a purely formal democracy, with no consideration for other material circumstances, is untenable even in a state, but much less on the international plane."

Let us analyze these assumptions. Does the Charter envisage the so-called "primary responsibility" of the five great powers which enjoy a privileged position in the Security Council? This question was debated at the San Francisco Conference, in Committee III/I. On that occasion, states Kelsen, the Soviet delegate made a statement to the effect that the privileged position of the great powers in the Security Council was enjoyed by virtue of the responsibilities and duties which were imposed upon them. Even the Cuban delegate, who was otherwise opposed to the right of veto, pointed out that the responsibility of the permanent members of the Security Council was greater than that of the non-permanent members. However, their responsibility was not defined in the Charter. Article 24, para. 1 of the Charter states: "In order to ensure prompt and effective action by the United Nations, its Members confer on the Security Council primary responsibility for the maintenance of international peace and security, and agree that in carrying out its duties under this responsibility the Security Council acts on their behalf." Hence, the responsibility is borne by the Security Council as a whole, and not just by its permanent members. The paragraph quoted above clearly shows that there is no difference in the responsibility borne by the permanent and non-permanent members.

Therefore, we may speak of the privileged position of the great powers, the permanent members of the Security Council, but not of any definite legal responsibility borne by them.

Second, any attempt to correlate the right of veto with the principle of sovereign equality of states would be indefensible.

The possibility that five non-permanent and two permanent members of the Security Council would use the veto is so remote that it is more hypothetical than real, for the simple reason that the great powers are interested in every international issue because of their foreign policy aims.

The right of veto by a permanent member constitutes its individual right. However, the theoretical possibility that nine non-permanent members of the Council would use the veto would amount to a collective exercise of a right. Where then is there any sovereign equality between a permanent and a non-permanent member of the Security Council? Their status differs both politically and legally, even though their legal responsibility is equal, as defined in the Charter.

The argument that the rights of the great powers derive from the duties assumed by them under the Statement of 7 June 1945, which sought to justify the use of the right of veto by a permanent member of the Security Council, can be countered by pointing out that by virtue of making a statement such as the above, four great powers may validly restrict specific acknowledged rights to someone's benefit, but rights can under no circumstances be unilaterally extended, as is done by the great powers when they interpret the right of veto in the Security Council in this way (e.g., the "double veto").

Third, it is true that the United Nations is not the same as a national parliament, particularly when disputes affecting the maintenance of international peace are concerned. However, this argument cannot be used to justify the right of veto for the permanent members of the Security Council. Practice has shown that these members have resorted to the veto not in order to protect minority interests but rather to protect great power interests.

Although the United Nations most probably could not have been created without conceding the right of veto to the great powers, this right could also have carved out for them a sphere of competence based on their very extensive powers as well as on certain, not very clearly defined, duties. However, the political antagonisms between the great powers soon flared up, often producing exceedingly strained situations. The principle of unanimity on which their joint operation was to function not only proved to be ineffective but actually became a stumbling block to the peaceful settlement of disputes. In fact, the right of veto lost its practical impact the moment the United Nations had to cope with the first open act of aggression in its history. When it became clear that the principle of unanimity could no longer be taken as a basis for maintaining international peace, the United Nations had no other choice than to make a *de facto* revision of the Charter by transferring competences of the Security Council to the General Assembly in cases when the former could no longer function as the main organ for the maintenance of peace and security.

As the membership of the United Nations grew, it was believed that the Security Council would take second place in importance. It was even thought that the diminished powers of the Security Council would cause the right of veto, as envisaged in the Charter, to disappear. This trend was viewed as a process of democratization in international life and perhaps even in international law. However, as the Organization came nearer to its goal of universality, the General Assembly became an unwieldy instrument, even though it has retained its importance as a forum for shaping world public opinion and a platform from which the lesser powers can make foreign policy declarations. The Security Council again appears to be a suitable organ through which the great powers, primarily the two superpowers, can conduct world affairs. The Security Council now finds it a very useful practice to work on the basis of consensus rather than voting.

IX. The Economic and Social Council

The growth of technology and advancement of civilization have promoted the economic interdependence of states. Every day there is an even greater exchange of raw materials and manufactures, for no country in the world can produce everything necessary for its economy from its national resources. This economic exchange must be legally regulated. Work began in this sphere under the League of Nations. At a conference held in June 1928, a final act was adopted banning restrictions on imports and exports; an international conference convened in February 1930 to discuss the question of economic treaties; on 12 June 1933, sixty-six states got together to discuss international monetary and economic problems. However, all these efforts by states to effect a legal regulation of the economic system on a world scale were unsuccessful.

After the Second World War, a more energetic approach was taken to international economic questions. The monetary and financial conference at Bretton Woods, held from 1–22 July 1944, led to the creation of two international organizations, as U.N. specialized agencies: the International Monetary Fund and the International Bank for Reconstruction and Development. The Conference also made a number of recommendations to the participating governments. Today, on the basis of the Charter, member states are obliged to cooperate in the international economic sphere and to undertake joint and separate action to this end. Unlike the Covenant of the League of Nations and as an addition to the Dumbarton Oaks proposals, the Charter provides for one additional main organ — the Economic and Social Council.

The Economic and Social Council is composed of 54 members, 18 of whom are elected each year by the General Assembly for a three-year term. Unlike in the Security Council, states may be immediately re-elected.

The Economic and Social Council has the following competences:

    a. to prepare or initiate reports on international economic, social, cultural, educational, health and related matters. The Council also makes recommendations on these questions to the General Assembly, to members of the United Nations and to the specialized agencies for which such recommendations would be of interest.

    b. to make recommendations concerning the respect for and observance of human rights and fundamental freedoms for all.

In order to carry out these tasks, the Economic and Social Council may:

    a. prepare draft conventions for submission to the General Assembly;

    b. convene international conferences on all matters falling within its competence;

    c. negotiate agreements and define the terms under which specialized agencies will be linked with the U.N. Organization (these agreements must be approved by the General Assembly); coordinate the work of the specialized agencies by means of consultations and make recommendations to this end, as well as recommendations to the General Assembly and members of the United Nations;

    d. provide information to the Security Council and give assistance at its request.

The Economic and Social Council also performs other tasks assigned to it by the General Assembly.

Every member of the Council has one representative in this organ, and only one vote. The great powers are elected to the Council as a matter of course. Small and medium-sized states do not object to this practice, because the great powers must take a part in international economic life in keeping with their great economic power.

Decisions in the Economic and Social Council are made by a simple majority of those members who are present and voting.

The Council meets whenever necessary, but it must convene at least twice a year. It may set up subsidiary organs, commissions and committees, which may work even when the Council is not in session. There are two types of commissions: commissions for technical matters within the competence of the Council, such as, for example, commissions for employment and economic development and for public finance, the Commission on Human Rights, the Commission on the Status of Women, the Commission on Narcotic Drugs, and four regional economic commissions: the Economic Commissions for Europe, Asia and the Far East, Latin America and the Middle East. *Ad hoc* committees may be set up for special matters, such as the committee for negotiations with specialized agencies, etc.

If the discussion of a matter is of interest for a member state or specialized agency, their representatives may be invited to take part in the discussion, but without the right to vote. The Economic and Social Council may organize special consultations with non-governmental organizations whose affairs fall within its competence.

Because many major economic problems today are dealt with by special United Nations institutions, such as the U.N.D.P., which handles questions of assistance to developing countries, UNIDO, which promotes industrial development, UNCTAD concerned with trade and development, and other bodies, the Economic and Social Council is increasingly acting as a coordinator. As a result member states now prefer to discuss their economic and social problems within the General Assembly committees.

X. The Trusteeship Council

Under the mandate system established after the First World War, the colonies of the defeated states were partially internationalized by being placed under the supervision of the League of Nations. After the Second World War, the system of trusteeship replaced the old mandate system, and the Trusteeship Council was set up as one of the main U.N. organs.

There are three kinds of members in the Trusteeship Council: those who administer trust territories, the permanent members of the Security Council which do not administer such territories, and enough other members elected for three-year terms by the General Assembly to make up a number equalling that of countries which administer trust territories and those which do not. This "equality" is rightly thought to be merely nominal. Because decisions are carried by a simple majority, the interests of the colonial bloc can prevail by winning only one vote from the opposite bloc.

The Trusteeship Council is one of the six main organs of the United Nations. However, it carries out its functions under the supervision of the General Assembly. Therefore any resolutions which run contrary to the interests of the peoples within the trust territories are opposed in the Assembly by the majority, which is anti-colonialist.

The Trusteeship Council discusses reports submitted by the administering authority; it receives and investigates petitions, consulting the administering authority when doing so; it carries out periodical tours of these territories and undertakes measures in accordance with the agreement on trusteeship. The administering authority submits a report to the General Assembly every year based on a questionnaire prepared by the Trusteeshp Council concerning the political, economic, social and educational progress of the inhabitants of these territories. The Trusteeship Council may seek the assistance of the Economic and Social Council and specialized agencies in performing its tasks.

Only a small number of trust territories still remains today, so that the continued existence of this organ is questionable.

XI. The Secretariat

The Secretary-General is the chief administrative officer of the United Nations. The Charter assigns him, but not the Secretariat as a whole, very important functions. It is contended by some that the Secretary-General is actually one of the main organs of the United Nations and that the Secretariat serves as his office. At first it was thought that he should act as president of the Organization. Later, the General Assembly restricted his powers by adopting various regulations and by establishing the administrative tribunal which evaluates his decisions. The functions of the Secretary-General are of an administrative and executive nature. As head of the U.N. administration, he may take part in meetings of the General Assembly, Security Council, Economic and Social Council, and Trusteeship Council. At each regular session of the General Assembly he submits an annual report on the work of the United Nations.

The Secretary-General may bring any matter threatening international peace and security to the attention of the Security Council. Upon the approval of the Security Council, he informs the Assembly on topics on the agenda of the Security Council which concern international peace and security. In addition to administrative powers, then, the Secretary-General also enjoys political pre-rogatives provided for under Article 99 of the Charter. He also receives reports containing information on non-self-governing territories and registers and pub-lishes international treaties.

The Secretary-General acts according to his own judgment. Neither he nor his staff receive or ask for instructions either from governments or from any other authority outside the United Nations. It is the duty of the Secretary-General and his staff to refrain from any action which would not be in keeping with the status of an international official, responsible only to the United Na-tions. It is the duty of the members of the United Nations to observe the strictly international character of the Secretary-General and his staff.

XII. Specialized Agencies

Introduction — Article 24 of the Covenant of the League of Nations en-visaged international organizations which would work under the supervision of the League, on the basis of joint agreements. Indeed, all future international organizations and all commissions established to deal with matters of world importance were to enter into a relationship with the League of Nations. This idea received its definitive shape in the Charter of the United Nations. Article 57 envisages specialized agencies created under international agreements. These agencies have international responsibilities, as defined in their basic in-struments, in the economic, social, cultural, educational, health and related fields.

Membership in the specialized agencies is not only open to members of the United Nations. Other countries may also join these international organiza-tions. According to the agreements concluded by some specialized agencies, U.N. members have the right to recommend that an application for mem-bership be refused.

The United Nations coordinates the policy and activities of the specialized agencies by means of recommendations and gives the initiative for the creation of new specialized agencies.

The specialized agencies must send regular annual reports to the Eco-nomic and Social Council. This organ has a coordinating committee composed of the U.N. Secretary-General and the executive heads of the agencies. The agreements also provide for a reciprocal participation of representatives of the Economic and Social Council and of the specialized agencies in each other's work. Representatives in the Economic and Social Council do not have voting rights, but they do have the right to submit formal recommendations and amendments, if requested by a full member of the Economic and Social Council or by any of its commissions and subsidiary bodies. Similarly, on the basis of the agreements, there is a reciprocal exchange of information. Recommendations can only be made by the United Nations, in its capacity as the central international organization in the contemporary community of nations. The specialized agencies are authorized to make international agreements with one another, provided they inform the Economic and Social Council about the nature and contents of these agreements. Many such agreements have already been concluded.

The specialized agencies agree to support the Security Council in implementing its decisions intended to maintain or establish international peace and security. They have also agreed to help the Trusteeship Council if so requested in order to promote the welfare and development of the peoples in non-self-governing territories.

The specialized agencies are legal entities. Under the Convention on the Privileges and Immunities of Specialized Agencies of November 21, 1947, they may conclude international agreements; they may acquire and transfer property and, finally, they have the right to initiate legal proceedings.

The agreements concluded with the thirteen specialized agencies contain standard provisions concerning representation of the United Nations and of the agency in question at meetings, the possibility of introducing topics for each other's agendas when so requested, exchange of information and documents, coordination of personnel and statistical services, and budgetary and financial arrangements. It is noteworthy that the specialized agencies have agreed to consider every recommendation by the United Nations and to make reports on the measures they have undertaken. The close link between the United Nations and the specialized agencies is demonstrated by their obligation to assist the Security Council in implementing its resolutions for the maintenance or establishment of international peace and international security. The specialized agencies cooperate with the United Nations in regard to promoting the welfare and advancement of peoples in non-self-governing territories. In 1947 the Economic and Social Council set up the Administrative Committee on Coordination (ACC) to supervise the proper implementation of the agreements on international cooperation and to eliminate any duplication of work and effort. The majority of the agreements concluded between the United Nations and specialized agencies provide for the right to send recommendations to the United Nations on matters within their competence.

So far, the following specialized agencies have been created: the International Labour Organization (ILO), the Food and Agriculture Organization of the United Nations (FAO), the United Nations Educational, Scientific and Cultural Organization (UNESCO), the International Civil Aviation Organization (ICAO), the International Bank for Reconstruction and Development (World

Bank), the International Monetary Fund (IMF), the International Development Association (IDA), the Universal Postal Union (UPU), the World Health Organization (WHO), the International Telecommunication Union (ITU), the World Meteorological Organization (WMO), the International Finance Corporation (IFC), and the Inter-Governmental Maritime Consultative Organization (IMCO).

2. The International Labour Organization — ILO existed even before the Second World War, unlike most of the other specialized agencies, which are of a more recent date. This organization was set up in 1919 at the Paris Peace Conference. Its original constitution was an integral part of the Treaty of Versailles. The matters with which this international organization is concerned are for the most part laid down in the preamble to the constitution. These include working hours, manpower utilization and prevention of unemployment, wages, industrial safety, protection of the interests of workers, pensions, disability compensation, protection of workers employed in foreign countries, recognition of the principle of equal wages for equal work, recognition of the principle of freedom of association, and technical assistance to underdeveloped countries. On 10 May 1944, the well-known Philadelphia declaration was adopted and included in the ILO constitution. This declaration reaffirmed the principles on which the ILO was founded. The declaration proclaims that all human beings, without discrimination, have the right to aspire both to material welfare and to spiritual development, freedom and the dignity of the human personality and economic security under equal conditions. In this declaration, the ILO endorsed the following important principles: labor is not a commodity; freedom of expression and association is essential for progress; poverty in any part of the world threatens the welfare of everyone.

At first, membership in the ILO was conditional on membership in the League of Nations. Later, countries which were not League members were accepted. According to its constitution, every member state of the United Nations may become a member if it accepts the obligations contained in its basic legal instrument. Non-member states may also join this international organization upon the approval of two thirds of the Conference.

The ILO has a very specific structure, which differs from that of the other U.N. specialized agencies. The International Labour Conference is the supreme policy-making organ and meets at least once a year. Every member state sends four delegates to the Conference, two government delegates, one delegate representing labor and one delegate representing management. Every delegate has a separate vote. The main task of the Conference is to set international labor standards either in international conventions or in recommendations. The conventions adopted by the ILO are binding on those states which ratify them. Recommendations need not be ratified, but it is the duty of every member state, within a specific time period of twelve to eighteen months from the time of the conference, to recommend to its competent constitutional bodies the adoption of the convention or the approval of the subject matter of the recommendation. The United Nations supervises implementation of an adopted convention. It may impose sanctions against any state violating a convention. What is more, states which have not ratified a given convention must submit annual reports on the state of their domestic "law and practice" in regard to the subject matter of the convention and must explain why the convention has not been ratified.

The Governing Body is the executive organ of the ILO. It is composed of 56 members: representatives of governments, labor representatives, and management representatives. In addition to electing the Director-General and supervising the work of the International Labour Office and the organization's committees and commissions, the Governing Body also lays down policy and working programs. The International Labour Office, with its headquarters in Geneva, constitutes the permanent secretariat of this organization.

3. The Food and Agriculture Organization — FAO — began operations on 16 October 1945, when its constitution was signed in Quebec. The primary goal of this organization is to improve nutrition in the world and to raise living standards; to achieve this goal, the organization promotes increased production and better distribution of all food and agricultural products from farms, forests, and fisheries. A special task is to improve the living conditions of rural populations and thus contribute to an expanding world economy.

The founding members of this international organization are listed in an annex to its constitution, but other countries may be admitted by a two-thirds majority vote at the Conference if they are willing to accept the obligations set forth in the constitution.

FAO organs include the Conference, Council and Director-General. The Conference is the supreme policy-making organ and is composed of one representative from every member state. It determines policy and approves the budget. The Council is made up of representatives from 42 countries elected by the Conference. The Council supervises the coordination of the work of intergovernmental organs in regard to the production, consumption, and distribution of food and agricultural commodities.

4. The United Nations Educational, Scientific and Cultural Organization (UNESCO) — adopted its constitution on 4 November 1946. The purpose of this international organization is to contribute to the peace and security by strengthening international cooperation in the sphere of education, science and culture, in order to further universal respect for justice, for the rule of law, for human rights and fundamental freedoms without discrimination. By using the means of mass communication, UNESCO seeks to promote popular education and the spread of culture and to encourage teaching and broader knowledge in the world. UNESCO programmes include elementary education, compulsory schooling and the raising of the level of teaching about the United Nations and human rights, and the exchange of scientific and educational experts.

Member states of the United Nations are automatically members of this organization. If a state is suspended or expelled from the United Nations, it is also suspended from this organization.

UNESCO organs are the General Conference, the Executive Board, and the Secretariat. The General Conference is composed of representatives from all member states and convenes every two years. It lays down policy and working programs and approves the budget for the next two-year period. The Executive Board is composed of 40 government representatives and sees to the implementation of programs. The Secretariat has a Director-General and an international staff. Every UNESCO member state has its own National Commission which, in addition to assisting in the implementation of UNESCO programs, acts as a liaison between UNESCO and the educational, scientific and cultural institutions in its own country and in all countries of the world.

5. The World Health Organization (WHO) — According to the constitution of WHO, health is not merely the absence of sickness or infirmity but a state of complete physical, mental and social well-being. Hence its purpose is to help all peoples of the world achieve the highest possible standard of health. To this end it acts as a leading and coordinating body in international health activities; it assists governments in improving public health services, gives necessary technical assistance, works to eradicate epidemics and other diseases, proposes conventions, agreements and rules on international health questions and undertakes all measures to achieve these purposes.

Membership in WHO is open to all states. Every country wishing to be a member of this international organization must submit an application, which is approved by a simple majority of votes.

The main organs of WHO are the World Health Assembly, the Executive Board and the Secretariat. The Assembly, which meets every year, is the chief body determining policy, the program of work, and also approves the budget. The Executive Board consists of representatives from 30 states elected by the Assembly and acts as the executive organ of the Assembly. The Secretariat consists of a Director-General and technical and administrative staff. This international organization also has technical committees of specialists from all parts of the world, who advise on technical matters involved in the adopted programmes.

6. The International Monetary Fund — *IMF* was esablished on 27 December 1945, when representatives of those countries whose quotas amounted to 80 percent of the resources of the Fund had deposited their instruments of ratification of the Bretton Woods Agreement. It is the task of this specialized U.N. agency to promote international monetary cooperation and the expansion of international trade as an important factor affecting the living standard of every nation. A special task of the IMF is to seek to stabilize foreign exchange rates, to promote the concluding of current exchange arrangements, and to prevent competitive exchange depreciations. The IMF undertakes fiscal and monetary measures to help countries overcome foreign exchange difficulties. The resources of the IMF are created by subscriptions from members as determined by the agreement. One part, as a rule 25 percent, is deposited in gold, and the remainder in national currency. The IMF also earns revenues from short-term investments and charges on its transactions.

Organs of the IMF are the Board of Governors, the Executive Directors, the Managing Director, the technical and administrative staff. The Board of Governors is the supreme organ and has been vested with virtually all the powers of the IMF. The board is composed of one governor and one alternate appointed by each member country. The number of votes enjoyed by the governors is in proportion to the quota. The executive directors take care of the day-to-day operations of the Fund and those affairs for which they receive authorization from the Board of Governors. Five of the executive directors are appointed by the members with the largest quotas, and the other fifteen are elected by the governors representing the other members. The managing director is appointed by the executive directors and presides over all their meetings. He is also head of the operating staff of the IMF and conducts its technical affairs.

The International Monetary Fund is a useful consulting center for its members on all current fiscal and foreign exchange problems.

7. The International Bank for Reconstruction and Development (World Bank) — As early as at the Bretton Woods Conference, the United Nations agreed that the primary purpose of this organization should be to provide assistance by making capital available, at low interest rates, for projects which would develop the productive resources of the states receiving the loans. The Bank also assists private foreign investment by providing guarantees and participating in loans and other investments. If private capital is not available, the Bank provides loans on reasonable terms out of its own capital or from funds raised by it.

The IBRD has a board of governors, executive directors, and a president. The board of governors is vested with all the powers of the Bank. It is composed of one governor and alternate appointed by each member state. Every member state has 250 votes, but it may gain more votes by increasing its subscription to the Bank's capital. The board of governors has devolved many of its powers on the executive directors, of whom there are presently 20. The executive directors elect the president, who is in charge of the current affairs of the Bank.

The Bank has assisted many countries in their economic development by providing loans and other services, and particularly by giving advice. However, this assistance has not been able to meet the ever growing needs of the large number of developing countries. Sometimes the Bank's policy is rightly criticized, for instance, when it grants loans to the Republic of South Africa, which has been condemned by the General Assembly in a series of resolutions for its racist policy and violation of human rights.

8. The International Development Association — *IDA* is a new lending agency which was created on 24 September 1960, to make long-term loans to developing countries on easy terms and in some cases even interest free. The IBRD is responsible for administering the Association, which was set up to supplement its activities. The board of governors and executive directors of the World Bank hold the same functions in the IDA. The president of the Bank is also president of the IDA.

9. The International Finance Corporation — *IFC* became a specialized agency of the United Nations on 20 February 1957. Although this organization also works closely with the World Bank, it is a separate legal entity with its own funds. The Corporation is open to all states which are members of the World Bank. It is the purpose of this specialized agency to promote the economic growth of member states, particularly developing countries, by investing in private enterprises. The Corporation often makes its investments in association with private investors and does not require government guarantees of repayment. The IFC also acts as a clearing house for investment opportunities for both domestic and foreign capital. The Corporation is controlled by the Board of Governors, which consists of the Governors and alternates of the IBRD who represent countries which are at the same time members of the Corporation.

10. The International Civil Aviation Organization (ICAO) — A special convention signed at the 1944 Chicago Conference established the International Civil Aviation Organization. The purpose of this specialized agency is to promote the principles and technology of international civil aviation, by providing assistance to member states in planning and developing international air transport.

States accepting and ratifying the Chicago Convention on International Civil Aviation become members of this international organization. Other states may also be admitted to the ICAO by a four-fifths majority vote by the Assembly.

There are three main bodies in this agency: the Assembly, composed of member states, each having one vote, the Council, and the Secretary-General. The Assembly determines policy, approves the budget, and decides on all matters which are not in the exclusive competence of the Council. The Assembly is convened by the Council every three years. The Council is presently composed of representatives of 30 states elected by the Assembly on the basis of their importance in international civil aviation and with an eye to an equitable geographic distribution. The Council is an executive body; it appoints the Secretary-General and administers the finances of the ICAO. It also sets standards in order to make international provisions regulating international civil aviation as uniform as possible; it collects and publishes useful information. The Secretary-General appoints the staff of the Secretariat and supervises its work.

11. The Universal Postal Union (UPU) — The Berne Treaty which came into force on 1 July 1875, created the General Postal Union, which was given its present name at the Second International Postal Congress in Paris in 1878. The Universal Postal Convention has undergone several revisions.

The purpose of this international organization is to ensure the normal functioning and improvement of various postal services. Members of the UPU have formed a single postal territory within which there is an unhindered reciprocal exchange of letter-post items. The provisions of the convention lay down the basic rates, weight and size limits of mail. All members are obliged to comply with the provisions of the convention. Almost every country in the world is a member of the UPU. The Universal Postal Union is composed of the Universal Postal Congress, the Executive Council, the Consultative Council for Postal Studies and the International Bureau. The Congress meets once every five years to amend or supplement the Universal Postal Convention.

12. The International Telecommunication Union (ITU) — This international organization has been in existence since 17 May 1865. An international convention on telecommunications was adopted on 2 October 1947, at a conference held in Atlantic City and came into force on 1 January 1954. The ITU has been a U.N. specialized agency since 10 January 1949.

The International Telecommunication Union promotes international cooperation in order to improve the rational utilization of telecommunications and to promote the expansion of technical services. Most important, the Union apportions the radio spectrum for radio communications services and registers the radio frequency assignments to individual stations. It also fosters the adoption of measures to assure the safety of life with the help of telecommunications; it carries out studies in this field, makes recommendations, and compiles and publishes useful information for its members.

The International Telecommunication Union Organization is composed of the Plenipotentiary Conference as the supreme organ, administrative conferences, the Administrative Council, the General Secretariat, the International Frequency Registration Board, International Telegraph and Telephone Consultative Committee and the International Radio Consultative Committee.

13. The World Meteorological Organization (WMO) — International cooperation in the field of meteorology dates back to 1853, when an international conference was held in Brussels to work out a program for compiling meteorological data from observations made by ships at sea. The International Meteorological Organization was founded in 1878 in Utrecht; a convention adopted in Washington in 1947, which came into force on 23 March 1950, established the World Meteorological Organization. WMO has been a U.N. specialized agency since 20 December 1951.

14. The Inter-Governmental Maritime Consultative Organization (IMCO) — The purpose of this international organization is to create suitable machinery for cooperation between governments in the sphere of legal regulation and practice in regards to technical matters, particularly safety at sea; it considers all questions concerning shipping, which are referred to it by any organs or specialized agencies of the United Nations; it organizes the exchange of information and drafts international conventions and agreements on maritime affairs.

The IMCO has an Assembly composed of representatives of all of its members, an 18-member Council, a 16-member Maritime Safety Committee and a Secretariat, which is headed by a secretary-general.

15. The International Atomic Energy Agency — *IAEA* is not a specialized agency of the United Nations. It is an autonomous inter-governmental organization which operates "under the aegis" of the United Nations. It was created for the purpose of promoting the peaceful use of atomic energy. The agreement on the Agency's working relationship with the United Nations was approved by the General Conference of the agency on 23 October 1957, and by the U.N. General Assembly on 14 November 1957. This international organization was created in order to accelerate and enlarge the contribution of atomic energy to peace, health and prosperity in the entire world. According to its statute, the IAEA must, to the best of its ability, see to it that the assistance provided by it, at its request or under its supervision, is not used in order to further any military purpose.

The chief functions of the Agency are to assist research and practical application of atomic energy for peaceful purposes, including the generation of electric energy. In doing so, the Agency should devote special attention to underdeveloped regions. The Agency is also to assist in securing services of procuring material and equipment. It promotes the exchange of scientific and technical information on the peaceful use of atomic energy; it encourages the exchange and further training of scientists in this field; in cooperation with the competent U.N. organs it sets standards for protection and safety of health, which may be threatened during the use of atomic energy. The Agency concludes agreements with U.N. specialized agencies having a particular interest in atomic energy.

16. The World Intellectual Property Organization (WIPO) — was established by a convention signed in July 1976 in Stockholm, which came into force on 26 April 1978, after it had been ratified by ten member states of the International Union for the Protection of Industrial Property and seven members of the International Union for Protection of Literary and Artistic Works. Since the agreement with the United Nations was concluded in 1974, it has had the status of a specialized agency. Its organs are the General Assembly, the Conference, the Coordinating Committee, and the Secretariat. WIPO has its headquarters in Geneva.

17. The United Nations Industrial Development Organization (UNIDO) — was established by the convention adopted on 8 April 1979 in Vienna and came into force at the end of the same year after 21 ratification instruments were submitted. This organization had been acting as a specialized body of the United Nations since 1966. UNIDO's organs are: The General Conference; the Board for Industrial Development; the Committee for Programme and Budget; and the Secretariat. UNIDO has its headquarters in Vienna.

XIII. Regional Arrangements and Agencies

The United Nations Charter permits the concluding of regional arrangements and the establishment of regional agencies for the purpose of maintaining international peace and security, provided they are in accordance with the purposes and principles of the United Nations. Actually, regional arrangements and agencies are approved if they fit in with the political and legal system of the United Nations. The Charter calls upon member states to make every effort to settle local disputes by means of these regional arrangements or agencies before referring them to the Security Council. The regional agency is thus competent in the first instance for the peaceful settlement of local disputes. The Security Council may not interfere with any proceedings in this respect on the part of a regional agency and indeed is obliged to assist it. The Security Council is also authorized to use these agencies when implementing enforcement measures. Every measure taken by a regional agency or on the basis of regional arrangements concerning international peace and security must be reported to the Security Council.

Present-day regional arrangements and agencies include: the Organization of American States, the Arab League, NATO, the Western European Union, the Council of Europe, the Nordic Council, the European Coal and Steel Community, the European Economic Community (Common Market), the Warsaw Pact, and the Council for Mutual Economic Assistance of European People's Democracies (CMEA)

XIV. Other International Organizations

There are many international organizations formed by states which operate outside the framework of the United Nations. Some writers refer to them as administrative unions. These international organizations are increasingly of a regional character, because the United Nations is taking over the functions of universal organizations. These "administrative unions" include, for instance, the International Union for the Protection of Industrial Property, the European Payments Union, and the Danube Commission. All these international organizations, or unions, deal with special aspects of international law, such as international railway, monetary, copyright, and river navigation law and other special international law.

There are also a large number of so-called *non-governmental organizations* (NGOs), whose activities have an international character but whose members are not states but other legal entities and individuals. Because of the special experience and the technical knowledge they possess, non-governmental organizations are often consulted by the Economic and Social Council. These organizations, which have acquired a consultative status in relationship to the United Nations, are divided into two categories: Category A and Category B. Category A covers those non-governmental organizations which have a basic interest in the economic and social problems dealt with by the Economic and Social Council. These would include for instance, the International Chamber of Commerce, the International Cooperative Alliance, the Interparliamentary Union and others. Category B includes non-governmental organizations of more restricted interest in the activities of the Economic and Social Council, such as the international institutes for public law, for criminal law, for finance, for administrative sciences, the International Union of Architects, etc. There are over one hundred other non-governmental organizations listed by the United Nations.

Chapter Three: Man As a Subject of International Law

I. Introduction

Theoretical Concepts — United Nations Charter — Universal Declaration of Human Rights — Human Rights Covenants — Proclamation of Teheran

1. Theroetical Concepts — The struggle for recognition of human rights has a long history. It was waged in the slave-owning states of antiquity and is still continuing to this day in various forms. Of relevance for international law is the period of transition from feudal to capitalist society, when the bourgeoisie was challenging the feudal privileges that used to be handed down from generation to generation, when it was looking for new manpower and demanding free competition in the market place, under the watchword of freedom for the individual and equality of all people, regardless of origin. At that time, Hugo Grotius defined international law as regulating not only relations between states but also relations between individuals, relations between the subjects of different states.

As the powerful bourgeois states began to take shape, they became more interested in their state prerogatives. Their legal theoreticians began to elaborate the theory of state sovereignty, dividing international law into public and private. According to their notions, international law only regulated relations between states. The individual was completely ignored as a subject of international law. International protection of the interests of individual persons existed only insofar as they were protected by the laws of the states of which they were citzens, as the so-called classical political rights won in various bourgeois states were valid only within that state and not in other countries. This international order also drew a distinction between those states which were considered civilized and those countries which were exploited by the powerful European bourgeois states.

The theoreticians of that time asserted that international law existed for the sake of state interests and not to promote the interests of individuals. Consequently, its purpose was to protect state interests in the first instance, and insofar as the interests of individual citizens became involved, they were protected by their state. The interests of individuals were thereby protected by virtue of the fact that they were citizens of given states. If individuals are mentioned in international law, it is only in connection with states which wish to regulate a certain relationship with one another and must therefore bring their internal legislation governing the behavior of their subjects into accord. On the basis of these notions, which belong to a theory that we would refer to as "negatory" in regard to recognition of man as a subject of international law, the individual is an object of inter-state regulation and not a subject governed by international law.

For three full centuries the idea has prevailed that international law regulates only relations between states and not relations between individuals. Jellinek, Oppenheim, Tripel, and Gidel held this opinion. It has not even been abandoned in modern-day writing on international law, although its proponents are not so dogmatic any more, as it is no longer popular to deny human rights even in the international sphere.

Modern proponents of this theory base their arguments on the dependence of the individual on the state: physical persons in international law acquire rights and duties on the basis of international treaties, which are the result of the mutual consent of states; another kind of dependence of the individual on the state is seen, according to these theoreticians, in the exercise of human rights in the international sphere. If an individual suffers injury, he is not able to take recourse to any of the international courts for enforcement of his rights but must seek diplomatic remedy (the state of which he is a citizen takes up the dispute). This second reason has served some theoreticians as the basis for their negatory view (Greene). Others, however, such as Sieber, include this notion in the general definition of subjects of international law.

Modern Soviet legal theory is unanimous in denying the personality of the individual in international law, although Soviet theoreticians use different arguments. Yanovski refers to international law as a legal discipline which regulates relations between sovereign states. He follows the line of reasoning taken by Levin in 1948, to the effect that a subject of international law must take part in creating norms of international law. Krilov has argued his negatory view in the following way: to recognize a direct international personality to the individual would be tantamount to allowing imperialist states to protect the rights of individuals. This view has been elaborated by a large number of internationalists in the socialist countries (Tomko, Morozov), and was even propounded by the International Association of Democratic Jurists at their meeting in Brussels in 1963.

However, there is a growing body of specialists in international law who reject the above theory and allow for a full international personality of the individual. In contrast to the individualists, these theoreticians see the person as a special subject, alongside states and international organizations.

The adherents to this theory develop their arguments in different ways. Reuter, for instance, points to the rights and obligations man has already possessed for a long time in the international context, and goes on to seek ways and means for the enforcement of these rights. In his opinion, the absence of machinery for the realization of human rights at the international level testified only to the incomplete nature of the legal personality of the individual. O'Connell speaks of the "international personality" of the individual, because the rights and duties which a person holds in international affairs are not the same and can never be the same as the rights and duties of states, in view of their different activities. The prominent legal specialists Alfaro and Cassin also join in to acknowledge the international personality of the individual. The former invokes the Declaration on Non-Self-Governing Territories and the decisions of the Economic and Social Council, while the latter refers to the Universal Declaration of Human Rights.

The two theories described above are poles apart. One recognizes and the other denies man as a subject of international law. In the middle ground between these two extremes there is a large body of authors whose views represent a kind of compromise. They work on the assumption that man cannot be an object of regulation by international law without having the status of an international subject. Daam feels that "to a certain extent" the individual is also invested with international rights and duties, while Bishop concludes, in view of the vital interest of the individual to enjoy protection under international law as well, that in a foreseeable future we will develop a procedural mechanism which will enforce the protection of human rights. Birkin propounds a similar view, pointing out that from the standpoint of *de lege lata* not very much has been achieved in regard to the position of the individual in international law, but that, *de lege ferenda*, the individual will assume an increasingly important place in the relations regulated by international law.

The majority of Yugoslav experts hold a similar view. Professors Radojković and Avramov acknowledge only the tendency to recognize the individual as a subject of international law. They link this tendency with the mechanism for the exercise of rights by their holders. Avramov states that international practice has to a certain degree confirmed the notion that the individual's international personality has been recognized through the protection of human rights. Andrassy is inclined to agree, because "the study of the individual as a subject of international law is acquiring more and more new and compelling arguments."

The special status of the individual in international law is discussed in the works of some internationalists who accord man as an individual only a certain kind of personality. Verdross, for instance, speaks of a passive personality. This passive personality is the consequence of a physical person's inability to submit a complaint against a given state to international bodies. Guggenheim sees the individual as an intermediate subject of international law, because, in general, the individual is given rights or duties only through the agency of the state of which he is a citizen. Bartoš views man as "a reflexive subject of international law, i.e. a subject upon whom rights are conferred not directly but through the medium of the international legal order." The rules of international law which protect the individual would, therefore, be only "reflexive rights," i.e. "the reflection of the objective legal order" for him.

In contradistinction to all these concepts are those theories which see man as the exclusive subject of international law. These are the so-called "individualist" theories. They follow diverse lines of reasoning to arrive at the conclusion that man should be recognized as a subject of international law and find a variety of justifications for such a conclusion.

According to Westlake, the rights and duties of states are none other than the rights and duties of individuals. Krabbe goes even further by stating that only individuals are subjects of international law. Georges Scelle agrees with Krabbe's idea but gives it his own interpretation. According to him, international society is composed of individuals, and for this reason man must be the subject of international law, while the state constitutes an apparatus for regulating the common interests of individuals. Hence the state is not a subject of international law; only the people making up international society are subjects. According to Remmau's conception, states are members of the international community, while man is the subject of international law. In reaching this conclusion, he has been influenced by German federal law, i.e. the relationship between the federation and its members. Kaufmann is of the same opinion and in support he cites the decisions handed down by the U.S. Supreme Court and the German Federal Court in the years before the Second World War. On the basis of these judgements, the rights of individuals may derive directly from international treaties.

After the First World War, a group of internationalists appeared (Jouffre de Lapradelle, Scelle, Birkin, Niemeyer, Lauterpacht, Kelsen, Verdross, Segal), which was joined by a notable number of Greek jurists (Politis, Tenekides, Seferiades, Spiropoulos), propounding the view that man is a subject of present-day international law and that he appears in this capacity largely as a result of the development in international social relations. Politis's plea that the state must no longer be an iron cage in which the individual is a prisoner is well-known. Today the notion is becoming increasingly accepted in legal theory that the state is only a means, while man is the ultimate purpose of any law and hence of international law and that, therefore, the individual must be regarded as a subject of international law.

Authors who subscribe to the negatory theory either totally or with some reservations make reference to international protection of the individual. Thus, terminologically, the theory is accepted that the rights of the individual are protected through the agency of the state to which he belongs. However, to-day international law recognizes specific rights to individuals and imposes specific obligations, regardless of whether or not these rights and duties feature in the internal legislation of the state. Quite aside from any sanction by municipal law, contemporary international law recognizes the personality of the individual, regardless of the scope (so far still partial) of his rights and duties and regardless of the absence of effective machinery to guarantee their realization. For this reason we prefer to speak of the international rights and duties of man rather than of the international protection of the individual.

2. The United Nations Charter acknowledges man as a personality in international law.

The Preamble to the Charter states: "We the peoples of the United Nations determined . . . to reaffirm faith in fundamental human rights, in the dignity and worth of the human person, in the equal rights of men and women and of nations large and small . . . have resolved to combine our efforts to accomplish these aims." In other articles of the Charter, human rights are defined in greater detail. Article 1, para. 3, calls for the promotion and encouragement of respect for human rights and fundamental freedoms "for all, without distinction as to race, sex, language, or religion." Chapter IX, which regulates international economic and social cooperation, reiterates the demand for a universal and effective respect for human rights, without discrimination. Chapter XII concerning the international trusteeship system, contains similar provisions. The U.N. Charter provides for two main organs to see to the enforcement of these rules. The Economic and Social Council is authorized to make recommendations "for the purpose of promoting respect for, and observance of human rights and fundamental freedoms for all." Under Article 13 of the Charter, the General Assembly is authorized to assist in the realization of human rights and fundamental freedoms.

These provisions on human rights in the U.N. Charter constitute general rules of positive international law, even though the Charter does not provide guarantees for their enforcement. At any rate, under Article 38 of the Statute of the International Court of Justice, these are general rules of law contained in a basic legal act of the present-day international community.

3. The Universal Declaration of Human Rights — On 10 December 1948, the General Assembly adopted under Resolution 217 (III) the Universal Declaration of Human Rights, as the culmination of three years of work by the Commission on Human Rights.

The Universal Declaration contains traditional political rights, personal rights enjoying legal protection, economic and social rights and the right to share in cultural life and scientific advancement. The corresponding duties of individuals to the community are also envisaged. The rights and freedoms enumerated in the Declaration may not be exercised contrary to the purposes and principles of the United Nations. The Declaration prohibits any discrimination based on the political or international status of the country or territory to which a person belongs. The Declaration was proclaimed as "a common standard of achievement for all peoples and all nations, to the end that every individual and every organ of society, keeping this Declaration constantly in mind, shall strive by teaching and education to promote respect for these rights and freedoms and by progressive measures, national and international, to secure their universal and effective recognition and observance, both among the peoples of member states themselves and among the peoples of territories under their jurisdiction."

From the standpoint of society in general, the Declaration undoubtedly constitutes a progressive document. A political and legal standard of human rights on a universal scale has been established. The question remains, however, of the import of the Declaration from the legal standpoint. Kelsen categorically denies the legal effect of the Declaration. According to this writer, the Declaration as a "common standard of achievement" may have a moral but not a legal significance. However, Bartoš very properly argues that the Declaration is a "reflection of the legal conviction of the majority in the United Nations, and that it is therefore the legal conviction of civilized nations. Such a source of law is not only an ideal for the United Nations but also a legal platform for the preparation of further texts. All the organs of the United Nations are obliged in their further work to adhere to this seminal document. Hence every action impairing the *status quo* in a state should be taken to be contrary to this document." On the other hand, Bartos also feels that the states cannot be expected to carry out an immediate change in their present legal and social standards, because there are states which do not have the material means, for instance, to provide social insurance forthwith, as expressly required by the Declaration.

The Declaration undoubtedly has a legal as well as a moral character. It was adopted in a lawful proceeding. Its provisions are in accordance with the Charter, and insofar as they go further than the Charter, they certainly do not violate it. The legal value of the Declaration is undoubted, although we feel that the extent to which it is binding is open to debate. The Universal Declaration of Human Rights is an instrument of a constitutional character which defines in precise terms the general rules of law contained in the Charter and assigns them varying degrees of binding force.

4. Human Rights Covenants — In 1948, the Commission on Human Rights prepared the first draft of a covenant on human rights. From 1948 to 1957, the provisions to be included in this historical document of international law were studied in the organs of the United Nations. In 1951 it was decided in the Economic and Social Council and in the General Assembly that two covenants should be prepared, one concerning economic, social and cultural rights, and the other setting forth civil and political rights.

On 17 December 1966, the U.N. General Assembly unanimously adopted the International Covenant on Civil and Political Rights and the International Covenant on Economic, Social and Cultural Rights. A third document, the Optional Protocol to the Covenant on Civil and Political Rights, was passed by a majority of votes.

The covenants are a further elaboration and close legal definition of the principles of international human rights contained in the Charter and the Universal Declaration of Human Rights, "recognizing that . . . the ideal of free human beings enjoying civil and political freedom and freedom from fear and want can only be achieved if conditions are created whereby everyone may enjoy his political and civil rights, as well as his economic, social and cultural rights."

The covenants are open for signature by member states of the United Nations or any of its specialized agencies, by states parties to the Statute of the International Court of Justice, and by any other state which is invited by the General Assembly to accede to them. The covenants are subject to ratification, and instruments of ratification must be deposited with the U.N. Secretary-General; the covenants were to come into force three months from the day the thirty-fifth instrument of ratification or accession was deposited. The provisions of the covenants apply to all parts of federal states, without any limitations or exceptions. Today the covenants are in force, as 35 member states have ratified them.

5. The Proclamation of Teheran — In commemoration of the twentieth anniversary of the adoption of the Universal Declaration of Human Rights, an international conference on human rights was held in Teheran in 1968 to discuss the further development and enforcement of political, civil, economic, social and cultural rights and the elimination of all forms of discrimination, particularly the policy of *apartheid.* The conference was attended by representatives of 84 countires and 48 inter-governmental and non-governmental international organizations.

The program of the conference had been drawn up by a preparatory committee and included an evaluation of the measures undertaken in the human rights filed by the United Nations and its specialized agencies, and an assessment of the methods and techniques used in observing and promoting human rights and fundamental liberties. A future program for safeguarding human rights and other liberties for all peoples in the world without discrimination was also formulated.

Contrary to expectations, the Teheran Conference did not produce a charter on human rights that lived up to the Universal Declaration of Human Rights. Taking place at a time of heightened tensions in the world, the conference reached the best possible compromise under the circumstances, embodied in a text called a proclamation. It ranked about the same as one of the better resolutions of the main organs of the United Nations, the only difference being that it was adopted at an international conference, convened to study a special domain in the International Year of Human Rights.

Nevertheless, the Proclamation of Teheran defined the major humanitarian issues, albeit partially and in a compromise form. Of significance were the affirmation of the high value and universality of the Universal Declaration on the Granting of Independence to Colonial Countries and Peoples, the Convention on the Elimination of All Forms of Racial Discrimination and other adopted conventions and declarations in the field of human rights. Finally, the Proclamation of Teheran represents one further document whose general endorsement of the rights and obligations deriving from the Universal Declaration and the above-mentioned conventions represents a moral and political legal basis. *Apartheid* is described as a crime against humanity, and the struggle against this crime is acknowledged as legal. The wholesale abrogation of human rights as the result of aggression and armed conflicts was condemned; the causes and effects of flagrant violations of human rights were noted, such as discrimination and the growing gulf between the economically advanced countries and the developing countries, which is increasingly handicapping the effective observance of human rights in the international community. Finally, all peoples and governments were called upon to safeguard the principles proclaimed in the Universal Declaration of Human Rights, so that all human beings would enjoy "a life consonant with freedom and dignity and conducive to physical, mental, social and spiritual welfare."

The compromise that the superpowers had reached with one another before the conference and the atmosphere of strained relations (the Middle East and Vietnam hostilities) greatly impeded the work of the five-nation drafting committee (Mr. Artucio for Uruguay, Mr. Daftari for India, Professor Jankovic for Yugoslavia, Professor Kanyiehamba for Uganda, and Professor MacDonald for Canada), effectively preventing the drafting of a better text as regards content and form.

II. Fundamental Human Rights

Right of Peoples to Self-determination — Civil and Political Rights — Economic, Social and Cultural Rights — Prohibition of Slavery — Nuremberg Principles — Genocide — Prohibition of Discrimination — Refugees — Minorities — Right to Asylum

1. The Right of Peoples to Self-Determination — The right of peoples to self-determination was being discussed as far back as the Renaissance, but it was particularly topical during the French Revolution. The actual beginning of this right dates from the first socialist revolution in 1917 and the writings of its leader, Vladimir Ilyich Lenin. Lenin indefatigably championed recognition of this right, basing his arguments on the Second International's London congress in 1896, when for the first time the proletariat raised the issue of the self-determination of peoples, and on the congress of the Russian Social Democratic Workers Party of 1903. Lenin did not base his theory on the 17th and 18th century petty bourgeois postulates which considered this right to be utopian, with the result that peoples remained oppressed within the borders of certain states. He called for the creation of independent national states by secession from alien national collectives.

Woodrow Wilson was also a proponent of the self-determination of nations. This right was proclaimed in his Fourteen Points of 1919, and he specifically mentioned this right in an address to the American Congress. He stated that this right was not a phrase but an imperative principle. Wilson proposed that the right of peoples to self-determination should be incorporated in the Covenant of the League of Nations, but the colonial powers managed to thwart this attempt. Wilson's ideas should be considered against the background of the involuted international situation created after the First World War. American capital was interested in certain underdeveloped regions (primarily colonies), but the colonial powers wanted to keep it out. The proclamation of the principle of self-determination of peoples would result in many colonies gaining their independence, but at the same time it would open the floodgates to foreign capital. Between the two world wars, the right of peoples to self-determination evolved from an internal expedient into an international political principle.

During the Second World War, the right of peoples to self-determination became highly controversial. Item 3 of the Atlantic Charter recognizes "the right of all peoples to choose the form of government under which they will live." In London, the Allied Powers acknowledged the right to self-determination, thus rebutting Hitler's thesis of *Lebensraum,* according to which only the great nations, first and foremost the German Reich, had the right to "living space." The Dumbarton Oaks proposals did not include the right to self-determination, but at the insistence of many small nations present in San Francisco this right was included in the U.N. Charter. Article 1, para. 2, and Article 55 of the Charter specifically deal with this right. The right of peoples to self-determination today is no longer an international political right but an international legal principle, despite views to the contrary, which in some cases are put forward as official policies of governments (e.g. the Netherlands). This principle, which is only mentioned in the Charter, has been further elaborated in the Covenants on Human Rights. Both covenants begin by setting forth provisions on the right of peoples to self-determination. This first article of both conventions was approved after long debate and is given below:

> 1. All peoples have the right to self-determination. By virtue of this right, they freely determine their political status and freely pursue their economic, social and cultural development.
> 2. All peoples may, for their own ends, freely dispose of their natural wealth and resources without prejudice to any obligations arising out of international economic cooperation, based upon the principle of mutual benefit, and international law. In no case may a people be deprived of its own means of subsistence.
> 3. The States Parties to the present Covenant, including those having responsibility for the administration of Non-Self-Governing and Trust Territories, shall promote the realization of the right of self-determination, and shall respect that right, in conformity with the provisions of the United Nations Charter.

In our opinion, this article sanctions the right of every individual to opt freely for the political, economic, social and cultural status of that community to which he belongs. This is actually a personal right, which is exercised collectively. If this were only a collective right of a people and not a personal right, then, among other things, it would be pointless to include it in a covenant on human rights.

The same article imposes the obligation upon all states, including the non-self-governing territories and trust territories, and all others which in any way control the exercise of this right by other people, to observe this right and to promote its realization. Later, a provision was included in this article to the effect that the right of peoples to self-determination implied a permanent sovereignty over their natural wealth and resources. It was also stated that no people could be deprived of their own means of subsistence, regardless of whether or not a state can invoke a right which it had acquired. Some new conceptions in international law have thus come into being: first, that the exercise of the right to self-determination is not the privilege of those peoples who have had this right recognized in special international treaties; second, that the principle of legitimacy in regard to rule over colonial peoples — publicly endorsed in the League of Nations, Lord Cecil being one of its most vociferous supporters — becomes invalid.

2. Civil and Political Rights — *England's Magna Carta (Magna Carta Libertatum* of 1215) contained provisions concerning individual liberties in addition to rules on feudal organization; in another text (the Bill of Rights of 1688), the political rights of citizens (the right of petition, freedom of speech in parliament, and so forth) were mentioned in addition to restrictions on royal prerogatives. However, these legal documents from the 13th and 17th centuries were compromises between the peerage and the monarchs. They were primarily intended to settle questions of government powers and only secondarily guaranteed citizens political rights. Human rights were not established in them as a principle.

The French Declaration of the Rights of Man and the Citizen proclaimed the political and some personal rights of the members of the bourgeois class. This was an act which was invoked by citizens throughout Europe at that time. However, the rights defined in the French Declaration only referred to the so-called "civilized world." These were rights of "citizens," but not rights for the millions of "aborigines" in the many colonies held by European powers.

The rights of all people, without restriction to region and without discrimination, were set forth in the Charter of the United Nations and in the Universal Declaration of Human Rights, and thus for the first time in the history of mankind acquired a universal character. These rights were given broader scope and received legal force only in the Covenant on Civil and Political Rights. The rights enumerated in this document represent the maximum possible achievement at the present level of development of international relations. At the same time, this maximum possible realization of human rights is the minimum standard of human rights, below which states as a rule must not sink.

In listing the civil and political rights of man, the Covenant begins with the principle of self-determination of peoples and their inalienable sovereignty over natural wealth and resources. A nation must be free before it can talk about the freedom of the individual. The other articles cover a broad range of democratic rights and liberties. There were very few opponents to adoption of these rights, because they were largely rights which had already been enshrined in the constitutions of the majority of countries: the right to life as the inalienable right of every individual; the right to freedom and security of the person; the right to freedom of movement and free choice of place of abode; the right of equality before courts and tribunals; the right to freedom of thought, conscience and religion; the right of peaceful assembly; the right of peaceful association, including association in trade unions; the right to take part in the conduct of public affairs; the right to vote; the right to be given equal treatment before the law. It is specifically stated that no one may be held in slavery or servitude or may be subjected, without his free consent, to medical or scientific experimentation.

One of the basic assumptions of the Covenant on Civil and Political Rights is that the democratic freedoms and rights of man are directly dependent on the safeguarding of peace and security. History has shown more than once that whenever preparations for war are made, democratic freedoms and human rights are abrogated. For this reason, prohibition of war-like propaganda and discrimination receive special mention in the covenant.

The covenant provides for two kinds of measures in enforcing these civil and political rights: a. measures for implementation of provisions of the covenant on a national scale and b. international measures.

a. All parties to this covenant have undertaken the obligation to observe all the rights recognized by the covenant. If any of these rights have not yet been recognized by some of the signatory states, these states undertake to adopt legislative or other measures to ensure the enjoyment of such rights by all individuals in their territory. In order to safeguard civil and political rights as fully as possible, every state signatory undertook the duty to provide for each person an effective legal remedy and to develop the judiciary for their proper implementation.

Departures from specific articles of the covenant are possible only in the event of an exceptional public emergency threatening the survival of the nation. Even in this instance, however, states cannot enforce measures which are inconsistent with their obligations under international law.

b. The international measures provide for the formation of the Human Rights Committee, composed of 18 members of high moral character and recognized competence in the field of human rights. The Committee began its work in 1976.

3. Economic, Social, and Cultural Rights — Economic, social and cultural rights were subjects of long debate in the United Nations. Their enforcement did not depend simply on the will of governments but on actual social and economic conditions. Mindful of this fact, and mindful of the insistence by some states that these rights should not be included in a legal text, the United Nations recommended at first that only civil and political rights should be dealt with in the covenant. At its 11th session in 1950, the Economic and Social Council considered the draft of the covenant and decided to ask for an opinion from the General Assembly on the possibility of adding economic, social and cultural rights. At its fifth regular session, the General Assembly noted that the first eighteen articles of the draft did not mention some of the most elemen-

tary human rights and that amendments were necessary. On that occasion, the General Assembly took the view that civil and political freedoms were closely and reciprocally linked with economic, social and cultural rights, and decided that these rights should be included in the covenant as well. The General Assembly called upon the Commission on Human Rights to carry out this task. At its 13th session, the Economic and Social Council considered whether or not it was possible to put two categories of human rights into one document, viz., civil and political rights along with economic, social and cultural rights. The General Assembly was asked to decide on this point.

The Covenant on Human Rights was discussed at length at the sixth regular session of the General Assembly. It was decided on that occasion to draw up two covenants on human rights, one which would contain civil and political rights, and another which would cover economic, social and cultural rights; they were to be simultaneously approved by the General Assembly and handed over to the states for their signatures.

Such a decision gave some states an excuse for not ratifying the Covenant on Economic, Social and Cultural Rights, thereby evading the responsibilities imposed upon them not only by the U.N. Charter but also by the Universal Declaration of Human Rights. On the other hand, there was the danger that these same states would not have ratified a single covenant on human rights, and then civil and political rights would have been excluded from the scope of international law. The United Nations finally opted for the adoption of two covenants, although this method meant a division of rights which are closely linked.

In the final text of this covenant, the following rights in addition to the right of self-determination, are envisaged as "the ideal of free human beings enjoying freedom from fear and want": a prohibition of discrimination as to race, color, sex, language, religion, and political or other opinion; the equality of men and women; the right to an adequate standard of living for everyone and his family and to the continuous improvement of living conditions; the right to health care, and so forth.

Special attention was devoted to rights which are not sufficiently protected in some countries. In countries where the right to work does not exist, the citizens are exposed to the constant threat of unemployment. For this reason, the covenant enunciates in its articles not only the right to work but also other rights in this connection: the right of every person to enjoy just and favorable conditions of work; the right of everyone to form trade unions with others and to join a trade union; the right to social welfare, including social insurance.

The family, which is described in the covenant as "the natural and fundamental group unit of society," has been awarded special protection. This protection includes the right to a marriage of free consent, protection of mothers before and after childbirth and special measures of protection of behalf of all children and young persons, with special protection from economic and social exploitation.

Finally, the right of every individual to education and to participation in cultural life is specified.

The Covenant on Economic, Social and Cultural Rights also provides for two kinds of measures: a. internal measures to be taken by states and b. measures on the international level. Because the economic, social and cultural rights are formulated in the covenant more as a program of principles whose full realization is to be achieved progressively, the measures for their implementation are milder and of more limited scope than the measures provided for in the Covenant on Civil and Political Rights.

a. Each signatory state is obliged under the covenant to take steps "to the maximum of its available resources, with a view to achieving progressively the full realization of the rights recognized in the present covenant." Limitations on these rights are only possible as prescribed by law, provided they are compatible with the nature of these rights and are solely for the purpose of promoting the general welfare.

b. On the international level, states signing the covenant have undertaken the obligation to submit reports to the Economic and Social Council through the Secretary-General concerning the observance of the rights set forth in the covenant. These reports are sent periodically and contain information on difficulties encountered by states in their efforts to fulfil their obligations under the covenant. The Economic and Social Council may pass on the reports to the Commission on Human Rights, which makes "general recommendations" on them and may also give information about the reports to the specialized agencies concerned with furnishing technical assistance and all organs authorized to give assistance, for the purpose of facilitating the better implementation of the provisions of this covenant.

4. Prohibition of Slavery — Up until the beginning of the 19th century slave trade was not prohibited. What is more, states vied with one another to gain a monopoly in this area of international commerce. The cutthroat competition of Spain in the 16th century and Portugal in the 17th century is legendary. In 1713, the English and Spanish kings concluded the Treaty of Utrecht, on the basis of which in thirty years' time England acquired the exclusive right of importing Africans to the Spanish colonies in America.

At the 1815 Vienna Congress, a declaration of principle was adopted which proclaimed the slave trade to be a violation of European international law. In the course of the 19th century, slavery was abolished in several European countries. France prohibited salvery in its territory as early as 1791, but slavery was legal in its colonies up until 1848; England abolished slavery in its colonies in 1834; the slaves were freed in the United States in 1865 after the Civil War, and Brazil abolished salvery as late as 1888.

In 1885, an international conference was convened in Berlin to settle a number of questions concerning the Congo. The conference decided that the European powers which held territory and zones of influence in the Congo river basin should undertake measures to abolish slavery, and that the slave trade should be ended. Purchased slaves could no longer be resold. Slave traders who persisted in their activities would be punished. The international Brussels Conference was convened soon after, in 1889, to deal with the abolition of slavery. In 1890 this conference adoped a convention which laid down a series of measures for countries in which slaves were bought, sold, and transported. Military posts and patrols were instituted to supervise the implementation of the convention. Imports of alcohol, firearms and ammunition were prohibited as a supplementary measure. This additional measure was reviewed at the Paris Peace Conference in 1919, for the purpose of extending the scope of its application and making it more stringent. In Saint-Germain, two conventions were signed, one on trade and armaments and the other on sales of alcohol in African and Asian regions. A new office was created, under the supervision of the League of Nations, to collect information on the implementation of the convention.

Article 23 of the Covenant of the League of Nations called for the abolition of slavery of all kinds, regardless of race. The assembly of the League of Nations adopted a convention on slavery on 25 September 1926, to serve as supplement to the conventions of 1885 and 1890. States were obliged to provide for all the necessary measures in their territories to eliminate slavery once and for all in all its forms. The mutual assistance of states was envisaged for this purpose. The League of Nations was entrusted with the task of supervising the implementation of this convention, and states submitted reports to it on any instance of slavery and on the measures taken to abolish it.

The United Nations adopted the Supplementary Convention on the Abolition of Slavery, the Slave Trade, and Institutions and Practices Similar to Slavery, which entered into force on 3 April 1957. This convention concerns both traditional types of slavery and every legal status sanctioned by a state in which the right of freedom of the individual and his self-preservation in public and private life is restricted, e.g. bondage because of debts, the selling of children into slavery by parents, etc. The right of a husband to hand his wife over to another, the duty of a widow to marry a specified person, self-immolation of widows, etc., are all equated with slavery.

The selling of women and children is a special form of slavery. In 1902, in Paris, twelve states signed the first international convention on the abolition of the white slave trade. In 1910 this convention was supplemented and signed by a large number of European countries. The signatory states were obliged to help one another in suppressing this form of slave traffic, in particular by policing borders, and to punish violators of this convention under criminal law. As early as 1921, the League of Nations held an international conference on the white slavery issue, and a new convention was adopted. The seduction and abduction of females under the age of 21, regardless of consent, was deemed punishable by law. The abduction of women over 21 years of age was also to be considered a criminal act if deception or coercion could be proven. In 1933, a convention on the abolition of traffic in adult women was adopted under the auspices of the League of Nations. This convention prohibited traffic in women, even consenting adult women. In 1947, at Lake Success, a protocol was signed amending the conventions of 1921 and 1933, and in 1949 the conventions of 1904 and 1910 were amended. Under Resolution 317 (IV), the U.N. General Assembly adopted a convention on the abolition of traffic in human beings and exploitation of prostitution by other persons. All the earlier provisions on the abolition of this kind of slavery were thus codified, and new measures were introduced for regulating this international problem. Contemporary international law protects persons of both sexes, adults and minors, from falling into slavery.

5. The Nuremberg Principles — On 11 December 1946, the U.N. General Assembly adopted a resolution endorsing the principles of international law recognized in the charter and judgments of the Nuremberg tribunal. In the same resolution, the General Assembly invited the Commission for Codification and Development of International Law to formulate these principles, which it did, submitting them to the General Assembly in the next year.

In addition to the enumeration of international crimes contained in the Charter of the Nuremberg tribunal, which has been discussed in the chapter on international responsibility of states, the main Nuremberg principles are the following:

> First. The perpetrator of an international criminal act is not absolved of responsibility if the internal legislation of his country does not envisage such criminal acts;
> Second. A head of state or member of government may not be relieved of responsibility for perpetrating international criminal acts by virtue of his office.
> Third. The perpetration of international criminal acts by order of his government or superior does not free the offender of responsibility under international law if he had the possibility of a moral choice.

The formulation of the Nuremberg principles thus affirmed the international personality of the individual in international law. Mankind is made up of individuals, and each member is responsible for the injury and killing of other people in any act of aggression, regardless of whether or not his national law provides for criminal liability and punishment for these criminal acts.

6. Genocide — The Convention on the Prevention and Punishment of the Crime of Genocide gives the individual certain rights under international law as a member of a specific group and at the same time imposes responsibility upon him for the perpetration of criminal acts, as provided for in the convention.

On 11 December 1946, the U.N. General Assembly unanimously adopted Resolution 96 (I) on the crime of genocide, with no abstentions. The above convention was prepared pursuant to this resolution.

The word "genocide" was coined by Professor Lemkin from the Greek word "genos" (race, people) and the Latin "occidere" (to kill).

Genocide is the abrogation of the right to exist for national, ethnic, racial or religious groups, with the intent to destroy them in whole or in part. Genocide includes: a. the killing of members of a group; b. bodily or psychological harm to members of a group; c. deliberate subjection of a group to living conditions which will lead to its complete or partial physical destruction; d. measures carried out to prevent births within the group; e. compulsory transfer of children from one group to another. According to the convention, punishable acts include genocide, agreement to carry out genocide, direct public incitement to perform genocide, an attempt at or complicity in genocide.

The convention contains the very important provision that the perpetrators of criminal acts of genocide and all those persons responsible for this deed shall be punished, regardless of whether they are state administrators, officials or ordinary citizens. This provision implies that first, public administrators (heads of state) no longer enjoy absolute inviolability, and second, the criminals may not be exculpated by the internal legislation of their state. So far as extradition is concerned, genocide is considered to be an international criminal and not political act. Hence the convention obliges signatory parties to perform extradition in such cases.

The court of the state on whose territory the criminal act of genocide is carried out is competent to try the persons accused of these acts. The convention at the same time provides for the creation of an international criminal court which would be competent to try these cases. Its competence would extend to the signatory states which have recognized its jurisdiction.

Genocide has been known throughout history. In antiquity, Carthage was razed to the ground; in the Middle Ages, entire religious sects were exterminated; at the beginning of the new era, the American Indians were decimated simply because they were members of a people who defended their land and way of life from European invaders. In the twentieth century we have seen the massacre of Armenians in Turkey. After the First World War, fascism made genocide a part of its political program and employed it on an unprecedented scale. This ancient international criminal act only became punishable after the Second World War. Yugoslavia was the first country in the world to include genocide in its penal code of 1951 (Chapter XI, Article 124, which lists criminal acts against mankind and international law).

7. Prohibition of Discrimination — a. Prohibition of discrimination in regard to sex. The legal regulation of the status of women prior to the Second World War centered on the protection of special rights of women, but after the Second World War, the emphasis was shifted to protection of human rights in general. The United Nations Charter, the Universal Declaration of Human Rights, and other acts by the United Nations have rejected discrimination between people based on difference in sex, and the phrase "human rights" refers to the rights of every physical person, whether male or female. International law rejects theories of a biological and intellectual inferiority of women and recognized the equality of the sexes.

The status of women in the legal order of the United Nations is regulated today not only by legal acts on protection of human rights but also by provisions in special conventions adopted for the purpose of protecting certain women's rights. There are many such conventions, the most important the Convention on the Political Rights of Women of 20 December 1952. For the first time, states in the United Nations undertook a legal obligation to provide the following equal rights for men and women:

> — the right of women to vote in all elections;
> — the right of women to be elected, under equal conditions as men, to all public elected bodies;
> — the right of women to perform all public functions established under internal law.

The convention, therefore, contains provisions giving women political equality with men. Furthermore all these political rights give women the opportunity to fight for the realization of their economic and social rights in a variety of institutions. These democratic trends were expressed in 1953 by the adoption of the Declaration of Women's Rights at the World Congress of Women held in Copenhagen. The declaration proclaims civil, social and economic rights in addition to political rights and opens the way for the legal regulation of these rights.

b. *The Declaration on the Elimination of All Forms of Racial Discrimination.* In line with the provisions of the United Nations Charter, the Universal Declaration of Human Rights and the then draft covenants on human rights, and at the initiative of the African countries, the General Assembly adopted on

20 November 1963, the Declaration on the Elimination of All Forms of Racial Discrimination. This declaration condemns all discrimination based on race, color of skin or nationality, as a violation of human rights and fundamental liberties, as an impediment to friendly and peaceful relations between nations and as a threat to international peace and security. As a more precise definition of acts of racial discrimination was necessary to put an end to such a policy, the declaration calls upon all states to ensure all persons equal access to any position or public service; to promulgate legal measures for the prohibition of such discrimination; to put an end to the policy of racial segregation, particularly the policy of apartheid, to secure the enjoyment of political and civil rights and the right of equality before the law. States were further called upon to prohibit any propaganda concerning the superiority of one race aimed at justifying or inciting racial discrimination, and to prohibit incitement to violence against any race or group of people of another color of skin.

Specific measures were also laid down for the elimination of racial discrimination. The declaration states that everyone has the right to effective assistance and protection from an independent national court competent to adjudicate on such matters, and it goes on to proclaim that all necessary steps will be taken in the area of teaching, education and information in order to remove prejudices and improve understanding between nations and racial groups. The declaration seeks to ensure the legal effect of the measures implementing the principles it proclaims by calling upon states to take all the necessary steps, including adoption of legislation, to outlaw organizations which abet or incite racial discrimination. The United Nations, on its part, will give all possible assistance in the realization of these purposes.

Albeit the measures for the elimination of racial discrimination are described in rather broad terms in the declaration, it is notable that protection is extended not only to races and racial groups but also to individuals belonging to various racial groups, for the purpose of securing for such individuals the complete enjoyment of human rights and basic liberties. The procedure for enforcement of the rights of individuals was to be provided for in the Convention on the Elimination of All Forms of Racial Discrimination.

c. *The Convention on the Elimination of All Forms of Racial Discrimination.* On 21 December 1965, the U.N. General Assembly adopted Resolution 2106, which proclaimed the International Convention on the Elimination of All Forms of Racial Discrimination.

Prior to the adoption of this convention the various legal documents of the United Nations had only spoken of respect for human rights and fundamental liberties, "without distinction as to race, sex, language or religion." This wording is also to be found in the Universal Declaration of Human Rights, the Declaration on the Granting of Independence to Colonial Countries and Peoples, and other documents containing provisions on human rights. There was not even any clear provision on the concept of racial discrimination in the Declaration on the Elimination of All Forms of Racial Discrimination. Hence Article 1 of the Convention defines the concept of racial discrimination. According to this definition, racial discrimination refers to all differentiation, exclusion, restriction or granting of precedence on the grounds of race, color, ancestry, and national or ethnic origin and aiming at or resulting in the violation or compromise of the recognition, enjoyment or enforcement — under equal conditions — of human rights and fundamental liberties in the political, economic, social and cultural spheres or in any other area of public life. Thus racial discrimination was clearly spelled out in political and legal terms and should facilitate efforts to eliminate this international crime.

In regard to content, the convention did not go much further than the declaration. It affirmed the basic principles of the declaration as obligations under international law, adding a more elaborate system of enforcement measures.

The contracting states thereby condemn all forms of racial discrimination, including racial segregation and *apartheid.* All propaganda and the idea and theory of the superiority of one race over another are condemned. To this end, states are obliged: not to undertake any act or proceeding which would entail racial discrimination; not to support, defend or assist racial discrimination; to annul all laws and regulation resulting in racial discrimination; to proclaim an offense punishable under law any propagation of ideas based on racial superiority or hatred or the incitement to the performance of such acts; to outlaw any organization and participants in propaganda activities which propagate or incite racial discrimination. Signatory states also undertook the obligation to guarantee all persons equality in the enjoyment of civil, political, economic, social and cultural rights.

In addition to national measures, the convention also provided for a system of measures of an international character, notably the Committee on Racial Discrimination to be composed of eighteen legal experts, elected for four years by the signatory states. The committee is authorized to consider reports submitted by the acceding states concerning their legislative, judicial, administrative and other measures. Provision is also made for a special procedure according to which a state party to the convention which considers that another state party is not implementing the provisions of the convention can take this matter to the committee.

The committee may be approached directly by individuals or groups of individuals, if they feel that they are the victims of a violation of any of the rights in the convention. Two conditions must be met: a. the petitioners must have first exhausted all available domestic remedies, unless recourse to these remedies would cause an unjustifiable delay; b. the petitioners must be under the jurisdiction of a state which has recognized the competence of the Committee.

The importance of this convention appears even greater when it is compared with some conventions adopted within the European Council, in which states, even though they have identical social systems, could not agree on the manner of implementing these rights. It was a significant advance in the protection of human rights on an international level for agreement to have been reached that individuals can have recourse to the Committee if they feel that their rights have been violated. Furthermore, this agreement was reached on a subject which is extremely sensitive and controversial.

8. Refugees — After the First World War, and especially after the Second World War, the need was felt for regulating the problem of refugees under international law. Refugees are considered to be those persons who leave their country in large numbers and seek refuge and domicile in another country. After the First World War, the League of Nations had to deal with the problem of Greek and Russian refugees, and after 1933 there was the additional problem of Jewish emigrants fleeing from Nazi Germany. The office of High Commissioner for Refugees was established with Fridtjof Nansen as high commissioner. Nansen introduced the so-called Nansen passport, which served as an identity document for refugees. After the Second World War, refugees from some European, Asian and African countries created a problem which demanded the attention of the United Nations. Immediately after the war, the refugee question was assigned to the United Nations Relief and Rehabilitation Administration (UNRRA) and an inter-governmental committee. In 1947, the United Nations set up a specialized agency known as the International Refugee Organization (IRO). This agency, which was temporary, was authorized to see to the legal protection, repatriation and resettlement of refugees. It soon became evident, however, that this legal protection was not sufficient, and that it would be far more effective if accompanied by economic assistance. For this reason, in 1954, economic assistance began to be granted to refugees. A special fund for this purpose was set up within the United Nations. In 1949 the General Assembly decided to dissolve this international organization and to transfer its functions to the High Commissioner for Refugees. On the basis of an authorization by the General Assembly, the Economic and Social Council set up at its thirteenth session an advisory committee for refugees to assist the High Commissioner in solving refugee problems.

In 1951, an international conference was held in Geneva under the auspices of the United Nations, which unanimously adopted a convention relating to the status of refugees. Yugoslavia was one of the twenty-six countries which sent representatives to take part in the work of the conference. Yugoslavia ratified this convention on 15 December 1959. The Convention relating to the Status of Refugees constitutes a codification of materials concerning the rights of refugees and, under Article 37, supersedes previous treaties regulating this matter: the accords of 5 July 1922 and 31 May 1924, the conventions of 28 October 1933, 10 February 1938, and others.

Having defined the persons who may be considered refugees, the convention provides protection for them, in view of the fact that they have been deprived of the protection of the state from which they have fled. In the convention, the status of refugees is regulated by several standards. Under the most favorable standard, refugees enjoy equal treatment with the nationals of a territorial state. The provisions which define this standard are quite numerous. The refugee in this case enjoys the same religious, copyright and patent rights. The same standard is applied to a refugee both in regard to his rights to receive public assistance and in regard to labor legislation and social security; the fiscal levies paid by refugees may not be higher than those which, under the same conditions, are paid by the nationals of that country.

The acquisition of property and the rights pertaining to this property correspond with the standard under which the refugee is treated as an alien.

Refugees will enjoy the most favorable status agreed upon for citizens of a foreign country on the question of the right of association. The specific conditions are enumerated under which this right is recognized; the association must be without political or monetary aims. The same standard is also agreed upon for paid professions.

Finally, a refugee shall have the same status as a citizen of the state from which he has fled concerning his right to appear in court.

Mindful of the fact that the refugee has severed every tie with the state from which he has fled, the Convention relating to the Status of Refugees contains a number of articles concerning government assistance which should be given to refugees. If a refugee wishes to travel abroad and cannot obtain travel documents from his home state, the state party to the convention in whose territory the refugee is located may issue him paper, in conformity with Article 27. Refugees are also granted certain freedoms. They are allowed a free choice of domicile and free movement in the state in which they are located; they are absolved from criminal proceedings over irregularities in their manner of entry and residence formalities, if they come directly from the territory where their life and liberty were in jeopardy; in this case, they must immediately report to the authorities of that country. They can only be expelled according to a special procedure if national security and public order so require. However, under no circumstances may a refugee be expelled to a place where his life and liberty would be in jeopardy because of race, religion, nationality, membership in a social group or because of political views, unless he represents a threat to the security of the country in which he is located or because of conviction for a particularly heinous crime.

The 1951 Refugee Convention was amended on 23 November 1957 , at The Hague by the concluding of "arrangements on refugee seamen," which were ratified by Yugoslavia on 12 March 1963. This agreement regulated questions concerning refugee seamen who have no permanent place of residence. The conditions are defined according to which a refugee seaman is considered to have his regular place of abode in a specific territory, while other articles of the agreement concern personal papers which the refugee seaman should acquire. Generally speaking, the agreement follows the principles of the 1951 convention.

Despite the remarkable progress that has been made in alleviating the plight of refugees, there are still some unresolved problems, such as, for instance, the question of obligatory reception of refugees. It is thought that protection should be provided until these persons lose their refugee status, either by voluntary repatriation or by the taking of new citizenship, as the purpose is to protect refugees during the time when they have lost the protection of the state from which they have fled and have not yet gained a legal status in a new state.

In New York on 31 January 1967, a protocol on the status of refugees was adopted. This protocol extends the legal scope of the convention to cover new groups of refugees by awarding the status established by the convention to persons who became refugees because of events which took place after a given date. By acceding to the protocol, signatory states obligate themselves to apply the convention, without regard to the time limits originally set down in the convention.

9. Minorities — A minority is a group of individuals who belong to a specific category and differ from the majority of a population as regards race, language or religion. This is the most widely accepted definition, although writers agree only that there is still no proper definition of a minority. It is difficult to find a definition which would cover all minorities in the world. For instance, numbers, i.e. whether one belongs to a majority or minority, cannot always be taken as a criterion. In the Republic of South Africa, the blacks make up the majority, but are treated as a minority. However, such cases are rare, and the above definition, albeit not totally comprehensive, describes most minority groups, particularly in Europe.

Minorities have existed since antiquity. Some writers believe that the minority originated in the freedom of cult which was granted to vanquished peoples. Some writers view the protection of religious persons, granted by the Peace of Westphalia in 1648, as pivotal in the rise of minorities. Still other authors point to the declaration contained in the final act of the 1815 Vienna Congress concerning the protection of the Polish national minority as a landmark in international law. Actually, the need to protect minorities in a country usually arises after war, when it becomes necessary to protect the status of persons who have been threatened because they differed from the majority of the population in a state in their religion, language or race. Minority protection has been an institution in international law which has been applied as a rule in peace treaties or in acts following the conclusion of such treaties. However, even though this institution has an international legal character, to this day it has not acquired the features of a general rule of international law. It has remained a regional institution, applied wherever the need arises for regulating minority relations with regard to historical, political or legal conditions. There is no rule of international law which would require a universal regulation of the legal regime for minorities throughout the world.

The final act of the 1815 Vienna Congress protected the interests of the Polish national minority. In the course of the 19th century, the then European great powers championed protection of the Christian peoples in the Turkish Empire. Under their pressure, on the eve of the signing of the Paris Peace Treaty of 1856, Turkey published the famous Sultan's decree known as *hatti-humayouni*, according to which Turkey assumed the obligation to take all necessary measures to ensure full freedom for every religion, regardless of the number of believers, and to admit such persons into the government administration, regardless of nationality. Article 9 of the Treaty of Paris states that the Sultan informed the great powers of this edict and thus was admitted to the European Concert. The Treaty of Berlin, of 13 July 1878, imposes in Article 62 an obligation on Turkey to give full observance to religious freedom, collectively guaranteed by the great powers. And the newly-created states of Serbia and Montenegro were awarded independence under the conditions of religious non-discrimination. The same obligation was imposed on Bulgaria and Romania. Peace treaties after the First World War imposed obligations to protect minority rights on the following countries: Austria, Hungary, Bulgaria, Turkey, and Later Czechoslovakia, Poland, Yugoslavia, Romania and Greece. Some states, such as Finland for the Aland Islands, Albania, the Baltic states and Iraq pledged to protect minorities upon admittance to the League of Nations.

During the Second World War, Hitler manipulated the German minorities in other countries for his own military and political ends, so that by the end of the war minority protection as an institution of international law had been considerably compromised. German minorities in many countries had been turned into fifth columns and threatened the existence of the states in which they lived. The United Nations Charter does not mention any special minority rights; it simply calls for respect for human rights and fundamental liberties for all, without distinction to race, sex, language or religion. Treaties on minority groups concluded between the two world wars were not formally annulled, but the legal machinery for enforcing them no longer exists.

The peace treaties concluded at the end of the Second World War (1947) calls for protection of minorities, but the accent is laid on observance of human rights and fundamental liberties without discrimination. These peace treaties did not provide for effective measures of international control over the enforcement of provisions on protection of minorities.

Between the wars, Yugoslavia concluded a series of bilateral agreements with its neighbors on the protection of minorities. However, these treaties gave more protection to the minorities in Yugoslavia than to Yugoslav minorities in the other countries. The Yugoslav Constitution grants full rights to minorities and provides the possibilities and means for their development. The Special Statute on Minorities which was appended to the Memorandum of Understanding between the Governments of Great Britain and Northern Ireland, Italy, the United States of America, and Yugoslavia in Trieste regulated this question between Yugoslavia and Italy. The Statute provided reciprocal guarantees that neither country will discriminate against minority groups, and that these minority groups will enjoy equal rights with all other citizens, both in regard to political and civil rights and in regard to rights of a national, economic, cultural and educational nature. This minority statute constitutes an elaboration of the fundamental *human rights* as set forth in the Universal Declaration of Human Rights, adopted by the U.N. General Assembly on 10 December 1948.

10. The Right to Asylum — Can states decide on providing asylum at their own discretion, or is asylum one of the international human rights? We are speaking here of the territorial right to asylum as opposed to the diplomatic right to asylum when a person fleeing from persecution by territorial authorities can take refuge in the building of a diplomatic representation.

The Universal Declaration of Human Rights contains the following statement: "Everyone has the right to seek and to enjoy in other countries asylum from persecution." The draft declaration had contained the stipulation that everyone had the right to seek and *to be granted* asylum, wording which would suggest that the right of asylum was considered to be a human right. However, the final text of the Universal Declaration was altered to read, "to enjoy . . . asylum." Similarly, when the human rights covenants were being drawn up, it was proposed that the right of asylum should be given a special place in the covenants, implying that every person has the right to seek and to be granted asylum on the territories of the signatory states. Certain states, however, remarked that such a provision would mean opening their borders to no small number of persons, perhaps even persons who in certain states would be undesirable. The United Nations Commission on Human Rights respected these arguments, and in the final texts of the covenants the right of asylum does not figure as a special human right.

The Convention relating to the Status of Refugees adopted in 1951 provides for the protection of refugees on the territory of any of the states parties to the convention, with recognition of only a certain measure of protection from persecution.

In the absence of a definitive document on the right to asylum, the United Nations started work on drawing up a declaration. The draft declaration was submitted in 1960 to the General Assembly for discussion and adoption, but a final text was not agreed upon. Finally, on 14 December 1967, the General Assembly adopted the Declaration on Territorial Asylum. One of the most important provisions of this declaration is that no person may be persecuted or compelled to return to any state where he might be subjected to persecution, nor can he be refused admittance into a state at the frontier.

All these instruments and international practice to date give no grounds for viewing the granting of asylum as mandatory. Each state, in accordance with its sovereignty and its economic and political conditions, may grant asylum or not, according to its discretion.

III. Regional and Universal Protection

European and American Systems — Optional Protocol to the International Covenant on Civil and Political Rights — The Question of the High Commissioner

1. The European and American Systems – The European Convention on Human Rights and Fundamental Freedoms was adopted in Rome on 4 November 1950. Pursuant to the convention, two bodies were created: the European Commission on Human Rights and the European Court of Human Rights. In principle, individuals may not appeal directly to the European Court: only states and the European Commission may appear as parties before this court. However, according to Article 25 of the convention, the Commission may receive petitions from all persons, non-governmental organizations or groups of persons claiming to be the victims of a violation of the rights enunciated in the convention by any of the states parties, provided that the state party against whom the complaint is directed has recognized the jurisdiction of the Commission. As the Commission may also be a party before the court, the rights of all these persons can be protected before this organ, albeit in an indirect way.

The European system has served as an example for the Western Hemisphere. At the 1959 meeting of the Organization of American States, the foreign ministers decided to set up an Inter-American Commission on Human Rights and to prepare an Inter-American Convention on Human Rights on the European model.

The Inter-American Commission on Human Rights is authorized to receive communications from individuals. The communications are studied by a sub-commission, which then passes them on to the Commission with its report and recommendations, and its opinion on which petitions should be brought to the attention of the states against whom they are directed. The states in question are obliged to give information, which is made available to the petitioner. The procedure continues if it is seen that a sizable number of complaints have been submitted against one state, and if this state refuses to provide the sought-for infomation and explanations. In order to establish the tacts, the Commission carries out an inquiry on the spot and prepares a report on the human rights situation in the country in question. It is also competent to make recommendations to the state and to publish its findings. At its 1965 session, the Inter-American Conference decided that in the case of violations of certain rights, the Commission may send recommendations to governments concerning the petitions submitted by individuals.

The Inter-American Convention on Human Rights is still in draft form. In contrast to the European Convention, the draft Inter-American Convention provides for protection not only of civil and political rights but also of economic and social rights. The procedure for the protection of all these rights depends on their nature: a commission and court, whose functions would be analogous to their European counterparts, are envisaged for dealing with violations of civil and political rights. The mechanism of enforcement of economic and social rights consists in the submission of periodical reports by states parties. Recommendations and opinions are then sent to the states parties to expedite the realization of these rights.

2. The Optional Protocol to the International Covenant on Civil and Political Rights — The Covenant on Civil and Political Rights provides for a procedure in which only the signatory states may submit complaints concerning cases of non-observance. The majority of states did not wish to be put in a position where an international forum would pass judgment on them in this sphere, and for this reason the right of individual petitions is not even mentioned in the covenant. The Optional Protocol to this covenant was intended to remedy this situation, so that the right of persons enjoying the rights guaranteed in the convention to seek protection of their rights would be recognized by states acceding to the protocol. The protocol states that the Human Rights Committee is competent to receive and consider petitions (from individuals who claim to be victims of violations of a right set down in the covenant), providing that all available domestic remedies have been exhausted, and providing the same matter is not being examined "under another procedure of international investigation or settlement." According to the protocol, the Committee shall reject any complaint which is anonymous, which it considers to be an abuse of the right of petition, or which is considered to be incompatible with the provisions of the covenant. The Committee brings complaints it has deemed admissible to the attention of the state against which the complaint has been made. Within six months the state concerned must provide the Committee with explanations concerning the matter and must provide information on the measures that have been taken to remedy the situation.

3. The Question of a United Nations High Commissioner for Human Rights — Ever since the first proposals were made by the delegation from Uruguay, and especially since the latest proposals initiated by Costa Rica and the group of countries supporting it, there has been no end to debate in the United Nations on the setting up of an independent office of a High Commissioner for Human Rights to help implement international protection of human rights. In 1967, resolutions on the establishment of this office were adopted. The recommendations made so far contain three basic conceptions of the terms of reference of this office: a. the receiving and investigation of petitions submitted by individuals, b. the receiving and rejection of petitions from individuals in the High Commissioner's capacity as representative of the Human Rights Committee, c. a general safeguarding of human rights and submission of reports and opinions to United Nations organs.

One of the primary questions concerns the justification for creating an office in which an individual would be charged with implementing the protection of human rights. The prevailing view in the United Nations seems to be that only collective bodies can deal with human rights problems. Furthermore, the progress achieved in this field, both on a regional and on a world-wide basis, has been the work of collective bodies so far. Finally, such a High Commissioner would be working parallel to existing bodies and those provided for under the human rights covenants.

PART TWO

LEGAL REGULATION OF INTERNATIONAL RELATIONS

Chapter One: Organs of International Relations

I. Introduction

Concept — Features of Old and New Diplomacies — Evolution of Diplomatic Law and Modern Codification — Codification of the Rules of Consular Relations and Immunity

1. Concept — International subjects (states and international organizations) maintain intercourse with one another through their organs, i.e. through the intermediary of the persons authorized to represent their interests, and thus cause due international legal effects. The internal organization of these organs is regulated by internal regulations of states. This section of international public law will deal with the central organs of states competent for international intercourse (head of state, government, and foreign minister), with diplomatic agents, foreign service officials and consuls.

2. Features of Old and New Diplomacies — Diplomatic relations generally developed in Europe. Diplomatic centers were located in several European capitals. The other continents were rated second in importance. Parts of Asia and Africa were mainly significant as the imperial dominions of the great powers. Prior to the beginning of the twentieth century, America was isolated, geographically by the oceans, politically by the Monroe Doctrine. The great diplomatic personages seldom left the European countries and even less often crossed the ocean.

The modern technical resources have reduced the space to an incredible degree. There is virtually no state in the world that can supply its industry from its own raw material sources alone. There is no nation on our planet that is not interested in the international political situation. More and more statesmen express the opinion that peace is the common weal of the entire mankind. The diplomatic centers are no longer restricted to one single continent. New Delhi,

Peking, Djakarta, and Cairo are today just as important diplomatic centers as Paris, London, Moscow, Vienna, or Berlin.

As a rule, diplomacy was conducted between the great powers only. All the metropolises were located in Europe. Diplomatic relations between the great powers were designed to regulate their essential interests. The small and medium-sized countries were interesting only because of their strategical positions or as raw material sources. More often than not, they were forced to oscillate between the large diplomatic partners. When major international issues were discussed at international congresses and conferences, solutions were sought only within the sphere of interest of the great powers, while disputes were seldom settled in public but rather through the diplomatic channels or behind the scenes. This was the diplomatic method. Bismarck, for example, at the Berlin Congress in 1878, would immediately adjourn sessions if any disagreement broke out between the great powers. Every international congress or diplomatic conference adopted its own rules of order and procedure in accordance with the balance of forces between the great powers. This is how it was ruled whether decisions would be adopted according to the principle of unanimity or by majority vote.

Diplomatic channels are not the only means of international intercourse. Even today they cannot be abandoned, but as international life becomes democratized, many new forms of international cooperation have been brought into use. These include in the first place international organizations, of which there are hundreds today, and which operate on the basis of legal regulations and a fixed procedure. A new form of diplomacy is evolving, the diplomacy of international organizations, more especially diplomacy within the United Nations, and with it there is a new kind of diplomat, specialized for international organizations.

The great powers used to believe that they were responsile for the conduct of foreign affairs of the small and medium-sized powers as well. Hence the theory of protection of small nations by the large ones. This theory has its deep roots in the examples of interventions in the Mediterranean and Asia, especially in China; or the conference of ambassadors of the great powers of 1913, which dealt with relations between the small countries. The vestiges of such conceptions have not yet been uprooted. One of such vestiges in our present-day international community is the official justification for the right of veto for the five great powers in the U.N. Security Council.

Each country is today the master of its own destiny. Its foreign political program, as well as the character of its diplomacy, depend on its internal socio-economic order and development, and not on its location within someone's interest. Responsibility depends on the acts of states in international intercourse, which are assessed on the basis of the rules of international law. Diplomacy is the foreign political activity of a country, which is conducted by its diplomatic apparatus. It is today required to coordinate its activity with the principles and rules of international law, based above all on the United Nations Charter. Diplomacy is increasingly the conduct of foreign political affairs of a country on the basis of these principles and rules. It is an important feature of contemporary diplomacy, notwithstanding the numerous violations of its rules.

The extension of diplomatic relations to the entire world, and the introduction of more order in its activity on the basis of international law, has called into question the application of the old methods. To begin with, it is today more and more difficult to conduct the so-called secret or "black" diplomacy. As diplomacy is being taken outside the narrow scope of rulers and politicians and transferred to political parties, parliaments, political congresses, in other words to the broad popular masses — thus making every individual interested in international affairs — this kind of political activity has acquired new aspects and a new character. Its conduct is no longer the privilege of a certain rank of politicians but more and more involves political activity by virtually an entire nation.

The character of contemporary diplomacy also tends to alter the structure of the diplomatic personnel. The cadres of professional diplomats have, of course, remained, but they are more and more being replaced with prominent politicians, scientists, soldiers and businessmen. They may carry out their mission within three or four years and then go back to their old jobs, or continue their careers as professional diplomats. Because of the highly complex international life, modern diplomacy requires today a large staff of experts of different kinds.

3. Development of Diplomatic Law and Contemporary Codification — Virtually all diplomatic rules have long been based on the unwritten international customary law. An exception was the rules on the ranking of diplomatic representatives, dated 19 March 1815, which is found in the Appendix D of the Final Act of the Vienna Congress. According to them, there are three classes of diplomatic representatives: ambassadors, envoys and chargés d'affaires. These, then, within their own class, are ranked according to the date of the official notification of their arrival, there being an express prohibition to rank diplomatic agents on the basis of kinship by blood or marriage between courts. The same applied to political alliances. Three years later, under the Protocol of the Congress of Aix-la-Chapelle of 21 November 1818, the Vienna rules were amplified when the five royal and imperial courts decided to set up a new class, that of resident ministers, which would be situated somewhere between an envoy and a chargé d'affaires. This division has remained in force until very recently. These acts codified this portion of international public law, until the Vienna Conference on Diplomatic Relations and Immunities of 1961.

As regards regional codification, mention should be made of the Havana

Convention of diplomatic representatives, of 20 February 1928, providing for a distinction between regular and extraordinary diplomatic agents. According to this convention, regular are those diplomatic representatives who permanently represent the government of a country in another state, whereas extraordinary are those who have been charged with a special mission or have been accredited to represent their government at an international conference or congress. The convention regulated their privileges and immunities, ceremony, selection, functions, and the beginning and end of mission. Between the two world wars, attempts were made to codify this branch of international law, but they were not successful.

The question of the codification of diplomatic law was raised soon after the setting up of the United Nations Organization. Diplomatic relations and immunities were on the list for codification by the International Law Commission. Two conventions were adopted in this sphere: the United Nations Convention on Privileges and Immunities, of 13 February 1946, and the Convention on the Privileges and Immunities of Specialized Agencies, of 21 November 1947. However, as can be seen, these two conventions regulate the privileges and immunities of the representatives of member states and international officials, or as Bartos put it, "diplomatoid" personnel.

The question of the codification of diplomatic relations and immunities was again raised in the United Nations General Assembly in 1952, at Yugoslavia's insistence, in view of the bitter experience of her diplomatic officials in the Cominform countries. The International Law Commission, on the basis of a U.N. General Assembly resolution, gave the codification of this branch of diplomatic law priority treatment. Finally, at its ninth session in 1957, it decided to draft three conventions covering this sphere. The first, on the so-called sedentary, regular diplomacy; the second on the so-called flying or *ad hoc* diplomacy, in which representatives of states attend bilateral or multilateral negotiations as plenipotentiaries or experts, or as members of delegations at international conferences, or the meetings of international bodies, and special intergovernmental contacts of an official character; the third convention was to apply to diplomacy within international organizations. It was also decided to draft for the time being only the outline of the first convention. In 1958, the International Law Commission finally adopted the draft rules regulating diplomatic relations and immunities. In 1959, the U.N. General Assembly requested the U.N. Secretary-General to convene, by the spring of 1961, an international conference in Vienna, with the purpose of codifying in a convention the rules governing diplomatic relations and immunities. It did take place in 1961.

The Vienna Convention on Diplomatic Relations was designed to "help foster friendly relations among countries, irrespective of any differences in their constitutional and social systems." It attempted to encompass all the legal civilizations in the world. It did not neglect the fundamental ideas and even the many rules formulated at the Vienna Congress in 1815, especailly those which received endorsement in the course of a long practice. The Vienna Conference on Diplomatic Relations of 1961 unanimously took the view that the codification of the existing rules in the sphere of diplomatic law should be combined with a progressive development of this portion of international law. Thus some new solutions have been arrived at on the basis of the "aims and purposes of the United Nations Charter in respect of the sovereign equality of states and of international peace and security and development of friendly relations among nations." Those customary legal rules that were not embraced by this convention remained in force as the rules of international customary law. In 1961, two other protocols were adopted in connection with the questions on which no compromise solution was found in the text of the convention, namely the protocol on the acquisition of citizenship, according to which the members of the mission who do not have the citizenship of the state to which they are accredited and the members of their families may not acquire the citizenship of that state by virtue of its legislation; next, the Protocol regarding the mandatory referral of disputes to the International Court of Justice.

4. Codification of Rules on Consular Relations and Immunities — Until the adoption of the Vienna Convention on Consular Relations in 1963, no codification of rules governing consular services had been made, although efforts to this end had been made by international jurists (Bluntschli in 1868, Field in 1876, Fiore in 1890 and others), and draft conventions and rules on the rights of consuls were proposed (the Institute for International Law in 1925, the Inter-American Commission of Jurists in 1927, Harvard University in 1932).

Consular relations and immunities were among the fourteen questions for codification on the list of the International Law Commission, outlined as early as in 1949. However, the question was taken into consideration by the Commission only in 1955, when the Czech professor Žurek, who was appointed rapporteur, made the first draft of the rules of consular relations and immunities.

The Convention on Consular Relations, which is similar, especially in its preamble, to the Convention on Diplomatic Relations, was adopted in Vienna in 1963. The codification of consular rules, despite the rich practice and bilateral and unilateral conventions, was more difficult because of the absence of written legal sources and of fairly uncertain legal customs, frequently interpreted in different ways in various parts of the world. Furthermore, the question of consular rules directly affects economic interests and security of states much more than diplomatic law, making codification and progressive development of this part of international law more difficult. However, all the difficulties notwithstanding, a number of consular relations were regulated, including their immunities and privileges, the status of career and honorary consuls, and two protocols were adopted at the Vienna Conference on Diplomatic Relations of 1961.

II. Head of State

In the era of absolutism, the monarchs, who used to be the heads of state, were regarded as subjects of international law. Today, at any rate, a head of state is not a subject of international law but only an organ of his state who represents it in international relations without a special authority. The head of state enjoys this right for as long as he fulfils that function. Once the function is terminated, under international law he loses this entitlement as well as all the privileges appurtenant to him as head of state.

Until the 19th century, the rule was that the head of a state was empowered to fully represent his state, namely, that he had an unlimited entitlement as regards the conduct of his country's foreign affairs. As democratic institutions gained acceptance, this right was restricted constitutionally; the head of state was made competent to proclaim the state of war, conclude peace, receive, accredit and withdraw diplomatic representatives, and possibly to ratify international treaties.

Under international law, no distinction is made today between heads of state. Their external and internal functions have been regulated on the basis of internal constitutional provisions. In the international practice of the states maintaining the system of monarchy, certain distinctions are made between monarchs and presidents of republics, but these relate more to honors than to rights. As regards the special kind of a so-called collective head of state, *e.g.* in Switzerland, the U.S.S.R. and other East European states, the act of this kind of head of states has the same effect as the acts of an individual head of state. The sovereignty of a state having a collective head is as a rule represented by the praesidium of an assembly *in corpore* (*e.g.* the praesidium of the National Assembly of the F.P.R.Y., according to the Constitution of 1946).

Until the First World War, the head of a state had no responsibility under international law whatever. The modern international law has made a considerable headway in determining the responsibility of a head of state for international crimes against peace and mankind, for war crimes, more specifically for the crime of genocide, regardless of whether or not he has been freed of any responsibility under the constitution and the legislation of his country.

In international law, the rights, and privileges of a head of state mainly apply in connection with his stay abroad. A foreign head of state enjoys exterritoriality and a complete criminal immunity. The residence which he occupies is invulnerable. He has a right to freely and without restriction communicate with his own country. Should he commit a crime or in any way infringe the laws of the countries in which he is residing, he might be denied hospitality. It is only in grave cases that he might be deported.

A head of state abroad is entitled to the highest honors established under protocol. These include the right to a title, to military honors, to an official welcome, etc. Certain privileges result from comity, such as the exemption from customs dues, taxes and so forth. The wife and the minor children of a head of state also enjoy the mentioned entitlements and privileges. A head of state is not entitled to rights and privileges in the event of an incognito stay abroad, until he reveals himself. From that moment he automatically is invested with the rights and privileges appurtenant to him.

The President of the Republic represents the S.F.R.Y. at home and abroad. He informs the Assembly on the situation and problems of home and foreign affairs and proposes the consideration of various questions and the adoption of decisions.

If the Presidency of the S.F.R.Y. is not able to meet, owing to a state of war or in the event of an immediate war emergency, the President of the Republic may issue edicts having legal force on the questions pertaining to the competence of the Assembly of the S.F.R.Y. He must present these edicts to the Assembly for endorsement as soon as the latter is able to meet again.

III. Government and Minister of Foreign Affairs

1. Government — The foreign political acts of a government express certain state interests. Whatever form they might have (resolution, declaration, etc.), the foreign political acts of a government are binding upon a state. It is similarly held in international law that a prime minister is authorized to make statements on behalf of his government. His statements and his acts, made on behalf of the government as a whole, are also binding. Other states may not inquire whether or not he had the right to make them or issue them on the basis of the constitution or legislation of his state. It is sufficient for a person to hold the office of prime minister. This is, for example, the principle applied in the rules of order of the United Nations Security Council, according to which a prime minister represents his state without powers, automatically and on the basis of his office.

According to the Constitution of the S.F.R.Y., the Federal Executive Council is competent to propose internal and foreign policies to the Federal Assembly.

The Federal Executive Council ratifies those international treaties that are not within the competence of the Federal Assembly.

2. Minister of Foreign Affairs — Heading the ministry of foreign affairs, or the state secretariat for foreign affairs, or whatever its title may be, is the responsible minister, or federal secretary, who is in charge of the entire foreign service. The latter encompasses all the officials in the foreign service, as well as its diplomatic and consular agencies. The foreign minister's duty is to receive foreign representatives, to hold talks and negotiations with them, to maintain supervision in the drafting of all foreign policy and other acts, to supervise the execution of international treaties and all obligations assumed by his country, to protect the rights and privileges of the diplomatic agents accredited in his country, to safeguard the interests of the state as a whole, and particularly of its nationals who may be abroad, etc. The minister is the representative of his government having the powers to safeguard the interests of his country in the sphere of foreign affairs. All the external acts of his country must go through his department for which he is fully responsible. In view of the nature of his powers, every one of his acts and statements is binding upon the state. This was the basis for the judgment of the Permanent Court of International Justice in the Hague on 5 April 1933, in the dispute between Denmark and Norway concerning East Greenland. Namely, on 22 July 1919, the Norwegian minister of foreign affairs declared that Norway was renouncing its sovereignty over Greenland for the benefit of Denmark. Later Norway challenged this right to Denmark, claiming that the foreign minister was not authorized to take over the prerogatives of the Norwegian parliament in regard to the ceding of national territory. The Court took the view that third states were not expected to examine the competence of a foreign minister on the basis of the country's internal legislation and constitutional order. According to international law, a foreign minister is *ex officio* empowered to make statements on behalf of his government which are binding upon his state.

IV. Diplomatic Agents

Concept — Types of Diplomatic Agents — Classes and Ranking of Diplomatic Agents — Diplomatic Corps — Appointment of a Diplomatic Mission — Diplomatic Language — Functions of Diplomatic Agents — Diplomatic Immunities and Privileges — Termination of a Diplomatic Mission.

1. Concept — Diplomatic agents are persons authorized to represent a state abroad.

The 1961 Vienna Convention laid down the precise classification of the different diplomatic representatives: the head of a mission is a person whom the government has accredited and authorized to act in this capacity; the members of a mission may belong to the diplomatic personnel, having a diplomatic capacity, and the staff of the mission, comprising administrative and technical personnel as well as members of the service staff of the mission. The Convention uses the term diplomatic agent. It is applied to the head of a mission and its diplomatic personnel.

The head of a mission or member of the diplomatic personnel may represent their state in any international organization. The Vienna Convention also makes provision for accreditation of one and the same person by several states to be head of a mission in another state, subject to the latter state's agreement. Bartos was right to criticize this innovation in the 1961 Vienna Convention on diplomatic relations, saying that "it may be fatal for the relations of a state with other states, with which it has different interests. Furthermore, it is far from certain how the personal status of the head of such missions will be viewed if he has been accredited to different states at various times, if he has been accredited in different classes and finally, who will be responsible for his actions if he makes a personal mistake. In such an event, which state will be informed that its head of the mission has become a *persona non grata?*"

Every sovereign state has the right to send diplomatic representatives (active right of legation), as well as the right to receive foreign diplomatic representatives (passive right of legation). It is a rule that non-sovereign states do not enjoy these rights. However, there have been cases in diplomatic practice where non-sovereign states have exercised this right with the consent of the state to which it owed allegiance (the suzerain state). On the basis of the Sultan's Edict of August 1830 (para. 20) and the 1838 Constitution (para. 18), Serbia had the right to appoint a permanent agent to Istanbul (*chargé d'affaires*), and on the basis of 1835 and 1839 edicts was authorized to maintain its diplomatic agents in Moldavia and Wallachia. Similarly, before independence, Bulgaria had its diplomatic agents in several foreign capitals and received representatives of foreign countries.

In a federal state, only the central government has the right to send diplomatic representatives abroad. The members of the federation as a rule do not have this right, although there are some well-known exceptions (e.g. Bavaria as a Roman Catholic land maintained diplomatic relations with the Holy See during the First and the Second Reichs).

2. Types of Diplomatic Agents — Writers on international law in earlier centuries generally recognized three types of diplomatic representatives: regular, extraordinary, and secret.

Regular diplomatic representatives are the persons authorized to represent their state permanently in another state.

Extraordinary diplomatic representatives are the persons authorized to carry out a special mission abroad (accredited to a foreign government) at international congresses or diplomatic conferences, or at the sessions of an international organization or its organs. Earlier it was considered that extraordinary diplomatic representatives were mainly expected to perform ceremonial duties, *e.g.* at solemn occasions, coronations of monarchs, state funerals, anniversary celebrations, etc., or certain "business missions" — for instance, to discuss a controversial matter, to negotiate a loan, to adjust borders, etc. The great complexity of international life today makes it necessary for extraordinary diplomatic representatives to perform widely diverse but important diplomatic functions.

Secret diplomatic representatives used to be authorized persons who conducted affairs of state in a foreign country in confidence and in secret. They enjoyed guaranteed safety and inviolability as ministers plenipotentiary without exterritoriality or diplomatic ceremony. The classic example is the monk Père Joseph (Le Clerc du Tremblay), nicknamed "éminence grise," who performed secret diplomacy for Cardinal Richelieu. Today, international law recognizes only public diplomatic activity and, therefore, the status of any secret diplomatic representatives is not and could not be governed by the rules of international law.

3. Head of Mission — Class and Rank — Prior to the 1815 Vienna Congress, there were a multitude of diplomatic titles. Every monarch wished to acquire as high a ranking as possible for his representative, and for this reason bestowed strings of titles upon him and cited the high rankings which his diplomat held at his court.

In view of the multiplicity of titles and capacities of diplomatic representatives, the question of their rank was until the Vienna Congress a serious problem for states and often provoked serious political consequences. The scramble for diplomatic ranks was actually a struggle for prestige by sovereigns and states. Thus, for instance, when the Treaty of Karlowitz (1699) was being concluded, the question of precedence of the delegates from Turkey, Austria, Poland, and Venice could not be solved, so that finally as many entrances as there were delegations were opened into the conference hall. In this way, all the delegations could enter the hall at the same time and take their places. Thus they could no longer argue over the order in which the delegations would enter the hall.

The rules of the Vienna Congress envisaged three classes of diplomatic representatives. Ambassadors and the papal representatives — legates and nuncios — belong to the first and highest class. Envoys extraordinary and ministers plenipotentiary, and others accredited to sovereigns, belong to the second class. The third class included *chargés d'affaires,* accredited to ministers of foreign affairs. In 1818, the Congress of Aix-la-Chappelle added a protocol to the Vienna treaty. It introduced yet another class in between the envoys extraordinary and ministers plenipotentiary and the chargés d'affaires. These were the so-called resident ministers. Thus, up until the 1961 Vienna Conference on diplomatic relations, there were four classes of diplomatic representatives: ambassadors, ministers plenipotentiary and envoys extraordinary, ministers resident, and *chargés d'affaires.*

Resident ministers were envoys from semi-sovereign states or from sovereign states to semi-sovereign states. These ministers were also appointed when regular diplomatic relations had not yet been established between two states. In modern diplomatic practice there are no longer any resident ministers.

According to the 1961 Vienna Convention on diplomatic relations, the heads of missions were divided into three classes: a. ambassadors or nuncios, accredited to heads of state, and other heads of missions of a corresponding rank; b. envoys, ministers or internuncios accredited to heads of state; c. *chargés d'affaires* accredited to ministers of foreign affairs. There is no difference, nor can any distinction be drawn, between heads of missions on the basis of their class. Exceptions are allowed in respect to precedence and etiquette.

States negotiate the class to which the heads of their missions should belong. However, they acquire ranking within their class according to the day and hour of taking office. A head of a mission is considered to have assumed his functions when he submits his credentials or when he notifies his arrival and submits a copy of his credentials to the minister of foreign affairs or to some other minister, according to the custom in the receiving state; but this custom must be applied in a uniform manner. The order in which the credentials or copies of the credentials are submitted is determined according to the day and hour of the arrival of the head of the mission (art. 13 of the Convention).

Chargés d'affaires are accredited by the minister of foreign affairs to the ministry of foreign affairs of the other country.

There are two kinds of *chargés d'affaires:* the *chargé d'affaires* who is especially accredited and represents the head of a mission, and the *chargé d'affaires ad interim,* who is not accredited but is the senior official who replaces the head of the mission in his absence.

4. Diplomatic Corps — The rule is for all the heads of missions in a country to be considered members of the diplomatic corps. However, today there is a growing tendency to include in the diplomatic corps all those who are on the diplomatic list in a country.

The diplomatic corps is not a legal person. Although it does not represent a cohesive entity, it may appear as such in a ceremonial capacity. For instance, the diplomatic corps as a whole takes part in celebrations of a national holiday, various congratulations, expressions of condolence, and so forth. There have been instances in the past when the diplomatic corps protested against violations of diplomatic immunity and privileges (*e.g.* the protest of the diplomatic corps to the Italian government because of infringements contained in a verdict by the Italian court of appeals in 1924).

The diplomatic corps is headed by its doyen, who leads the corps at ceremonies and to whom a territorial state may make announcements which are to be conveyed to the entire corps.

5. Appointment of a Diplomatic Mission — Before sending diplomatic representatives, states must give their assent for the opening of a permanent diplomatic agency. Permanent diplomatic relations are established by an international agreement, and it is only after this that diplomatic representatives are exchanged. In order for these relations to develop in as favorable an atomosphere as possible, the states ask each other's approval for the heads of their respective missions.

The approval of a person to serve as head of a foreign state's mission is called *agrément. Agrément* is an old institution in international law and is intended to avoid appointment of any *persona non grata* to a country. Today the failure to seek *agrément* is considered an insult and slight to the receiving state. Hitler's practice of not asking for *agrément* was particularly responsible for this customary rule being established as international law. For instance, after the murder of Dolfuss, Hitler appointed von Papen ambassador without first asking for *agrément.*

It is a customary rule that refusal to give *agrément* must be explained, although the 1961 Vienna Convention envisages that the receiving state is not obliged to give the accrediting state reasons for refusing to grant *agrément.* However, there have been instances when *agrément* for a particular person was delayed for so long that the other state finally proposed a new person. It is considered that receiving states should not refuse to give *agrément* because a proposed diplomatic representative does not have the qualifications for this function. The question of qualifications, *i.e.* whether someone can be a diplomat or not, is a matter of discretion of each state. Refusal on these grounds might be interpreted as interference in the internal affairs of the other state if the qualifications of a proposed diplomatic representative were given a close scrutiny by the other state. Sex or religion are also not reasons for refusal to give *agrément.* However, states do have the right, and as a rule exercise it, to refuse *agrément* to a person who is not a citizen of the state which intends to accredit him. *Agrément* is also properly refused to a person who had earlier taken an unfriendly attitude toward the receiving country or had worked against its interests, or the interests of its citizens. Dishonorable actions may also be a reason for refusing *agrément,* which is usually done tacitly.

Agrément is given to the head of the mission. However, approval is also needed for the military, naval and air attachés. *Agrément* is sometimes also called consent.

After *agrément* is received, the diplomatic representative is appointed by decree or edict, that is to say, by an internal act of law.

Under the Yugoslav Constitution, the president of the Republic appoints and recalls ambassadors and envoys of the Socialist Federal Republic of Yugoslavia by decree, and receives the credentials and letters of recall of foreign diplomatic representatives accredited to him (art. 217), while *chargés d'affaires* are appointed and recalled by the Federal Secretary for Foreign Affairs.

The new head of a mission carries his *letters of credence* with him. We usually say letters of credence, although in fact there is just one document. They can also be called credentials. These credentials, then, identify the head of the mission as having been appointed as such, and contain his name, occupation (i.e. diplomatic class), and the subject matter of the mission of the diplomatic agent, always with the express desire of fostering good or friendly relations between the two states. The letters of credence are a formal document and must contain the full title of the state and its head. In order to preclude any formal omissions liable to have political repercussions — for instance, if a mistake were made in the name of the state or head of state — the new head of the mission first submits a copy of his credentials to the minister of foreign affairs of the country to which he is coming.

Letters of credence are handed over at a formal ceremony. How much of ceremony there will be depends on the individual state. After he has submitted his credentials, the diplomatic agent acquires the right to perform diplomatic functions in the country concerned.

The state is free to appoint whomever it wishes as other members of the mission, but it must first notify the ministry of foreign affairs of the receiving state both of their arrival in the country and of their departure. Notification must be given both for members of the mission and for members of their families and suites. This notification is necessary for the enjoyment of their privileges and immunities.

6. Diplomatic Language — Up until the 17th century Latin was the language of diplomacy. The stature of Louis XIV and the general international prestige enjoyed by France at that time, as well as the political hegemony of the Bourbon period, gave French precedence over Latin as the diplomatic language in Europe of the day. The use of Latin as the language of diplomacy waned steadily, until finally French became the generally accepted diplomatic language in the 19th century. All important international treaties were written in French, for the Final Act of the Vienna Congress to the Hague Conventions (1889 and 1907).

After the First World War, English began to vie with French as the diplomatic language. The Versailles Peace Treaty was drafted in both languages and, significantly, both versions are considered authentic. The Permanent Court of International Justice introduced both French and English as official languages. After the Second World War, the number of diplomatic languages proliferated. The Charter of the United Nations was written in English, French, Chinese, Russian and Spanish. According to Article 111 of the Charter, all these languages are "equally authentic." Today, all these languages are considered to be languages of diplomacy. In the organs of the United Nations, however, the working languages are French and English, and since 1950 Spanish has also been a working language. Today there is no longer any single language which could be considered the language of diplomacy, but in practice French and English are still being favored.

7. Functions of Diplomatic Representatives — The main functions of diplomatic representatives are to act on behalf of the state they represent: by protecting the interests of their state and its citizens to the extent allowed by international law; by being authorized to negotiate with the government of the receiving state; by informing their government on conditions and developments in the state to which they are accredited; and by submitting reports on events there; and, finally, by promoting friendly relations and fostering economic, cultural and scientific ties between the state which they represent and the state to which they are accredited. Diplomatic representations, or diplomatic agents, perform all official business in the ministry of foreign affairs (in Yugoslavia known as the Federal Secretariat for Foreign Affairs) of the state to which they are accredited, or this ministry acts as an intermediary.

The activity of the diplomatic agent is first and foremost to represent his state. This means that in the country where he has been posted or at the international conference to which he has been sent, he acts not on his own behalf but on behalf of the state which he represents.

An equally important function of the diplomatic agent is to protect the interests of the state which he represents and its citizens. He is, therefore, authorized to take all necessary steps to promote the national and individual interests of the citizens of his state.

No provision — according to the 1961 Vienna Convention on diplomatic relations — may be construed as prohibiting any diplomatic mission from performing consular functions. This was a compromise formula adopted in 1961 at the Vienna Conference when, upon a Spanish initiative, it was insisted that a diplomatic mission should at the same time perform consular functions.

It is considered that every accredited diplomatic agent is authorized to conduct negotiations in one or more states to which he has been posted, in the country to which he has been sent with his powers, or at an international conference which he is attending as a delegate of his government.

The term negotiations should be interpreted in its broadest sense. Negotiations include all contacts, regardless of whether they concern the broaching of questions, gaining information about the other side's viewpoints, or making concrete offers and proposals. The head of the mission needs no special authorization to conduct negotiations. However, if agreement reached in the course of negotiations is to have the effect of an international agreement, it must be confirmed in writing, in some form or other, as a treaty, protocol or exchange of notes.

The diplomatic agent is obliged to inform his government about all important events of a political, economic, scientific, cultural and other nature. The receiving state has no right to obstruct the work of foreign diplomats in this respect. What is more, it is obliged to facilitate a normal performance of these functions. Normal performance of these functions implies the use of authorized channels for the sending of official reports.

The U.N. Charter enjoins states to promote international friendly relations, particularly in the spheres of the economy, culture and science.

Finally, diplomatic representatives perform all their functions in accordance with the rules of international law. This means that they are forbidden to interfere in the internal affairs of the state to which they are accredited. This is actually their so-called negative function. The diplomatic representative is obliged to refrain from interfering in the internal affairs of that country, even when he is outside the country on leave of absence, for instance, so long as he holds the post of an accredited diplomatic representative there.

8. Diplomatic Immunities and Privileges — The functions of diplomatic agents that we have enumerated require them to have an independent and specially protected status. Even in ancient times the rights of envoys were guaranteed, since diplomats were held to be sacrosanct. Although diplomatic practice in this respect has not always been consistent through the centuries — for example, foreign envoys have been deprived of liberty or even been killed in case of an outbreak of hostilities (a custom of the Porte) — it is true that the rights and privileges of diplomatic representatives have been generally respected, particularly in Europe after the Peace of Westphalia (1648).

When the Constituent Assembly in France abrogated all privileges in 1786, the diplomats in Paris were alarmed and asked the ministry of foreign affairs whether this applied to diplomatic privileges as well. The Constituent Assembly soon afterwards published a special decree proclaiming respect for the immunities and privileges of diplomatic agents. In 1810, Fouché advised Napoleon to enact a law abrogating diplomatic privileges and immunities because of the theft of plans in the ministry of the army, in which the Russian and Austrian ambassadors had been involved. Napoleon, it seems, would have taken Fouché's advice, had he not been warned of the harmful consequences of such an action by his ministry of foreign affairs. This was probably the last attempt in Europe to abolish diplomatic privileges and immunities by legislation, although there have been violations up to the present day.

Diplomatic immunities and privileges constitute a body of international customary rules, or rules laid down by convention which states submit to, regardless of whether they have expressly or tacitly stated their acceptance. The assumption is justified that newly created states are automatically obliged to apply and respect diplomatic immunities and privileges from the moment when they undertook to establish diplomatic relations with other states.

There is a controversy, however, on the legal basis of the so-called fiction of exterritoriality.

The *theory of exterritoriality* of diplomatic agents was expounded by Grotius and further elaborated by Binkershoek. This theory is based on the fiction that a diplomatic representative is not subject to the laws of a territorial state, since he and his dwelling are deemed to be outside its territory, that is to say, never to have left the territory of his own state. This theory came under sharp criticism, particularly at the end of the 19th and begining of the 20th centuries. (See Fauchille's criticism in French literature and Geršič's criticism in Yugoslav literature.) Caillier more recently has made the acute observation that the theory of exterritoriality extends diplomatic privileges to such an extent that a diplomat has virtually become exempt from the obligation to respect the laws of the receiving state. According to these authors, criminal acts committed on the premises of a diplomatic mission, even if the perpetrators are citizens of the territorial state, would come under the jurisdiction of the courts of the country to which the representation belongs and not of the local courts. It is in fact the territorial state which has jurisdiction over such criminal acts. Furthermore, the territorial state has extensive jurisdiction in the sphere of civil law.

Today, the term exterritoriality is still used to indicate the body of diplomatic immunities and privileges of a diplomat or members of a diplomatic mission, but the fiction as a legal basis for explaining the special legal status of diplomatic agents is rejected.

In our opinion, the legal grounds for diplomatic immunities and privileges should be sought in the protection of the general interest *in the international community.*

The diplomatic agent protects a given interest of his country. There is no doubt about that. He is authorized to protect the national interests of his country and its citizens. This capacity, on the other hand, by no means gives him the right to jeopardize the interests of the host country by interfering in its internal affairs. Hence, in the last analysis, the diplomatic agent must try to promote the common interests of both states. However, the realization of bilateral interests must not damage the interests of third states protected under international law. The safeguarding of bilateral interests must be in accordance with the *general interest* of the international community, although the peaceful settlement of disputes or of a situation likely to disturb the peaceful course of international affairs is often sufficient to make such regulation accordant with the general interest.

Authors classify diplomatic immunities and privileges in various ways. Some writers, such as Genet, divide immunities and privileges into "real," *i.e.* those which are enjoyed by the mission alone, and "personal," *i.e.* those which concern the person of the diplomatic representative. Others, particularly older writers, such as Rivière and Danevski, divide the rights of diplomatic representatives into essential rights and subsidiary rights. In Yugoslavia, Geršić adopted this latter division, classifying inviolability and exterritoriality as essential rights. Most authors simply enumerate generally accepted immunities and privileges. Diplomatic privileges and immunities may be classified in three groups, although all three are overlapping. These groups would be immunities and privileges in respect to the premises of the mission and its archives, those which pertain to the work of the mission, and, finally, personal immunities and privileges.

a. *Immunities and privileges in respect to the premises of the mission and its archives* — The building and all other premises of the diplomatic mission are inviolable. The authorities of the territorial state are not allowed to enter them without the permission of the head of the mission. The host state is obliged to take all necessary measures to prevent anyone from entering the premises by force, damaging them or disturbing the peace in the mission, and especially bringing the dignity of the country concerned into jeopardy. No kind of search, requisition, or confiscation can be carried out on the premises of the mission.

The head of the mission, as well as the country to which it belongs, are exempt from all taxes, either federal or local, for the premises, regardless of whether they are owned by the mission or rented. However, an exception is made for taxes levied on the payments for services specially performed.

The archives and correspondence, as well as all the records and documentation of the mission, are inviolable. Inviolability is not confined to the building of the mission and diplomatic premises. The records, correspondence and documents are inviolable wherever they are, even when carried by a member of the mission. The territorial state is not allowed to make any distinction between official and private archives and correspondence, since the very act of classification would be an infringement on this important rule of diplomatic law.

b. *Immunities and privileges concerning the work of the mission* — The government and authorities of the territorial state are expected to provide all necessary facilities to enable the diplomatic mission to function properly. The mission is entitled to apply to the government and authorities of the host country for assistance and ordinary information. It is the duty of the receiving state to be forthcoming in this respect.

Members of the mission have the right to freedom of travel and movement in the territory of the state to which they are accredited. Without this right they would be prevented from carrying out the recognized function of informing their government about developments in the state where they are posted as diplomatic agents. The territorial state has the right to enact laws or other ordinances to designate zones in which freedom of movement would be restricted or prohibited for reasons of national security. Obviously, the designation of zones which are out of bounds should correspond to actual security needs and should not be done maliciously with the object of harassing a state or group of states.

Members of a mission not only have the right to freedom of movement in the territory of the host country, but also the right of free intercourse, for official purposes, both with their government and with their diplomatic and consular agencies, whether they are in the same country or in third countries. This right also extends to their fellow citizens located in that country and to members of international organizations, specifically the United Nations, its specialized agencies, etc.

The mission has the right to use all suitable means of communication, including diplomatic couriers and coded dispatches in maintaining contacts with its government and other missions and consulates of its country. The host country is obliged to protect these official communications. If a mission wishes to use a radio transmitter for this purpose, it is obliged, under the 1961 Vienna convention and under the international conventions on telecommunications, to seek special permission from the government of the host country.

The diplomatic correspondence of the mission is inviolable, which means that its mail may not be opened and detained, nor may the seal on it be damaged. Diplomatic mail must be clearly and unmistakably marked as such. Diplomatic mail refers to the so-called diplomatic pouch, which contains diplomatic documents or the usual service requisites.

Diplomatic mail is most often carried by a diplomatic courier. He is under the protection of his state and enjoys the right of immunity. He can under no circumstances be placed under arrest or be detained when carrying out his duties as courier. The diplomatic courier must be provided with a letter identifying his capacity and the number of packages comprising the diplomatic pouch.

The same provisions, rights and obligations apply to *ad hoc* diplomatic couriers, except that their immunities cease once they deliver the diplomatic pouch entrusted to them.

c. *Personal immunities and privileges* — One of the oldest rules of international customary law, which is still in force today, is the granting of diplomatic immunity and privileges to the head of a mission, together with his official and unofficial suite. Nowadays the suite of a head of a mission includes his family and members of the mission and their families. The extent of diplomatic privilege, especially for the lower ranks of diplomats, is a matter of courtesy, and it is up to the state to decide whether diplomatic privileges shall be extended to various officials of the mission. Today the tendency is for diplomatic immunities and privileges to be granted to an increasing number of persons.

Diplomatic immunity and privileges are also enjoyed by members of the administrative and technical staff of the mission, together with their families, provided they are not citizens of the host country, or permanently resident in it. Immunity from prosecution is not valid for acts committed outside the performance of their functions. The rationale is that an ambassador's secretary, filing clerk or radio operator may know as many secrets as any member of the diplomatic personnel, and therefore needs the same kind of protection from any possible pressure from the local authorities. If service personnel are not citizens of the host country or permanent residents, they enjoy immunity, but only in the course of their duties.

The person of a recognized diplomatic agent is inviolable. He may not be placed under any kind of arrest and no coercive measures may be taken against him. His dwelling is inviolable and so are his documents, correspondence, and property.

A diplomatic agent may not be prosecuted under criminal law or any civil and administrative proceedings. Exceptions are made in suits involving privately owned real estate in the host country, unless the diplomatic agent is empowered to own the property on behalf of his government and for the purposes of his mission; in the suits involving a legacy where the diplomatic agent is the executor, administrator, heir or legator, appearing as a private citizen and not on behalf of his country; finally, in the suits resulting from any business or professional activities performed by the diplomatic agent in the host country outside his official duties.

The diplomatic agent is not obliged to appear as a witness before a court of the host country.

The diplomat's country may waive the judicial immunity of its diplomatic representatives. In criminal cases this waiver must always be given expressly. In civil and administrative cases, it may be given either expressly or tacitly. It is deemed to have been given tacitly if the diplomatic agent appears as the defendant in a suit without claiming immunity. If the diplomatic agent is the plaintiff, he *ipso facto* loses the right to claim judicial immunity in respect to any counter-charges, provided they are related to the case. The waiving of judicial immunity in civil or criminal proceedings should not be confounded with immunity against the carrying out of the sentence. A special express waiver is needed to carry out the sentence.

The diplomatic representative is exempted from all taxes with the exception of indirect taxes, taxes on private real estate and inheritance, taxes on private income, and so forth.

Diplomatic immunity and privileges begin the moment the diplomatic agent enters the territory of the receiving state and cease when he loses these functions or leaves the country. They remain in force even in the event of an armed conflict. The territorial state must allow the diplomatic representatives of the belligerent country and their families to leave the country without interferencce. In transit through the territory of third countries on official business, diplomatic representatives and their families also enjoy inviolability, immunities and privileges. Diplomatic couriers in transit also enjoy these rights.

9. Termination of a Diplomatic Mission

9. Termination of a Diplomatic Mission — The time factor is possibly one of the main reasons for terminating a diplomatic mission. There is a growing tendency for diplomatic agents to be kept at one post abroad no longer than three to five years, although these time periods are not stated in the letters of credence. The diplomatic mission is also terminated once its job is completed: for instance, a ceremonial mission sent on the occasion of the proclamation of a new state; the coronation of a ruler; the inauguration of a president of a republic; the funeral of a head of state; etc.; or participation at diplomatic conferences. Another common reason may be, for instance, the diplomat's death, recall or request by the host country for his removal if proclaimed *persona non grata.* The head of a mission or any member of the diplomatic personnel may be proclaimed *persona non grata.* The 1961 Vienna Convention on diplomatic relations made provision for a special group of so-called non-acceptable persons among the non-diplomatic personnel. A person may be proclaimed *persona non grata* or "non-acceptable" even before entering the country to which he may have been accredited. Finally, another important reason is a break in diplomatic relations or war. In both cases, the diplomatic representatives and the entire personnel of the mission together with their families must be allowed to return to their country.

V. International Officials

At the close of the 19th century, Geršić made the far-sighted observation that "as a result of increasing cultural solidarity and common interest in communications, states are evidently tending to replace separate administrative operations with a joint international organization to administer certain affairs and relations of a general international nature." He noted at that early date that, "we are already today on the threshold of a new epoch of an international administrative organization which will give a completely new and different shape to the intercourse of cultured nations. In the course of time, this process will engulf one branch of administration after the other, and this international organized form of administration will undoubtedly be competent to gain increasing importance and application in international life." Geršić was already making attempts to distinguish the officials of the "international administration" from the group of diplomatic agents, stating that "since these organs operate and perform official duties in the sphere of international affairs, they may rightfully be called international administrative bodies."

In Geršić's days there were several international unions and commissions established for certain joint administrative duties. On the basis of an exhaustive scientific analysis, he foresaw a new institution in international law, which only began to assume a distinct shape between the two world wars (the staff in the Secretariat of the League of Nations, in the International Labour Organization, in the Reparations Commission, etc.). After the Second World War, in view of the proliferation of international organizations and agencies, international officials received recognition under international law.

The legal status of international officials today is regulated on the basis of international treaties between the interested states, for each international organization and agency separately. These treaties give the officials of an international organization rights and privileges in the countries which are members of the international organization concerned. National delegates to the United Nations and officials of this international organization enjoy the privileges and immunities necessary for an untrammeled exercise of their functions in the Organization. According to Article 105 of the Charter, these privileges and immunities are enjoyed in the territory of each member of the United Nations. These rights were soon elaborated in the U.N. Convention on Privileges and Immunities, adopted on 13 February 1946, and in the Convention on Privileges and Immunities of Specialized Agencies adopted on 21 November 1947.

Privileges and immunities are enjoyed in the first instance by the Secretary-General of the United Nations, by all his aides and their spouses and minor children. They enjoy the same measure of privileges, immunities, various exemptions and facilities as the heads of diplomatic missions. However, under the 1946 Convention, officials of the United Nations designated by the Secretary-General with the approval of the General Assembly enjoy judicial immunity only during their appointment, exemption from taxes on the salaries and payments received from the United Nations, foreign currency and customs privileges. Privileges are granted solely in the interest of the United Nations and not for their personal advantage. The Secretary-General is authorized to strip an official of his immunities if his activity has been detrimental to the interests of the United Nations. If the Secretary-General committed abuses, the Security Council would be authorized to deprive him of his immunities.

Experts of the United Nations who are not officials enjoy privileges and immunities only during the time spent performing the mission for the United Nations. Generally speaking, they enjoy immunity from personal arrest, detainment or confiscation of personal effects, judicial immunity for acts committed in the performance of their mission, inviolability of all mail and documents, the right to use ciphers and to receive mail in communication with the United Nations, monetary and foreign currency privileges. This group of international officials is also given privileges and immunities in the interest of the United Nations and not for their personal advantage.

The United Nations is authorized to issue its officials with a valid travel permit, called "the United Nations *laissez-passer*". The Secretary-General, his aides and directors enjoy the same privileges as heads of diplomatic missions on the basis of this travel permit.

The officials of specialized agencies also have similar immunities and privileges under the 1947 Convention.

Judges of the International Court of Justice, by nature of their office, cannot be officials of the United Nations, even though the World Court is one of its organs. Therefore, they are not included in these two conventions. However, while not being officials of the United Nations, the judges of the International Court of Justice should in our opinion be classified as international officials, since they are not representatives of member countries. They have diplomatic privileges and immunities during the exercise of their functions, according to Article 19 of the Statute of the International Court of Justice.

Following an exchange of letters between the president of the International Court of Justice and the minister of foreign affairs of the Netherlands, dating 26 June 1946, members of the Court enjoy the same treatment as heads of diplomatic missions accredited to the Queen of the Netherlands. They are not accountable to local jurisdiction for acts performed in their official capacity, within the limitations of their duties.

VI. Consuls

Concept — History — Types of Consuls — Classes and Ranking of Heads of Consulates — Consular Corps — Appointment of a Consular Mission — Functions of Consuls — Relationship between Consular and Diplomatic Representations — Consular Immunities and Privileges — Termination of a Consular Mission.

1. Concept — Consuls are authorized persons who protect the interests of their country and its citizens in the territory of another state in administrative, legal and economic affairs and in education, culture and science. The rule is that consuls do not have a political function. They are official representatives of a state without a diplomatic capacity. They perform their duties in accordance with the laws of the country on whose behalf and for whose interests they work, and in compliance with international agreements and international customs. If there is no diplomatic mission in the country to which the consul is posted, he may also be assigned a political role. In this event, the head of the consulate, without changing his consular status, may be authorized to perform diplomatic acts, but only with the agreement of the host country.

The Vienna Convention on consular relations envisages that a consular officer may be authorized to represent his country at any inter-governmental organization. Acting in this capacity, the consular officer has the right to all privileges and immunities awarded a representative to such an inter-governmental organization.

2. History — At the time of the Crusades, developed commercial centers — such as, for instance, Marseilles, Genoa, Venice and Dubrovnik — founded commercial colonies in various ports on the Mediterranean, Aegean, and Marmora. Their settlements soon extended as far as the shores of the Atlantic Ocean and Baltic Sea. Hanseatic and Flemish towns soon followed their example. Each of these mercantile colonies elected a headman called consul. He was authorized to maintain order in the settlement and to enforce the legal regulations of his country, since at that time the principle of personal rather than territorial law prevailed. The consul exercised judicial authority over his fellow countrymen. The consuls were not diplomatic representatives at that time either. Diplomatic functions were performed by envoys, sent from time to time as the need arose. As permanent diplomatic representatives came to be appointed, at the time of the growth of absolutist states and centralization of government, consuls were no longer elected by the members of a mercantile settlement but commissioned by the state and charged with the duty of protecting the interests of its subjects. However, since the territorial principle was gaining ascendance — personal law was applied if it was in accordance with the public order of the territorial state — the character of consular functions changed. Consuls no longer had police or judicial authority over their fellow countrymen. They became organs of their state, authorized to protect the interests of its citizens before local authorities. Essentially this nature of the functions of consular representatives has remained unchanged since that time. The consuls in so-called infidel lands, for example in Turkey, Egypt, Tunisia, Morocco, etc., were an exception. The consuls in these countries continued to be privileged and had political and judicial authority. The special status and rights of "European consuls" in the Levant were regulated by specially concluded agreements, so-called *treaties of capitulation.* The oldest treaty of this kind was concluded with the Ottoman Empire in 1528.

3. Types of Consuls, Class and Rank of Heads of Consulates —

There are two types of consuls: career officers *(consules missi)* and honorary officers *(consules electi).* Career officers are, as their name implies, professional consuls; they are the permanent officials of the state and can hold no other office. Honorary consuls are distinguished citizens, most often of the territorial state, who perform consular duties without remuneration. As a rule, these are businessmen who perform these tasks for personal, business, or other reasons.

Every state is free to decide whether it will appoint or receive honorary consular officers.

Four classes of heads of consulates are generally recognized, regardless of whether they are career or honorary officers. These are the consul general, consul, vice-consul and consular agent.

The *consul general* is a consul of the first class, commissioned by the head of state, or in some countries exceptionally by the minister of foreign affairs. His consular area is the largest. The second class includes *consuls,* with a smaller consular area, who are also commissioned by the head of state, or infrequently by the minister of foreign affairs. Vice-consuls are in the third class, a class with an even more restricted area, and they are under the supervision of the consul general or consul. The vice-consul is nominated by the minister of foreign affairs. *Consular agents* form the last class. They are appointed by the consul general or consul, with the agreement of the host country. The consular agent works within the terms of reference of his powers, (the so-called *licence*), issued by the consul general or consul.

The heads of consulates are ranked in their classes according to the date of issue of *exequatur.* If two or more heads of consulates have been given *exequatur* on the same date, the order of precedence is determined by the date of submission of their letters patent to the host country. Provisional officers are ranked after all the heads of consulates. Among themselves they are ranked according to the dates on which they undertook the office of a provisional officer. Honorary consular officers, when heading consulates, are ranked in their respective classes after career officers who are heads of consulates. Heads of consulates have precedence over consular officers who do not hold this post.

4. Consular Corps — This is the body of all consuls in a place, including heads of consulates as well as official of the same rank. The highest administrative authority of the host country in the place of residence of consular representations establishes a list of the consular corps on the basis of consular immunities and privileges enjoyed by them. The consul having greatest seniority is called the doyen of the consular corps and has the same function as the doyen of the diplomatic corps.

5. Appointment of a Consular Mission — Newly appointed heads of consulates are issued letters patent by their governments. The consul general and the consul are issued this document by their heads of state, less frequently by the minister of foreign affairs, but always by the latter in the case of a vice-consul. In the letters patent, a state informs the other state of the appointment of a consul, giving his name, title and class, and citing the consular area and headquarters of the consulate. If the receiving country agrees, the state may substitute for the letters patent a notification with all envisaged consequences. The appointed head of a consulate acquires this capacity only when the host country agrees that he may perform such functions. If it does, the host country issues him an *exequatur,* which serves as proof of his acceptance. The *exequatur* also provides a guarantee that the consul will be protected in the course of his duties, which means that he will enjoy immunities and privileges to which he is entitled. If the state refuses to grant *exequatur,* it is not obliged to state the reasons for its refusal. The 1963 Vienna Convention on consular relations permits the possibility of provisional recognition pending the issue of the *exequatur* so that he can attend to his office. As soon as the head of the consulate is permitted to exercise his functions, the host country must immediately inform the competent authorities in the consular area, to enable the head of the consulate to carry out his duties.

6. Functions of Consuls — As a rule the consul protects the interests of his country in his area. However, he may perform consular functions outside his consular area, if allowed by the host country. He may also undertake the exercise of consular functions in some other state, if the interested states do not object. The 1963 Vienna Convention on consular relations also envisages the possibility of the consulate of one state performing consular functions on behalf of a third country, if the receiving country does not object.

It is the consul's duty to oversee the observance and enforcement of treaties in force between his state and the territorial state and to intervene in cases of violations of treaty provisions. He is expected to take care that his interventions should not have a political character. Interventions of a political nature are the domain only of diplomatic and not of consular representatives.

The consul protects the interests of citizens — physical and legal persons — of his state in accordance with the laws and other rules in force in the country where he is posted, and on the basis of international agreements, international customs, and the 1963 Vienna Convention on consular relations. The consul assists citizens of his state in matters of repatriation and inheritance in the territory of the host country. He protects the interests of minors and incapacitated citizens of his country, particularly in cases where it is necessary to appoint a guardian or trustee; organizes legal defense; speaks on behalf of citizens of his country, or takes measures to secure for them a defense attorney before the courts or other authorities, protecting the rights and interests of these citizens when they cannot defend their own rights and interests.

To facilitate the exercise of their functions, consular officers have freedom of communication with the citizens who have been placed under arrest or detained in some other way, to see that they are represented in court. Consular officers, however, must refrain from intervening on behalf of a fellow citizen who has been detained if the interested party expressly objects to this.

The consul is charged with a number of duties of an administrative character, such as the issuance of passports and travel permits for fellow citizens, as well as the issuance of visas and other documents to persons wishing to travel to that country. Consuls also issue affidavits and act as registrars. In fact, they perform all those duties which at home are normally handled by a notary public, in respect to documents issued by or to be used in the receiving state or the country of the consul.

An important consular function is to foster the growth of trade, economic, cultural, and scientific relations between the two states and to promote friendly relations between them. He must therefore keep abreast of the commercial, economic, cultural, and scientific life in the host country, submit reports on this to his government and supply information to interested parties.

The general protection of shipping is in the jurisdiction of the consul. He is entitled to supervise and inspect ocean-going and river ships which carry the flag of his country, and the airplanes registered in his country, including their crews. The consul gives assistance to these ships and airplanes and to their crews. For this purpose he receives the travel declarations of these ships, inspects and stamps visas on ship papers, and conducts enquiries into incidents which may have occurred during their passage. He also settles all disputes between the captain, officers, and seamen.

The functions of consuls are increasing day by day. Consuls are more and more active in cultural and even sports exchanges; they perform functions in the realm of tourism, social security, etc. It is safe to say that the duties of consuls cover the entire range of foreign relations, except for those reserved exclusively to the diplomatic agents.

7. Consular and Diplomatic Missions — Consuls are not hierarchically subordinate to the head of the diplomatic mission in the same country but are directly accountable to their government. However, the head of a diplomatic mission has the right to supervise consulates in the state to which they are accredited, and may even temporarily remove a consul from his post.

With the agreement of the host country, the head of the consulate may be authorized, if there is no diplomatic mission in that country, to perform diplomatic functions as well, The authority to perform diplomatic duties does not entitle him to diplomatic privileges and immunities.

Today it is becoming increasingly common for consular sections to be opened as parts of diplomatic missions and not as separate consulates. The names of the members of the diplomatic mission who perform consular functions are submitted to the ministry of foreign affairs of the receiving country. Although performing consular functions, these officials continue to enjoy their diplomatic privileges and immunities.

8. Consular Immunities and Privileges — Consular immunities and privileges are certainly not so extensive as those enjoyed by diplomatic agents. Consular officers have functional immunity. They are exempt from the jurisdiction of judicial and administrative authorities of the receiving country for acts committed in the course of their consular duties. An exception is when civil suits are brought concerning contracts concluded by the consular officer in his private capacity, or suits by a third person for damages arising from an accident caused in the host country by a vehicle, ship, or airplane.

Consular officers may not be arrested or put under temporary detention except in case of a serious criminal offense and on the basis of a warrant issued by the competent judicial authorities. If criminal proceedings are brought against a consular officer, he has the duty to appear before the competent authorities. The proceedings must be conducted with due respect for his person and in a way which will least disrupt the performance of consular duties.

The following rules are in force in respect to giving evidence: the consular officer may not be forced to give evidence. Consular officials and members of the service staff, however, must not refuse to give evidence, so long as they are not required to reveal facts concerning the exercise of their functions.

In addition to these immunities and privileges, consular officials enjoy the following additional rights: exemption from the obligation of registering as aliens and of having to obtain a residence permit, exemption from fiscal levies and imposts, etc.

The consul has the right to communicate with all citizens of his country whenever they are within his consular area, for the purpose of protecting them and their interests. This incontestable right of consuls derives from the nature of their consular duties. Consuls also are entitled to communicate with the authorities of the host country and with the authorities of their own government. In this communication the consulate may use all convenient means of communication, including diplomatic or consular couriers, diplomatic or consular pouches, and cipher dispatches. The consulate may erect and use a radio transmitter, but only with the agreement of the host country. Consuls are entitled to the honors due them on every occasion. They are acknowledged the right to exhibit their national arms and flag on the offices of the consulate.

The premises of the consulate are inviolable. The authorities of the host country may not enter consular premises, unless given permission by the head of the consulate, by persons he designates or by the head of the diplomatic mission. The receiving country has the special duty of preventing forcible entry into the premises of the consulate, damage to the consulate, a breach of the peace or threat to its dignity.

The archives of the consulate are inviolable at all times and in all places.

Almost all the aforementioned privileges and immunities are also granted to honorary consular officers. They are, however, not extended to members of the family of the honorary consular officer who is employed in a consulate headed by an honorary consul; the consular archives of the consulate headed by an honorary consul are inviolable at all times and in all places, provided they are kept separate from other papers and documents, and particularly from the private correspondence of the head of the consulate and every person working with him.

9. Termination of the Consular Mission — The state which has appointed a consul may recall him at any time. The functions of the consul also cease if his country retracts the letters patent. In both cases, the receiving state must be notified. On the other hand, the host country may withdraw its *exequatur*. The country of the consul is then obliged to take measures in the shortest possible time to transfer the consul whose *exequatur* has been withdrawn.

The termination of a consular mission occurs upon the consul's death or resignation.

The functions of the consul cease when consular relations are broken off. A break in diplomatic relations may, but need not, entail a break in consular communications, if the states breaking off diplomatic relations agree to continue consular relations. Consular functions cease and the consulate is closed down in the event of an outbreak of war between the two countries. Protection of citizens is entrusted to a protecting power or some other neutral state, while the building of the consulate may be placed for safekeeping in the charge of another state which is not involved in the armed conflict.

Chapter Two: International Acts

I. Unilateral Legal Acts

Concept — Classification

1. Concept — A unilateral legal act in international law is the duly expressed legally relevant interest of an international subject. Its purpose is to establish any changes in or put an end to a given legal situation. The interest of this international subject must not be in contradiction with the legally protected general interest of international law. This means that states may not make use of a unilateral legal act in order to acquire greater rights than have been granted to them under the positive rules of international law. If a unilateral legal act of one subject should challenge the legally protected interest of another subject, the latter can, under certain conditions, nullify the effect of the former's unilateral legal act by putting forward his own interest, which is protected under the universally valid rules of international law. Before the unilateral legal acts expressing the legal interest of a subject of an international law can have a legal effect, they must receive tacit or express consent from the other interested subjects. This requirement stems from the specific nature of international law, in which the subjects are states, equally sovereign among themselves, whose mutual legal acts cannot be compared with the acts of government in the internal legal system of state. Bartos correctly holds that unilateral legal acts in international law are only "relatively, conditionally and up to a point unilateral."

2. Classification — The main types of unilateral legal acts are notification, recognition, protest and renunciation.

Notification is an official statement having an international purport that is presented to a subject of international law. Such a statement may supply information concerning a policy, demand, event or fact that has taken, is taking, or is about to take place. A statement of this kind is official, which means that the notification must be presented by a diplomatic agent.

As a rule, notification is made directly. It may be given indirectly if no normal diplomatic relations are maintained or if there is a state of war. The state receiving the notification cannot subsequently claim not to be familiar with the facts contained therein.

Notification is usually mandatory in the event of a declaration of war; notification of the state of war to neutral states by a belligerent; notification of blockade; notification on re-entry into force of the treaties concluded prior to the war and envisaged under a peace treaty; registration of international treaties in accordance with Article 102 of the U.N. Charter.

Recognition is a unilateral legal act which acknowledges a given situation or accepts the demand of an international subject: *e.g.,* the recognition of a new state or government, of an insurgent as a belligerent, etc.

Recognition may be granted expressly, tacitly or implicitly (*e.g.,* establishment of diplomatic relations with a new state implies its recognition).

Protest is a unilateral legal act which challenges the legality of a new situation or of a demand by an international subject.

Protest is an important institution in international law, deriving from the generally valid rule *qui tacet consentire videtur.* It is an unwilling acquiescence to a demand or situation. It is a legal remedy to protect an interest of an international subject. Protest has legal effect if it has been issued or transmitted by a diplomatic agent.

Renunciation is the unilateral act by a subject of international law whereby it renounces some of its entitlements. Renunciation must be made expressly, and it must be very closely defined. Peace treaties frequently contain various types of renunciation: *e.g.,* renunciation of demands for reparations, territory, rights and so forth.

II. International Treaties

1. Introduction

Concept and Definition — Name and Form — Components of Treaty and Language — Subject Matter — Classification of International Treaties — Codification of International Treaties Law

2. Concept and Definition — International comity requires states, as the basic subjects of international law, to maintain relations for the purpose of dealing with numerous questions of a mutual and general interest. The most suitable instrument laying down the rules of conduct and behavior of states is the international treaty. During the first fifteen years following the Second World War, more than 400 volumes of different treaties were registered with the Secretariat of the United Nations. In recent years the number of treaties concluded has increased even more. The growing regulation of relations between subjects of international law — mainly states but also international organizations — is one of the most distinctive features of contemporary international life.

An international treaty is a bilateral or multilateral legal act coordinating the interests of the contracting parties with the purpose of causing effects envisaged under the rules of international law.

Legal doctrine is not unanimous as to the substance of the term international treaty. There are two schools of thought. According to the consensualist theory, the treaty is an agreement of wills that has been reached on an issue by two or more contracting parties. For this theory, consensus is the only essential element of international law, without which this legal act cannot exist, while its formal aspects are not of substantive importance. According to the formalist (or normalist) theory, the treaty denotes the existence of a formal act which comprises the consensus of the contracting parties. The formal nature of the act and its existence are deemed to be essential in the concept of the treaty.

The majority of contemporary international jurists support the consensus theory. They define the international treaty as a bilateral or multilateral act arising from the concordance of wills of two or more subjects of international law with the purpose of causing certain legal effects, or of establishing, abolishing, or altering a relationship between them, pursuant to international law.

Since the definition of a concept or institution is indispensable in matters requiring codification, it is understandable that the United Nations International Law Commission, in its draft rules governing international treaty law which provided the basis for the international covention, should have supplied its own definition of the international treaty. According to it, a *treaty* denotes any international agreement concluded between states in written form, contained in a single, or in two or more mutually related instruments, whatever their appellation may be, which are pursuant to the rules of international law.

As it is known, in the course of the Commission's work, different special rapporteurs proposed different definitions of a treaty. They are all of interest in trying to understand the essence of a concept as it is understood today. The first rapporteur, Brierly, defined the treaty as a written agreement between two or more states or international organizations, establishing a relationship pursu‑ ant to international law between the contracting parties. Lauterpacht, on the other hand, held that treaties are agreements between states — including under this heading organizations of states as well — for the purpose of creating legal obligations and rights for the contracting parties. Similarly, Fitzmaurice points out that the treaty is an international agreement in the shape of a formal instrument, concluded between two or more collective entities which have the capacity of subjects of international law and are possessed of international personality and treaty-making power, and is designed to create rights and obligations or establish relationships which are regulated under international law. For Valdock, the international treaty is an agreement which must be regulated under international law and is concluded between two or more states that are subjects of international law and are possessed of an international legal personality.

Like the majority of writers, contemporary international law and the current practice of states and international organizations are generally adopting the consensualist theory. It has been adopted in the rules on the registration of international treaties in the United Nations General Assembly; and according to it, an international treaty is a written act signifying the concordance of wills between states for the purpose of establishing rights and obligations. The text need not be expressed in its solemn form; it is sufficient that there be an exchange of letters of agreement between states for such a contract to be regarded as a treaty, provided, of course, that the acts are designed to create a certain international obligation.

3. Name and Form of Treaty — Contemporary international law makes no distinction between treaties on the basis of their appellation. Thus a large number of other appellations are used for various types of contracts. In the doctrine of international law there are different definitions, although practice does not conform to any specific rules. Currently in use are the following terms:

— *Treaty,* the most widely used appellation, is applied to the most important types of agreement, those of a political character in the first place (treaties of peace, alliance, friendship and cooperation, or neutrality). It usually denotes multilateral agreements of quasi-legal character, and so-called law-making treaties. It is also exclusively applied to the acts establishing international organizations, international unions, etc. Trade arrangements of long-term character are usually called treaties (treaties on trade and navigation, for example).

— *Convention* is most frequently used for contracts which do not have a political character, especially for instruments creating legal rules of general character (The Hague Conventions; the Barcelona Convention; the Convention on the Abolition of Slavery; the Convention on the Privileges and Immunities of the United Nations and its Specialized Agencies; the Convention of the International Labour Organization; the Convention of the Universal Postal Union, etc.).

— *Pact* is most frequently applied to political treaties that have an especially solemn character (for example, the Kellogg-Briand Pact, etc.).

— *Covenant* and *charter* are used in the same sense as pact (*e.g.,* the Covenant of the League of Nations, the Charter of the United Nations).

— *Agreement* generally applies to treaties of an economic and technical character, or of a financial and humanitarian significance, and in some cases also to political treaties having a special purpose (agreement on the extension of military aid and cooperation, agreement on the granting of military basis, etc.).

— *Protocol,* in the sense of a treaty protocol, is an agreement of complementary character, designed to amend or provide interpretation of other treaties, etc.

— *Declaration,* in the sense of treaty-declaration, is an international instrument which establishes joint policies by the signatories of this declaration. It is also used for the acts which lay down certain legal principles.

— *Final Act* is a formal document which enumerates treaties or conventions that have been concluded at an international congress or conference (for example, the Final Act of the Peace Conference in Lausanne of 1923).

— *General Act* is an instrument that enumerates treaties or conventions. It is usually an act which itself has become an international treaty, where the enumerated treaties or conventions are simply incorporated or appended. (For example, the General Act for the Pacific Settlement of International Disputes, signed in Geneva on 26 September 1928.)

— *Compromise* denotes one means of peacefully settling an international dispute.

— *Statute* is an agreement of contractual character on the establishment of an international organization, or on the foundation of a special organ or body.

— *Concordat* is an agreement between the Holy See and the head of a state, which regulates the interests of the Roman Catholic Church in that state.

— *Modus vivendi* designates all manner of provisional agreements, or a temporary agreement to extend the validity of a treaty from one year to the next.

Since modern international law makes no legal distinction whatever between the various appellations of contracts, it is the practice of the United Nations Secretariat to register and publish any international treaty whatever its appellation might be.

There are no rules in international law to prescribe the form or procedure for the conclusion of an international treaty, although the constitutional laws of some states do contain suitable provisions for both. The doctrine of international law is trying to categorize treaties according to their form or according to the person appearing on behalf of the contracting parties. Thus there are treaties in the form of an agreement between states (examples of this practice most often date back to the 19th century. But there are some in the present century too, such as the Treaty of Versailles and the peace treaties concluded with the former enemy states after the First and Second World Wars), or treaties between heads of states (for example, the peace treaties of 1814 and 1815, and the Paris Treaty of 1856), or treaties in the form of international agreements (this type is in wide use today, in view of the general tendency toward simplification and less formality), or in the form of agreements concluded between competent ministries, or government organs, or agencies.

International treaties may be concluded in different forms, provided the contracting parties have agreed on the subject matter and the treaty has been drawn up in written form.

4. Components of Treaty and Language — Since international treaties may be concluded in a variety of forms, their component parts may also differ. Here again there are no rules of international law as to which parts the text of a treaty must have. Practice has shown that every treaty, whatever its form, contains several more or less fixed portions, which are known as the preamble, main body, and final part of the treaty.

All international treaties as a rule have a title that describes the kind of treaty and its subject matter (*e.g.*, treaty of alliance, agreement on trade or navigation, treaty on the extension of military assistance). Only treaties concluded in simplified form need not have a title in their original text (agreements arrived at through an exchange of notes or letters, etc.). In addition to subject-matter, the title in bilateral treaties usually also states the names of contracting parties.

In earlier treaty practice, which was in force until the end of the 19th century, the title was usually followed by invocation of the divinity. Following the treaty practices of the ancient world, invocation was very widely used in the middle ages and even afterwards. Today, for understandable reasons, its traces can only be found in the concordats that the Roman Catholic Church concludes with states.

The preamble or introduction to a treaty is part of the text and is set out directly after the title. The preamble states the reason for concluding the treaty and the names of the representatives who took part in negotiations, mentioning that their powers had been verified.

The main body of the treaty is the most important part of the text, because it states the provisions that create rights and obligations in connection with the subject matter. The content of this portion depends on the subject matter that the treaty wants to regulate and relationships that are to be established or regulated. In addition, this part of the treaty may also contain certain complementary clauses defining the concepts which appear in the other provisions of the main body.

The main body is followed by the final or concluding provisions. They usually deal with the entry into force of the treaty (*e.g.,* on the day of signature, or after ratification instruments have been exchanged or deposited), termination (*e.g.,* following its abrogation or expiration), revision, accession, and so forth. It also contains provisions relative to reservations, registration and publication, possibly also a colonial or federal clause, as well as stipulations regarding the original copies of the treaty, their number and languages, signifying the original language. The text of the treaty ends with the date and place of its conclusion, signatures and the seals. The main body is often amplified by additional articles that are appended. They have the same legal force as the treaty itself and form its integral part. They are called appendices, annexes, protocols, additional protocols, etc. Appended to peace treaties are usually geographical and topographical maps.

The contracting parties are quite free to select the language or languages in which a treaty is to be drafted. Today two or more languages are generally used, although for special reasons states may opt for one language only. Reasons are various and may be political (*e.g.,* insistence on the principle of the sovereign equality of states) or purely practical (*e.g.,* suitability of a language for a given subject matter, its richness and precision, etc.). Hence there are no uniform and general rules on the use of language, although it is desirable that the treaty itself should determine which text or texts are to be regarded as authentic.

5. Subject Matter — The subject matter of a treaty comprises one or more obligations undertaken by the contracting parties, or unilateral undertaking of only one of them. Most international treaties contain the obligation of two parties, or of several parties equally if it is a multilateral treaty. The binding nature of the treaty may be expressed by the fact that both parties assume the same obligations. However, there are many treaties in which different obligations are assumed. In others only unilateral obligations are established. This type of treaty often gives proof of an existing inequality between the contracting parties, or may arise as a result of pressure or hegemony of a bigger and stronger state. This, however, need not always be the case, because a unilateral obligation may be the consequence of a certain earlier service rendered or the commission of a wrongful act.

The subject matter of a treaty constitutes one of its principal elements. Contemporary international law does not allow states complete freedom as regards the subject matter of a treaty. Recent practice has shown the tendency of prohibiting the conclusion of treaties which run counter to international law. Their content may not be unlawful. A treaty will be unlawful if its implementation encroaches on the imperative norms of universal international law (*jus cogens*) or if its fulfilment is physically impossible. This prohibition does not mean that the treaties may not transgress any positive rule of public international law. In contemporary public international law there are two rules that can be departed from or changed (*jus dispositivum*) by means of the treaties concluded by states, but there are also norms of an imperative character, which cannot be changed. States are, of course, not free to conclude treaties which condone slavery, genocide, armed attack against a third country, preparations for and conduct of a war of aggression, white slavery, etc. The United Nations Charter in Article 103 provides for the nullity of treaties that are contrary to the norms of international law. "In the event of conflict between the obligations of the members of the United Nations under the present Charter and their obligations under any other international agreement, their obligations under the present Charter shall prevail," states the above mentioned article.

The contemporary practice of states, the main body of international jurists, and United Nations Law Commission have accepted the necessity for state negotiated treaties to be consistent with the positive international legal order. It also regulates the question of the subject matter of treaties. We should also mention that the treaty, in addition to being permissible, must also be practically feasible. A treaty which is not practically feasible of fulfilment cannot produce legal effects, and the agreement of wills of the contracting parties in the main body could only be a fiction.

6. Classification of International Treaties — In the theory of international law, international treaties are classified in a number of ways, according to different criteria. Here are some of the principal classifications:

a. *According to the number of contracting parties* — In terms of the number of contracting parties, international treaties may be bilateral or multilateral. The former are concluded only between two parties, the latter have three or more contracting parties. However, a bilateral treaty may eventually become a multilateral one, if it is subsequently acceded to by other states. As regards the subject matter, the treaties concluded between two states generally regulate a specific aspect of their relations, either to bring about certain actions, or to provide for legal effects of such actions. This, however, cannot be regarded as a hard and fast rule, for there are an enormous number of bilateral agreements resulting in the emergence of general rules governing relations on long-term bases, such as the treaties on ownership of property on both sides of national frontiers or on local border areas of commerce.

Legal theory sometimes singles out so-called *collective treaties* as a separate kind of agreement. They contain rules compulsory for all states. According to some writers, they are compulsory by virtue of the fact that such treaties represent an international custom. Thus they are frequently called treaty laws of a constitutional character. They bind even those states which neither participated in their conclusion nor subsequently acceded to them. For example, although the Geneva Convention on Prisoners of War of 1929 was not in force between the U.S.S.R. and Germany, the International Military Tribunal in Nuremberg held criminally liable and convicted German war criminals for crimes against the Soviet war prisoners. The Nuremberg Tribunal did so rightfully, because the provisions of the Geneva Convention represent a general legal rule of international law. This standpoint is corroborated by such international legal acts as the United Nations Charter. The Charter was likewise a collective treaty regulating international peace and security, setting out obligations and rights for member states as well as non-member states.

b. *According to sphere of operation* — In jurisprudence, treaties are most frequently divided according to their sphere of operation into *treaty laws* and *treaty contracts*. Grounds for this division are based on the presumption that treaty laws contain general rules of international law valid over a longer period, whereas treaty contracts regulate a specific international relationship, of a limited duration, establishing a series of reciprocal rights and obligations (*e.g.* a loan agreement, a commercial treaty, etc.). However, this distinction is not fully acceptable, because in practice many international agreements have features pertaining to both types of treaty. It may be applicable only insofar as it emphasizes the differences that may exist between the two as sources of international law; the treaty laws are much more important as sources, since they extend to a large number of states and concern issues of a wider or of a general significance. Treaty contracts usually apply only to relations between two states, and their significance as sources of law should be assessed in this light.

c. *According to the geographical factor* — In a geographical sense, international treaties may be general or regional. A general international treaty applies to a large number of states, irrespective of the part of the world in which they are located. Regional treaties are restricted to states from a specific part of the world.

d. *According to possibility of accession* — Parties to a treaty may be its original signatories and those which joined later by accession, if the latter was provided for by the original contracting parties. Treaties containing no provision on subsequent accession are called *closed treaties*. Others are known as *open treaties,* and they acknowledge in advance the right of accession to other states which did not participate in their drafting. There are also so-called *semi-open treaties,* and the states wishing to accede to them must first consult with the original contracting parties.

The U.N. International Law Commission was faced with the question of how to deal with the right of all states to accede to treaties of multilateral and general character. This question was especially interesting because in the process of decolonization following World War II, a large number of new states were interested in participating in many conventions which had been promulgated and had come into force long before their emancipation. However, these instruments stipulated that the question of their revision and amendment, as well as of accession, was reserved for the states that concluded them. In the case of conventions and treaties adopted within the League of Nations — and there are a large number of those — this meant that only the former colonial powers which ruled the non-self-governing territories were entitled to decide on the amendment and extension of validity of these international instruments.

Two completely opposed standpoints were taken on this question within the U.N. Commission. According to one school of thought, on the basis of the principle of sovereign equality, states are free to choose their treaty partners and cannot be forced to allow for the accession of all interested states to multilateral treaties of a general character. Others hold that because of the significance of the issues involved and because the international community wants the largest possible number of states to participate in the treaties of this character, they should be open for accession to all states (the so-called all-states clause). In its final draft of the rule of accession, the Commission stood by the traditional view that accession to a treaty is possible only subject to an express provision to this effect, or if the original contracting parties should decide so subsequently.

e. *According to subject matter* — In terms of subject matter, international treaties may be of many different kinds. The most important types of treaties are political, commercial, technical, administrative, or procedural. Within these there are further distinctions, *e.g.,* political treaties include treaties of friendship, alliance, mutual assistance, neutrality, etc. While such classification may be interesting from a theoretical standpoint, in practical terms it has no use.

f. *According to form* — In this respect, treaties may be divided into written and verbal treaties. This division can stand if it is accepted that international treaties may also be concluded verbally. However, we believe that all treaties must be concluded in a written form. Verbal treaties are so-called gentlemen's agreements, contracted between heads of state. They are based on international comity rather than on international law. Such treaties have no legal force.

g. *According to the method of conclusion* — In terms of procedure and method of conclusion, treaties may be solemn or concluded in simplified form. The solemn treaties, which are treaties in the true sense of the word, are concluded according to a special procedure and are subject to ratification by the highest competent authority. The treaties concluded in simplified form are usually by an exchange of notes and letters. Agreements in this form come into force by acceptance, approval or, in rare cases, by ratification. The competence of the organs which endorse or approve an agreement depends on the constitutional practice of different states, but the procedure itself is quite simple.

7. Codification of International Treaty Law — The codification of the rules of the international law of treaties and their progressive development is not just a question of legal technique but a legal and political question on which relations between states depend to a very great measure. Since interests of states, and especially their protection, play a crucial role in the contemporary international community, accession to treaties is generally a political question.

Work on codifying the rules of the international law of treaties was started by the U.N. International Law Commission in 1949, at its first session. In the course of several years of work, four special rapporteurs succeeded one another. Each one submitted his own report emphasizing the points and conceptions which he regarded as essential for the Commission's work. Although the Commission's work was thus enriched, it was also impeded to a certain extent, because on the election of each new rapporteur the topics under consideration were revised and the discussions duplicated. With the election of Waldock as the fourth rapporteur, the Commission's work was accelerated.

In 1966, at its 18th session, the Commission was finally able to conclude its work on drafting the rules of the law of treaties. Its proposal served as the basis for the drafting of an international convention on the law of treaties, which was adopted at the diplomatic conference in Vienna in 1968 and 1969.

III. Treaty Making Power

Introduction — Treaty-Making Power

1. Introduction — Treaties are most often concluded by states. However, the contemporary development of international relations and the creation of a large number of different international organizations, headed by the United Nations Organization, raised the problem of the treaty-making power of these new subjects of international law. Basically, treaty-making power is possessed only by the sovereign states, so that the question of their international treaty-making capacity does not arise. Within the terms of their competences and function, international organizations, by exercising their treaty-making capacity, also exercise their international personality, even if their statutes do not specifically invest them with international legal personality enabling them to conclude international treaties.

The question of the treaty-making power of international subjects has two aspects: a. treaty-making capacity depending on the kind of state, and b. treaty-making power and competence of international organizations to conclude international treaties.

2. Capacity — Treaty making is one of the oldest and most characteristic attributes of the sovereignty and independence of states. "The right of a state to conclude an international treaty is a feature of its sovereignty," was the judgment handed down by the Permanent Court of International Justice in the Wimbledon Case. Therefore, if a state enjoys normal and full independence, the only limitation on its effective exercise of power to conclude international treaties may stem from the need to conform with written rules of international law concerning the validity of the treaty.

The U.N. International Law Commission ruled that each state has the ability to make international treaties, except that the member states of a federal state may do so only if permitted under their federal constitution, and within those limitations.

Although all states are capable of making international treaties, the treaty-making power of some of them may nevertheless be limited. Attempts have been made to categorize states according to their treaty-making capacity. The fullest categorization would be as follows: a. fully sovereign states; b. federal states; c. confederations of states; d. states in personal union;

e. states in a real union; f. the Vatican; g. permanently neutral states; h. international organization of states; i. semi-sovereign states, *e.g.,* vassal states or protectorates.

The case of states under a. is quite clear, and as regards federal states, the rule is that international treaties are made only by the federal state as a whole and not by its federal units (*e.g.,* the United States of America, Canada, Australia). In the case of Switzerland, although international treaty making is in the federal government's competence, the national constitution nevertheless permits the cantons a limited treaty-making ability, and many of them have entered into separate arrangements with other countries (Similar cases were those of the members of the Federal State of Germany between 1871 and the end of the First World War, and of Germany under the Weimar Constitution of 1919. And similarly, Article 32 of the Federal Republic of Germany's Constitution of 1949 provides for the *Länder* to have a limited ability of making treaties with other states, subject to approval from the federal government). With composite states and unions of states, the treaty-making capacity is determined in different ways. In personal unions and confederations of states, treaties are usually concluded by each member state separately. In a real union, on the other hand, it is only the union as a whole that has the treaty-making ability and competence. The Holy See (Vatican) is not a state in the sense accepted by international law; but having been recognized as an international subject, it is able to conclude international treaties, especially the concordats. The permanently neutral states are limited to a certain extent in the exercise of their sovereign rights, especially as regards their ability to conclude treaties. They may not conclude treaties of alliance, collective assistance or guarantees. As to territories under international control, the practice is for such territories not to have treaty-making power. Treaties are made on their behalf by the competent state or international organization.

Legal doctrine and international practice are agreed that some *international organizations* and bodies can make international treaties. They include inter-governmental organizations, especially the United Nations Organization and its specialized agencies. As regards other international organizations, the opinions of writers differ. In the contemporary theories of international law, considerable attention is being devoted to the question of the subjectivity of international organizations and of their ability to conclude international treaties.

The topicality of this problem has been underlined by the U.N. International Law Commission, and all the rapporteurs have provided that the contracts concluded by international organizations do fall within the domain of the international law of treaties. However, in the final draft of the rules of the law of treaties, which covered only the treaty-making activity of the states, the provisions on the power of international organizations were omitted. They did stipulate in a separate clause that the agreements concluded by international organizations shall be subject to the basic principles of the law of treaties.

The subjectivity of international organizations is regulated mainly by their statutes and through the existence of certain rights and functions pertaining to their activities. Confirmation for it is found in the large numbers of agreements made between them as well as with states. Therefore, those international organizations which have a prominent manifestation of legal personality, especially in the domain of treaty-making, must be granted subjectivity, enabling them to participate in treaty acts as contracting parties.

Since a treaty is the result of the congruence of wills of two or more subjects of international law to coordinate their interests, it must be concluded by competent organs. On the whole, the will of an international subject is valid and produces its effect only if it originates from competent organs and if the latter did not overstep the limits of their powers or competence.

The question of what organ is competent to conclude an international treaty is one of recent date. It has become especially topical following the emergence of democratic states and the introduction of the principle of the division of power. It is held today that the municipal law of states is expected to deal with this question. The organ having the power of international treaty-making is the same one that represents the state in its foreign relations. Limitations on this competence exist in the form of requirements for approval or consent from the legislative body or another competent organ (depending on the constitutional provisions), in accordance with the type of agreement and the character of the obligations assumed. The competence of treaty-making organs of international organizations is laid down in their statutes and often depends on the functions and jurisdiction of the organization itself, so that in the final resort the question of competence is determined through practice and through the interpretation of the relevant statutes.

The internal rules of each state designate the organs competent to conclude international treaties. These include the head of state, the prime minister, the collective organ of the state, individual members of government or parliament, or persons empowered by them. International treaties are most frequently concluded through diplomatic representatives who must possess special powers issued by the competent organs.

The Vienna Convention on the Law of Treaties laid down that in terms of their functions, and without having to be issued with powers, representatives of states are the following persons: a. heads of state, prime ministers and ministers of foreign affairs for all acts relating to treaty-making; b. heads of diplomatic missions, for the adoption of the texts of treaties concluded between the accrediting state and the state where they are accredited; c. representatives of states at international conferences or in international organizations, for the adoption of texts by that conference or by that organization.

The full powers issued to representatives of states for the purpose of treaty making stipulate the range and limits of their powers. If these are exceeded, the agreement is considered null or void. If some special limitations are involved, failure by the representative to abide by them will not nullify his consent, except in case the other negotiating states had not been informed of this limitation before the representative had given his consent. In this event the treaty will be regarded as invalid.

In the internal legal order, the free consent of a contracting party is a prerequisite for the validity of the contract. *A contract concluded under duress by misrepresentation or in error, shall be considered void.*

Some attempts have been made to determine the characteristics of the congruence of wills that must be attained before a treaty can come into being and produce its effect.

According to one group of writers, the rules of municipal law concerning the lack of will and good faith in treaty-making do not fully apply because of the specific nature of international relations and the peculiarities of international law. According to others, however, conditions for the validity of international treaties are found in the analogous rules of municipal law. They hold that an analogy should be made because the corresponding rules in the domain of the internal law of states are far more developed and carry tradition and continuity.

The textbooks of international law usually cite three kinds of cases where the lack of expressed congruence of wills may make a treaty invalid or void. These include: deception, misapprehension and duress (constraint against the person of the representative of a state and constraint against a state by the threat or use of force, and bribery). However, a full analogy with municipal law is not possible. For example, the misapprehension of a representative as regards the legal position does not affect the validity of an international treaty, because it is assumed that all contracting parties have to be familiar with all circumstances pertinent to a case, including the legal provisions of the contracting states. Therefore, the analogous rules of internal law must apply since ignorance of the law cannot be taken as an excuse. As regards misapprehension of facts, this kind of error can legally become the grounds for the nullification of the consent of a state, if it concerns a fact or a situation assumed by the given state to have existed at the moment when the treaty was concluded, and to have constituted a crucial basis for its consent to be bound by the treaty. As to duress, it may be applied against two objects: the representative of a state, or a state. In the former case the declaration of consent shall have no legal effects if it was made under duress exercised against its representative. In the latter, however, a treaty shall be null and void if it has been concluded under the threat of force or with the use of force, in violation of the principles of the U.N. Charter.

A state may claim deception as grounds for the annulment of its consent to be bound by the treaty, if it was led into conclusion of the treaty through misrepresentation by another state participating in negotiations. Misrepresentation makes the treaty revocable at the demand of the injured party.

The grounds for withdrawing consent to be bound because of the bribery of its representative was introduced as a completely new concept by the U.N. International Law Commission (Article 47 of the Draft Rules of the Law of Treaties). It envisaged that the bribery of a representative may be taken as grounds for the repeal of his state's consent to be bound. This was eventually endorsed by the Vienna Convention. The bribing of the representative of a state is made equal to misrepresentation.

The third condition for the validity of a treaty is that the subject matter of a treaty be legal. This element, like the previous two, is necessary before a treaty can become effective.

Under municipal law, the subject matter of a contract must be physically possible and legal. The same rules apply to international treaties.

IV. Origin of Treaty

Introduction — Adoption and Authentication — Signature
— Ratification — Accession — Acceptance — Approval —
Conclusion of a Treaty in Simplified Form — Registration
and Publication — Entry into Force

1. Introduction — The method of negotiation depends on the type of treaty that is to be concluded. Negotiations of multilateral treaties are usually conducted at international conferences, whereas negotiations for the conclusion of a bilateral treaty are the subject of talks between foreign ministers, most frequently, or the diplomatic representatives of the interested countries. Since there are no general international rules concerning the conduct of negotiations, these may be pursued verbally and through direct contact by negotiating persons. Negotiations may also be conducted in writing, by means of diplomatic notes or letters sent by authorized persons. Negotiations may even be conducted by telephone.

In the 17th, 18th and 19th centuries, the practice was for monarchs to take a direct part in negotiations (*e.g.*, the Congress in Erfurt of 1808; the Vienna Congress of 1815; the Ljubljana Congress of 1821; the Congress in Verona of 1822). In more recent times, we may quote as an example President Wilson's participation in the negotiations and signing of the Treaty of Versailles. We are also witnesses today of increasingly frequent personal encounters at the highest level (*e.g.*, Yalta, Potsdam, and subsequent summit meetings). Following the negotiations thus conducted, treaties came into effect by the act of signature. The bourgeois revolutions during the 18th century and the promulgation of democratic constitutions in many countries on the principle of division of power brought innovations into the method of conducting foreign affairs. Negotiations and the first stage of the conclusion of the treaty (signature), are thus entrusted to the executive organs of government, whereas the final process of treaty making is referred to the legislative organs, which either seek authority to carry out ratification or carry it out themselves.

In the course of negotiations, each meeting ends with a protocol which is signed by the negotiators. If negotiations fail to bring about the conclusion of a treaty, all the earlier acts and statements have no legal significance and produce no operative effect for the negotiating parties.

2. Adoption and Authentication — Once agreement has been reached on general principles, the text of the treaty is drafted , and then it is adopted and authenticated. The text must be adopted by all parties to the negotiations.

The earlier practice was for the text to be adopted by unanimous agreement of all the states participating in its formulation. The recent practice of concluding treaties at large international conferences or within international organizations has brought majority vote into favor. At international conferences, a text is usually adopted by two-thirds majority, unless the participating states agree by the same majority of votes to adopt a different rule.

The authentication of a text is necessary to enable the negotiating states to become familiar with the content of the treaty before they decide whether or not to become contracting parties. From that moment onwards, the text may not be altered, and following the procedure of authentication it becomes final and authentic. Which procedure will be used to verify a text will depend on the decision of the negotiating states. In the absence of this procedure, this may be done by the signing, the signing *ad referendum*, or the initialling of a text or final act of a conference which incorporates the text. The initialling is done by the representatives of states. For example, the General Act for the Pacific Settlement of International Disputes was adopted in Geneva on 26 September 1928, by the Assembly of the League of Nations. It was signed by the president of the Assembly and secretary general for the purpose of authentication only. The same practice was used in cases of several conventions which were concluded under the auspices of the United Nations, *e.g.* the General Convention on Privileges and Immunities in the United Nations, and the Convention on the Privileges and Immunities of Specialized Agencies.

According to the Vienna Convention on the Law of Treaties, the text of a treaty is established as authentic and final: a. following the procedure envisaged in the text of the treaty or established by the drafting states; b. in the absence of such a procedure, through signature, signature *ad referendum* or the initialling of the text of a treaty or the final act of a conference which incorporates the text by the representatives of those states.

3. Signing of Treaty — Under the conventional method of treaty making, signature is deemed to signify its adoption. It comes after the termination of the stage of negotiation. The effect of the signing, according to the earlier practice, depended on ratification or other forms of the entry into force of a treaty.

Legal doctrine has for a long time adhered to the theory that the head of state, or the monarch, is bound by a treaty to which the signatures of his plenipotentiaries have been affixed, provided, of course, they have not gone beyond their terms of reference. This signing was regarded as the final conclusion of a treaty, which came into effect the moment the signatures were affixed. In contrast, ratification was regarded as a formality and obligation incumbent on a head of state or monarch with declarative and retroactive effect. This view has been supported by the writers who look for an analogy in the private law institution of mandate and the relationship between the grantors and recipients of powers. As new democratic constitutions came into being at the end of the 18th and early in the 19th centuries, the concept of ratification and its significance completely changed. Ratification has become an essential element for the entry into force of a treaty, and its signature marks only one stage in the drafting of the treaty and the establishment of agreement by the negotiating parties.

The recent treaty practice, in accordance with the tendency of simplifying the procedure of treaty-making, has shown an increased number of treaties coming into force upon the act of signature, so that signature and ratification are now given equal significance in the definitive expression of the consent by parties to become bound. This tendency was noted by the International Law Commission, which in Article 10 of the draft rules of the Law of Treaties provided for the following cases in which the consent of a state to be finally bound by a treaty is expressed through signature: a. when the treaty specified the signing to have such an effect; b. when it is established in some other manner that the negotiating states have agreed that the signing should have such an effect; c. when the intention of an interested state to acknowledge such an effect to the act of signature arises from the full powers of its representative or has been expressed in the course of negotiations.

In addition to signature, which normally signifies consent by the contracting states to be bound by the treaty, there is also the institution of *signature ad referendum*. This institution is similar to the initialling, and many writers make no distinction between them at all. The signing *ad referendum* is a conditional affixing of signatures, which means that the treaty is signed subject to consent by the government of the interested state. In the event of its positive stance, the treaty need not be signed again, for a statement by the government concerned represents the recognition of the affixed signature. This is most frequently used in the conclusion of multilateral treaties, especially of important multilateral conventions.

As regards the procedure of signing, the practice is for the treaty to be signed by all the empowered persons simultaneously. Should this not be possible for any reason at all, the treaty usually stipulates the date by which the state which was not able to affix its signature in good time should do so subsequently.

4. Ratification — In the classical procedure of treaty making, the stage of signature has a specific significance, but it does not make the treaty thus signed definitive. Its entry into force depends on ratification. Consequently, the ratification of international treaties is a constituent element in the process of treaty making.

Broadly speaking, ratification is the final statement of intent of a state, which participated in negotiations and signed the treaty, to accept as its international obligation the agreed text of an international instrument. Once the ratification instruments have been exchanged in the case of bilateral treaties, or deposited in the case of multilateral treaties, the international treaty becomes final and valid.

The modern conception of ratification as the final act in binding states is grounded on the new doctrine and on recent practice of states as regards the role and significance of the act of signing. Ratification as a confirmatory act after the signing is being gradually abandoned, as seen in the rejection of the private law principle on the retroactive effect of ratification.

The U.N. International Law Commission, working on the codification of the rules of the law of treaties, has devoted special attention to the role of ratification. Holding the view that the signing of ratification expresses the final consent of a state to be bound, the Vienna Convention envisages consent through ratification in the following cases a   when the treaty provides for such a consent to be expressed by ratification; b. when it is otherwise established that the negotiating states agreed to make ratification necessary; c. when the treaty is signed subject to ratification and d. when the intent of a state to sign the treaty subject to ratification is stated in the powers of its plenipotentiary or had been expressed during negotiations.

Shifts in jurists' opinions about the relationship between the act of signing and ratification have another important consequence besides the non-retroactive effect of ratification. For a large number of states, the signing of certain types of treaties is equally as important to ratification as the expression of a state's consent to be bound. This implies that the signing need not necessarily represent the indispensable prior stage to be followed by ratification; the two procedures can be equally treated as a method of opening contractual relations. Unless a treaty stipulates ratification, or this is inferred from the method of its conclusion and the terms of reference of the plenipotentiaries, whether a treaty enters into force by signature or by ratification is no longer relevant. On the contrary, today, two treaties make no provision for their entry into force, and most of them do so in a variety of ways including signature, signature subject to ratification, signature by one and signature plus ratification by the other party, exchange of notes, accession, acceptance or approval, and so forth. Bearing in mind this variety of practice and juridical opinion, the International Law Commission took the view that in the absence of a relevant clause, the entry into force of treaties is regulated according to the interpretation of the intent of the parties. This view is all the more acceptable since there is no rule for or against ratification as the uniform method of inaugurating a treaty. Thereby the question of the need for ratification has been suitably resolved in the Vienna Convention in conformity with the contemporary treaty practice of states.

The problem of competence is highly significant in determining the exact import of ratification. Like any other legal act, whether in municipal or international law, ratification must originate from the competent organs of a state before it can produce a valid effect. Meeting such provisions is an essential condition for the full validity of ratification and the legality of the assumed obligation, both internationally and internally. The rule is to observe the constitutional provisions of the state which carries out ratification. This is the presumption when dealing with the problem of constitutionality of a treaty and the legality of the act of ratification. The treaty-making practice has confirmed this rule, and most treaties state that the treaty would be ratified "in accordance with the constitutional provisions and rules," or "in accordance with the relevant constitutional methods," or "in the form prescribed by the laws or the contracting states," etc. (For example, the Treaty of Alliance, Cooperation and Mutual Assistance, concluded between Yugoslavia, Greece, and Turkey on 9 August 1954, Article 14; the Charter of the United Nations Organization, Article 110; the Covenant of the Arab League of States, concluded in Cairo on 22 March 1945 by Egypt, Iraq, Transjordan, Lebanon, Saudi Arabia, and Yemen, Article 20; the Treaty of Friendship and Mutual Assistance concluded in Warsaw by the U.S.S.R., the German Democratic Republic, Poland, Czechoslovakia, Bulgaria, Hungary, and Albania; the North Atlantic Treaty, Washington, 4 April 1949, Article 11, etc.) The confirmation of the above rule is also found in judiciary practice, *e.g.* the *Ambatielos* case, of 1 July 1952.

It happens occasionally that a treaty is ratified and the other party or parties are informed thereof, without the treaty being concordant with the provisions governing the competence of the organs that concluded it. In such cases validity of the treaty is questionable because of *unconstitutional ratification.*

Ratification may be unconstitutional for two reasons: a. the final decision on binding the state was not taken by the organ that is competent to act in such a case, and b. the ratifying organ did not act in terms of its competence, although it acted as the authorized organ (*e.g.,* it failed to obtain prior approval or consent from the legislative body, if this was required under the constitutional provisions).

Since an incorrectly ratified treaty may produce its effect both internally and internationally, unconstitutional ratification raises the problem of the validity of the treaty both in the home country and abroad. There are three different views in the theory of international law whether incorrect ratification is fully valid from the standpoint of international law. Internally, its validity is not challenged if ratification is in conformity with the formal constitutional provisions and has been performed by a competent organ, although such ratification may be contrary to the material content of constitutional provisions of the ratifying state. The constitutionality of such acts is not tested, because the majority of states do not usually check whether an international treaty is internally concordant with its national constitution.

Therefore, according to one view, unconstitutional ratification is valid from the standpoint of international law, even though it may have been performed contrary to the constitutional provisions, as the limitations in regards to the competence of organs have no international effect. According to another view, which is prevailing today, an anticonstitutional ratification cannot be valid. On the contrary, it results in the invalidity of the treaty. To acknowledge its validity would be contrary to legal doctrine. The practice of states, and also judiciary practice, provide sufficient examples in support of the latter conception (*e.g.,* the treaty between Chile and Peru of 20 January 1835, was proclaimed invalid, because it was ratified by a non-competent government; Romania denied the validity of the trade agreement concluded with Austria on 14 August 1920, because prior approval had not been obtained from the parliament for ratification; the judgment of the Permanent Court of International Justice in the East Greenland case, etc.).

According to the advocates of the third view, international law allows each state to decide on the organs and procedure for the conclusion of a treaty, and therefore it is only interested in the external manifestation of its intent. They, therefore acknowledge any purely theoretical value of the thesis on the invalidity of an unconstitutional ratification, considering that the consequences arising from such ratification can show their negativity only on the international plane.

The U.N. International Law Commission took the middle view. It held that a state could not claim as the grounds for the nullification of its consent the fact that this consent had been expressed in contravention of a provision of internal law which regulates the question of competence of the organ concluding an international treaty, except if the violation of its municipal law had been obvious.

The most significant feature of ratification is that it is not mandatory but of a discretionary character. A state has the right not to ratify a treaty at all, and is not under the obligation to start the procedure of ratification within a specified time.

Another important characteristic of the institution of ratification is that it cannot have a retroactive effect. The treaty comes into force immediately upon its ratification, but not from the moment of signature as was the case when the rule of private law applied. An exception is made for the treaties that come into force with signature because that date is decisive for their full validity.

Another characteristic of ratification is that it may not be conditional. A state can either ratify a treaty or refuse to do so, but it cannot set up conditions or alter the treaty upon its ratification. The revision of the treaty can only be carried out subject to the consent of all the parties concerned (*e.g.,* by way of reservations).

International law does not have definite rules governing the manner and procedure for states to become bound by the treaties. States have full freedom to determine the procedure of ratifying international treaties and of assuming rights and duties in accordance with their municipal, and above all, constitutional provisions. Depending on the sociopolitical systems of states, at various times there have been different methods of regulating the ratification of international treaties. Thus in absolute monarchies and dictatorships, the exclusive competence in the matter of treaty making rests with the head of state, whatever might be his style. In the system of the political division of power, competences are regulated between the legislative bodies and the executive organs, or the head of the state. In some systems, the final decision on binding a state by international treaties rests exclusively with legislative organs (collegial bodies).

5. Accession — Accession is the procedure in which states which did not take part in the conclusion of a treaty declare in a special document their consent to be bound by it.

Today's treaties which contain an accession clause make accession independent of the coming of the treaty into force, which was not possible in the earlier practice and according to the original understanding of accession. They do so in two ways: a. a clause of the treaty makes accession possible before the date of the treaty's entry into force, and b. the entry into force is made conditional upon the depositing of the instruments of accession.

This viewpoint was endorsed in Article 15 of the Vienna Convention on the Law of Treaties. The consent of a state to be bound by a treaty is expressed by accession in the cases: a. when a treaty or amendment thereto provide for such a consent by accession; b. when it cannot be otherwise established whether the negotiating states had agreed that such a consent may be given by accession; c. when all the parties subsequently agree that such a consent may be given by the accession of an interested state.

6. Acceptance — By definition, acceptance is the act by which a state, in the place of signature or ratification or accession, or of all these procedures together, expresses its consent to be bound by the provisions of a treaty.

Acceptance is a new institution in the international law of treaties. It has been in use only since the end of World War II. The aim of introducing this institution was to facilitate the constitution of new international organizations and to foster their contractual relations. Its practical purpose was to enable the states to avoid the complex and often very long procedures of ratification or accession to treaties, while abiding by their constitutional provisions and other internal acts which determine the competence of organs in concluding international treaties. This institution appeared in the form of a clause which is formulated in one of the following variants: the treaty shall come into force a. upon its signature, without reservation of acceptance; b. upon its signature with the reservation of acceptance to be followed by acceptance; and c. with acceptance (*e.g.,* General Agreement on Tariffs and Trade of 1947; Convention on Inter-Governmental Maritime Consultative Organization of 1948; Convention on Safety at Sea of 1948; the Havana Charter on International Trade Organization of 1948). In this manner, the institution of treaty acceptance was regarded as a suitable instrument which offered states freedom to interpret "acceptance" as meaning an instrument of acceptance *eo nomine,* or a formal instrument of ratification, or a less formal assent to the treaty concluded — according to the requirements and constitutional provisions of its municipal law.

Although originally treaty acceptance was expected not to parallel but to circumvent the conventional method of treaty ratification, practice has shown that states are not inclined to renounce the institution of ratification, and since 1950 acceptance has been used on rare and exceptional occasions (*e.g.,* the Agreement on the Importation Of Educational, Scientific and Cultural Goods of 1950). The crucial turnabout in the practice of the United Nations was the promulgation of the Convention on the Prevention and Punishment of Genocide of 1948, and the Convention on International Broadcasting of News and Right to Correction of 1949.

The Vienna Convention also provided that "consent of a state to be bound by a treaty shall be expressed by acceptance or approval under similar conditions as those applied to ratification."

7. Approval of Treaties — The institution of treaty approval as a means of definitive conclusion of treaties appeared in the practice of states considerably after the institution of acceptance.

In this practice it acquired certain specific features which in a way set this institution apart from others. Usually a signed treaty is not subject to ratification as a condition for its entry into force, but at the same time the latter is made to depend on approval or endorsement by the competent organs of the contracting states. Approval is most frequently used in the form of "signature subject to approval," and a clause is inserted in the treaty text stating that the treaty was open for the procedure of approval without a subsequent or preliminary signature. Both these forms are used in practice.

The treaty comes into force following the *exchange of notes* on the approval made. Formally, this procedure differs from that of the exchange of ratification instruments, although the procedure of the exchange of notes on approval fulfils all the functions of the ratification procedure. The exchange of notes on approval, in contrast to the similar procedure of ratification, need not be carried out at the same time, for there can be a time gap between the note which proposes the entry into force and the note which confirms it. In such cases, the date of the last note is the moment of the entry into force. The Vienna Convention on the Law of Treaties has also provided for approval to be a means for states to express their consent to become bound by international treaties (Article 11, para. 2).

8. Conclusion of a Treaty in Simplified Form — Parallel with the conventional conclusion of international treaties which involves the stages described above , the new treaty-making practice has created separate procedures whereby states enter into treaty relations in a simplified form, without prejudice to the legal force of the concluded international acts. The new method is to conclude agreements through an exchange of notes, exchange of letters, etc. Under this method, one party to the agreement sends the other a note or a letter in which it proposes the text of the agreement that is to be concluded. The other party may express its agreement with the proposed text and declare its intention to regard the adopted text as its international commitment. This type of agreement is usually concluded without the formal intervention of competent organs, and, as a rule, it requires no ratification. The purpose of such agreements is most frequently to extend, revise or amplify existing agreements (*e.g.* the trade agreement between the F.P.R.Y. and the Republic of Chile, concluded on 14 and 21 April 1954, through an exchange of notes). Similarly, the subject matter of agreements concluded in this form may vary considerably.

9. Registration and Publication — Article 18 of the Covenant of the League of Nations, and later Article 102 of the United Nations Charter, attempted to regulate the registration and publication of international treaties. The establishment of secretariats for both world organizations laid the foundations for the solving of these questions on the broadest international basis.

Article 102 of the United Nations Charter provides "every treaty and every international agreement entered into by any member of the United Nations after the present Charter comes into force shall as soon as possible be registered with the Secretariat and published by it." In regards to sanctions for failure to attend to this duty, it states that "no party appertaining to any such treaty or international agreement which has not been registered, . . . may invoke that treaty or agreement before any organ of United Nations."

Since Article 102 of the United Nations Charter did not regulate certain questions pertaining to the procedure of registration, these were suitably resolved once the rules on the application of Article 102 were adopted. The rules were passed under a resolution of the United Nations General Assembly in 1946. They envisaged: a. that the treaty or agreement must be concluded by at least one party that is a member of the United Nations Organization; b. that it must be concluded after the entry into force of the Charter; c. that it must have entered into force prior to registration (Article 1, paras. 1 and 2). Provision is also made for the registration of every subsequent modification by the parties to a treaty, or to the provisions thereof, their scope or their application.

The practice of the United Nations regarding registration and publication of treaties was confirmed in the Vienna Convention, which states that "the treaties concluded by parties to the Convention on the Law of Treaties shall be registered with the Secretariat of the United Nations as soon as possible."

10. Entry into Force — As to the entry into force, account should be taken of the date when the international treaty obligation enters into force, and the moment when it becomes binding on the parties to it.

Parties are free to set the date of the treaty's entry into force. They usually do so in an express clause to this effect. However, the date of the entry into force may also be set implicitly by the treaty itself. If the treaty fails to make provision for it in one of the two ways, then the dates fixed for the exchange or deposit of the ratification instruments, or for acceptance, approval or signature, may be taken as indicative of the intent of the parties to make it the date of the treaty's entry into force.

A treaty enters into force in the manner and at the time provided for under its clauses or under the agreement of the states participating in the negotiations. This should be the basic rule. In the event of the absence of such a clause or of such an agreement, according to the Vienna Convention, the date of entry into force is taken to be the moment when it is established that all the negotiating states have given their consent to be bound by the treaty.

The entry into force of multilateral treaties does not mean they become binding on all states that are parties to them. Therefore, in addition to the so-called objective entry into force, there is also the operative effect of the treaty for each party that has given its consent to be bound by the treaty after it has come into force (*e.g.*, the Geneva Convention on the Law of the Sea and the Vienna Convention on Diplomatic and Consular Relations).

Modern practice makes allowance for provisional entry into force. When a treaty entes into force prior to its ratification, on the basis of one of its clauses, then it does so provisionally and subject to its subsequent ratification (*e.g.*, the Agreement on Air Services between Great Britain and Argentina, of 7 May 1946, made express provision in Article 12 for its provisional entry into force on the date of signature, and a definitive entry into force once it had been ratified by both contracting parties). Because of the urgency of their subject matter, the practice has been introduced for certain types of agreements (*e.g.* of an economic and commercial character) to be provisionally entered into force. Almost one half of all the trade agreements concluded between Yugoslavia and Italy have had a provisional entry into force. Instead of introducing a clause on the provisional entry into force into text of a treaty, the parties may make a separate protocol or exchange letters agreeing to a provisional entry into force.

V. Observance, Application and Interpretation of Treaties

Observance — Application — Interpretation

1. Observance — It is a basic rule of international law that parties to a treaty have a duty to perform in good faith all the obligations arising therefrom.

The observance and fulfilment of an obligation that has been assumed is the rule of conduct in all legal orders, be they of international or internal character. The rule *pacta sunt servanda* is encountered in all the stages of development of the international community, although in its evolution it has been under the influence of different ideas and conceptions which have affected its very foundations.

The rule *pacta sunt servanda* is today beyond dispute. It has been mentioned in the preamble and Article 2 of the United Nations Charter: "All members, in order to ensure to all of them the rights and benefits resulting from membership, shall fulfil in good faith the obligations assumed by them in accordance with the present Charter." The rule *pacta sunt servanda* is a rule of international law, and the principle of fulfilment in good faith stemmed from the need to protect and safeguard the interests of all the parties to a treaty regime.

The Vienna Convention has also provided that "every treaty in force binds the contracting parties, and they must fulfil it in good faith."

Since a treaty creates both rights and obligations for the contracting parties, the latter have the duty to take all the necessary legislative and other measures to perform the contract. This means that the parties may not invoke their internal provisions (of a constitutional or legislative character) as the reason for failing to fulfil their treaty commitments. According to international customary law, non-fulfilment of treaties is regarded as the basis for international liability of states and for their obligation to make up for damages. A clause may also be inserted to the effect that non-fulfilment of a treaty entitles the other party to revoke the treaty or to renounce its further observance.

2. Application — The problem of treaty application should be considered in terms of a. duration and the principle of non-retroactive effect of treaties; b. territorial application, and c. substantive application (reservation to multilateral treaties).

a. *Duration of treaties* — The time of duration is usually stipulated in the treaty (*e.g.* the U.N. General Convention on Privileges and Immunities, in Article 35, envisages that "the convention shall be in force between the United Nations and each acceding member as long as the party remains a member state of the United Nations Organization, or until a revision of the Convention has been made and adopted by its members"), either by setting special conditions for its membership in relation to the other parties, or by establishing the time of duration — five, ten or twenty years (*e.g.,* the Convention on the Prevention and Punishment of the Crime of Genocide provided for the validity of ten years, whereupon it would be extended for periods of five years for all the parties which do not renounce it within less than six months before the expiration on the current period). Treaties having a perpetual duration without the right of revocation, the so-called perpetual international treaties, are not current in modern practice.

Another aspect of the problem of treaty duration deserves special attention. It is the principle of non-retroactivity of treaties. Viewed *ratione temporis,* provisions of a treaty do not bind a party in regard to any fact which took place or situation which ceased to exist before the treaty entered into force with respect to that particular party, unless provided otherwise in the treaty. This basic rule on the non-recognition of the retroactive effect of the treaty should not be taken as absolute, since parties are free to envisage the retroactive effect of any or all of the treaty provisions. The fact remains, however, that as a general rule a treaty cannot be considered to have been concluded with the intention of producing a retroactive effect unless such an intention has been expressly provided for, or stems from the treaty obligations (the existence of a general rule was also confirmed in the judgment of International Court of Justice in the *Ambatielos* case).

b. *Territorial Application of Treaties* — Although nost international treaties are operative over the entire territory of the parties to it, the question nevertheless arises as to the exact determination of the sphere of their territorial application. The basic principle of international law was that once a state assumed treaty obligations, the other parties had the right to demand that a treaty be applied to all its territories, including the entire territory of that state and the territories for which it is internationally responsible. This principle, created in the era of the colonial empires, was modified in the course of time, and the exercise of the right of self-determination of nations gave them the right to decide on their own destinies and, as the prerogatives of sovereign power changed hands (with the overthrow of the colonial rule), to refuse to accept the clauses of treaties that had been foisted upon them without their wanting it. The generally accepted principle today is that each state has the duty to apply a treaty throughout its own territory, although in actual fact the application of this principle can still give rise to difficulties because of the existence of various colonial and federal articles and of various constitutional acts promulgated by composite states. Despite any possible difficulties, the principle of the territorial application of treaties in the narrow sense (to the national territory of the state) must continue to be observed subject to nothing else arising from the agreements (*e.g.*, the Antarctica Treaty of 1 December 1959 explicitly determines the territory where it shall be applicable).

The Vienna Convention, in its Article 29, interprets the concept of territorial application as follows: "Unless a different intent arises out of a treaty, or it is determined in some other manner, the application of a treaty shall extend over the entire territory of each party."

c. *Reservations to Multilateral Treaties* — The institution of reservations to international treaties is of a recent date. In the course of the 19th century, when concluding certain international treaties of a multilateral character, states tried to evade the effect of certain provisions and even entire parts of a treaty. The practice of making reservations was more widespread in the course of the first half of the twentieth century. Resort to this institution was justified by the tendency of states not to give an unreserved adherence to international treaties, without determining their position in the treaty regime. In the course of time the question of reservations became a problem for the law of treaties, and its regulation was attempted on several occasions. The right to make reservations was welcomed by those states which did not want to sacrifice any of their interests, even those of a minor significance, to the general interest as expressed in an international treaty. On the other hand, the work of large international conferences and the entry into force of the conventions which they adopted are closely related to the problem of reservations which, as a means of coordinating different interests, were designed principally to expand the treaty obligations, albeit to a limited extent. Rather than face a complete nonparticipation of a state in a treaty, they preferred its partial participation. Following the growing practice of reservations and in view of the need for them in a highly developed network of relations between states, the possibility of making reservations was accepted, and it was specially provided for and regulated in the texts of the conventions adopted under the auspices of the League of Nations and generally in that period. This practice was eventually confirmed in the United Nations Organization, and finally settled in the Vienna Convention.

International jurists define the reservation as basically a unilateral legal act, as a formal unilateral statement, whereby a state disapproves of a certain provision or provisions of a treaty, or gives them a specific interpretation. In the absence of such reservations in the treaty text these provisions would otherwise be applicable. However, as a unilateral legal act, before it can enter into force and become valid, a reservation must receive the consent of the other parties whose interests are involved.

The Vienna Convention defines the reservation as "unilateral statement, however phrased or named, made by a State when signing, ratifying, accepting, approving or acceding to a treaty, whereby it purports to exclude or to modify the legal effect of certain provisions of the treaty in their application to that state."

In principle it is held that every state has the right to make a reservation, either upon signatures or ratification, or on any other occasion when it definitively becomes a party to the treaty. Some limitations do exist in the rules governing the right of states to make reservations. Thus the Vienna Convention provided that no reservations can be made in the following cases: a. if the treaty expressly prohibits reservations; b. if the treaty allows only certain reservations; c. if in a treaty which contains no provision on reservations a reservation is made which is not in accordance with the object and purpose of the treaty.

Reservations as unilateral manifestations of intent cannot produce effect until consent to the proposed reservations is obtained from the other interested parties. Therefore, before a reservation can enter into force, the other parties to the treaty must agree to it.

In practice there are several ways of giving this agreement. International treaty practice has accepted that consent shall be granted expressly by introducing a clause on reservations in the text of the treaty.

On the basis of this clause, certain types of reservations, or reservations in general, may be formulated. In this manner states agree in advance to the possibility of making reservations. Contemporary practice is increasingly favoring the making of reservations (*e.g.* Article 39 of the revised General Act of 28 April 1949 has a reservations clause; see also Article 64 of the European Convention for the Protection of Human Rights and Basic Freedoms, of 4 November 1950; Article 42 of the Convention on the Status of Refugees, of 28 July 1951, etc.).

On the other hand, if the treaty involved is a constitutive act of an international organization, then — unless the treaty itself should determine otherwise — the reservation must be expressly accepted by the competent organ of this organization. Another example supporting the claim that a reservation cannot produce a legal effect until it receives agreement from all contracting parties (a principle that was endorsed by the International Court of Justice in 1951 in its advisory opinion following the placing of reservations on the Convention on the Prevention and Punishment of the Crime of Genocide) is that of the treaty negotiated by a limited number of states, whose object and purpose suggest that the application of the treaty as a whole by all the contracting parties is a condition for the consent of each one of them to be bound by the treaty. In every case it is necessary for the reservation to be accepted by *all* the contracting parties.

Another way of agreeing to a reservation is for other parties to sign the treaty simultaneously with the state which has made a reservation. Thereby it is considered that they are tacitly in agreement with the reservation formulated.

The international practice of adopting multilateral conventions, especially under the auspices of international organizations or by them, gave rise to another method of regulating the granting of agreement to a reservation. Thus there came into being the so-called *tacit agreement,* which is designed to regulate the eventual position of the reservation-making state within a period of time. After a certain time it is held that the states which fail to answer the notification of a reservation tacitly agree to it.

3. Interpretation of Treaties — A fundamental premise of classical international law is that contracting states should themselves interpret a contractual instrument which they conclude with one another.

To a very large extent, the effect of the treaty and its fulfilment depend on how the contracting parties understand their treatyobligations. It is not a rare occurrence for a dispute to arise between parties owing to different interpretations attached to one or several provisions, to the meaning and content of a word or phrase, or to the treaty as a whole. Since misinterpretation may also be due to an insufficiently clear or ambiguous wording, the task of treaty interpretation is to determine the true meaning and substance of the treaty provisions, as well as the true intent of the contracting parties. Usually altered circumstances and conditions are the reason for seeking a common interpretation of certain treaty clauses.

From the standpoint of international law, interpretation is a separate procedure which is carried out according to certain methods and on the basis of certain rules founded upon international law. Thus in the course of long practice, certain basic principles have evolved in the interpretation of international treaties. The most significant among them are the following: a. interpretation is designed to establish the true intent of the contracting parties; b. interpretation must not be at odds with the basic principles of international law; c. the presumption must always be that the contracting parties did not intend to conclude a treaty whose object is impossible, or illegal, or with the intention of not performing it; d. international treaties must be so interpreted as to be in agreement with the mandatory rules of international law; and e. an international treaty must be interpreted in good faith and in accordance with the customary, ordinary meanings attributed to an expression, in the context and in the light of its objective and the intention of the contracting parties.

The methods applied in the interpretation of international treaties are also in use in the international laws of states: grammatical, historical and logical. Bearing in mind the current judicial practice, more particularly the practice of the International Court of Justice in The Hague, it might be stated that the principal method in the interpretation of treaties is the grammatical and logical interpretation. The historical method of interpretation is more and more being considered as complementary, especially in cases when the text of the treaty is insufficiently clear.

The Vienna Convention on the Law of Treaties has taken the view that a treaty must be interpreted in good faith and in accordance with the customary and everyday meanings which are given to expressions, in their context and in the light of their purpose and intent.

VI. Effect of Treaties and the Principle *Pacta Tertiis Nec Nocent Nec Prosunt*

In the course of long years of practice, a general legal principle evolved according to which treaties produce an effect only between the contracting parties. Following this principle such a treaty is *res inter alios acta* for third states. It was considered that the relative effect of the treaty, i.e. only between the contracting parties, means that in principle treaties may neither harm nor benefit third states *(res inter alios acta nec nocere nec prodesse potest)*. This is the view that was taken by the International Law Commission as it laid down that "a treaty may not create obligations or rights for a third state without its consent."

The rule at the base of this general premise of treaty law derives from Roman Law, but it has undergone certain changes. Justification for this rule in international law is not found in the general conception of private law but is based on the sovereignty, equality and independence of states as contracting parties.

In support of this general rule is the existence of a large number of decisions by national and international tribunals (*e.g.,* in the advisory opinion on the competence of the European Danube Commission, the Permanent Court of International Justice did not apply to Romania the decisions of the London Convention of 1883, because Romania did not participate at that conference; in the judgment on the territorial jurisdiction of the International Commission on the river Oder, the Permanent Court of International Justice refused to apply the Barcelona Convention of 1921 to Poland, because the latter failed to ratify it).

The United Nations International Law Commission backed the present contractual practice of states and the standpoint of the contemporary theory of international law.

Based on the premise that treaties are applicable only to the contracting parties and may create no obligations or rights for a third state without its consent, the Vienna Convention provided for exceptions to this rule by instituting rights and obligations through international treaties. Thus a state may undertake an *obligation* pursuant to a treaty to which it is not a party under the following conditions only: 1. that the original parties intended such a provision to be a means of creating an obligation, and 2. that the interested state *expressly* agrees to be bound in this manner.

On the other hand, a *right* may be created only if such was the intention of the original contracting parties (to create the right for one state, group of states or for all states) and if the interested state or states are agreeable to it. In contrast to the creating of an obligation, here the assumption of the state's consent suffices, and it will be valid until it is proved to be otherwise.

VII. Fulfilment of Treaties

Contracting states have the duty to fulfil treaties in good faith and completely. An exception may be made only in the event of certain objective obstacles or difficulties which are recognized by international law as objective circumstances preventing the execution of a treaty.

Since as a rule the fulfilment of an international treaty depends on the contracting parties, the assumed commitments must be performed as state obligations. The state has the duty to use every possibility, means and method to achieve this end.

Since time immemorial, the fulfilment of a treaty was secured by certain legal means — conclusion of separate guarantee, treaties, pledging of territories, occupation of territories, lien on state revenues, guarantees by third states, collective guarantees, right of retention, etc.

Many of these forms have disappeared in contemporary international law, but some have been retained, Thus, for example, Great Britain pledged certain colonies with the United States as a guarantee for the repayment of a loan contracted in the course of the Second World War. The occupation of a territory as a method of performing contracted obligations by a state, once in very frequent use, is today permitted only by way of exception. Another type of international guarantee was the Allied occupation of Germany, on the basis of the act of unconditional surrender by all the German armed forces on 8 May 1945, and the decision by the Potsdam Conference. After the creation of the United Nations Organization and the adoption of the U.N. Charter, occupation for the purpose of securing the fulfilment of an international treaty has not been permitted and is in violation of the principles of the U.N. Charter. For this reason, guarantees by third states are now most frequently sought or the placement in lien of certain financial resources.

The guarantee by third states is a very old institution and has been used often. It may be individual, given by several states (in the period between the two world wars, many treaties were concluded subject to guarantee by the great powers) or collective (collective guarantee was contained in Article 10 of the Covenant of the League of Nations, and the treaties on minorities, concluded after World War I, were similarly under the guarantee of the League of Nations). This method has also been in use since the Second World War (*e.g.,* the United Nations Security Council guaranteed the independence and the integrity of the Free Territory of Trieste).

International organizations may participate in the execution of international treaties (the United Nations provisional government in West Irian, on the basis of the agreement between the Netherlands and Indonesia of 1962). Collective guarantee with the establishment of a special supervisory mechanism have been envisaged under the statute of the International Labour Organization.

The rule is that a treaty must be fulfilled exactly as provided for by the parties in the treaty. If the method of fulfilment has not been defined, it is to be performed according to the established customary rules of international law. Similarly, international treaties must be executed within the set time limits. If these have not been stipulated in the treaties, the assumption is that their execution must follow forthwith.

Modern international law prohibits a unilateral mandatory execution of international treaties (*e.g.,* in 1882, Great Britain bombarded Egypt because of non-payment of a debt). For the non-fulfilment of treaties, the contracting parties have available to them many legal remedies under international law. (International treaties usually contain provisions for the settlement of disputes, application and execution — submission to the International Court of Justice, arbitration, diplomatic negotiations, etc.) For certain special types of agreements of a technical or commercial character special bodies — mixed commissions — are frequently set up to take care of the treaty execution.

VIII. Amendment of Treaties

Treaty Amendment in Classical International Law —
Regulation of Amendments to Multilateral Treaties

1. Treaty Amendment in Classical International Law — The basic principle applying to the amendment of treaties was that a treaty may be altered only subject to agreement between contracting parties. It applied mainly to bilateral treaties.

In contrast to the denunciation of treaties, revision is the procedure by means of which the parties to a treaty agree — either spontaneously or at the demand of a third party — to introduce into the treaty certain modifications in order to adjust it to newly arisen circumstances. Revision is performed either by diplomatic means or by special procedure. The best way of achieving results is for the treaty itself to contain a specific clause to this effect, *i.e.* a clause empowering the contracting parties, after a lapse of time and at the demand of one of them, to renew negotiations for the revision of the original text of the treaty.

In the doctrine of international law, the majority of writers consider that treaty amendment is a legal question and that it should be handled in a corresponding manner. A different viewpoint is held by McNair, for whom the problem of revision is a purely political problem and a political issue. He based his view on the fact that in principle no state has a legal right to demand revision in the absence of a specific provision of the treaty to this effect.

As early as at the London Conference of 1871, which was convened on the occasion of the unilateral abrogation of the Paris Treaty on the Neutrality of the Black Sea, it was established that the basic principle of international law was the prohibition of a unilateral abrogation or modification of contracted provisions, and that it could be permitted only subject to consent by the contracting parties. Similarly, Article 19 of the Covenant of the League of Nations stipulated that the Assembly of the League of Nations may, from time to time, invite League members to reexamine those agreements which had become inapplicable owing to lapse of time or changed conditions. However, since no agreement was reached as to the method of applying this article, it remained ineffective. On the other hand, when the Charter of the United Nations was drafted, a similar provision was not included in its text, although in the opinion of certain writers such a procedure may be applied in certain cases pursuant to the provisions of Articles 1, 11, and 14 of the Charter.

2. The Need to Regulate the Revision of Multilateral Treaties
— The question of finding a suitable procedure for amending multilateral trea-

ties is mainly motivated by practical considerations: firstly the need to avoid the rule of unanimity by all the contracting parties, and secondly, the need for new rules which are imposed by practice. The use of multilateral treaties as instruments of regulation of certain complex relations by a large number of contracting states gave rise to the conviction that treaties themselves must make provision for a method of their eventual modification. In the period following the Second World War, this kind of clause became very frequent. Modifications were being made by a majority of votes, either by simple majority or in other proportions (*e.g.* the Convention of the Universal Postal Union of 1957, Article 23; the Convention on the World Meteorological Organization, Article 28; the Agreement on the International Financial Association of 1955, Article 7; the United Nations Charter, Article 108). Multilateral conventions to set up international organizations also provide for agreement by contracting parties to be bound by any amendments which may be made by the conference of the organization, as its highest body, in the manner and following the procedure approved in advance, except when a state expresses its opposition within a given period (*e.g.*, the Convention on the Creation of the World Health Organization, the International Civil Aviation Convention, the European Agreement on Road Signs, etc.). There is in addition a third manner of amending multilateral conventions. It consists in collaboration between each contracting state and the competent administrative organ of the international organization under whose auspices the convention was adopted, with the proviso that the right of final decision is left to the supreme bodyof this organization (*e.g.* the Convention on the Prevention and Punishment of the Crime of Genocide, Article 16; the Convention on Customs Facilities to Benefit Tourism, of 4 July 1954, the United Nations Charter, Article 109, etc.). Besides these main types, there is another which applies to specific stituations in which international organizations appear as parties to an agreement. This practice is directly related to their treaty-making power. Thus, for example, in the agreement between the United Nations, on the one hand, and the Universal Postal Union, the International Telecommunication Union and the World Meteorological Organization on the other, provision was made for the amendment procedure, stipulating that it would begin within six months from the date of a demand being submitted to this effect by one of the parties.

The question of the drafting of rules for the amendment of treaties attracted the special attention of the United Nations International Law Commission. The Commission took the view that the rights and status of the contracting parties, during the validity of an international treaty and especially of an agreement of a multilateral character, must be correlated with the need for the maintenance of their independence and equality and the need for changes which may arise for various reasons. In order to avoid any similarity with the practice of treaty revision in the period between the two world wars, when the stronger states imposed solutions on the weaker ones, the Commission used the expression "treaty amendment." Considerable attention has been given to the rules on treaty amendment.

The Vienna Convention provides for the amendment of treaties by agreement between the contracting parties.

The amendment of multilateral treaties is modification *stricto sensu* with the effect of changing treaty provisions in regard to all contracting parties. In view of the need for each party to determine its rights and positions each one is entitled to ask to be notified about any proposed amendment so that it can: a. take part in deciding on the measures that should be taken in connection with the proposal and b. take part in negotiations and the conclusion of any treaty designed to amend the earlier one.

The legal effect of an agreement to amend the original treaty is expressed in the following: each state, as it becomes a party to a treaty, after the agreement on its amendment has come into force, shall consider itself: a. party to such a revised treaty, and b. party to the original treaty in respect of each party that is not bound under the amendment agreement. Obviously, all this is subject to a state's having no other intention.

Multilateral treaties may be amended only between certain contracting parties. This is attained by *inter se* agreements. Namely, individual parties may conclude an agreement on the amendment of a treaty only in mutual relations, and under the following conditions: a. that such a contingency has been stipulated by the treaty; b. that it should be without prejudice to the enjoyment by other parties of their contracted rights or to the fulfilment of contracted obligations; c. that the modification should not apply to those provisions the renunciation of which is incompatible with the effective performance of the treaty as a whole; and d. that amendment is not prohibited under the treaty.

IX. Termination and Suspension of Treaties

Introduction — Termination of or Withdrawal from Treaties by Agreement of Contracting Parties — Provisional Suspension of Multilateral Treaties by Agreement of Some Contracting Parties — Abrogration of Treaties Having No Termination Clause — Abrogation of Treaties Containing the Abrogation or Withdrawal Clause — Duration — Realization of the Purpose of the Treaty — Later Impossibility of Implementation — Abrogation Owing to Non-Fulfilment by Another Contracting Party — Termination or Suspension of a Treaty Owing to its Violation — Renunciation of Treaty Rights — Termination or Suspension of a Treaty Because of the Conclusion of a New Treaty — Conditions for Abrogation — Termination of a Treaty which is Incompatible with the Subsequent Imperative Norm of General International Law — Change in Circumstances (rebus sic stantibus)

1. Introduction — The international law of treaties, like all other spheres of international law, is affected by the vicissitudes of international life. Treaties are subject to various changes in the course of their duration; they may become obsolete; they may change, become suspended or terminated. The reasons may be various. They may be of a political nature, but they may also depend on the will of the contracting parties, or may have arisen following a procedure which international law acknowledges as the cause for the termination or suspension of a treaty.

The validity and duration of a treaty are terminated on the basis of almost the same reasons as in municipal law, subject to certain peculiarities specific in international law. These reasons include: expiration of the treaties; their implementation; agreement by the contracting parties; disappearance of the subject matter of the treaty; impossibility of implementation; etc. Certain reasons are especially peculiar to international law, e.g. termination or suspension of a treaty as a result of its violation. Here are the main reasons for the termination or suspension of international agreements.

2. Termination of or Withdrawal from a Treaty by Agreement of the Contracting Parties — To begin with, a treaty may be terminated by agreement between the contracting parties, attained following the entry into force of the treaty (*mutuus dissensus*). The doctrine states that the parties which concluded a treaty may agree to terminate it by agreement, express or tacit. The presumption is that only the contracting parties are interested in the fate of the treaty and that a third party has not acquired on the basis thereof any interest that should be protected. The agreement by the contracting parties to terminate or withdraw from the treaty may be achieved by the conclusion of a new treaty which annuls the existing treaty, or of a new treaty which regulates the same subject matter. It is also possible to achieve a tacit agreement by substituting all the provisions of the former treaty with the provisions of the new one, although a tacit agreement may also be inferred from the behavior of the contracting parties. The new treaty may expressly provide for the cessation of the validity of the old treaty, but it is not indispensable.

The Vienna Convention on the Law of Treaties has provided that "a treaty may be terminated, or a party may withdraw from it only a. in accordance with the provision of the treaty which allows such a termination or withdrawal; b. at any time by agreement of all contracting parties." It should be emphasized, however, that the general rule on the agreement to terminate a treaty is subject to certain modifications which depend on the type of treaty. In the case of a collective or multilateral treaty, the text may provide for a *majority decision* to be necessary for its termination (*e.g.,* Article 422 of the Versailles Treaty, Article 26 of the Covenant of the League of Nations, Article 108 of the U.N. Charter, and the majority of the statutes of international administrative unions). In a similar manner, the effect of a treaty may also be abrogated under an agreement by the parties involved.

3. Provisional Suspension of Multilateral Treaties by Agreement of Some Contracting Parties

3. Provisional Suspension of Multilateral Treaties by Agreement of Some Contracting Parties — The appearance of a large number of multilateral treaties imposed the need — because of the specific nature of relations arising between parties to a treaty — to draft special rules to govern exceptions. The possibility of suspending multilateral treaties on the basis of agreement by some of the parties and in relations between them has attracted the special attention of the International Law Commission. The Vienna Convention allows that if a treaty contains no provision on its termination, two or more parties may conclude an agreement for the provisional suspension of the treaty, *only in relations between them,* provided such an agreement, a. does not prejudice the enjoyment of rights by other contracting parties or implementation of their own obligations; b. is not incompatible with an effective fulfilment of the treaty by all contracting parties.

4. Abrogation of Treaties Having no Termination Clause — A general premise of classical international law is that treaties containing no termination clause may not, in principle, be abrogated unilaterally, *i.e.* without the consent of all the other contracting parties. In other words, the consent of all parties must be obtained in such cases, and it may be given, or presumed, in various ways before notice has been issued, but also after it.

In contemporary treaty practice there is a considerable number of international treaties that contain no duration or termination clauses relating to the right of contracting parties to abrogate or withdraw from the treaty regime. Recent examples are the four Geneva Conventions on the Law of the Sea, the Vienna Convention on Diplomatic Relations, etc. These conventions do not contain a termination clause, and the question arises whether such instruments may be regarded as perpetual, or whether they are subject to termination by unanimous agreement, or imply the right of each party to unilaterally withdraw from the treaty subject to prior notice.

The settlement of these issues depends on several factors: on the intent of the parties involved, on the character of treaties, etc. In the dilemma whether to adopt the idea of a free denunciation of such treaties, or to defend the principle of preserving acquired rights and prevent abrogation wherever it has not been expressly envisaged, the Vienna Convention adopted a middle-of-the-road solution, stating that a treaty containing no termination or withdrawal clause cannot be denounced except when it is established that the contracting parties had the intention of allowing this possibility.

5. Abrogation of Treaties Containing the Abrogation or Withdrawal Clause — Very frequently the text of the treaty regulates the possibility of a unilateral abrogation by the contracting states. In this case an international treaty ceases to be valid by unilateral abrogation.

It is a general rule that a treaty can only be revoked in accordance with all the conditions provided in it (as regards time, procedure, etc.). Practice has shown that in most cases the treaty text itself provides for the possibility of a unilateral denunciation (*e.g.,* the Convention on Married Women's Nationality of 20 February 1957, Article 9). There are, however, a large number of agreements stipulating that a unilateral revocation would be valid only subject to the consent of all other contracting parties.

Since the earliest days unilateral abrogation of international treaties has created serious international disputes and harmed cooperation between states, creating tensions (in recent times we have the example of Yugoslavia's protest against unilateral denunciation of treaties by the East European Countries after 1948).

6. Duration — The rule is for agreements to be concluded for a definite time period. Upon expiration of this period the agreement ceases to be valid and is no longer applied.

The duration of an agreement is seldom stipulated in the case of agreements of a law-making character.

When the agreed time has lapsed, the agreement automatically ceases to be valid, but the parties may come to prior agreement on the atuomatic extension of the agreement. On this occasion the term is again set for the treaty's validity.

7. Realization of the Purpose of the Treaty — Once the object and purpose of the treaty have been implemented, it ceases to be valid because the objective for which it was concluded has been achieved (*e. g.* a treaty on frontier is terminated once the boundaries between the parties have been drawn).

A treaty can also be terminated when its objective has been attained by some other means and its retention becomes pointless.

8. Later Impossibility of Implementation — According to the general rules of international law, a treaty is also terminated when its execution becomes physically impossible (*e. g.*, by *force majeure*, the disappearance of the object of the treaty, etc.).

Such a solution no longer is acceptable in all cases. The International Law Commission has therefore stipulated that a treaty need not necessarily be terminated because of the subsequent impossibility of execution, but that only its effect be suspended; for example, when the impossibility of implementation is of a provisional character.

9. Abrogation Owing to Non-Fulfilment by another Contracting Party — In international law, in analogy with the rules of municipal law, the principle of treaty termination can be applied in case of its non-implementation by one of the parties. Its effect is to release the other contracting party from the duty of performing its obligations under the treaty. However, contemporary practice as well as doctrine do not fully accept this standpoint because of the enormous significance which the implementation of the treaty has for relations between contracting parties in various spheres, and more specifically because of the equality of the parties, since non-fulfilment of the contract upsets the balance between equal partners and brings the innocent party into a disadvantaged position.

It is held at present that non-fulfilment of an agreement by one of its parties does not automatically render the agreement null and void, but only has the effect of allowing the innocent party a choice of either remaining party to the treaty and demanding its execution or of denouncing it. On the other hand, in view of the wide spectrum of relations between states in bilateral and multilateral treaties, various consequences may arise in connection with the non-fulfilment of a treaty. Accordingly, this reason for the termination of a treaty was not elaborated by the International Law Commission, which pointed out that the question should be dealt with within the context of the problem of termination or suspension of a treaty owing to its violation, implying that the concept of a *substantive violation* of a treaty also covers the "violation of the provisions of a treaty which [are] essential for the implementation of the objective or aim of the treaty."

10. Termination or Suspension of a Treaty Owing to its Violation — The majority of authors acknowledge that the violation of a treaty by one of its contracting parties may entitle the other to revoke it, or to suspend the performance of its contracted obligation. However, opinions differ regarding the range of this entitlement and the condition under which it can do so. Thus, certain writers, in the absence of international organs to safeguard the execution and observance of treaties, are inclined to grant the innocent party greater rights in the event of the violation, even the right to cancel the treaty. Others again are rather inclined, because of the possibility of a misuse of this right for trivial and non-essential reasons, to grant it in a very restricted form and under specified conditions of the existence of a "material" or "substantive" violation of the treaty.

The International Law Commission, on its part, held that account should above all be taken of the kind of treaty that is involved, as relations involved in bilateral treaties are quite different from those of a multilateral and legislative character because of their subjective matter as well as because of the respective interests of the parties. In the Commission's opinion, therefore, the violation of a treaty however important and grave it is, does neither render the treaty *ipso facto* terminated, nor does it entitle the innocent state to simply invoke the violation as a pretext for the cancellation or termination of a treaty.

The Commission eventually decided that the contracting parties must have full freedom to deal with the question of the effect of a violation of a treaty and its consequences in the manner which they consider to be most suitable. In this sense it adopted the provisions of Section V of the Vienna Convention on the Law of Treaties.

11. Renunciation of Treaty Rights — Certain writers mention renunciation as a means of terminating a treaty. They point out that similar to a creditor's right to waive a debt claimed from his debtor, the same option must be recognized to a party to an international treaty. The condition for it is that renunciation is not presumed but the beneficiary must make an express statement to be waiving his advantage. Examples from practice support this view ; *e.g.*, soon after the signing of the peace treaty with Italy in 1947, the Allies released Italy from the clauses that prevented it from rearming; a similar situation existed in regard to West Germany; also, Yugoslavia waived its right to war reparation by Bulgaria after signing the peace treaty with that state.

Since renunciation presupposes two subjects whose interests are directly involved in the act, it is obvious that this method of terminating treaties could not be applied in the case of law-making treaties and those of multilateral character, since those involve a number of rights and obligations created not in the interest of one state but in the general interest of all the contracting parties. Today it is hardly possible to expect a state to renounce the rights it enjoys under the United Nations Charter. Such a renunciation would in fact be detrimental to the interests and rights of other signatory states.

12. Termination or Suspension of a Treaty Because of the Conclusion of a New Treaty — The termination or suspension of treaties for this reason applies when the parties, without expessly terminating or amending the original treaty, conclude another treaty that is so incompatible with the earlier one that the contracting parties must be assumed to have intended to abrogate it.

The Vienna Convention stipulates that a treaty shall be deemed to have ceased to be active once its contracting parties have concluded another treaty relating to the same subject matter, under the following conditions: a. if the treaty infers, or suggests in some other way, that the parties had intended to regulate the matter in future under the later treaty; b. if the clauses of the later treaty are so incompatible with those of the earlier one that both treaties cannot be applied at the same time.

13. Conditions for Abrogation — If the treaty has been concluded subject to conditions for abrogation, it shall cease to be valid once this condition has been fulfilled. In that case the treaty is terminated from the moment of incipience of the circumstance envisaged as the condition. The termination of the treaty takes place automatically , and there is no need for it to be expressly stated (*e.g.,* through an express clause in the later treaty, or implicitly by substituting the content of the earlier treaty with that of the later one).

14. Termination of a Treaty that is Inconsistent with a Later Imperative Norm of General International Law — International treaties may cease to be valid because they are not consonant with the general rules of international law having a mandatory character, which cannot be circumvented by means of treaties (the rule *jus cogens*).

As to the effect of the mandatory norms of general international law in regards to the earlier international treaties, the Vienna Convention, in its section concerning the termination of the treaties, provides that if an extant treaty is contrary to the the new norm *(jus cogens superveniens)*, then the existing treaty is to be regarded as invalid and is to be terminated. The treaty shall be null and void from the date of entry into force of the new international norm having the *jus cogens* character. It does not cancel it *ad initio*, but it prevents its further existence and application.

15. The Clause *Rebus sic Stantibus* — A substantial change of circumstances has a significance for the effect of treaties, and it was, therefore, decided by the International Law Commission to introduce the clause *conventio omnis intelegitur rebus sic stantibus*, known in the Middle Ages. The purpose of this institution is to recognize as the general norm a specific reason for the suspension of or withdrawal from a treaty.

Since the clause basically means a change of circumstances, the cessation of the effect of a treaty or withdrawal from a treaty may be justified by invoking a change in the circumstances that existed at the moment the treaty was made, which could not have been foreseen by the contracting parties. The condition for the application of this motive is that the changed circumstances must have arisen independently of the will of the parties involved and made the further implementation of the treaty harmful for one of the parties.

An essential change in circumstances may be invoked as a reason for terminating treaties or withdrawing from them only if it affects those circumstances which actually motivated the parties to agree to be bound by the treaty.

The clause *rebus sic stantibus*, in the opinion of the majority of theoreticians of international law, does not imply unilateral abrogation of a treaty but is used to back the demand by one party for a formal revision of the treaty or for its termination, depending on the degree of change in the circumstances.

Opinions differ among jurists about importance, role and effect of this clause and about its very nature. Writers such as Jelinek and Anzilotti see in this clause a rule that helps to interpret the will of the parties, especially their intent at the moment of the conclusion. Therefore, this clause may not be invoked as a reason for abrogation. On the other hand, Scelle sees in altered circumstances an unforeseen event which compels parties to readjust treaty relationships between them, either by agreement or by the decision of a competent judiciary or arbitration body. Other writers believe that the clause *rebus sic stantibus* owes its existence and justification to the fact that it serves the vital interests of states. Therefore, a state's right to survival may be a reason for unilateral abrogation on account of changed circumstances that are liable to harm its interests. An opposite standpoint is taken by the supporters of the view that the clause may be invoked only in exceptional cases, when circumstances have changed so much as to make it clear that the parties would not have bound themselves if they had been able to envisage such a substantive change. A middle-of-the-road stance considers the clause *rebus sic stantibus* to be inherent in every treaty, and that any change in circumstances necessarily leads to the termination of the treaty, on the basis of the tacit intention by contracting parties which is presupposed in all cases.

There are many examples in the practice of states for the invocation of the clause *rebus sic stantibus* as justification for the termination or alteration of contracted obligations on the basis of changed circumstances.

The Vienna Convention has made the following provisions:

> 1. A party may invoke unforeseeable changed circumstances to abrogate a treaty, except a. if the existence of these circumstances represented the essential basis of the consent of the parties to be bound by the treaty, and b. if the effect of the change is to radically alter the quantum of the obligations that are to be fulfilled under the treaty.
> 2. The substantial change of circumstances may not be invoked, a. in the case of a treaty drawing national boundaries, and b. if the change stemmed from the violation of either a treaty or some other international obligations vis-à-vis the other parties and was committed by the party invoking it.

X. Effect of War on International Treaties

The effects of war have not been the same for all kinds of treaties and have depended on the ruling conception of the nature of the war. Thus the classical doctrine of international law in the early 19th century held that declaration of war terminated all international treaties previously concluded between the belligerents. This conception reflected the current practice of concluding international contracts mainly of a political character and traces its roots back to ancient times, when the institution *diffidatio*, to solemnly proclaim, all the existing contracts with the belligerent required each belligerent side as abrogated. This view, with certain insubstantial modifications, prevailed until 1815. Subsequently, in accordance with the restrictive interpretation of war as a relationship between states which does not directly affect their citizens, the practice was adopted for a large number of treaties to remain in force depending on the subject matter to which they were related. At the turn of the century the concept of war evolved towards being regarded as a phenomenon which interested not only the governments of the states involved in the conflict but also their citizens. Peace treaties concluded after the First World War have shown an obvious orientation in favor of the denunciation of the majority of international treaties between the former belligerents. Subsequently, the view evolved that the war in itself does not terminate contracts, although it necessarily has an effect on contractual relations, depending on the category of the treaty. With the outbreak of war then only certain categories of contracts are terminated; in fact the treaties designed to regulate warfare actually begin to be applied as hostilities start.

This standpoint has remained valid to this day, even though the United Nations Charter prohibits war. The outbreak of hostilities or conflicts is possible either in self-defense or as part of collective measures against an aggressor state. This is why the above mentioned distinction among treaties according to the effect of war on them remains topical and valid.

The contracts that are terminated upon the outbreak of hostilities include in the first place bilateral agreements. The most important of these are purely political contracts (treaties of friendship, guarantees, alliance, neutrality, etc.). Exceptions are also possible here (*e.g.*, the treaties which created and guaranteed the permanent neutrality of Switzerland, although essentially political, are not terminated with the outbreak of a war, since their purpose is to create a permanent system), although the rule remains and in fact is amplified with the category of the treaties which are held to be incompatible with the state of war (*e.g.*, treaties on extradition, trade and economic agreements, etc.). These treaties are also abrogated; or their effect is terminated, but the final decision as to which agreements should be regarded as abrogated by war, and which would only be suspended, will depend on the victorious side. Thus the peace treaties with former enemies concluded after the Second World War contain a separate clause which stipulates that each allied power should inform Italy, or Hungary, or Bulgaria, etc., within six months of the entry of a peace treaty into force, which prewar bilateral treaties it wishes to remain in force or bring back into existence. All the articles which were not in accordance with the peace treaty should be regarded as abrogated. The same applies to the treaty of peace concluded with Japan (Article 7). As regards Austria, the Allies took a different view. Since Austria was incorporated into Germany through the *Anschluss*, they did not apply the principle of abrogation of treaties concluded with that country prior to 1939.

Yugoslavia applied the mentioned provisions of the peace treaties with the former enemy states from World War II and informed them which treaties it would regard as remaining in force and which would be reinstated (*e.g.*, in its note of 25 February 1948, Yugoslavia told the government of Italy which treaties it wished to continue as valid, *i.e.* the Convention on Legal and Judicial Protection of citizens, the Convention on Extradition, both dated 6 April 1922, and the Convention on Livestock Contagions, of 12 August 1924).

The category of agreements whose effect is only suspended by war covers law-making multilateral treaties. This is because it is held that law-making treaties, as well as certain treaties of a multilateral and general character, are in the interest of the entire international community and all its subjects directly or even indirectly. It is, therefore, held that such agreements remain in force, notwithstanding the outbreak of a war or armed conflict (the Hague Conventions for example). The same group may include the numerous conventions constituting the international unions, as well as the conventions of a purely legal character which interests states other than the contracting parties (*e.g.* the Universal Postal Convention). In principle, such conventions are not abrogated, but their effect is only suspended for the parties at conflict during its duration. Subject to there being no other provisions, these conventions resume their effect after the end of the war.

The third category covers those treaties which in fact begin to be applied with the outbreak of a state of war or a conflict, since their purpose is precisely to regulate relations during wartime (*e.g.*, agreements on the treatment of prisoners of war, the sick and wounded, the shipwrecked, etc.). This category also covers the agreements concluded through the intermediary of a protecting power, such as those on the exchange of war prisoners, on the establishment of a neutral zone, etc.

XI. State Succession and International Treaties

State succession is the assumption of rights and obligations related to the territory of a state by another state as a result of a change of sovereignty in the said territory. On this basis, the state succeeding to a territory takes over the legal relationships of the state to which the territory belonged or in which it held sovereign rights.

The changes due to state succession are of a complex character, and the legal effects of the transfer of sovereign powers have a special significance for international treaties and their further validity. These changes are also important with respect to the status of public property, financial commitments and debts, nationality, legislation, property relations and other non-contractual rights and obligations.

Contemporary international law has not yet evolved suitable legal rules which would adequately regulate relations between the predecessor and successor states in regards to the international contracts concluded prior to the emergence of a new government in a territory. The question became especially topical in the era of decolonization, when a large number of new states came into being. Although contemporary doctrine has not taken a definitive stand, practice is being created by the predecessor states, generally the colonial metropolises. By concluding a special agreement with the successor state, they establish the volume of the rights and obligations taken over from an earlier period. Successor states have attempted to assume a more definite stance in re-

gard to the agreements which were applied in their territory prior to the acquisition of independence, and solutions were adopted to regulate the status of successor states in respect of the earlier treaties. According to Bartoš, legal theory
admits four possible solutions: a. *tabula rasa* is proclaimed in respect of contracts between a newly emerged state and the predecessor state, and the new
state is not bound by the old contractual relations, nor does it inherit any contracted commitments; b. the new state has the right to select which treaties to
retain in force; c. the new territorial sovereign is assumed to be generally succeeding the old one, with the proviso that the successor state must be entitled to
subsequently abrogate those international contracts which it believes do not
suit its interests, although until the abrogation they would be in force and binding; d. a deadline may be set by which the parties would decide, by means of a
subsequent agreement, which contracts would remain in force, with the proviso
that from the moment of the emergence of the new state until the expiration of
the deadline, all the treaties inherited from the predecessor state would be
deemed to be in force.

Irrespective of practice, which is still in the process of evolution, it is clear
today that the theory of general succession by the new territorial sovereign is
not acceptable in any shape or form. This theory has reflected the stance and
interest of the colonial and big powers and tends to protect their acquired rights
on the basis of the earlier treaties. Therefore, in regulating the status of the
newly emerged states, especially those created in the period of decolonization,
the assumption must be made that all international contracts concluded by the
earlier holder of sovereignty shall cease to be valid, and those of the successor
state shall begin to be applied. This principle should be applicable to all treaties, but international practice and doctrine have shown that certain exceptions do exist. They include those international agreements which relate to a
definite sphere (*e.g.,* agreements on international servitudes, agreements on
the regime of waters, etc.), or which tacitly imply the extension of the validity
of certain agreements, irrespective of their nature or specific features. States
may also agree, by contract, which international treaties will remain in force
on the occasion of the succession. The existence of different solutions is the result of different relationships and circumstances in which they arose. As regards the practice of Yugoslavia, the recognition of Serbia's independence at
the Berlin Congress of 1878 was made conditional upon the obligation of taking
over the international treaties that had been concluded by Turkey. In the case
of the Kingdom of Serbs, Croats and Slovenes, created after the First World
War, the peace conference did not permit a break in the continuity of Serbia's
international subjectivity, and retained in force certain international treaties,
by extending them to the entire territory of the Kingdom. Similarly, all the
multilateral treaties and conventions in which Serbia appeared as the signatory remained in force and were taken over by the state which later became the

Kingdom of Yugoslavia. With the creation of socialist Yugoslavia following World War II, the view was taken that the international legal continuity did not cease between it and the former Kingdom of Yugoslavia, or Serbia, in regards to international agreements that they had concluded. The government of the F.P.R.Y. recognized in principle the earlier obligations arising from bilateral international agreements. It also recognized all the earlier international multilateral agreements. Similarly, all the international rights and obligations of the F.P.R.Y. have been extended to the territory acquired from Italy, whereas the international agreements concluded by Italy had ceased to be valid in regard to Yugoslavia.

Chapter Three: Peaceful Settlement of Disputes and the Safeguarding of Peace

Introduction

The clashing interests of international subjects are likely to cause international disputes and may bring about international conflicts. International law has the means of resolving international disputes in a peaceable manner and of safeguarding peace, as well as rules for settling international conflicts. This chapter will deal with the means of achieving a peaceable settlement of disputes and safeguarding peace.

According to some authors (*e.g.* Oppenheim), international disputes may be of a legal or political nature. In their opinion, legal disputes are those arising from acts by the legislative, judicial or executive organs of a state, its armed forces or individuals residing in its territory, whereas political disputes are those resulting from the conflicting political interests.

Most of the authors agree that in practice it is difficult to distinguish legal from political disputes. It may be even more difficult to adopt this division theoretically, because a dispute is a sum total of conflicting demands, regardless of whether they might be preponderantly of a legal or political nature. Any political dispute has its legal side, just as every legal dispute has its political substance. In view of the present state of international relations, we believe that it is still difficult to set up judicial institutions for the settlement of disputes that would be both of a political and a legal character, although the need is already being felt for such international tribunals as, for example, an international criminal court. This is why we have today the International Court of Justice at The Hague, which actually deals with legal disputes, and the U.N. Security Council, which handles political differences, in addition to other means which may be used for the settlement of both kinds of disputes. In any case, both the legal and political disputes come within the domain of international law.

MEANS OF A PEACEFUL SETTLEMENT OF DISPUTES

I. Negotiations

Negotiations are the first and extremely important means of a peaceful settlement of international disputes. It is certainly one of the most successful means, because many disputes are actually removed in this manner, provided both the litigant sides are interested in having the dispute successfully resolved. It is true that the course of negotiation may also be affected by certain other factors which have little to do with the object of dispute. In that case negotiations under way turn into a kind of diplomatic haggling, which means that either some interest other than the one calling for settlement is at stake, or one side is intent upon forcing its own interest on the other side through various means of diplomatic or other pressure.

The negotiations usually begin with a statement in which a party in a dispute states its case. A dispute may be terminated as early as in this initial stage of the negotiations, during the acceptance of the statement or the first exchange of statements. The settlement of the dispute may be continued with a further exchange of statements, if the interested parties expect to be able to achieve the desired result in this way. The parties also may, immediately or after several exchanges of statements, undertake to organize one or several diplomatic meetings.

The parties accepting negotiations are under no obligation whatsoever. The acceptance of the negotiations as a means of a peaceful settlement of disputes only commits the parties to begin the negotiation. Hence the result of the negotiations may be the decision to abandon this method as futile, or to accept the opponent's demand, or to conclude an agreement. This means of peaceful settlement of international disputes is frequently recommended and suggested by Yugoslav diplomacy as highly suitable in the present-day international relations.

II. Inquiry

An international commission of inquiry is a body which is expected to establish the facts of an international dispute without any bias and to submit a report about it to the parties to the dispute. The task of fact-finding may also be given to a person who is held in high standing by both parties.

A commission of inquiry is established under an agreement between the contesting parties. The agreement must make mention of the commission's terms of reference and of the time limit by which the commission must be appointed and begin its work. Representatives or attorneys of either side may be appointed to the commission, and the two parties must agree on the rules of procedure. After the completion of their task, a report is made and signed by all the members of the commission, and is then read at its public sitting, in the presence of the representatives and attorneys of the parties to a dispute. The report of the commission of inquiry commits them to nothing; it simply serves as a basis for further negotiations.

The Hague Convention for the Pacific Settlement of International Disputes of 1899 contains six articles applicable to the commissions of inquiry. The second Hague Conference of 1907 worked out the rules on the commissions of inquiry, making good use of the experience acquired from the incident in the North Sea of 1904, involving the British fishing trawlers which were fired upon by the Baltic Fleet. On the basis of the facts established by an international commission of inquiry (comprising five senior naval officers from Britain, Russia, the United States, France and Austria), Russia paid the victims of the incident a compensation of 65,000 pounds sterling.

Many treaties today provide for the establishment of commissions of inquiry — should ever a need for them arise — in the event of any international disputes. The use of the commissions of inquiry has been envisaged under Article 34 of the U.N. Charter for the purpose of establishing facts liable to threaten international peace and security. The United Nations has used this means on several occasions, in cases involving Greece, Palestine, Korea, Hungary, etc. In 1950, under its Uniting for Peace Resolution the U.N. General Assembly established a permanent commission of inquiry called the Peace Observation Commission consisting of fourteen members and designed to supervise and report on situations in any area of the world where international tensions are liable to jeopardize international peace and security.

III. Mediation

Mediation is assistance to the parties to a dispute, in the form of counsel from a third state, group of states or a person enjoying international prestige (*e.g.* mediation by Count Bernadotte in the Palestine question), with the aim of attaining a specific solution to an international dispute. Mediation may be requested, but may also be offered. It can even be undertaken during an armed conflict, while the hostilities are in progress, for the purpose of ending them, (for example, the mediation by U.S. President Roosevelt in the Russo-Japanese War terminating in the Portsmouth Peace of 1905).

Certain authors, particularly the older international law experts, make a distinction between mediation and good offices. Thus good offices might be viewed as a collection of steps by third states designed to make negotiations between the conflicting parties possible, whereas mediation would consist in direct negotiations on the basis of the mediator's proposals. Other authors who claim that this distinction has disappeared in practice and that good offices are also covered by mediation are also right. This has also been confirmed in the U. N. Charter. Article 33 makes mention only of mediation and not of good offices as well.

Mediation may consist in the transmission of demands and replies, but should never transcend its advisory framework. Mediation means an active participation in a dispute, but the proposals and advice given by the mediators have no compulsory force.

Mediation may also be regarded as a duty under an international treaty. Article 8 of the Paris Peace Treaty of 1856 — in the case of the dispute between Turkey and the signatories of this Treaty — held the contracting parties under the obligation to seek mediation from the other signatory powers before resorting to force. The Hague Convention for the Pacific Settlement of International Disputes defines mediation as a right of states outside a dispute to offer their good offices, or mediation, the performance of these offices not being regarded as a hostile act. This convention also provides for a special kind of mediation according to which each party appoints one state which is not involved, empowering it to carry on negotiations on behalf of the litigant, which during that time maintains no contact with the other, at least in the matter under dispute. Provision is made for a thirty-day mandate, unless required otherwise.

The League of Nations developed the system of mediation by placing itself in mediating service in the event of any international dispute (Article 11; para. 3 of Article 15 of the Covenant of the League of Nations.). According to Article 11 of the Covenant, any war or threat of war is a matter of concern for the entire League of Nations, and the League of Nations is therefore obliged to undertake suitable measures for the successful maintenance of peace among nations. The application of this instrument was advanced even further after the Second World War. According to the United Nations Charter, the Security Council is competent both to offer and to demand mediation in an international dispute. The U.N. Secretary-General can also have a mediating role. At the proposal of the Yugoslav delegation in 1950, the U.N. General Assembly appointed a permanent commission for good offices which is available to states in the settlement of their disputes.

IV. Conciliation

Conciliation is a proceeding in which the parties take their dispute for settlement to a commission or selected person, with the idea of having it studied from both a factual and legal aspect. The commission or the selected person submits reports containing suggestions for the settlement of the dispute. It is a rule that the parties are not under the obligation to adopt any proposed solutions. Hence the proposals of this kind are not deemed to have the character of arbitration or a judicial settlement. Suggestions for the settlement may be made available to the parties until such time as they reach an agreement. Conciliation commissions, and even their composition, may be envisaged in advance under treaties to that effect, so that in the event of any dispute, they could immediately be set into motion.

Viewed historically, this instrument has evolved from the practice of international commissions of inquiry. Conciliation was especially common between the two world wars. It was institutionalized in the Covenant of the League of Nations, according to which the role of conciliation was to be performed by its organs (Article 15 of the Covenant). Conciliation as an instrument for the settlement of disputes was recommended by the resolution of the third session of the Assembly of the League of Nations, held in 1922. It was particularly favored in their diplomacy by Switzerland and the Scandinavian countries. Prewar Yugoslavia was bound by a number of treaties to resort to this means in the event of a dispute. Conciliation was also known in the treaty practice of the American states. For some kinds of disputes, conciliation was provided for in the peace treaties of 1947.

The difference between the commissions of inquiry and of conciliation consists in the former acting only as fact-finder, whereas in conciliation, factual and legal aspects of the difference are considered. A distinction should also be made between conciliation and mediation. In mediation we have, as a rule, third states which take part in the settlement through their good offices and counsels. As a rule, conciliation is done through commissions composed of several persons. However, in mediation as well as in conciliation a single individual may also be appointed. In this case the following distinction remains: conciliation is a proceeding to consider the factual and legal aspects of the dispute, whereas mediation consists of advice and different offices which are offered to the parties to the dispute. Yet in practice these instruments are so close to one another that it is difficult to distinguish between them on the basis of their characteristics. Thus, for example, in conciliation any proposed solution is understood in advance to be non-binding. However, the signatory parties to an agreement may undertake in advance the obligation to regard any decisions of the conciliation commission as definitive and even binding (Article 45 of the

Convention on Danube Navigation of 1948). Whatever variants there might be among the means of settling international disputes, they all have in common settlement in a pacific manner.

V. Arbitration

Concept and Types of Arbitration — Development — Arbitral Procedure — Contemporary Codification of Rules on Arbitral Procedure — Role of the International Court of Justice in Arbitral Procedure

1. Concept and Types of Arbitration — Arbitration is a peaceful settlement of an international dispute by one or several arbitrators. Arbitration is a judgement on the basis of legislation in force. The judgment passed by an arbitrator or a court of arbitration is binding on the parties to the dispute and must be carried out, provided, of course, that states have voluntarily accepted this method of settling their controversies.

The overriding principle in arbitration is that of the autonomy of will. According to the advisory opinion of the Permanent Court of International Justice of 1923, no state may be compelled, without its consent, to submit its disputes with other states to mediation or arbitration or any other kind of peaceful settlement. Consent may be given once and for all in the form of a freely-assumed obligation, but it can also be granted in individual cases, irrespective of any existing obligation. Hence if states wish to settle their dispute by way of arbitration, they must first conclude a convention (*ad hoc* arbitration) which is called a *compromis.* This agreement should contain the name of the arbitrator, the description and composition of the arbitral tribunal, subject of controversy and the procedure. States may also commit themselves in advance to arbitration in the event of any dispute. This kind of arbitration is called *institutional,* and is envisaged either by a clause in their treaties, or by special arbitration treaties providing for the contingency of any dispute between the signatories.

The composition of an arbitral tribunal is not essential. The arbitrator may be an individual, a person of high standing, a high government official or a head of state. Very frequently the president of the Swiss Confederation or the president of the Swiss Supreme Court is chosen as arbitrator. In the Middle Ages, controversies between Christian states were usually settled by the Pope as the supreme arbitrator. An arbitral tribunal may take the form of a forum, for example at a law school. Following a dispute between Britain, Venezuela, and the U.S.A., arbitration was entrusted to a commission which sat in Paris and which was composed of American and British members, headed by Professor Martens. It was common for the conflicting states to put up their own arbitrators, who would then select a third. In modern arbitration the composition of the tribunal is known in advance. There is no doubt that the most advanced form of international adjudication was achieved by the establishment of the International Court at The Hague, known between the two world wars as the Permanent Court of International Justice. Permanent justices can be far more independent vis-à-vis the litigant parties than *ad hoc* arbitrators, which undoubtedly raises the prestige of the permanent judge and increases his objectivity. Furthermore, over many years of international judiciary practice, they acquire greater knowledge and skills than the *ad hoc* arbitrators, who may only deal with one kind of dispute.

2. Development — Arbitration is the oldest method of resolving international disputes. It was known among the ancient Eastern peoples, but some authors (Le Fur) believe that its origin goes back even further. Arbitration was used by the Sumerians, ancient Greeks, and later by the Italian city states. Late in the Middle Ages states used to submit to the arbitration of the Pope as the highest moral authority. Arbitration fell into disuse during the absolutist period, but it came into favor again at the end of the 18th century, after the 1794 treaty between Britain and the United States to establish a portion of the frontier in Canada. Since then it has been more and more frequently in application. Between 1794 and the end of the 1900s, there were 170 cases of arbitration.

The so-called "Alabama" dispute between Britain and the United States, resolved in 1872, helped to spread the utilization of this method. Britain was made to pay the United States about 16 million dollars for failing to observe neutrality in the American Civil War, thus inflicting on the United States damages to the mentioned amount. Great Britain duly implemented the decision of the arbitral tribunal and paid up within the set time limit of one year.

The Hague conferences made frequent use of arbitration. In 1899, Russia proposed obligatory arbitration, at least for certain cases, for example for all questions of compensation for damages, for the interpretation of international treaties, etc. Germany, on the other hand, which was preparing for war, was against a compulsory introduction of this institution into positive international law. Since all decisions were to be taken in unanimity, obligatory arbitration was not adopted at the first Hague Conference. In 1907, at the second Hague Conference, another attempt was made to agree on introducing obligatory arbitration in the first Hague Convention, but again without success. A partial result was achieved when the following declaration was inserted in the convention: "In questions of a legal nature, and especially in the interpretation or application of international conventions, arbitration is recognized by the signatory Powers as the most effective, and at the same time the most equitable, means of settling disputes which diplomacy has failed to settle." Although obligatory arbitration was not adopted, a permanent court of arbitration with its seat at The Hague was established at the first Hague Conference, and a procedure for a peaceful settlement of disputes was provided under a separate convention. Yet the Permanent Court of Arbitration was not a real tribunal. Essentially it consisted of a panel of arbitrators, acknowledged authorities in questions of international law, nominated by the signatory powers. Each of these had the right of nominating four arbitrators for a period of six years. The names of the arbitrators were entered in a panel. In the event of a dispute, states took arbitrators from this panel for members of the arbitral tribunal which would eventually decide on the dispute. In addition to this panel, the Permanent Court of Arbitration consisted of the International Bureau, which in fact served as the registry for the court, and the Permanent Council of the Court, made up of diplomatic representatives accredited to the Netherlands and the Dutch minister for foreign affairs. The task of the Permanent Council was to control the International Bureau and to handle administrative questions concerning the business of the Court. During the first twenty-five years of its existence, only 35 jurists were chosen as judges in the 18 different cases heard by the Court, and only 12 of them were selected a second time. An exception was the eminent French professor of international law, Louis Renaud, who was a judge in seven cases. The Permanent Court of Arbitration is still in existence, and its main function is to nominate suitable candidates for election to the International Court of Justice.

Between the two wars, several hundred arbitration treaties and conventions containing a clause on arbitration were concluded. The League of Nations endorsed arbitration as one of the most important means for settling international disputes peacefully. A collective convention known as the General Act for the Pacific Settlement of International Disputes was adopted by the League of Nations on 26 September 1928 and came into force on 19 August 1929. The signatory states were given broad opportunities for resorting to arbitration under this Act. In 1949 the U.N. General Assembly adopted the Revised General Act containing minor changes (the name United Nations Organization was substituted for the League of Nations). The General Act came into force the following year, but only a small number of states acceded to it.

3. Arbitral Procedure — The Hague Conferences of 1899 and 1907 set up the machinery for arbitration which was available to states but was not compulsory. The procedure was laid down on the basis of the experience of arbitral tribunals and the draft adopted by the Institute for International Law in 1875. According to the first Hague Convention of 1899, the main principles for arbitration were the following: there could be no arbitration without a previous *compromis,* which had to contain the usual elements; rules of procedure were to be determined by the judge; if the tribunal was composed of several persons, a president and registrar must be appointed; states may be represented before the tribunal by their representatives and attorneys; as a rule the Court sits at The Hague; in the first phase the proceedings would be in writing; the parties were expected to present their arguments in written form and submit evidence; in the second phase the agents and attorneys for the parties would plead their cases orally, give additional evidence and answer the questions of the tribunal.

After the oral proceedings were concluded, the judges retired to deliberate. Their deliberations were private. The judgment was to be reached by majority vote, with the written opinion and signatures of the president and registrar. The judgment was final and without appeal. A review was permitted if provided for in the *compromis,* provided a new fact had come to light which would have an effect on the outcome of the hearing. In the case of review, the same tribunal which had first heard the case was to hear the new evidence. Interpretation of the *compromis* was in the competence of the court and not of the parties.

The fourth chapter of the Revised Hague Convention of 1907 (Articles 86 to 90) provided for *summary proceedings* on disputes of a technical nature. Under this procedure, the parties to a dispute would each nominate one judge, and these two would select a third. All arguments would be presented in written form, and there would be no oral hearing unless deemed necessary in order to hear witnesses and expert opinion. This type of arbitral procedure was introduced to reduce court costs and to expedite settlement of disputes when possible.

4. Contemporary Codification of Rules on Arbitral Procedure — In its first session in New York in 1949, the U.N. International Law Commission selected arbitral procedure as one of the priority tasks in the codification of international law. Professor Georges Scelle was designated rapporteur, and he was responsible for the many-times-revised text of the Draft Convention on Arbitral Procedure, later known as the Draft Model of Rules on Arbitral Procedure.

Working on the Draft Convention on Arbitral Procedure, the International Law Commission sought to formulate the main principles which would govern arbitral procedure between states, from the arbitration treaty, the establishment of the tribunal, *compromis* and terms of reference of the tribunal, to the judgment, and its review or annulment. On the other hand, the Commission did not specify the details of procedure, since it became convinced that procedure should vary from case to case. The comments on the draft convention prepared by the U.N. Secretariat state that the draft only concerns itself with procedure. Professor François, then chairman of the U.N. International Law Commission, stated in the Legal Committee in 1953 that the draft was a convention not on arbitration but on arbitral procedure, since it did not seek to create new obligations but rather envisaged certain procedural guarantees for the entire course of the proceedings to give it effect, *i.e.* if parties resorted to arbitration, they would then have to follow a specified procedure.

Work on establishing this procedure followed two lines. First, existing rules of arbitral procedure in the broad sense were codified, and second, new rules were laid down providirg procedural guarantees to give effect to the obligation to resort to arbitration. The Commission did not consider codification of the so-called classical rules of arbitral procedure to be its prime task, nor did it consider codification of these rules to constitute the substance of arbitral procedure. The intention of the Commission was to promote the *progressive* development of international law in this sphere by means of such codification. The new rules were not unknown in the theory of international law, and some parts were already being used in practice. The draft, however, built these new rules into a coherent system in which few faults can be found, especially since the trend has been to strengthen the function of the judiciary in international law.

In its codification of existing rules, the Commission started with the traditional concept of arbitration formulated in the well-known Article 37 of the Convention for the Pacific Settlement of International Disputes (1907), according to which international arbitration settled disputes between states on the basis of legal principles by judges whom they themselves selected. Thus, for instance, states voluntarily submitted to arbitration; they designated the arbitrators; they agreed upon the terms of reference for the court, the procedure and the law on which the arbitrators would base their judgment. However, this part of the draft convention on arbitral procedure was not subjected to criticism, either by the minority opinion in the U.N. International Law Commission which criticized the draft, or by the majority in the General Assembly which refused to adopt it. States were opposed to those provisions of the convention intended to promote the progressive development of international law, specifically procedural guarantees formulated to give effect to the obligation to resort to arbitration. These procedural guarantees were for the most part concerned with the competence of the International Court of Justice, and we shall give them a separate consideration.

5. The Role of the International Court of Justice in Arbitral Procedure — The possible jurisdiction of the International Court of Justice was envisaged even before the setting up of an arbitral tribunal, in case the parties did not agree on the existence of the dispute, or in case their dispute was liable to arbitration. If the parties did not reach a prior agreement, one of them could petition the International Court for a decision on this prior question, and its decision was final. In its decision, and in anticipation of the establishment of an arbitral tribunal, the International Court of Justice could lay down interim measures which the parties would have to accept in order to protect their own interests. The reason for such proceedings can be found in concrete cases in the past, when arbitration could not be resorted to, since there was no authority to decide whether or not there was a dispute or whether a dispute involved those obligations for whose nonfulfilment arbitration was prescribed. For this reason it was difficult to establish the competence of a judicial body which, prior to the setting up of an arbitral tribunal, would ensure the effectiveness of arbitration. This effectiveness was guaranteed by the nature of the decision of the International Court of Justice, as it was definitive.

Furthermore, if one of the parties failed to name one or more arbitrators, on the basis of the *compromis* or any other agreement, within three months as provided by this draft, a president, vice-president, or judge of the International Court of Justice would be authorized to replace him. The president of the International Court of Justice was to have the same authority in the absence of regulations on the composition of the arbitral tribunal that was to be set up after consultation with the contesting parties. The International Court of Justice was also to have authority to exclude one of the arbitrators in the event of an objection by either of the parties.

If the parties fail to agree on the law according to which the arbitral tribunal would pass judgment, the draft envisages this tribunal to be "inspired" by para. 1, Art. 38 of the Statute of the International Court of Justice, concerning the use of legal sources. If for any reason the tribunal that decided a case cannot be asked for a decision on the interpretation and legality of its judgment, one of the parties may submit such a dispute to the International Court of Justice after three months.

Finally, the International Court of Justice has considerable competence in regard to review and annulment of the judgment after the expiration of three months.

A request for review is submitted to the tribunal passing judgment. However, if for any reason this is not possible and there is no other agreement or settlement provided for between the parties, one of the parties may submit this request to the International Court of Justice.

The International Court of Justice is authorized to annul judgments at the request of one of the parties, if the tribunal has exceeded its authority, if one of its members is suspected of corruption, or if a basic rule of procedure has been seriously violated. The time limit for such an appeal is from 60 days to six months.

Let us take a closer look at these rules of the draft convention intended to promote the progressive development of this sphere of international law by laying down specific competences of the International Court of Justice.

First of all, the most important question is that of suitability for arbitration, that is, whether a dispute is subject to obligatory arbitration under a treaty. The problem arises when this question must be settled prior to the setting up of a tribunal, when there is no authority to decide on the existence or non-existence of a dispute and, in particular, to decide on whether a dispute is covered by an obligation of arbitration. The Commission took the viewpoint that provision must be made for a procedure to settle this question, since the history of arbitration has shown that many decisions were never made because of this lacuna in arbitration treaties, when it was left to the parties to a dispute to decide this kind of question between themselves, which they practically never managed to do. Hence the Commission ruled that in the event of a disagreement between the parties, or at the request of either, the International Court of Justice would be competent and its decision would be final.

These guarantees giving effect to the arbitral procedure came under fire in the Legal Committee at the eighth and tenth regular sessions of the U.N. General Assembly.

States were unwilling to undertake a general obligation to submit to an arbitral procedure in all cases. As adoption of this arbitral procedure posed a certain legal obligation on states, they feared the possible implications for their sovereign rights, any of which could be involved in the arbitration of any eventual dispute.

States are willing to have recourse to a number of means for the peaceful settlement of disputes, specifically arbitration — even under the old procedures — and, in particular, an international judicature in the form of the International Court of Justice. In their opinion, the attempt made in the draft convention was a denial of the traditional distinction between international arbitration and permanent international judicial settlement. Their stand was that the arbitral procedure provided for by the draft was a shift from the traditional concept of international arbitration to a permanent obligatory judicial determination in which these two institutions begin to merge. Thus the draft convention neglected the principle of the autonomy of will of the parties, which was an essential part of the classical form of arbitration. Finally, at the thirteenth session of the General Assembly, the draft model of rules of arbitral procedure was adopted, and it was recommended that member countries follow these rules in their legal dealings with one another.

In our opinion, there is justification for the procedural guarantees, which in the course of arbitral proceedings are ensured by the authority of the International Court of Justice in the interest of successful conclusion of arbitration. As provided for under the draft convention, the authority of the International Court of Justice in this instance is not a regular competence undermining the traditional form of international arbitration, which states would not like to see precluded as a means for the peaceful settlement of their disputes; rather, it is a competence to be exercised only if the parties to a dispute have not decided otherwise. If, however, the parties to a dispute, which have voluntarily submitted to arbitration, do not specify their procedure in the future for specific cases, then they tacitly accept the authority of the International Court of Justice.

VI. The International Court of Justice

Introduction — Establishment — Organization — Competence — Procedure

1. Introduction — The International Court of Justice is the principal judicial organ of the United Nations. It functions in accordance with Chapter XIV of the Charter (Articles 92 to 96) and with the Statute based on the Statute of the Permanent Court of International Justice. The Statute of the present International Court of Justice is an integral part of the Charter of the United Nations.

2. Establishment — The Permanent Court of International Justice was established under the Covenant of the League of Nations. Its draft statute was formulated by a commission of jurists, adopted by the Council of the League of Nations in San Sebastian in 1920, and that same year was submitted for approval to the first assembly of the League of Nations. By 1930, 34 states had adopted the optional clause of Article 36 of the Statute concerning the compulsory jurisdiction of the Court in their legal disputes. From 1922 up to the German occupation of the Netherlands (the seat of the Court was at The Hague), the Court handed down 31 decisions and gave 27 advisory opinions. The United Nations Charter changed the name of the court to the International Court of Justice. The old Statute was for the most part retained, with only minor modifications. The Court itself decides on other rules concerning its work and on details of procedure.

3. Organization — The Court consists of 15 independent judges. They are not representatives of their countries and are selected purely for their personal qualifications. These are persons of high moral fibre, who fulfil the necessary prerequisites for holding the highest judicial positions in their own countries. Although the judges of the International Court of Justice are not elected on the basis of their nationality, no two may be nationals of the same state.

The autonomy of the judges is guaranteed both in a moral and in a financial respect. They enjoy diplomatic privileges and immunities and receive salaries from the United Nations.

Before taking up his duties, each judge must solemnly declare that he will exercise his powers impartially and conscientiously. Judges are prohibited from holding any political or administrative functions. They may not engage in any other occupation of a professional nature. They are not permitted to act as agents, counsels or attorneys in any case, nor may they participate in deciding disputes in which they may have previously appeared in such a capacity. Judges may not be dismissed unless the Court unanimously decides to do so, and if a judge has ceased meeting the required conditions. In such an event, the court registrar informs the Secretary-General of the United Nations, and from that moment the position of the disqualified judge is considered vacant.

Judges of the International Court of Justice are elected by the U.N. General Assembly and Security Council from a list of nominations by the national groups in the Permanent Court of Arbitration. Three months prior to election, the U.N. Secretary-General sends a written request to the members of the Permanent Court of Arbitration or the national groups of those states which are not members of this court for nominations of persons qualified to undertake the duties of member of the Court. Each national group nominates up to four candidates, only two of whom may be fellow nationals. The national groups first consult the highest courts, law schools and other high institutions of law in their countries for suggestions. Next, on the basis of the nominations of these national groups, the Secretary-General makes an alphabetical list which he submits to the General Assembly and Security Council. These two principal organs of the United Nations proceed independently of each other in electing the judges. The electors must bear in mind not only the qualifications required of the judges but also the fact that in the Court as a whole, "the main forms of civilization and the principal legal systems of the world" should be represented. Those candidates are considered elected who have obtained an absolute majority of votes in both the General Assembly and the Security Council. If several nationals of the same state should happen to obtain an absolute majority both in the General Assembly and in the Security Council, the eldest is considered elected. If after the first session one or more vacancies are not filled, a second and third session will be held. If even after the third session there is still a vacancy, the General Assembly may ask a joint commission of six members to be set up (three to be nominated by the General Assembly and three by the Security Council) to nominate persons whom the General Assembly and Security Council would vote upon separately. When the joint commission achieves unanimous agreement in respect to the new nomination, this name is placed on the list of proposed candidates if it was not there before, and then elections are held in the General Assembly and the Security Council.

Judges are elected for nine years and are eligible for re-election. A judge who is due to be replaced must terminate the cases which he has begun. The Court elects its president and vice-president for three years, but they may be re-elected. The Court has its registrar and may appoint other officers as necessary. The seat of the Court is at The Hague, but it may hold sessions elsewhere whenever it considers this desirable.

As a rule the Court must sit in full. Nine judges constitute a quorum.

The Court may, from time to time, set up one or more chambers consisting of three or more judges to hear various categories of disputes. By way of example, labor disputes and cases concerning transit and communications were mentioned in the Statute. These chambers also decide disputes at the request of the parties concerned. Their judgment is considered to have been made by the Court. Every year a chamber may be formed of five judges to hear and pass judgment on cases by summary procedure, again at the request of the parties to the dispute. These special chambers, however, have not been used in the Court's practice. The Statute provided that judges who are nationals of either of the parties shall retain the right to participate in hearing the dispute before the International Court of Justice. However, if the Court appoints to the chamber a judge of the nationality of one of the parties, the other party may choose a person to sit as judge in the Court (national judge). Similarly, if the Court appoints to the chamber no judge of the nationality of either party, both parties may choose a person to sit as judge. These *ad hoc* judges participate in passing judgment on an equal footing with their colleagues. National judges are also appointed in advisory proceedings.

4. Competence — The International Court of Justice is authorized to settle disputes and to give advisory opinions.

Only states may be parties in cases before the International Court of Justice. There have been occasions when the Court heard cases which concerned the interests of private persons. However, in these actions the states of which they were nationals assumed the defence of their interests, and thus the private lawsuit became an international one.

The jurisdiction of the International Court of Justice depends on the voluntary consent of the litigants, under the general international law principle that no state can be sued without its consent. If, however, states agree to settle their disputes before the International Court of Justice, they must be parties to the Statute. Hence, only those states which are signatories of the Statute of the International Court of Justice may appear as parties to a dispute before this Court. This, of course, includes all the member countries of the United Nations. However, states which do not belong to the United Nations may also adhere to the Statute on the basis of the recommendation of the Security Council and decision of the General Assembly and in compliance with certain conditions. The conditions under which non-member countries may submit a dispute to the Court are laid down by the Security Council. The non-member state must adhere to the special provisions contained in treaties in force. However, these conditions must not be such that the parties are placed in a position of inequality before the Court. The Security Council has decided in principle that the International Court of Justice will be open to all non-member countries if they file a declaration accepting obligatory jurisdiction of the Court and undertake the obligations under Article 94 of the Charter to comply with the decision of the Court in every action to which they are a party. Thus today parties signatory to the Statute, such as Switzerland, San Marino, Liechstenstein, West Germany, etc., may submit disputes to the International Court of Justice.

The Court has jurisdiction over all lawsuits submitted to it. It is also competent for all cases expressly provided for in the U.N. Charter or in conventions and treaties in force, if the states in conflict decide to submit to its jurisdiction. They may do so if they conclude a *special agreement*. At the time when the Statute of the Permanent Court of International Justice was being drawn up, it was hoped to establish the compulsory jurisdiction of the Court for all disputes of a legal nature. However, this compulsory jurisdiction was not accepted then or later, when the Statute was revised after the Second World War. Instead of compulsory jurisdiction, Article 36 of the Statute gives states the option of accepting the jurisdiction of the International Court of Justice for all their legal disputes concerning: first, interpretation of a treaty; second, any question of international law; third, the existence of any fact which, if established, would constitute a violation of an international obligation; and fourth, the nature or extent of the reparation due for a breach of an international obligation. This is an *optional clause* of the Statute of the International Court of Justice, since it is up to the states whether or not they will accept it. When they do, it is binding for all the above-mentioned categories of disputes.

In addition to trying cases, the International Court of Justice gives *advisory opinions* on legal questions in accordance with international law. According to the Charter, the General Assembly and Security Council may seek advisory opinions on any legal question. However, other U.N. organs and specialized agencies may also request advisory opinions on legal matters which may arise in the course of their activities, subject to an authorization from the General Assembly.

The advisory opinions of the Court do not have the legal force of a judgment. This means that proceedings may be instituted later on the same matter, even before the International Court of Justice. Nevertheless, the advisory opinions of the Court carry considerable moral weight.

The Court settles disputes in accordance with the rules of international law but may also decide cases *ex aequo et bono* if the parties agree. However, so far there have been no judgments of this kind.

When deciding disputes, the Court observes (Article 38 of the Statute):

> 1. international conventions establishing rules recognized by the contesting states;
> 2. international custom, as evidence of a general practice accepted as law;
> 3. the general principles of law recognized by civilized nations;
> 4. within the framework of Article 59 (*sententia jus facit parte inters*) the Court may look to judicial decisions and the opinions of leading authorities on international law from various nations as a subsidiary means for determining rules of law.

5. Procedure — A dispute is brought before the Court either by the notification of a special agreement accepting its jurisdiction or by a written request to the registrar containing the names of the contestants and declaring the subject of the dispute. The registrar must forward this request to all parties concerned. He is also expected to inform members of the United Nations, by notifying the Secretary-General, and all other states having the right to appear before the Court (Article 40 of the Statute).

The Court, as necessary, may indicate all the interim measures which should be taken to safeguard the rights of each party. The proposed measures are immediately presented to the parties and the Security Council (Article 41 of the Statute).

The procedure before the International Court of Justice consists of two parts, written and oral (Article 43 of the Statute).

The written proceedings consist of pleadings to the Court, affidavits, sworn statements, depositions and, as necessary, counter depositions as well as all supporting documents and evidence. The depositions are submitted to the registrar of the Court, in the order and within the time limits laid down by the Court.

The oral proceedings consist of court hearings of witnesses, experts, agents, counsels and attorneys. It should be noted that the parties are represented by their agents, who may be assisted before the Court by counsels and solicitors. Agents, counsel and advocates of the parties before the Court all enjoy the privileges and immunities necessary for an independent performance of their duties (Article 42 of the Statute).

The official languages of the Court are French and English. However, the parties may agree to use only one of these two languages in the proceedings and judgment. If there is no agreement on the language to be used, each party may use the language it desires, but the judgment is pronounced in French and English, the authentic text to be determined by the Court. The Court may approve the use of some other language at the request of one of the parties. However, in this case it must make provision for translation into one of the official languages (Article 39 of the Statute).

The proceedings are presided over by the president. If he is prevented from presiding, the chair is taken by the vice-president or the senior judge present. The hearing as a rule is public. At the request of the parties, the Court may sit *in camera* (Articles 45 and 46 of the Statute).

The Court issues orders on the conduct of the case and specifies the form and time in which the parties must make their final summing-up speeches. It also undertakes all measures relating to presentation of evidence. The Court may also, prior to the hearing, call upon the agents to submit the necessary documents and to provide necessary explanations. The parties may refuse the Court's requests, in which case every refusal is entered into the records (Articles 48 and 49 of the Statute). The Court may appoint an individual, a body, an authority, commission or other institution to make investigations and give expert opinions (Article 50 of the Statute). After evidence and reports by witnesses have been received in the specified time limits, the Court may decline to accept any further oral or written evidence from either party. If the opposing party agrees to the additional proceedings, the Court will accept the evidence being proffered (Article 52 of the Statute).

If a party refuses to appear before the Court or fails to defend its case, the opposing party may demand decision in favor of its claim. However, in such an event the Court must review its terms of reference and determine whether the request of the opposing party is well founded in fact and in law (Article 53 of the Statute).

The hearing is closed after the arguments by the agents, counsel and advocates. It is declared closed by the president, and the judges then withdraw to deliberate. Deliberations are in private and remain secret (Article 54 of the Statute).

The Court passes its judgments by majority vote of the judges present. The presiding judge casts the deciding vote in the event of a tie (Article 55). The judgment must list the names of the judges who participated in passing the decision, as well as the reasons on which it was based (Article 56). If a judgment is not passed unanimously, the dissenting judges may file a separate opinion (Article 57).

Every member of the United Nations has undertaken the obligation (Article 94 of the U.N. Charter) to comply with the decision of the International Court of Justice in any case to which it is a party. If any party to a dispute fails to perform the obligations incumbent upon it under a judgment of the Court, the other party may have recourse to the Security Council, which may make recommendations or decide on measures to be taken to give effect to the judgment.

The judgment of the International Court of Justice is final and without appeal. If the intent and scope of the judgment are controversial, the Court shall give its interpretation upon the request of one of the parties (Article 60 of the Statute).

The Statute of the Court envisages the possibility of reopening a case only if the request is based on a highly relevant fact which was not known either to the Court or to the party seeking reopening, provided this ignorance was not due to negligence. The procedure to reopen a case is instituted by a judgment which specifically determines the existence of a new, decisive fact for the outcome of the decision, with the statement that grounds for the request have been deemed proper. The request to reopen a case must be made not later than six months after the new fact has come to light (Article 61 of the Statute). The Statute of the Court also provides for a statute of limitations under which no case may be reopened after the lapse of ten years from the date of a judgment (para. 5, Art. 61 of the Statute).

The International Court of Justice has not been resorted to as often as was hoped. Acceptance of the optional clause has been far from universal, and even those states which have accepted it have usually done so with numerous reservations. Despite the appeal by the General Assembly to member states to submit their legal disputes to the Court for settlement, the anticipated response has never materialized. Actually, the composition of the Court does not really provide a fair cross-section of legal systems in the world, and the rules of international law applied by the Court are still from that classical international law which evolved under the influence of capitalist countries in the 19th and 20th centuries. For this reason, the socialist countries and the newly-emerged states of Africa and Asia view this Court with scepticism and reserve.

Greater efforts to promote the codification and progressive development of international law will have the effect of strengthening the role of a reformed International Court of Justice, the principal judicial organ of the United Nations.

MAINTENANCE OF PEACE

I. Maintenance of Peace Under the U.N. Charter

The preservation of international peace and security is the primary purpose of the United Nations as stated in Article 1 of the Charter. To this end, the Charter provides for the taking of effective collective measures for the prevention and removal of threats to world peace, and it lists a number of ways in which international disputes and situations likely to lead to a breach of the peace might be adjusted or settled. Hence the Charter contains instruments not only for sanctions but also for the preventive removal of causes which might lead to an international conflict. The phrase, "to maintain international peace and security" used in the Charter has a definite meaning. The "peace" mentioned here is not a "formal" or "armed" peace, a peace fraught with new threats of war. It means that the peace sought by the United Nations is a peace with universal security in the world. That is why the Charter always couples these two concepts in the phrase "international peace and security." In pursuit of this goal, the members of the United Nations "shall refrain in their international relations from the threat or use of force against the territorial integrity or political independence of any state, or in any other manner inconsistent with the purposes of the United Nations" (para. 4, Art. 2 of the U.N. Charter). Chapter VI provides the mechanism for the peaceful settlement of disputes, or more precisely, it lays down a *preventive procedure,* while the following chapter gives the *enforcement measures, i.e.* those measures which would be used in the case of a threat to or breach of the peace, or aggression. Under the Covenant of the League of Nations, its members were obliged to try to settle every dispute by peaceful means. If the parties to a dispute had exhausted all peaceful means for settling their dispute without achieving a satisfactory settlement, they could resort to war. Hence war was not expressly outlawed by the Covenant and in fact was even deemed permissible under certain conditions. To be sure, acts prohibiting wars of aggression were soon passed: the 1924 Geneva Protocol; the 1927 Resolution of the Assembly of the League of Nations on the prohibition of wars of aggression; the General Act of 1928. Of particular importance was the Kellogg-Briand Pact or Pact of Paris of 27 August 1928, which outlawed war. However, in the words of Louis le Fur, it was generally acknowledged that this Pact was less comprehensive than the Covenant of the League of Nations, since the former had no sanctions whatsoever, while the Covenant at least had rudimentary sanctions. Notwithstanding the lack of machinery for enforcing the sanctions, the international law of that time prohibited wars of aggression.

Not only are wars of aggression prohibited under the United Nations Charter, but a procedure for maintaining international peace and security is laid down. States are no longer competent to decide who is an aggressor and who is the victim of aggression, since a system to determine the aggressive state and a mechanism to prevent breaches of peace and aggression have been set up. By the very fact that attempts at aggression cannot be ruled out, prohibition of the use of force is contingent upon the *individual and collective right of member countries to self-defense.* Every member country of the United Nations has the right to defend itself if it is the victim of armed aggression, but it must do so in accordance with the rules governing self-defense (Article 51 of the Charter and the General Assembly Resolution from the 5th session "On the Duties of States in the Case of an Outbreak of Hostilities").

II. Procedure for the Pacific Settlement of Disputes Under the Auspices of the United Nations

States are absolutely prohibited from resorting to force to defend or promote any of their interests, except in self-defense, but even then they must comply with existing regulations. The Charter makes it incumbent upon the parties to a dispute to seek a solution by negotiation, mediation, conciliation, arbitration or any other peaceful means of their choice (Article 33 of the Charter). This is an obligation undertaken by members of the United Nations. The Security Council is authorized to call upon the parties to a dispute to settle it in one of the above ways. If they fail in this, they are to bring it to the attention of the Security Council or the General Assembly. These two organs are competent to investigate any dispute and any situation liable to cause international friction or give rise to an international dispute. They are authorized to determine whether the continuance of such a dispute or situation is likely to endanger the maintenance of international peace and security. States which are not members of the United Nations may also bring their disputes to the attention of these organs, if they accept the obligation of a peaceful settlement as provided for under the Charter.

The Security Council may, at any stage of the dispute, recommend appropriate procedures or methods for settling the dispute. In doing so, it must take into consideration any procedure for settlement of the dispute that has already been taken by the parties. The Charter stipulates that the Security Council should refer parties to the International Court of Justice for settlement of their legal disputes (Article 36 of the Charter).

The framers of the Charter did not try to formulate a rigid set of procedures for the pacific settlement of disputes; instead, they listed a number of peaceful means for solving disputes which the parties should resort to, but they did not designate which means must be used in which cases, or even in what order they should be resorted to. This was done because almost every international dispute is different, and it would be extremely difficult to construct a detailed system which could apply to all cases. What is important is that a dispute is settled, not how it is settled.

If a peaceful settlement of a dispute is not achieved without the intervention of the United Nations, then the parties are obliged to submit it to the competent U.N. organs. The Charter does not specify which categories of disputes may be submitted to these organs. But, they certainly include disputes which, if not settled, could endanger international peace and security. However, the decision of one state to submit its dispute to an international forum of this kind and with these competences is proof enough that the dispute is of such a nature. Experience has shown that it may be left to the discretion of states to decide on the nature of a dispute which is to be submitted to the authorized U.N. organ.

III. Procedure for the Maintenance of Peace

Provisional and Enforcement Measures of the Security Council — Military Staff Committee — United Nations Armed Forces

1. Provisional and Enforcement Measures of the Security Council — Unlike the League of Nations, the United Nations finally decided, when drawing up its Charter in San Francisco in 1945, to create a system of collective measures in the event of aggression which would be effective at any given moment. The drafters did not just regulate the prevention of aggression; they went on to specify the measures to be taken in case of a threat to or breach of the peace, that is to say, measures to remove those situations which often give rise to acts of aggression.

The Security Council has the authority to determine whether there has been a threat to the peace, breach of the peace, or act of aggression. It is authorized to make recommendations or pass resolutions on what measures should be taken to maintain or restore international peace and security. This organ may first call upon the parties concerned to comply with any provisional measures that it may decide upon. Hence the Security Council may not immediately resort to direct enforcement measures, for in certain cases they might aggravate the situation, and it is the concern of the Security Council to prevent any worsening of already impaired relations. Hence these provisional measures must be without prejudice to the rights, claims, or position of the parties concerned. However, the Security Council must take their compliance with these measures into account in the case of further procedure. The next phase would be taking measures which would still be short of armed force in order to give effect to its decisions. The Charter enumerates these measures: "These may include complete or partial interruption of economic relations and of rail, sea, air, postal, telegraphic, radio and other means of communication, and the severance of diplomatic relations" (Article 41 of the Charter). However, if even these measures prove to be inadequate, the Security Council is authorized to "take such action by air, sea, or land forces as may be necessary to maintain or restore international peace and security. Such action may include demonstrations, blockade, and other operations by air, sea, or land forces of Members of the United Nations" (Article 42 of the Charter).

Members of the United Nations are bound (under Article 43) to make available to the Security Council, if it so requests, armed forces, assistance and other facilities necessary for the purpose of maintaining international peace and security. This obligation includes the right of passage through their territory. The numbers and types of forces, their degree of readiness, general location and the nature of the facilities and assistance to be provided are governed by agreements. These agreements are concluded between the Security Council and member countries, or between the Security Council and groups of members. They must be ratified by the signatory states in accordance with their constitutional regulations.

Under the Charter (Article 45), the Security Council's armed action must be prepared in advance, so that the United Nations can take urgent enforcement action. For this purpose, member countries must maintain national air force contingents which can be made immediately available for "combined international enforcement action." The plans for combined action and for the use of the armed force are made by the Security Council with the assistance of the Military Staff Committee.

2. Military Staff Committee — The Charter provides for the establishment of a Military Staff Committee "to advise and assist the Security Council on all questions relating to the Security Council's military requirements for the maintenance of international peace and security, the employment and command of forces placed at its disposal, the regulation of armaments, and possible disarmament." This Committee is responsible to the Security Council for the strategic direction of the armed forces of the United Nations. The Committee is composed of the chiefs of staff of the permanent members of the Security Council and their representatives and, under Article 47 of the Charter, is designed as an organ to advise and give assistance to the Security Council.

A decision by the Security Council to use international armed forces must receive the affirmative votes of the five great powers, permanent members of the Security Council. However, the great powers have yet to agree on the general principles for organizing the armed force which is to be made available to the Security Council by the U.N. member countries. Disagreement largely centers on the contribution of armed forces by the five permanent members of the Security Council. The U.S.S.R. is in favor of the principle of equal contributions, while the United States seeks a system of "comparable contributions." In other words, in the opinion of the U.S.S.R., the size of the armed forces made available to the Security Council should not be too large. The great powers should provide armed forces on the basis of the principle of equality, i.e. the armed forces — consisting of land, sea and air contingents — should be of the same strength and size. The principle of comparable contributions proposed by the United States calls for different military contributions by different states; for instance, one power would provide naval forces, another air-forces, a third land forces, and so on.

The right of veto may always be exercised when a threat to peace or breach of peace, *i.e.* aggression, has been ascertained. It may also be exercised on the question of the enforcement measures to be adopted in order to maintain international peace and security. It should also be noted that in these cases the rule *nemo judex in re sua* (no one may be a judge in his own cause) has not been envisaged. There is no suggestion in Article 27, para. 2 of the Charter that the parties concerned should abstain from voting on this matter. This is an indication of the trend towards a consistent application of the principle of unanimity of the five great powers in the Security Council. It has been seen that the application of this principle may be a stumbling block to the work of this organ. However, when the Security Council is paralyzed by the veto of one of its five permanent members, the General Assembly takes over its functions.

At its fifth regular session, the General Assembly created a new subsidiary organ — the Collective Measures Committee, whose task was largely to receive reports from states on preparations for collective armed action and to undertake other measures relating to this activity by the United Nations. In the opinion of some, the Collective Measures Committee replaced the Military Staff Committee. However, the terms of reference of the Collective Measures Committee are of far lesser scope and importance than those of the Military Staff Committee as laid down in the Charter. In practice, the United Nations has taken another course by forming the U.N. armed forces as the need arises.

3. United Nations Armed Forces — The Secretary-General of the United Nations established U.N. armed forces in Kashmir to maintain peace and order until the territorial dispute between India and Pakistan had been settled. These were actually more a peace-keeping than military force. In the Korean War, one party to the conflict was proclaimed victim of aggression by the Security Council (owing to the absence of the Soviet representative) and acquired the stationing of U.N. forces. Command of these forces was entrusted to the United States. In this conflict, according to Bartos, "the idea of collective action stems from the identity of war aims rather than from a special organization." The third instance differed from the first two. United Nations forces were formed after the abortive aggression against Egypt by Britain, France, and Israel. Hence, collective measures were applied after a completed act of aggression, on the basis of *ad hoc* agreements between the governments making their military contingents available to the United Nations and the Secretary-General. In this case the armed forces had a military rather than police capacity, since they kept the armies of the conflicting sides apart rather than maintaining order. The General Assembly resolution of 5 November 1956 set up a United Nations Emergency Force entrusted with the task of bringing about and controlling the cessation of hostilities. The U.N. Secretary-General adopted rules of procedure for these forces, according to which the United Nations Emergency Force is an auxiliary organ of the United Nations and as such derives its international character. The tasks of the United Nations Emergency Force are exclusively of an international character, and the members of this force must execute them and adjust their behavior strictly in accordance with the interests of the United Nations. Therefore, national contingents made available to the Secretary-General, on the basis of agreements between him and the respective governments, take on the capacity of an international army, the army of the United Nations.

The above examples show that the section of the Charter concerning the military forces of the United Nations and the Military Staff Committee could not be applied in practice. The intent of the framers of the Charter has not been followed in the manner stated in Chapter VII of the Charter. However, even though the machinery did not prove to be appropriate, it does not mean that the idea was a bad one. In the above cases the idea of an armed force was applied differently in different situations. There is still a need for the United Nations to have its armed forces, but on the basis of machinery which could be used in a number of possible variants. Perhaps it would have been impossible to create such machinery in the past. The Military Staff Committee has proved ineffective, and the General Assembly has formed the United Nations Emergency Force as concrete situations and cases have arisen (the Middle East, the Congo, Cyprus).

Chapter Four: International Conflicts

I. Coercive Means of Settlement of International Disputes

Retorsion — Reprisals — War

Retorsion, reprisals and war are coercive means used by states to settle their disputes.

1. Retorsion — Retorsion, or retaliation, by a state is a means of remedying a legal injury by another state in a way which does not violate the rules of international law. For instance, a state may impose higher customs tariffs or levy taxes on nationals of the offending state, and so forth. Although retaliation need not result in open hostilities, it may strain relations between the states.

2. Reprisals — Reprisals are a remedy involving force which a state resorts to in order to protect its interests or achieve an objective by injuring another state in a manner which violates the other state's rights. For instance, an innocent alien may be arrested in reprisal against his state. The United Nations Charter does not permit states to carry out reprisals either to protect an interest or to achieve an objective.

Prior to 1945, reprisals were an accepted institution in international law. They were defended as being "an injustice in the service of justice" or a "deplorable necessity." Reprisals were formally prohibited only in cases when restitution had already been made or damages had been compensated for. However, reprisals in peacetime have very often turned into measures involving the use of armed force, thereby posing a threat to peace and initiating hostilities.

Reprisals do not imply any right, nor do they result from the exercise of a right. A state which resorts to a reprisal is acting as a judge in its own cause,

and such a situation is legally untenable. As a rule, reprisals have been resorted to by great powers in order to compel smaller countries to make a concession or agree to a treaty which would run counter to their interests.

In the United Nations system of collective security, as established in the
Charter, reprisals are also prohibited as a form of self-help. There is a long list
of legally permissible means for redressing injuries in international relations,
from the mobilization of the public opinion of the injured state in order to influence the public opinion of the other state, to the publication of documents intended to influence the government and public opinion of third states, to the
good offices and mediation of third states, all the way to intervention by neutral states and by international organizations, especially the competent organs
of the United Nations.

In contemporary theory of international law, there are views that reprisals
are justified if they are taken to protect the interests of a state, provided they
cease as soon as their purpose has been achieved. By the same token, in time of
war reprisals are considered to be permissible if they do not violate the laws of
humaneness. However, the experience of past wars has unequivocally shown
that reprisals have specifically been intended for inhumane ends. In our opinion, reprisals should be abolished outright rather than allowed a limited application. Perhaps a restricted use of reprisals might be possible in isolated acts of
belligerence. However, why should reprisals be permitted when there are so
many other avenues open for the peaceful settlement of disputes? Indeed, the
use of reprisals in isolated acts of belligerence could be described as a breach of
the world peace. If an armed conflict has already commenced, in present-day
conditions of warfare it would be irrelevant to draw a distinction between permissible reprisals and acts of war. Hence we feel that reprisals must not be admitted as an institution in international law or as a form of self-help as long as
there is a competent international body for providing redress against unlawful
measures taken by the parties to a conflict. Unfortunately, however, reprisals
are still an institution in the law of war.

The United Nations Charter prohibits reprisals as an institution in international law, while various international conventions contain provisions *expressly* prohibiting:

> — reprisals against the wounded, sick, personnel, buildings or material
> protected by the First Geneva Convention;
> — reprisals against the wounded, sick, ship-wrecked, naval crews or mate-
> rials protected by the Second Geneva Convention;
> — reprisals against prisoners of war, pursuant to the Third Geneva Con-
> vention;
> — reprisals against persons and their property which are protected by the
> Fourth Geneva Convention;
> — reprisals against institutions devoted to science, art, education or hu-

manitarian or religious purposes, on the basis of the 1954 Hague Convention on the protection of property of cultural value.

3. War — War may be described as the defense of the interests of one or more states or the pursuance of objectives by means of armed forces. This is a *de facto* situation in the relations between states in which means of force are used. For a state of war to exist, at least one side must have an intention of making war. This intent may be manifested in the form of a declaration of war, an ultimatum — which becomes a declaration of war if its demands are not complied with — or the direct or indirect commencement of hostilities. Anything belonging to a country may be the object of hostilities (physical and juristic persons, property, transport and communications, etc.).

Prior to the First World War, every sovereign state was considered to have a legitimate right to wage war. This right was most often described as deriving from the right to self-preservation. We have seen that the Covenant of the League of Nations provided for a special procedure for the peaceful settlement of disputes between member countries, but it did not contain any provisions outlawing war.

Contemporary international law, as codified in the United Nations Charter, prohibits war. Any use of force, or a threat to use force, are prohibited. The Charter calls upon United Nations member states to "refrain in their international relations from the threat or use of force against the territorial integrity or political independence of any state, or in any other manner inconsistent with the purposes of the United Nations." The Security Council is competent to determine the existence of any breach of peace or threat to peace. However, Article 51 recognizes the right to "individual or collective self-defence if an armed attack occurs against a Member of the United Nations, until the Security Council has taken measures necessary to maintain international peace and security."

Although the Charter outlaws war, one or more states may violate this prohibition and initiate warfare. In this event the attacked state has the right to offer resistance in accordance with the procedure provided under the Charter and with the legal machinery adopted by the members of the United Nations. States are allowed to maintain their own armed forces on the basis of this individual right and for the purpose of taking part in collective action by the United Nations, in other words, for the fulfilment of their international obligations. Accordingly, *even if war has been prohibited by the Charter, the law of war has not become superfluous.* Although some commentators deny the need for the law of war today, and others feel that it has grown into a system of policing measures by the central international organization, armed conflicts since the Second World War — as, for instance, the Korean War — have proven the need for rules of war in our times as well. What is more, the belligerent sides in the Korean War in fact did accuse one another of violating the laws and customs of war.

II. Sources of the Law of War

Concept of the Law of War — Principal International Treaties as Sources of the Law of War — General Participation Clause and Martens Clause — Rules of Naval Warfare — Rules of Air Warfare — Liability for Violation of the Rules of War — Revision of the Rules of International Law of War

1. The Concept of the Law of War — The law of war, as part of international public law, is a body of contractual and customary rules of law which regulate the the relations between persons in international public law in time of war. The law of war thus assumes the possibility of restricting the use of the instruments of war and the manner of conducting warfare. The laws of war seek to impose as many civilized restraints as possible on this pathological state of relations between nations. Legal experts are aware that the outlawing of war will not automatically remove it as a sociological phenomenon in the life of the international community. However, they quite rightly feel that war can and must be subject to limitations, both in regard to the conduct of hostilities and in regard to the persons who by circumstance find themselves involved.

The law of war, then, is concerned not with denying the fact of war — which may be deplored, but whose existence cannot be refuted — but rather with challenging an unlimited right to select the means for inflicting injuries on the enemy (see Article 22 of the Hague Regulations on land warfare).

2. Principal International Treaties as Sources of the Law of War — The rules of war are contained in multipartite treaties and customary international law. The following multipartite treaties still in force serve as sources of the law of war:

1. The Declaration of Paris, respecting warfare on sea, 16 April 1856;
2. The St. Petersburg Declaration of 11 December (29 November) 1868, on the use of explosive bullets;
3. The Second Hague Declaration of 29 July 1899, prohibiting the use of projectiles designed for the "diffusion of asphyxiating or deleterious gases;"

4. The Third Hague Declaration of 29 July 1899, prohibiting the use of expanding (dum-dum) bullets;

5. The Hague Conventions and Declarations of 18 October 1907: (III) on the commencement of hostilities; (IV) respecting the laws and customs of war on land (these are the rules contained in the annex to the convention known as the Hague Regulations on land warfare); (V) respecting the rights and duties of neutral powers and persons in war on land; (VI) relative to the status of enemy merchant ships at the outbreak of hostilities; (VII) relative to the conversion of merchant ships into warships; (VIII) relative to the laying of automatic contact mines; (IX) respecting bombardment by naval forces in time of war; (XI) relative to certain restrictions with regard to the exercise of the right of capture in naval war; (XIII) concerning the rights and duties of neutral powers in naval war; and the Declaration prohibiting the discharge of projectiles and explosives from the air;

6. The Geneva Protocol of 17 June 1925, prohibiting the use of asphyxiating, poisonous or other gases, and prohibiting the use of bacteriological weapons in war;

7. The London Protocol of 6 November 1936, on the rules for the conduct of submarine warfare;

8. The Moscow Declaration of 1943, on the punishment of war criminals;

9. The London Agreement for the Prosecution and Punishment of the Major War Criminals of the European Axis, concluded in 1945, and the Charter of the International Military Tribunal;

10. The 1948 Convention on the Prevention and Punishment of the Crime of Genocide;

11. The Geneva Conventions on the protection of war victims of 12 August 1949: Convention for the Amelioration of the Condition of the Wounded and Sick in Armies in the Field; Convention for the Amelioration of the Condition of the Wounded, Sick and Shipwrecked of Members of Armed Forces at Sea; Convention Relative to the Treatment of Prisoners of War; Convention on the Protection of Civilian Persons in Time of War.

12. The Hague Convention on the protection of works of art and cultural monuments in the case of armed conflict, adopted on 14 May 1954.

Recent practice, dating to the late 1960s, in the application of humanitarian laws to contemporary armed conflicts has shown that the 1949 Geneva Conventions are no longer in keeping with the new development of international relations. After several years of consultations in the Red Cross (the League of Red Cross Societies and the International Committee of the Red Cross) and the United Nations circles, Switzerland (as the depositary of the Geneva Convention,) convened in 1974 in Geneva. The Diplomatic Conference on Humanitarian Law Applicable in Armed Conflicts. The conference, which was attended by the representatives of about 120 states, held four sessions (between 1974 and 1977), and, on 10 June 1977, adopted by consensus two protocols: the Additional Protocol to the Geneva Convention of 12 August 1949 on the Protection of the Victims of International Armed Conflicts (Protocol I, having 102 articles), and the Additional Protocol to the Geneva Convention of 12 August 1949 on the Protection of the Victims of Non-International Armed Conflicts (Protocol

II, having 28 articles). These protocols will come into force after being ratified by at least two signatories.

The two protocols, as suggested by their appellation, are not autonomous international treaties, but are to be applied in conjunction with the Geneva Conventions and may be acceded to only by those states that have previously become parties to the mentioned conventions.

Although Protocol I does not basically alter the provisions of the Geneva Conventions, it nevertheless does contain certain important changes in the approach to some essential problems of international law as applied to armed conflicts. To begin with, in accordance with Article 1, it has enlarged the concept of the international armed conflict. In addition to wars between states to which, in pursuance of the common Article 2 of the 1949 conventions, war and humanitarian law has been applied until now, henceforward these rules will also apply to anti-colonial and other armed conflicts which nations are waging to realize their right to self-determination guaranteed to them under the U.N. Charter. Prior to that, the colonial powers held that such conflicts were to be regarded as "internal" and refused to apply to them either the Hague or the Geneva Conventions. Furthermore, this protocol brought up to date and virtually revised many rules of the 1899 and 1907 Hague Conventions, which have been in force for more than seventy years. Although the principle of the formal equality of the belligerents relative to the application of the law has been left unchanged, the new rules (Chapter III of Protocol I) *de facto* puts the aggressor and occupier into a much more difficult position, while facilitating the defense of a victim of aggression. It is important to note that the provisions of Protocol I open up a number of new possibilities for the civilian population to join in the defense of their country while enjoying international protection, which is especially in the interest of states which, like Yugoslavia, have adopted a system of total national defense, or of national resistance to any aggressor.

Protocol II contains a number of obligations for the contracting parties to apply the basic rules of the Geneva Conventions in civil wars. Heretofore, in the practice of civil warfare, in pursuance of the common Article 3 of the 1949 Conventions, the authorities had the duty to apply only the general principles of humanitarian law, which had proved to be altogether inadequate.

3. The General Participation Clause and the Martens Clause

— The Hague Conventions contain two notable clauses. The general participation clause (*si omnes* clause) is found in Article 2 of the Convention Respecting the Laws and Customs of War on Land, in Article 6 of the Convention Relative to the Status of Enemy Merchant Ships, and in Conventions VII, IX, X and XI. According to this clause, the provisions of these conventions will be applicable only to the contracting powers and only if all the belligerents are signatories to the conventions. However, the Geneva Conventions of 1949 (under Article 2) must be observed, even if one of the parties to the conflict is not a signatory to them. Today the rules of the Hague Conventions are still in the vast majority of cases generally accepted rules of law and are enforced as such, regardless of whether the parties to a conflict are bound by them.

If there are no regulations in the codified law of war, the rules of customary international law are valid. This is the gist of the so-called Martens clause, contained in the Preamble to the Fourth Hague Convention Respecting the Laws and Customs of War on Land, which was adopted on 18 October 1907. It states that until such time as a more complete compendium of the laws of war is promulgated, the high contracting parties consider it useful to state that in cases which are not provided for by the regulations adopted by them, the population and participants in a war shall remain under the protection of the principles of international law as they derive from customs established among civilized nations, from the laws of humanity and the dictates of public conscience.

4. Rules of Naval Warfare — In addition to adopting the aforementioned conventions (from VI to XIII), the Second Hague Conference passed a resolution stating that in the absence of regulations of the international law of war, the principles contained in the Hague Regulations on Land Warfare should be applied wherever possible. Naval warfare was regulated to some extent in the 1909 Declaration of London, but this document was not ratified and never came into force. However, a considerable portion of the Declaration was adopted by many countries in their internal regulations, so that many of its provisions have become rules of customary international maritime law.

5. Rules of Air Warfare — There are no special rules regulating air warfare. But this fact certainly does not mean that warfare conducted in the air and actions mounted from the air are exempt from the rules of the international law of war. Air combat and air attacks are means of war, and their use is subject to the principles of international treaty and customary laws of war, on land and at sea. Of course it would be desirable if specific forms of air warfare were regulated by international law.

6. Liability for Violation of the Rules of War — Failure to observe and violation of the laws and customs of war carry international criminal liability, which is increasingly becoming punishable under the internal criminal laws of states.

All the Geneva Conventions of 1949 contain an identical article (52/I, 53/II, 132/III and 149/IV), according to which a party to a conflict may demand an inquiry into any alleged violation of the Geneva Conventions. The interested parties determine the manner in which this inquiry is to be instituted by agreement. If, however, they do not reach an agreement, they elect an arbiter who decides on the procedure to be followed. The Geneva Conventions state that if a violation is established to have occurred, the belligerent "shall put an end to it and shall repress it with the least possible delay." The parties to a conflict are authorized to punish the members of enemy armed forces and other persons responsible for violating the rules of the international law of war. For this purpose, protests may be delivered to the belligerents (to a commander of a unit, to the supreme command, or government) or negotiations may be initiated with the enemy, either directly or through the offices of a protecting power or some other neutral power.

7. Revision of the Rules of International Law of War — Over thirty years have passed since the end of the Second World War. In that time span there have been unprecedented advances in technology, particularly the technology of warfare, which have necessitated new thinking about the conduct of a modern war. Similarly, it cannot be denied that considerable progress has been made in organizing the present day international community. These two important developments must be kept in mind whenever a revision is undertaken of any part of international law, and particularly — in this instance — of the international law of war. However, very little has been done in this domain since the Second Hague Conference of 1907. The eminent jurist Kunz was right in saying that the absence of rules of war has taken its revenge on mankind. Between the two world wars, he called the attention of legal experts to the need for the adoption of new rules of the international law of war. The new Geneva Conventions adopted in 1949, although of great importance in the codification of the law of war, are still far from filling the gap. We might add that time, or military technology, and the concept of modern-day warfare have largely made even the 1949 Geneva Conventions obsolete. Hence the demand for a revision of the rules of warfare is justified both by the present level of war technology and by the corresponding changes in prevailing ideas about so-called total war.

Some well-known international organizations are working on revising the rules of war, such as UNESCO, the International Committee of the Red Cross, the International Committee for Military Medicine and Pharmacy, as well as professional and academic organizations, such as the International Law Association and the Institute of International Law. Renowned world jurists are also studying the problems of redrafting the rules of war, including François, Castrin, Kunz, Lauterpacht, and Stone, and such Yugoslav experts in international law as Andrassy, Bartoš, Radojković, and Tomšič.

Prior to any consideration of revising the laws of war, we must first answer the question of whether such a revision is an imperative need in present-day international affairs and international law. It may well be asked, why codify laws of war when war has been outlawed by the United Nations Charter?

Would such a project not suggest a lack of confidence in the political and legal machinery of the United Nations? Other arguments, which lead to the same conclusion, claim that codification is pointless because existing rules of war have proven to be ineffective in any case.

The prevailing view today is that the rules of the international law of war must be revised and codified, of course insofar as this is possible, *i.e.,* insofar as states will accept a comprehensive codification of this topic of international law. The first objection to codification on the grounds that war has already been outlawed may appear logical at first sight, but it cannot stand up to a realistic appraisal of international relations and the role of international law in regulating them. It is true that war has been outlawed by the United Nations Charter, but this same United Nations, as has been pointed out in the preceding section, may be involved in a military conflict with an aggressor state, and experience since the Second World War has shown that the rules of war are both useful and necessary. They are particularly indispensable in cases of so-called civil wars, particularly colonial wars. One view, related to this argument, is that there are legal and illegal parties to a conflict. This standpoint is held today by Scelle and Lauterpacht. Kunz is of the opinion that no discrimination should be made during a war and that non-discrimination in wartime should be the guiding principle in a revision of the modern-day rules of war. What this specifically means is that the U.N. forces taking part in a military action should not be treated on the basis of special rules.

Kunz is correct to state that the rules of war should be universal for all wars, be they "small" or "large," "peripheral," "central," or "total," and that these rules should be binding on all parties to the conflict, without distinction. Indeed, the purpose of rules of war is to strike a balance between military interests and humanitarian considerations. However, in our opinion, universally applicable rules of war would not preclude the distinction between legal and illegal parties to a conflict. It is this distinction that justifies the collective military action by the United Nations. War is outlawed, and if hostilities are conducted by anyone, they must be suppressed by force, provided, of course, that all other means have been exhausted, and the application of force must not contravene the rules of modern international law of war. If these rules are violated by the illegal party to the conflict during military operations, one more crime will be added to the series of international criminal acts already begun. If these rules are violated by the U.N. forces, the guilty parties will also be punished on the strength of these same rules of international law of war. In the instructions which the U.N. General Assembly approved for its armed forces in Egypt and Palestine, the commanders were enjoined to adhere to the principles and rules of the international law of war. Hence we feel that there is no contradiction between the existence of a general prohibition of warfare today, as contained in the Charter, and a revision and further codification of the rules of war, and for this reason the argument that the rules of war are superfluous is unacceptable.

The second argument to the effect that the laws and customs of war have been violated and therefore any further work on their codification would be irrelevant is quite an old one and has been shown to be unfounded. The lack of sufficient rules governing warfare has had grave consequences, and a complete absence of any restraints whatsoever would have tragic results for mankind. This is a fact which can hardly be denied today, in view of experiences of the past, which are very well known — for instance in regard to prisoners of war, the wounded and sick — and despite undoubtedly blatant abuses.

III. Commencement of Hostilities

The laws of war prohibit commencement of hostilities without a prior declaration of war. According to Article 1 of the 1907 Hague Convention III, the Contracting Powers recognize that hostilities between them must not commence without a previous and unequivocal warning, which should take the form either of a declaration of war, or of an ultimatum with a conditional declaration of war.

The declaration of war is a unilateral legal act which unambiguously informs the opposing side of the existence of a state of war. There are no rules governing the manner of declaring war. However, the declaration must be unambiguous; it must contain reasons and must be received by a competent organ — a diplomatic representative or minister of foreign affairs. The declaration of war is important in international law, because it is a legal act on the basis of which a state of war is established, which calls for special behavior by the belligerents and neutral powers in terms of the rules and customs of international law of war.

The declaration of war may be unconditional, or it may contain certain conditions. The latter is called an ultimatum.

Although the declaration of war is provided for in the above-mentioned Hague Convention, it is an ancient institution of the customary law of war. However, in the history of warfare very many wars have been initiated without such a declaration. In this case, a state of war is considered to exist from the moment when hostilities were begun, or when measures characterizing such a state were undertaken. It is enough for just one side to express the intention of waging war for a state of war to be considered to exist.

A state of war must be reported to other states without delay. It will not have a legal effect on neutral countries until they receive notification. Notification may be made by telegraph, according to Article 2 of the Third Hague Convention of 1907. However, this same article adds that the neutral powers cannot claim not to have been notified, if it is clearly ascertained that they were actually aware of the existence of a state of war. Under Article 51 of the U.N. Charter, every member state has the right to self-defense in the event of an armed attack against it, but it must inform the Security Council of the measures it has undertaken.

The word belligerency primarily calls to mind military action. However, in a broader sense belligerency may cover the severing of all kinds of relations, measures taken against physical and artificial persons, nationals of the enemy state, and so forth.

On 17 November 1950, the U.N. General Assembly adopted a resolution concerning the duties of states in the event of an outbreak of hostilities. This resolution provides the legal machinery for determining aggressor states. It also provides possibilities for the belligerents to forestall a war, despite the fact that hostilities had broken out. Therefore, *the declaration of war is relevant today if an attack is carried out against a state, or if a state is in a situation when it must take part in collective defense in the manner provided for under the U.N. Charter.*

War has a direct effect on international persons. In one way or another, it affects the entire system of international relations. Intercourse among nations is particularly affected, and neutral countries feel the effects of war no less than the warring states. First, diplomatic relations between the parties to the conflict are severed. The diplomatic representatives must then be allowed to return to their country or to go wherever they choose. They have the right to burn their files or to take their sealed documents with them. It is their right to place their building under the custody of a neutral diplomatic representation. Consular activities are ended in the same manner.

The effect of the outbreak of war is particularly notable in regard to international treaties, as has already been discussed. The belligerents may also conclude treaties in the course of a war. The subject matter of such treaties refers to the conduct of the war (cartels). These are treaties relating to the exchange of prisoners, treatment of internees, the creation of neutral zones (see Article 15 of the Geneva Convention on the Protection of Civilian Persons in Time of War), and so forth. Military commanders are authorized to negotiate and conclude these treaties. From the standpoint of international law, they need no special authorization to perform these functions, and the treaties enter into force immediately, or at a specified time, and no ratification is necessary. Of course, military commanders are authorized to conclude military treaties and agreements, but not political treaties, including political armistices. Regular organs for international relations are competent to carry out this second type of international treaty making.

IV. The Region of War

From the standpoint of the law of war, the *region of war* can be defined in a broad sense as the territory (land, sea and air) within which the belligerents may prepare and execute military operations. The *theatre of war,* in contradistinction to the region of war, is that part of the region on land, sea or in the air in which military operations are directly being conducted.

The region of war includes the territory of the belligerents, including inland waters and territorial seas, as well as the air space above their territories. These territories also include the lands under trusteeship of any of the belligerents, if they are used for military purposes, or if their population is recruited for service in the armed forces. The region of war also covers colonies, protectorates and condominiums. The belligerents may also conduct hostilities on the high seas and in countries which are not under the jurisdiction of either.

The parties to a conflict are prohibited from extending the region of war to territories under the sovereignty or jurisdiction of neutral states, to demilitarized zones or international neutralized zones, or to the inland waterways, territorial sea and air spaces of these territories. The parties to a conflict may also exclude parts of their territories from the region of war by agreement: for instance, for the purpose of creating hospital zones, safety localities and neutralized zones, pursuant to the 1949 Geneva Conventions. On the other hand, a neutral country may become a region of war in part or totally, if it was not willing or able to defend its neutrality, as was the case with Korea in 1904/1905, Denmark in 1940, or Egypt during the Second World War. States which permit bases to be established in their territories, regardless of the branch of the armed forces, may also become a region of war.

The territory in which hostilities are directly conducted is the theatre of war in the strict sense. This term describes that area between the front line and an internal line marking the rear. Of course these boundaries are constantly shifting with developments on the battlefield.

The definitions of the region of war in a broad sense and the theatre of war in a strict sense have largely become obsolete, even though they are still to be found in conventional textbooks. Such a distinction was justified when pitched battles were fought and military operations, as General Kolb put it, had the character of maneuvers. Today, in the age of total war, military operations are conducted simultaneously on the front and everywhere in the rear, so that the entire territory is a battlefield, or theatre of war. Ballistic missiles are also erasing any such distinction. It should be noted that partisan warfare and popular uprisings against occupying forces occasion a so-called territorial war, in which the distinction between the theatre of war proper and the region of war disappears. This was the case in Yugoslavia during the national liberation struggle (1941–1945).

V. Armed Forces

The armed forces of a country comprise regular and irregular armed forces. The regular forces include all land, naval, and air force units, as well as the citizens' army (the militia and volunteer corps), regardless of whether it is a special part of the army or is considered to be part of the regular troops. Each state determines which units are considered to be armed forces in its internal legislation. If, however, a citizens' army, including here resistance movements (*e.g.* partisans), is not considered part of the regular forces, it is considered to be an irregular force, and it is recognized to have the right of being a party to a conflict (a warring side, belligerent) if its combatants fulfil the following four conditions, in addition to the requirement that they belong to one of the parties to the conflict: first, that they are commanded by a person who is responsible for all his subordinates; second, that they have a fixed emblem which can be recognized at a distance; third, that they carry weapons openly; and fourth, that they comply with the laws and customs of war in their conduct of operations.

Under contemporary international law, the category of armed forces also includes the population of an unoccupied territory who, after an enemy invasion, voluntarily take up arms in resistance because there has been no time to organize a regular armed force, provided they carry weapons openly and observe the laws and customs of war. Actually, according to the Hague regulations, these rules refer to a national uprising, which is carried out either upon the command of the government or military authorities or spontaneously. In each of these cases it is considered to be a national uprising (levée en masse), whose legality cannot be contested if the aforementioned conditions are met. In this event the rebels have the rights and duties of members of regular forces. The members of regular forces must carry an identity card, which is issued by the competent organ of the armed forces.

VI. Parties to a Conflict

The term "party to a conflict" is more appropriate today than the terms "belligerent" or "warring side." It corresponds to the terminology which has been used since the Second World War in positive international law, and it corresponds to our view of the place that the laws of war hold in the system of public international law.

It is the rule that the term "parties to a conflict" denotes states which are in a state of war with each other. However, the central international organization, the United Nations, may acquire the status of a party to a conflict when, in conformity with the Charter, it resorts to collective armed measures to counter aggression. The member states of the United Nations which take part in the collective armed forces of the U.N. also have the status of parties to a conflict, each individually. This means that both the United Nations as a whole and each member country taking part in collective action must comply with the laws and customs of war. They bear direct responsibility for any breaches of these laws.

In civil wars the question arises of the recognition of the insurgents (rebel) as a party to a conflict. If an organized party (the *de facto* authority) wages an armed struggle against the state itself (the legal authority), it may be treated as a belligerent, provided this status is expressly recognized by the legal authority. In this case all the laws and customs of warfare will be in operation between the organized insurgent force and the armed forces of the state, as though an international armed conflict were being waged. If an insurrection is organized for the purpose of enforcing the right of peoples to self-determination, we feel that, on the basis of the U.N. Charter, the rebels should have the rights of a party to a conflict, as this principle has taken on legal force by virtue of its inclusion in the Charter. It would logically follow that rebels of this kind, on the basis of international law, should be given the status of a party to a conflict, and recognition of such a status should not be left to the will of the state under whose jurisdiction a nation is struggling for independence. In any case, the rebels in a so-called armed conflict, even if they do not have the status of a party to a conflict, are not at the mercy of the state under whose jurisdiction they fall. The fundamental humanitarian rules must be observed in hostilities with rebels which do not have the character of an international conflict. These principles have been laid down in Article 3, which appears in all four Geneva conventions of 1949. On the basis of this article, persons who have laid down their arms, who are not taking a direct part in hostilities, or who have been incapacitated by sickness, wounds, detention or any other reasons, "shall in all circumstances be treated humanely, without any adverse distinction founded on race, colour, religion or faith, sex, birth or wealth, or any other similar criteria." It is expressly prohibited for such persons to be murdered, mutilated, subjected to cruel treatment and torture, taken as hostage or subjected to outrages against their personal dignity. There is also a prohibition on the passing of sentences and carrying out of executions without trial by a regular court, or without necessary judicial guarantees at the trial of a condemned person. The wounded and sick of the rebel forces must be well treated and cared for.

VII. Recognition of the National Liberation Army of the Peoples of Yugoslavia as a Belligerent

In the course of the Second World War, Germany did not recognize the members of the National Liberation Army and Partisan Detachments of Yugoslavia as belligerents until a large number of the fascist troops had been taken prisoner. (Here we shall use the term "belligerent" or "warring side," because they were in common use in the terminology of positive international law until the end of the Second World War.)

From the very outset of the hostilities, Yugoslav partisans qualified as belligerents by fulfilling all the conditions laid down by Articles 1 and 42, para. 2, of the 1907 Hague regulations. First, they were led by a supreme commander; second, all the Yugoslav combatants wore the emblem of a five-pointed star on their caps; third, they openly carried weapons; and fourth, they observed the laws and customs of war, in compliance with the order handed down by the Supreme Commander on 8 November, 1941, demanding observance of the rules of warfare upon the pain of death. These are facts which testify to the indisputable legality of the national liberation struggle of the peoples of Yugoslavia from the standpoint of international law. It should also be pointed out that in the very beginning the Supreme Headquarters proclaimed the national liberation struggle of the peoples of Yugoslavia to be an integral part of the struggle of the Anti-Fascist Coalition, which the enemy had to recognize as a belligerent. According to Bartoš, the legal consequences of this fact had to be recognized. The exclusion of one nation from the Anti-Fascist Coalition, from the organized struggle of the United Nations, was certainly an artificial construction which was clearly intended to justify the crimes committed against the Yugoslav people.

In this connection the surrender of the Yugoslav Army in 1941 is persistently cited, particularly in the memoirs of German generals, as a legal argument for proving the "illegality" of Yugoslav fighting during the Second World War. This argument is untenable from the standpoint of the positive international law of that time. We would not even mention this attitude of German generals (*e.g.* Goerlitz), if their memoirs had appeared only in their own country. But they are being translated into other world languages and are being quoted in the professional literature of international law, particularly by authors who indiscriminately cite the views of "experienced generals."

Capitulation is an act of treason from the standpoint of the law of a country. Many military criminal codes impose a death sentence on those who surrender, regardless of the circumstances in which the surrender was made. However, from the standpoint of international law, a capitulation is a convention concluded between the competent military representatives, stipulating the terms for surrender of a fortress, a military unit or some defended place, or part of the territory which was under the jurisdiction of the military commander in question. Although capitulation has a legal effect under international law, the convention of capitulation does not give the enemy side sovereignty over any part of the territory. What did the Supreme Command of the former Yugoslav Army do when it authorized its representatives in Belgrade to sign an act of surrender for the entire Yugoslav Army on 17 April, 1941, *ie.,* to conclude an armistice, thereby surrendering the country into the hands of the enemy? It performed an act which has absolutely no validity from the standpoint of international law. Why is this so?

In the first place, the Supreme Command allowed itself to be taken prisoner and then delegated representatives to sign an act of surrender. However, according to international law, specifically the 1929 Geneva Conventions, which were signed and ratified in 1931 by Yugoslavia, a prisoner cannot even commit himself, because he has certain rights and certain duties, much less commit an entire army or, in the last analysis, sacrifice an entire nation.

In the second place, the representatives of the Supreme Command signed a document which they were not competent to sign on any grounds; the act of surrender which they signed was the armistice, a political act, for which, under international law, the political organs of a state are competent, but not, under any circumstances, the military commanders. Hence the surrender of the Yugoslav Army was, from the standpoint of positive international law, a legally invalid act.

However, regardless of the legal validity of the surrender of the Yugoslav Army, the people of Yugoslavia, soon joined the insurrection against the occupying forces all over the country. Such a development of events was condoned by the provisions of international law in force at that time. Article 42, paragraph 2, of the 1907 Hague Regulations states that an occupation applies only to the territory where authority is established and is in a position to assert itself. The enemy in Yugoslavia, despite his enormous military superiority, was not able to maintain his occupation during the Second World War, because the force of the organized resistance of the Yugoslav people was so great that liberated territories sprang up throughout the war, and popular government replaced the occupational authorities in them.

VIII. The Protecting Power

The interests of one side in a conflict in the territory of the other side are as a rule safeguarded by a neutral state. Such a state is called a protecting power by the Geneva Conventions. If the state in contention is not able to entrust a neutral state with the prerogatives of a protecting power, it may choose an international organization which provides all the guarantees of impartiality for the successful execution of these tasks. However, the provisions of the Geneva Conventions regulating the functions of protecting powers do not constitute an obstacle to the humanitarian activities of the International Committee of the Red Cross and other humanitarian organizations, subject, of course, to the consent of the parties to the conflict. In addition to the humanitarian functions prescribed by the Geneva Conventions, a protecting power in time of war may also safeguard other interests of the state in question, as well as the interests of its citizens (*e.g.* custody of the buildings and housing of the diplomatic representatives, consulates, judicial protection, inheritance, and so forth).

The protecting power carries out its functions through the agency of diplomatic and consular personnel, and it may also appoint delegates from among its nationals or the nationals of some other neutral countries. However, the delegates are subject to approval by the powers for which they are to carry out their functions. Representatives and delegates only have those powers provided for under the Geneva Conventions. In the course of their duties they are also obliged to give due consideration to the imperative needs of security of the state in which they are performing their functions. The protecting power is also authorized to provide its good offices to help resolve misunderstandings or disputes between the parties to the conflict, relating to protected persons under the Geneva Conventions or the application or interpretation of any of the provisions of these conventions.

Representatives and delegates of the protecting power enjoy full liberty in regard to selecting the places they wish to visit, and their visits may not be restricted either in number or duration, except in the case of exceptional military necessity, and even then only temporarily.

IX. Restraints in Warfare

Introduction — Limitations in Regard to Persons — Limitations in Regard to Property — Limitations in Regard to the Means of Warfare — Limitations in Regard to the Mode of Warfare

1. Introduction — The objects of attack in a war are the armed opponent and installations of a military nature. In warfare, the parties to a conflict, under Article 22 of the 1907 Hague regulations concerning the laws and customs of war, "have not an unlimited right as to the means they adopt for injuring the enemy." This article of the Hague regulations is interpreted very broadly. If the rules of positive international law (the Martens clause) do not explicitly prohibit the use of a means of warfare, this does not mean that it is therefore permissible. Every means contrary to the principles of the laws of war is prohibited, because the establishment of legal norms has not been able to keep up with the rapid advancement of military technology.

Limitations under international law apply above all to persons and property, and next to the instruments and modes of warfare.

2. Limitations in Regard to Persons — In time of war, all those persons who have the status of members of the armed forces in the conflict have the right to conduct hostilities. Unfortunately, they have the right to wound and kill one another. However, if a member of the enemy armed forces stops fighting, for any reason whatsoever — because he has been incapacitated by wounds, because of an unconditional surrender, or because he has no means of defense — his life must be spared, and he must be given the necessary care and assistance. The Hague regulations (Article 23) explicitly prohibit the killing or wounding of enemies in any of the aforementioned situations. This same article also expressly prohibits any proclamation to the effect that no one's life will be spared. A threat of this kind is usually made when the enemy is in difficulties. It is forbidden, and the conquered enemy who surrenders or who has been rendered incapable of fighting in any other way may be taken prisoner. He must be given the necessary assistance and care, and his life must not be taken. On the basis of this same regulation, the participants in a war are prohibited from forcing the citizens of the enemy state to take part in military operations against their own country, even if some of them may previously have been in their service.

According to the 1868 St. Petersburg Declaration, the sole legitimate objective of a state at war is to weaken the military forces of the enemy, so that the civilian population may not be the object of attack. Accordingly, the 1907 Hague regulations prohibit bombardment and attacks on undefended towns, villages, and buildings, and in the event of bombardment of military objectives the evacuation of the civilian population must be made possible. These provisions, of course, are valid only if the population does not take up arms against the enemy. Furthermore, Article 17 of the 1949 Geneva Convention provides for the conclusion of local agreements between the parties to the conflict for the evacuation of the population from besieged zones, especially the wounded, sick, the infirm, the elderly, children and pregnant women, as well as ministers of religion and medical personnel. Article 23 of this convention states that the contracting parties must permit a free passage for medicines and medical supplies.

3. Limitations in Regard to Property — All military installations may be objects of attack, including of course bombardment. These include military fortifications, munitions factories and war materiel, armories, transportation centers, and communications facilities which are used for military purposes. Undefended buildings, villages and towns are not to be attacked or bombed. Defended places are those in which organized resistance is made to the enemy, or at least this was the definition provided in the 1907 Hague regulations. However, today the concept of a "defended place" has been replaced by the concept of "military installations." The commander of an operative unit is obliged, in the event of bombardment, to notify the population or authorities — *e.g.* by means of leaflets, radio broadcasts, etc. — that the bombing of military objectives is to take place in a given locality, except in the event of an assault by storm. Article 26 of the Hague regulations states that the commander of the attacking forces must do everything in his power to notify the authorities before undertaking a bombardment, except in the case of a storm assault. Even today it is considered that a commander has this duty, if military considerations permit.

The 1949 Geneva Conventions also contain regulations prohibiting medical units and establishments, civilian hospitals, hospital ships, medical aircraft and transports of the wounded, sick and medical personnel and material from being the direct objects of attack. Similarly, under the 1949 Geneva Conventions, attacks are forbidden on hospital, neutralized zones, and safety zones. These zones are established under agreements concluded between the parties to the conflict. They are created for the purpose of providing shelter for those persons who must be removed from the area of military operations and must be given assistance and care. Specifically, medical zones are areas in which the wounded and sick are accommodated; safety zones provide shelter for both the wounded and sick and the infirm, elderly, children under 15, expectant mothers and mothers with children under seven; the neutralized zone provides safety for the wounded and sick, combatants and non-combatants and civilians who are not taking part in hostilities and whose activities are not of a military nature.

International law gives special protection to works of art. Article 27 of the Hague regulations and, more recently, the Hague Convention on the Protection of Cultural Property in the Event of an Armed Conflict, adopted on 14 May 1954, provide guarantees for the safekeeping of works of art and cultural monuments. Property of cultural value, as understood in the Convention, refers to moveable and immoveable property which represents the cultural legacy of a people. These include religious or secular architectural, artistic and historical monuments, archaeological sites, groups of structures which as a whole are of historical or artistic interest, works of art, manuscripts, books and other objects of artistic, historical or archaeological interest, as well as scientific collections and important collections of books, archives or reproductions of these objects. The buildings in which such property is kept, such as museums, libraries, etc., are also protected. Similarly, centers containing a significant number of the aforementioned works of art enjoy total protection.

In a certain sense, international law also provides protection for enemy property. The destruction or confiscation of enemy property is forbidden, except in the case of "military necessity" (Article 23 of the 1907 Hague regulations). Accordingly, the occupying power is not to destroy moveable or immoveable property in occupied territory unless such destruction is absolutely necessary for the performance of military operations (Article 52 of the 1949 Geneva Convention on the Protection of Civilian Persons in Time of War). However, the plundering of enemy property is prohibited under any circumstances, even when a locality has been taken by storm. Looting is a war crime, and its perpetrators will be punished under the international law of war.

A war trophy is the moveable enemy property seized on the battlefield. All objects which are used for military purposes may become booty. As a rule, these are weapons, ammunition and equipment. But they may also be other things, such as cash and securities, if they are found on the battlefield and serve military purposes. A war trophy is the property of the armed enemy forces and not that of individual combatants. The personal property of prisoners of war may not be seized as booty. Such property must remain in their possession and may not be taken away from them.

4. Limitations in Regard to the Means of Warfare — Article 22 of the 1907 Hague regulations states that parties to a conflict do not have an unlimited right to choose the means of inflicting injury on the enemy. The Preamble to the Hague Convention on the Laws and Customs of War on Land (1907) contains the Martens clause, which prohibits the use of any means of warfare which is contrary to the "usages established among civilized peoples," to the "laws of humanity," or the "dictates of public conscience." Hence, prohibitions in regard to the instruments and means of warfare are contained in treaties and in the customs of the international law of war.

International law implicitly prohibits the use of the following types of weapons:

> a. explosive projectiles under 400 grams, which burst into fragments or are filled with incendiary materials (the St. Petersburg Declaration of 1868). This prohibition extends to warfare on land and sea, but not to warfare in the

air. It is agreed that projectiles coated with phosphorus may be used in warfare against the enemy air force;

 b. expanding bullets and projectiles, the so-called dum-dum bullets (the Third Hague Declaration of 1899);

 c. poisons and poisonous weapons (Article 23a of the 1907 Hague Regulations);

 d. weapons, ammunition and war materials which needlessly increase human suffering (Article 23e of the 1907 Hague regulations);

 e. poisonous gases and bacteriological weapons (the Geneva Protocol of 17 June 1925);

 f. nuclear weapons. The use of nuclear weapons causes such terrible devastation that it cannot be justified by any "military necessity." The release of energy from the detonation of a nuclear device is accompanied by processes which are both poisonous and contagious, so that the use of such weapons would be prohibited even on the basis of existing rules of war, although there are justified demands being made today for an express prohibition of nuclear weapons in an international convention.

5. Limitations in Regard to the Mode of Warfare — It is an ancient and generally accepted usage that the parties to a conflict are prohibited from resorting to perfidy in the conduct of hostilities. The treacherous murder or wounding of persons belonging to the enemy nation or army are outlawed by Article 53b of the Hague regulations of 1907. The use of deceitful means to kill the enemy or put him out of action is thus prohibited by this article.

The international law of war forbids the misuse of flags of truce or white flags in general, the flag of the enemy army or state, the insignias and uniforms of the enemy, or the emblems of the Geneva Conventions (the Red Cross, the Red Crescent, or the Red Lion and Sun, etc.) for the purpose of deceiving the enemy.

According to Article 5 of the ninth Hague Convention relating to bombardment by naval forces in time of war, it is the duty of the population to mark monuments, buildings or localities by means of visible signs consisting of a rectangular panel divided diagonally into two colored triangular portions, the upper portion black and the lower portion white. This emblem is protected and must not be used in wartime for any purposes other than those for which it has been designated. Under paragraphs 1, Article 16 of the 1954 Hague Convention, a sign for indicating works of art and cultural monuments has been established: it is a shield pointed at the bottom and divided into four fields, colored blue and white diagonally.

Perfidy should be distinguished from *military stratagems,* which are not prohibited under the laws of war. Military ruses include various forms of surprise in order to gain tactical advantages, but not killing or wounding the enemy in an underhanded way.

Nor is the *spying* performed by belligerents prohibited, if it is reconnaissance by undisguised soldiers behind the enemy front lines for the purpose of obtaining information. Under the rules of war, each side in a conflict has the right to use spies (secret agents), but it does not have the right to protect them from punishment. If a spy is caught in the act, he may be punished without trial (under Article 30 of the 1907 Hague regulations). If a spy manages to escape, rejoin his own forces, and is subsequently taken prisoner by the enemy, he must be considered a prisoner of war and will not be held responsible for the previously committed act of spying (Article 31 of the Hague Regulations).

X. Relations Between Parties to a Conflict

As a rule, a state of war severs diplomatic and other relations between the sides in a conflict. However, they may maintain certain contacts through the intermediary of a protecting power or some other neutral state, the International Committee of the Red Cross or any other international humanitarian organization. In addition to these indirect contacts, the belligerents may make direct contact by individuals bearing a flag of truce or during the conclusion of an armistice.

The bearer of a flag of truce, or parleyer, is a person authorized by one belligerent to enter into negotiations with the other side. He travels under a white flag. The flag-bearer is entitled to inviolability, as is his party. (According to Article 32 of the 1907 Hague regulations, this inviolability expressly extends to buglers, drummers, flag-bearers and interpreters.) The parleyer may only be authorized to deliver messages, but he still enjoys inviolability. However, he does not have the right to disarm units under the pretext that the enemy has surrendered, as the Germans did in Yugoslavia in April 1941, because the sole function of a parleyer is to convey a message or to conduct negotiations.

An armistice is the cessation of military operations under a mutual agreement concluded by the parties to a conflict. If the duration of an armistice has not been specified in the agreement, the parties to the conflict may continue operations, but under the condition that they warn the enemy within an agreed time limit and in accordance with the terms of the armistice. The armistice may simply be a cease-fire for a specific or unspecified time period. It may be local or general. The armistice must be reported to the competent authorities and troops in good time. Hostilities may cease immediately after the announcement of the armistice, or within an agreed time limit. Violations of an armistice by either side in a conflict gives the other the right immediately to resume hostilities.

XI. Protected Persons in a Military Conflict

Introduction — Geneva Conventions — Wounded, Sick and Shipwrecked — Prisoners of War — Civilian Population

1. Introduction — The international laws regulating military conflicts provide for protection of prisoners of war, the wounded, sick, shipwrecked, and civilian persons. The rules which regulate this subject matter in the law of war have been codified in the Geneva Conventions, and these conventions represent an international code of human rights in time of war. The Geneva Conventions adopted in 1949 are still in force today. The four Geneva Conventions concern amelioration of the condition of the wounded and sick in armed forces in the field; amelioration of the condition of the wounded, sick and shipwrecked of armed forces at sea; treatment of prisoners of war, and protection of civilian persons in time of war.

2. The Geneva Conventions — The first Geneva Convention was concluded in 1864 and did no more than regulate the status of wounded soldiers in land warfare. This convention had only ten articles and contains the following basic principles: that the wounded and medical personnel of both sides are inviolable; that the wounded must be protected without discrimination; and that the emblem of the Red Cross is to designate protection from hostilities.

The Convention of 1864 stands as a landmark, not just in the evolution of international law but in the history of mankind. Prior to this convention, wounded soldiers were left to the tender mercies of the enemy on many battlefields.

The creation of national standing armies and the introduction of compulsory military service greatly increased the number of fighting men. Over 300,000 men, for instance, took part in the battle of Solferino in 1859 between the French-Sardinian and Austrian armies. In a relatively short time 40,000 men lay wounded in the field, but there were facilities for treating only 8,000. The terrible suffering of this enormous number of wounded after the Battle of Solferino was described by a Swiss citizen, Jean Henri Dunant, in a pamphlet *Un souvenir de Solferino,* which brought this serious international problem to the attention of the European public. In 1863 a committee of five Swiss citizens was created for the purpose of convening a diplomatic conference which was to adopt an international convention regarding the condition of the wounded. In 1864, twelve governments of the leading European powers sent their official representatives to the conference in Geneva, where the first Geneva Convention was adopted. Almost all the European states soon ratified this convention. It was applied in the war between Austria and Prussia in 1866 and in the Franco-Prussian war of 1870–1871.

Advancements in military technology and methods of warfare, not to mention the abuses committed, called for a revision of the Geneva Convention. A conference held in 1906 revised the rules of the earlier convention and extended protection to the sick as well as the wounded. At the Hague Conferences of 1899 and 1907, new rules were adopted for the protection of the wounded and sick in naval warfare, as well as of shipwrecked persons. The 1907 Hague regulations respecting the laws and customs of war on land laid down rules for the treatment of prisoners of war. After the First World War, the Geneva Conventions were revised at a conference held in 1929. The bitter experience of the Second World War prompted the convening of a diplomatic conference in Geneva, which sat from 21 April to 12 August, 1949. This conference drew up a total of 429 articles, a series of annexes and model treaties which are still in force today.

The Geneva Conventions must be observed in every armed conflict to which the contracting states are a party, be it a declared war or a conflict which one of the contracting sides does not recognize as a state of war. Similarly, the Geneva Conventions are applied in all cases of a partial or complete occupation of the territory of one of the contracting states, even if this occupation has been carried out with no armed resistance. Furthermore, even if one of the powers in a conflict is not a party to the Geneva Conventions, the contracting states remain bound by them in their mutual relations.

Persons in armed conflicts which do not have an international character, and which take place in the territory of one of the contracting states, have a special status. Such conflicts would include, for instance, civil wars and colonial or other uprisings. Prior to 1949, these persons enjoyed no protection under international law. The protection given to them under Article 3 of the Geneva Convention was very slight indeed. All it amounted to was a demand for humane treatment of persons who were not taking part directly in hostilities, implying here the members of armed forces who had laid down their arms or persons unable to fight as a result of disease, wounds, detention or for any other reason, with no discrimination. A particularly important provision prohibits the passing and execution of sentences without a previous trial, which must provide all the judicial guarantees recognized by civilized nations. Previously, according to internal regulations, for instance of the colonial powers, such persons could be summarily executed, without trial of any kind.

It should be noted, however, that the application of the provisions of Article 3 of the Geneva Conventions does not affect the legal status of the parties to a conflict. A clause to this effect was introduced into the Geneva Conventions of

1949 at the request of the colonial powers, in order to prevent rebels from citing this article as proof that they have been acknowledged by their opponent as a legal party to a conflict.

The contracting parties are obliged to undertake legislative measures in order to determine the punitive sanctions against persons who have performed or given orders for the performance of acts violating the conventions, particularly those acts which are designated as "grave breaches" of the Geneva Conventions. These are willful killing, torture or inhuman treatment, including biological experiments willfully causing great suffering or serious injury to body or health, compelling a prisoner of war to serve in the forces of a hostile power, or willfully depriving a prisoner of the rights to a fair trial; other breaches include destruction or appropriation of property which cannot be justified as a military necessity; unlawful deportation or transfer; illegal arrest, the taking of hostages, etc.

3. The Wounded, Sick, and Shipwrecked — The first two Geneva Conventions relate to the amelioration of the condition of the wounded and sick in the field and of the wounded, sick and shipwrecked in naval warfare. The contracting parties to these conventions undertook not only to refrain from attacking a wounded, sick or shipwrecked soldier, but also to move him to a medical unit and provide the necessary medical treatment. The Convention even requires that the contracting parties must search for and collect the wounded after each engagement, and for this purpose may conclude local armistices. Information about the wounded soldiers must be documented and sent to the national information bureau, which forwards it to the Central Prisoner of War Information Agency.

The treatment of the wounded, sick and shipwrecked soldiers must be humane. Prohibitions extend not just to the inflicting of bodily injuries or injuries to their dignity but also to any other discrimination. The only priority over medical treatment is given to military considerations. The dead must be buried or cremated, individually if possible. The bodies may only be cremated for reasons of hygiene or for religious reasons. Records must be kept on the graves of enemy soldiers.

The Geneva Conventions protect medical personnel. Medical personnel within their units may not be the object of attack. If they are in the power of the enemy, they shall continue to carry out their duties and shall not be considered prisoners of war. Military medical services include hospitals and other fixed medical establishments, mobile medical units, medical transports, and all personnel employed in these units. The 1949 Conventions draw distinctions among medical personnel. Permanent medical personnel include the persons engaged in searching for, collecting, transporting and treating the wounded and sick, those working on disease prevention, and the necessary clerical staff.

Auxiliary medical personnel are orderlies who carry the wounded after an engagement. These soldiers are exempt from attack only when performing these duties. Finally, civilians belonging to the Red Cross also are considered to be medical personnel. If the medical service is not able to carry out its functions, it may call upon the population to give voluntary assistance to the wounded, and for this reason no such civilian may be held liable by the opposing side. The medical personnel must wear a water-proof armlet bearing the emblem of the Red Cross on their left arms. The personnel must also carry an identity disc and a special identity card written in the national language and containing at least name and surname, date of birth, rank and serial number, as well as the capacity in which its bearer has the right to protection under the Geneva Conventions. These papers must be identical for every army.

Transports of the wounded, sick, and medical supplies may not be the object of attack and must be respected and protected. If these transports fall into the hands of the enemy, they will be subject to the laws of war, under the condition that the party to the conflict in every case must assume responsibility for caring for the wounded and sick within them.

The rules applying to medical aircraft are more strict. At the 1949 Geneva Conference, the view was taken that aircraft, even if used for medical purposes, presented a threat to the enemy. For this reason, special rules were adopted. The aircraft used exclusively for the evacuation of the wounded and sick and for the transport of medical supplies may not be the object of attack if flying on routes previously agreed upon by the sides in the conflict. However, medical aircraft must comply with every summons to land. After examination, the medical aircraft may continue its flight. If it is detained by the enemy side, the sick and wounded in it shall become prisoners of war.

Military hospital ships are those ships which the signatory states to the conventions have built or converted to serve exclusively for the purpose of providing assistance to the wounded, sick and shipwrecked, and for their treatment and transport. The same status is enjoyed by the hospital ships of national Red Cross societies, provided they have received an official commission from the side in the conflict and fulfil the conditions prescribed for military hospital ships. Under no circumstances may they be attacked or captured; they must be respected and protected even during a naval engagement, provided their names and characteristics are reported to the parties to the conflict ten days before being used for these purposes. There is a certain difference in the status of the sick and wounded on land and at sea. On land the enemy may use a medical unit or establishment which is in his power and may detain the personnel within them; whereas a hospital ship may not be seized, nor may its personnel be detained so long as they are in its service. However, for inspection purposes a hospital ship may be detained up to seven days. Naturally, hospital ships must refrain from performing hostile acts. Otherwise, any protection which they enjoy under the Second Geneva Convention ceases.

4. Prisoners of War — The Third Geneva Convention of 1949 regulates the position of prisoners of war.

The prisoner of war is the person of a specific category who falls into the hands of the enemy in an armed conflict. Prisoners of war are primarily members of the armed forces of one of the sides in a conflict, members of the militia and volunteer corps, or members of organized resistance movements, if they fulfil the above-listed four conditions. Members of regular armed forces belonging to a government or authority which has not been recognized by the power holding them also have the status of prisoners of war. For instance, the Germans did not recognize the units of General de Gaulle in the Second World War, because they did not recognize the committee which organized resistance against the enemy. Persons belonging to modern armies, crew members of airplanes, war correspondents, supply contractors, army entertainment groups and the like also have this status. Previously, such persons were interned, but now they have been granted the status of prisoners of war. Furthermore, the crew members of the merchant marines and civil aviation have this status, as does the population of an occupied territory who voluntarily take up arms with the advance of the enemy, provided they observe the laws and customs of war and openly bear arms. They are not to be considered bandits as before, but they cannot remain civilian persons because of their resort to arms. Finally, prisoners of war may also be persons released from captivity and then interned a second time. Persons successfully escaping from captivity but subsequently recaptured shall also be considered prisoners of war. Such persons are considered to have escaped if they reach their own territory, unit or ship. Finally, the heads of state, government ministers, members of parliament, and high government officials may also be granted the status of prisoners of war.

It is fundamental from the standpoint of international law that the prisoner of war should be in the hands of the power which has captured him, and not of individuals or of the military units which actually took him prisoner. According to international law, the person violating any of the rules of the Geneva Convention protecting prisoners of war, and the power which allowed such violations to occur, shall be held responsible.

Prisoners of war must be humanely treated, with no discrimination. Their person and their personal dignity must be safeguarded. Reprisals are prohibited. Prisoners of war also have the right to maintenance and medical care free of charge.

A prisoner of war continues to retain his full civil capacity. Because he is in the power of a state, a prisoner of war may only be transferred to the custody of a power which is a party to the convention relating to prisoners of war, and after it has been ascertained that the power concerned is willing and able to apply the provisions of this convention.

After falling into captivity, a prisoner of war must be evacuated as soon as possible from the battlefield. Evacuation must also be carried out humanely. During interrogation, the prisoner of war must not be forced to give information, except for his name and surname, rank, date of birth, and serial number. A member of the armed forces must carry an identity card, which must be shown on demand, but under no circumstances may it be taken away from him. Prisoners have the right to retain their personal belongings.

Prisoners of war may be used as labor force for the purpose of maintaining their physical and mental health, but due regard must be given to their sex and physical capabilities. Non-commissioned officers may only be used for supervisory work. Officers, however, must not be forced to work. The conditions of work must be suitable, and remuneration must be made. Prisoners must not be used to perform tasks which are unhealthy or dangerous (e.g. mine clearing).

For the purpose of protecting the prisoners' rights and representing them before the military authorities, a protecting power is to be appointed, the International Committee of the Red Cross or any other similar organization, to which prisoners may elect their representatives by free and secret ballot every six months. In officers' camps, the representative is the highest-ranking senior officer. The election of representatives must be confirmed by the power in whose custody they are being held. Representatives have the duty of looking after the physical, spiritual and intellectual welfare of the prisoners.

Prisoners must obey the laws, decrees and general orders which are in force in the armed forces of the detaining power. Hence, this power is authorized to mete out disciplinary measures or try prisoners in court for acts which, according to the laws in force, are characterized as criminal acts, or disciplinary offenses, but within the limitations prescribed by the Geneva Convention relating to prisoners of war. As a rule, military tribunals are competent to try prisoners of war, unless the legislation of the detaining power gives express authorization to civil courts to try members of the armed forces of that power for the same act for which the prisoners of war are being prosecuted. In any case, the prisoner of war may not be tried by a court which does not provide the basic guarantees of independence and fairness, or does not give the prisoners the right and means to defend themselves. A prisoner may only be tried under a regular court procedure, with the assurance of communication with the protecting power. The convention prohibits collective punishment for individual acts, corporal punishment, imprisonment in premises without daylight, and any form of torture or brutality. Military authorities and military tribunals can only mete out those punishments which are envisaged for the same acts for members of the armed forces of the detaining power. If a death sentence is pronounced, it may not be carried out before six months have elapsed from the day when the protecting power has been informed of the judgment. Disciplinary punishments may last for up to thirty days and include the discontinuance of special privileges, or even fatigue duty lasting from five to thirty days.

Upon the outbreak of hostilities or in all cases of occupation, each state must establish an official prisoner of war information bureau, which will be under its authority. The information bureau collects information about prisoners of war and submits it to a central agency in one of the neutral states. Such an agency was established for the first time in Basel in 1870. During the Second World War, it was located in Geneva and handled information concerning 36 million persons.

The convention provides for two types of repatriation of war prisoners: during the war and after the war. If the mental or physical fitness of a prisoner has been substantially impaired, or if medical treatment is expected to last more than one year, he must be directly returned to his own country. Upon the end of active hostilities, prisoners of war must be released without delay and must be repatriated.

After the Korean War (1952–1953) the problem arose of prisoners of war who refused to return home. Such a situation had not been envisaged by the Geneva Convention. On 3 December 1952, the U.N. General Assembly adopted a resolution prohibiting the use of force to carry out or prevent repatriation. The decision of whether to return to their own countries or to go to another country was left to the prisoners themselves. An international commission was set up for the purpose of determining whether such prisoners had voluntarily decided to return to their own country or to seek asylum in another country.

5. Civilian Population

5. Civilian Population — Total warfare does not spare any part of a state's territory from military operations. Of necessity, the entire population of a country is engaged in the war effort, and at the same time, in view of the modern developments of military technology (airplanes, guided missiles), the civilian population is exposed to the effect of enemy weapons, no matter where they might be. The experience gained since the Second World War has shown the need for rules of war to be adopted which would protect civilian persons in future armed conflicts. Such rules are contained in the Fourth Geneva Convention, which protects civilian persons in time of war.

The 1949 Geneva Convention on the Protection of Civilian Persons in Time of War applies not only to armed conflicts between states but also to situations of a partial or complete occupation of a country, regardless of whether or not resistance was encountered. In the first instance, the convention extends protection to civilian persons located in the territory of their state, as well as to those citizens falling into the hands of the enemy (occupation, internment). It mainly protects the latter category of civilians because of the terrible experiences of the Second World War, when millions of men, women, and children were tortured and lost their lives in concentration camps.

The general purpose of the convention is to protect the entire population of the countries engaged in a conflict, without distinction, and especially without discrimination as to race, nationality, religion or political convictions. Its goal is to ameliorate the sufferings of the population caused by war. To this end, the Convention provides for three types of zones:

> — *Safety zones.* These are localities protected from the effects of war, in which the wounded and sick, the aged and children under fifteen, pregnant women and mothers of children under seven may take shelter.
> — *Hospital zones.* These are locations in which only the wounded and sick are cared for. They are the same as the zones provided for in earlier conventions for military wounded.
> Upon the outbreak of war, and throughout its duration, the states in conflict may conclude agreements on the recognition of zones and localities to be subsequently determined. The contracting states may still in peacetime designate future safety and hospital zones.
> — *Neutralized zones.* The parties to a conflict may, on the basis of a written agreement, create the so-called neutralized zones in their territories for the purpose of protecting the wounded and sick, combatants and noncombatants alike, and civilian persons who have no functions of a military nature during their stay in these zones. The convention provides a model for such an agreement in an annex.

The creation of special zones for the protection of the civilian population was practiced in 1938 in the Spanish Civil War and in 1948 in the war between Israel and the Arab states (in Jerusalem). Despite these examples, which show the value of this institution, there are authors who doubt the possibility of setting up zones in any future conflicts, because of the nature of total war, in which even the smallest area is of military importance. However, these zones, particularly in wars conducted on a smaller scale, could be of value, regardless of their degree of effectiveness.

It should be pointed out that the convention protects persons who, in the event of a conflict or occupation, are under the control of one of the belligerents. The convention is only applicable to "protected persons." It does not protect the citizens of a state which is not bound by its provisions. The citizens of a neutral state are protected under the convention if the state of which they are nationals has no diplomatic representation in the state where they are located.

The power in whose territory protected persons are located may take security measures, but within the limits of humane treatment and with respect for their dignity. Measures designed to cause physical suffering, murder, torture, corporal punishment, or other brutalities are expressly prohibited. No one may be punished for an act which he has not committed. Collective punishments are prohibited, as is the taking of hostages. Protected persons may seek the assistance or visits of the protecting power, the International Committee of the Red Cross, and other humanitarian organizations.

The most important provisions of this convention are those relating to protected persons in occupied territory. In addition to the fact that these persons must be given humane treatment, it is notable that the type of occupation cannot affect their rights. For instance, the creation of quisling governments cannot affect the application of this convention. This provision marks a great stride forward in the international law of war, achieved since the Second World War. Heretofore, occupiers denied international protection to the population of the occupied territory, under the pretext that the domestic government was in power, there being only an insignificant change in the form of occupation.

The convention prohibits an occupying power from compelling protected persons to serve in its armed forces or navies. In fact, any type of pressure intended to encourage a voluntary enlistment is prohibited. Forced labor is not excluded, but is considerably restricted under the convention, and the precise conditions under which it may be used are spelled out.

Finally, the convention contains rules governing the treatment of interned persons, even though attempts to prohibit internment as a whole did not succeed at the Geneva Conference of 1949. The convention seeks to secure for an interned person the same treatment as that accorded to prisoners of war. The intention was to prevent a repetition of the treatment given internees in concentration and death camps such as Dachau, Mauthausen, Majdanek, and others. The state which detains internees is required to give them humane treatment, to maintain them, to provide medical care and to permit them to communicate with the outside world, their families and the protecting power.

The internee is in a more favorable position than the prisoner of war only inasmuch as he has the right to submit a protest against the decision on internment and, if his protest is rejected, to renew it every six months. An interned person has the right to be lodged together with his family, with the necessary facilities required for the continuance of his family life. Other provisions are similar to those regulating the status of prisoners of war.

XII. Military Occupation

Military occupation is defined as the imposition of control over the territory of another state by military force. If only a portion of the territory is captured, occupation is partial. If the entire country is captured by military force, occupation is total.

If military occupation is to have a legal effect, it must be effective, which means that it extends only to the territory in which the authority of the invading forces has been established and where it is in full control. From the standpoint of international law, the establishment and assertion of authority implies the establishment and maintenance of public order. In short, international law considers military occupation — and indeed war itself — as a *de facto* situation which must be subject to the rules of the international law of war.

The occupying power only enjoys the right of administration and the right of usufruct in the occupied territory. It does not have the right to change the social, economic, or legal order in the occupied territory. The occupying power may change existing legislation only if it is in the interest of the population in the occupied territory or if necessary for the security of the occupying army, property, and communications.

The proclamations of the supreme commander of the occupying forces have the force of law. They must be published in the language of the peoples in the occupied region. The population in the occupied territory must not be forced to pledge allegiance, serve in the enemy armed units, or provide information which would harm the interests of their country. The status of civilian persons under occupation has been discussed in the preceding chapter.

Although military occupation is recognized by international law as a *de facto* situation, at the same time the laws of war do not deny the people in occupied territory the right to rebel, to organize a resistance movement and drive the enemy from their soil by force of arms, under the conditions provided for in Article 1 and Article 42, paragraph 2, of the 1907 Hague regulations.

XIII. Neutrality

Concept — Rights and Duties of Neutral States — Neutrality at Sea

1. Concept — Neutrality can be described as the non-participation of third states in an armed conflict. It is the political stance of a state in regard to a conflict which has broken out, and it has certain legal consequences. From the moment that neutrality is proclaimed, a legal relationship is established between neutral states and the parties to the conflict. Their rights and duties will be discussed in due course. For the moment, suffice it to say that the relationship must be reciprocal. Neutrality as a specific legal status must be mutually respected. If it is not respected, either by the neutral state or by one of the parties to the conflict, the legal relationship is broken off, regardless of whether or not the ending of neutrality was provoked. What is being discussed here is temporary, voluntary neutrality, as distinguished from neutrality under treaty or permanent neutrality.

Neutrality as a rule begins when a declaration of neutrality is sent to the parties to a conflict, and it ends when the armed conflict is over. A declaration of neutrality is not considered to be necessary if states have specified in their internal legislation that they would take a neutral position in any eventual armed conflict. In this event, neutrality begins from the moment the conditions provided for in their internal legislation have been satisfied.

In view of the practices during the Second World War (*viz.*, Italy, Spain, Turkey), certain authors call the concept of non-belligerency a form of neutrality. However, it could hardly be described as a form of neutrality, even if it is called limited or partial. Non-belligerency is a political attitude towards one of the sides in a conflict, without the assumption of the legal consequences envisaged under international law. In the case of neutrality, the overriding legal consideration — provided, of course, it is acknowledged as an institution of international law — is reciprocity in the relations between neutral states and the belligerents. Reciprocity implies equal treatment by neutral states of all the parties to a conflict. However, there is no reciprocity in the state of non-belligerency because both sides in a conflict are not given equal treatment. Hence, non-belligerency cannot be equated with the legal institution which is known in international law as neutrality.

Both world wars have shown that the number of neutral states in such conflicts is steadily decreasing. Wars of global dimensions can hardly bypass the countries which might wish to have this status. The creation of the United Nations Organization has made it a matter of controversy whether neutrality can be enforced at all in the present-day world community, which is founded on the system of the U.N. Charter. According to Chapter VII of the Charter, member states must act in compliance with the decisions of the Security Council when the United Nations undertakes collective enforcement measures against an aggressor. The Charter thus requires the participation of all member states in the collective measures, in conformity with Chapter VII of the Charter, and makes no provision for a neutral attitude by one or more members of the United Nations. However, the experience of the United Nations has shown that its member states may be neutral in certain armed conflicts. In the Korean conflict, there were neutral U.N. member countries, such as, for instance, India, Burma, and Yugoslavia. Italy declared its neutrality in the Suez conflict. Furthermore, when the United Nations sent armed forces to Egypt, the question was openly raised in the United Nations whether only neutral countries could send their military contingents to the United Nations armed forces. Finally, Austria is a permanently neutral country but is at the same time a member of the United Nations. We can conclude from all these examples that expediency demands the existence of the institution of neutrality in the political and legal system of the United Nations. According to the letter of the Charter, there is no such thing as neutrality. According to United Nations practice, it does exist, and is not only tolerated but is even respected as an institution. In our opinion, this is one more example of the body of rules representing a *de facto* revision of the Charter.

2. Rights and Duties of Neutral States — Neutrality is a legal relationship in which the parties to a conflict are obliged to observe certain rights of the neutral state, and, on their part, the neutral states are obliged to refrain from certain acts in regard to the parties to a conflict, prevent them, or tolerate certain actions on their part. The Fifth Hague Convention regulated the rights and duties of neutral powers and individuals in war on land.

The territory of neutral states, including their territorial waters, is inviolable. The conduct of hostilities, *i.e.* armed fighting and war operations, is prohibited in their territory. The parties to a conflict are not allowed to use neutral territory for the passage of their troops, or for the transport of war materiel and food supplies. However, by the same token, troops may not be levied in neutral territory, nor may offices be established for the recruiting of volunteers for either belligerent side. A neutral state must not permit radio or telegraph installations to be established in its territory, or any other equipment intended for maintaining communications with the land or naval forces of the parties to a conflict. Nor may it use or permit the use for military purposes of such facilities which had been established before the war.

The neutral state has the right and duty to defend and protect its neutrality. To this end, it is entitled to prevent violations of its neutrality by any means, including force. The neutral state has the right to seek reparations in the form of compensation for damages or restitution of the *status quo ante*. If the troops of the parties to a conflict enter the territory of a neutral state, it will intern them; escaped prisoners of war will be left at liberty or may be interned. A neutral state may permit the transport of wounded and sick through its territory, provided military persons and war materiel are not transported with them. The Geneva Conventions apply to the sick and wounded who are interned in neutral territory. The citizens of neutral states cannot claim neutrality if they perform hostile acts against one of the belligerents, voluntarily put themselves into the service of the armed forces of a party to the conflict, or work on its behalf.

3. Neutrality at Sea — The Thirteenth Hague Convention of 1907 lays down the rights and duties of neutral powers in the event of naval war. The third paragraph of the preamble to this convention states: ''In cases not covered by the present Convention, account must be taken of the general principles of the Law of Nations."

It is the duty of neutral states to apply the convention rules impartially in regard to all the parties to the conflict. These rules may not in principle be changed in the course of the war by a neutral state, except "in a case where experience has shown the necessity for such a change for the protection of the rights" of the neutral states. The parties to a conflict are obliged to respect the sovereign rights of neutral states and to refrain from performing acts in their territory or neutral waters which would violate their neutrality. Hence, any hostile act against an enemy vessel, including interception or examination by a warship of one of the belligerents, is strictly forbidden. The parties to the conflict particularly must not use neutral ports and neutral waters for naval operations against the enemy. They are also not allowed to establish a prize court in neutral territory or on a ship in neutral waters. Similarly, a neutral state is prohibited from either directly or in any way supplying warships, ammunition or war materiel of any kind whatever to a belligerent. The authorities of a neutral state are expected to prevent in their territory the equipping or arming of a ship which is suspected of intending to take part in hostilities against one of the parties to a conflict, or of any other ship which has been converted for military purposes. However, on the basis of this convention, the neutrality of a state is not considered to be violated by the innocent passage of warships through its territorial waters. Innocent passage implies passage without damage done or war-like operations.

A neutral state must notify any warships in its roadsteads, ports or territorial waters that they are obliged to depart within 24 hours or within such other time as specified by its internal laws. A warship of one of the belligerents may not prolong its stay beyond the time limit prescribed by law, except in the case of a breakdown or damage, or bad weather conditions at sea. An exception is made for ships which are exclusively used for religious, scientific, or humanitarian purposes.

If the warship of one of the sides in a conflict does not comply with the request of the neutral state to depart within the given time limit, the state has the right to take the measures which it considers necessary for the purpose of preventing the ship from being used for the duration of the war. Detention of a warship implies detention of the officers and crew, who are subject to whatever restrictive measures the neutral state sees fit to impose.

XIV. The End of War

Debellatio — General Armistice — Capitulation — Peace Treaty

The parties to a conflict may end their hostilities in two ways: unilaterally or by agreement.

1. Debellatio — The unilateral cessation of hostilities implies the *final subjugation of the enemy (debellatio)*. The subjugated territory is usually annexed, so that a member of the international community of nations ceases to exist. Many states disappeared in this way in the period of unification of Germany and Italy in the 19th century. The age of imperialism abounds with examples of annexation by the great powers, which pursued their foreign policy aims by force of arms.

2. General Armistice — The parties to a conflict may end hostilities, primarily by agreement, in order to proclaim a *general armistice*. This is a phase which frequently precedes the conclusion of peace. A general armistice has a military and political character, and for this reason it is concluded, as a rule, by military officials with the concurrence of their government.

3. Capitulation — In the course of a war, there may be a *temporary* cessation of hostilities (armistice) in various sectors of military operations, most frequently for the purpose of collecting the wounded and dead, but it is not intended as a cessation of hostilities for the purpose of ending the war. Similarly, in the course of a war there may be a *capitulation,* which is a convention laying down the conditions for the surrender of a fortified place, a part of the fighting sector, a unit or the entire armed forces of one of the parties to a conflict. This is a military convention, and it has been provided for in the 1907 Hague regulations, according to which the belligerents must give due consideration to the rules of military honor when negotiating the capitulation. The Hague regulations also call for observance of the concluded capitulation by both sides. A capitulation may not contain political provisions, for it is typically a military convention. If it does contain political clauses, they are not valid from the standpoint of international law. To sum up, capitulations are military conventions which are concluded in the course of a war for a partial or complete surrender of the armed forces of one of the parties to the conflict. An unconditional surrender is a convention of a military nature, under which the armed forces of one of the parties to a conflict surrenders completely. This type of surrender was practiced by the Axis powers in the Second World War. After victory over the Hitlerite coalition, the Allies concluded an armistice with an unconditional surrender by all enemy forces.

International law recognizes this institution regardless of the attitudes taken by national legislations. The Swiss Constitution of 1874 forbids the military capitulation. According to Article 238 of the 1974 Constitution of the Socialist Federal Republic of Yugoslavia, "No one shall have the right to acknowledge or sign an act of capitulation, nor to accept or recognize the occupation of the Socialist Federal Republic of Yugoslavia or any of its individual parts." Such an act would be unconstitutional and punishable as a grave criminal offense. The Yugoslav policy, stated in this article of the Constitution, is in conformity with international law. Aggression is an international crime, and self-defense is a legitimate and "inherent right" of every state. Furthermore, defense against an aggressor is the duty of the state in the present international legal order.

4. The Peace Treaty — As a rule, a war is ended by a *peace treaty,* although there have been cases when war has been ended without a peace treaty (*e.g.* the war between France and Mexico, which was fought from 1862 to 1867).

A peace treaty is an international treaty concluded between the parties to a conflict for the purpose of re-establishing peaceful relations. It contains clauses regulating all questions concerning the future relations. In general, these include questions of territory; citizenship; repatriation of prisoners of war; various political questions, such as the dissolution of the political parties which had been involved in conducting the war; responsibility and extradition of war criminals; military matters, such as the dispersal or limited maintenance of military units, the manner of disarming the defeated army; war damages and restitution; and other matters of an economic and other nature.

Peace treaties also contain guarantees for their enforcement. They may also contain mechanisms or ways ensuring their implementation. However, these mechanisms may be determined in separate agreements or in annexes to the treaty. The peace treaties with Italy, Bulgaria, and Hungary concluded in 1947 provided for a body to execute certain provisions of the peace treaty, which was to be composed of the heads of the diplomatic representatives of the victorious powers.

The rule is that the state of war ceases from a legal standpoint at the moment the peace treaty enters into force. The treaty becomes effective with the exchange of instruments of ratification; of course, if ratification has been provided for by the treaty.

Peace treaties must be observed. Failure to comply with them either in part or as a whole, is a breach of international law.

References

1. Concept

Morelli, Gaetano. "Cours general de droit international public," *Recueil des Cours*, The Hague - 1956. -

Rolin, Henri. "Les principes de droit international public," *Recueil des Cours*, The Hague, 1950.

Svarlien, Oscar. *An Introduction to the Law of Nations*, New York, 1955.

Verdross, Alfred von. "On the Concept of International Law," *American Journal of International Law*, 1949.

Walz, Gustav Adolf. *Wesen des Völkerrechts und Kritik der Völkerrechtslengner*, Stuttgart, 1930.

2. Classification

Blagojević, Borislav. *International Private Law*, Belgrade, 1950.

Brigs, H. W. The "Legislative Jurisdictional Principle," in a Policy-Centred Conflict of Laws, *The International and Comparative Law Quarterly*, 1955.

Donnadieu de Vabres, Henri. *"L'universalité de droit international,"* *Revue de droit international privé*, 1938.

Pereterskii, I. S. "Sistema meždunarodnog častnogo prava," *Sovetskoe gosudarstvo i pravo*, 1947.

Wortley, B. A. "The International of Public and Private International Law Today," *Recueil des Cours*, The Hague, 1954.

3. Municipal and International Law

Kelsen, Hans. "Les rapports de systeme entre le droit interne et le droit international public," *Recueil des Cours*, The Hague, 1926.

Levin, D. B. "Sovremennii meždunarodno-pravovoi nigilizm," *Sovetskoe gosudarstvo i pravo*, 1948.

Papalambrou, Apostolos. "Le probleme de la 'transformation', et la question de la validité des actes étatiques 'contraires' au droit international," *Rèvue hellénique de droit international*, 1950.

Triepel, Carl Heinrich. "Les rapports entre le droit interne et le droit international," *Recueil des Cours,* The Hague, 1923.

Verdross, Alfred von. *Die Einheit des rechtlichen Weltbildes,* 1923.

Vladisavljević, Milan. *State and International Community,* Belgrade, 1934.

Verdross, Alfred von. "Les principes généraux du droit dans la jurisprudence internationale," *Recueil des Cours,* The Hague, 1935.

Vissher, Charles de. "Coutume et traité en droit international public," *Revue generale de droit international public,* 1955.

4. Sources

Cheng, Bin. *General Principles of Law as Applied by International Courts and Tribunals,* London, 1953.

Fleischmann, Max. *Völkerrechtsquellen,* Halle, 1935.

Grapin, _____ . *Valeur internationale des principes généraux du droit,* 1934.

Korovin, E. A. "Ob obščepriznanih normah meždunarodnog prava," *Sovetskoe gosudarstvo i pravo,* 1951.

Rousseau, Charles. *Principes generaux du droit international public,* Paris, 1944.

Sörensen, Max. *Les sources du droit international,* 1946.

Spiropoulos, Jean. *Die allgemeinen Rechtsgrundsätze im Völkerrecht,* 1928.

5. Codification

Alvarez, Alejandro. *La codification du droit international - ses tendences - ses bases,* Paris, 1912.

Bartoš, Milan. "Quelques observations sur la coexistence pacifique active," *Yugoslav Review for International Law,* 1960.

Friedmann, Wolfgang and oth. edit., *Transnational Law in a Changing Society,* New York, 1972.

Lauterpacht, Hersh. "Codification and Development of International Law," *American Journal of International Law,* 1955.

Pella, Vesparien. "La codification du droit penal international," *Revue générale de droit international public,* 1952.

Radojković, Miloš. "La Codification des principes de la coexistence pacifique," *Yugoslav Review for International Law,* 1962.

Sahović, Milan, edit., *Principles of International Law Concerning Friendly Relations and Cooperation,* Belgrade-New York, 1972.

Vissher, Charles de. "La Codification du droit international," *Recueil des Cours,* The Hague, 1925.

Yuen-Li-Liang. "Le développement et la codification du droit international," *Recueil des Cours,,* The Hague, 1948.

6. Development

Rappard, William. "Vues retrospectives sur la Société des Nations," *Recueil des Cours,* The Hague, 1947.

Roi, ____ . "Les Transformations du droit des gens depuis, 1919." *Revue générale de droit international public,* 1948.

Fenwick, Charles. "The Progress of International Law during the Past Forty years," *Recueil des Cours,* The Hague, 1951.

7. Modern Theories

Bartoš, Milan. *La doctrine Yougoslave sur le fondement du droit international public,* 1956.

Burton, John Wear. *Nonalignment,* New York 1966.

Castanos, Stelios. *Critique du droit international public moderne,* Paris, 1953.

Ganjukin, B. B. *Sovremenij neutralitet,* Moscow 1958.

Huber, Max. *Die sociologischen Grundlagen des Völkerrechts,* Berlin, 1928.

Janković, Branimir. "Principes du droit international," *Question actuelles du Socialisme,* Paris, 1954.

_____ . "De la Neutralité classique à la Conception moderne des pays nonalignés," *Révue Egyptienne de Droit international,* 1954.

Kelsen, Hans. "Science and Politics," *The American Political Review,* 1951.

_____ . "Theorie du droit international public," *Recueil des cours,* The Hague, 1953.

Krylov, Sergei Borisovitch. "Les notions principales du droit des gens," *Recueil des cours,* The Hague, 1947.

Quadri, Rolando. "Le Fondement du caractère obligatoire du droit international public," *Recueil des cours,* The Hague, 1952.

Lauterpacht, Hersh. *The Function of Law in the International Community,* London, 1933.

Manotas, Wilches Edgardo. *Le nouveau droit des gens,* Paris, 1948.

Mates, Leo. *Nonalignement,* Belgrade, 1970.

Pound, Roscoe. *Social Control and Function of Law,* 1942.

Stone, Julius. *The Province and Function of Law,* London, 1947.

Triyol, y Serra, A. Doctrines contemporaines du droit des gens, Paris, 1951.

Tunkin, Grigorij. *Voprosi teorii meždunarodnogo prava,* Moskva, 1962.

PART I — Subjects

Chapter One: States

1. Appearance and Disappearance of States

Bastid, Suzanne. "Les problèmes territoriaux dans la jurisprudence de la Cour Internationale de Justice," *Recueil des Cours,* The Hague, 1962.

Castren, Eric. "Aspects recents de la secession d'Etats," *Recueil des Cours,* The Hague, 1951.

Langer, Robert. *Seizure of Territory.* Princeton, 1957.

Sack, Alexander Nahum. *Les effets des transformations des Etats,* 1927.

Udina, Manlio. "La succession des etats quant aux obligations internationales autres que les dettes publiques," *Recueil des Cours,* The Hague, 1933.

2. Forms of States

Beante, ____ . *Le droit de petition dans les Territoires sous tutelle,* Paris, 1962.

Dollot, René. "Essai sur la neutralité permanente," *Recueil des Cours,* The Hague, 1939.

Dranov, B. A. *Černomorskie prolivi,* Moscow 1948.

Engelhardt, Edouard Philippe. *Les protectorats anciens et modernes,* Paris, 1896.

Hall, Hessel Duncan. *Mandates, Dependencies and Trusteeship,* London, 1948.

Liang, Yuen-Li. "Colonial Clauses and Federal Clause in United Nations Multilateral Instruments," *American Journal of International Law,* 1951.

Mathiot, André. *Les territoires non autonomes et la Charte des Nations Unies,* Paris, 1949.

Molodcov, S. V. "Raspad sistema kolonijalizma i ego vlijanije na meždunarodno pravo," *Sovetskoe gosudarstvo i pravo,* 1956.

Pinto, Roger. "Le Statut international de la Republique democratique Allemande," *Journal du droit international,* 1959.

Vedovato, Giuseppe. "Les acords de tutelle," *Recueil des Cours,* The Hague, 1950.

Viralli, Michel. "Droit international et de colonisation devant les Nations Unies," *Annuaire français de droit international,* 1963.

3. Recognition of States and Governments

Bierzanek, R. "La Non - Reconnaissance et le droit international contemporain," *Annuaire français de droit international,* 1962.

Briggs, H. W. "Recognition of States," *American Journal of International Law,* 1949.

Brown, Philip Marshall. "The Legal Effects of Recognition," *American Journal of International Law,* 1950.

Chen, Ti-chiang. *The International Law of Recognition,* London, 1951.

Chatelain, J. "Reconnaissance Internationale," *La Technique et les Principes du droit public,* t. II Paris, 1950.

Kunz, Josef L. *Die Anerkennungen von Staaten und Regierung im Völkerrecht,* Stuttgart, 1928.

Lauterpacht, Hersh. *Recognition in International Law,* London, 1947.

Lazarev, M. I. "K voprosu o priznani v meždunarodnom prave," *Sovetskoe gosudarstvo i pravo,* 1948.

Lorimer, J. "La Doctrine de la reconnaissance, fondement du droit international," *Revue de droit international et de législation comparée,* 1884.

Misra, K. P. "India's Policy of Recognition of States and Governments," *American Journal of International Law,* 1961.

Wright, Quincy. "Some Thougts about Recognition," *American Journal of International Law,* 1950.

McNair, Arnold Duncan. "Juridical Recognition of States and Government," *British Year-Book of International Law,* 1921–1922.

Spriropuolos, Jean. *Die de facto Regierung in Völkerrecht,* 1926.

4. Basic Rights and Duties of States

Bartoš, Milan. "Yugoslavia's Struggle for Equality," *Foreign Affairs,* 1950.

Etude. *preparatoire relative a un projet de declaration des droits et devoirs des Etats,* U.N. Publication, 1948.

Korowicz, Marc. *La souveraineté des Etats et l'avenir du droit international,* Paris, 1945.

Kelsen, Hans. "The Draft Declaration on Rights and Duties of States," *American Journal of International Law,* 1950.

Löwenstein, Karl. "Sovereignty and International Cooperation," *American Journal of International Law,* 1954.

Modžorjan, L. A. "Poniatie suvereniteta v. meždunarodnom prave," *Sovetskoe gosudarstvo i pravo,* 1955.

Usakov, Nikolai Aleksandrovich. *Suverenitet v savremenom medžunarodnom prave,* Moskva, 1963.

Weinschel, Herbert. "The Doctrine of the Equality of States and Its Recent Modification," *American Journal of International Law,* 1951.

5. Abuse of Rights in International Law

Jankovic, Branimir. "Interdiction de l'abus de droit en droit international," *Annuaire de l'Association des Auditeurs de l'Academie du droit international de la Haye*, 1959.

Josserand, Louis. *De l'Abus des droits*, Paris, 1905.

Kiss, Alexander. *L'Abus de Droit en Droit international*, Paris, 1953.

Politis, Nicolas Socrate. "Le probleme des limitation de la Souveraineté et la theorie de l'abus de droit dans les rapports internationaux," *Recueil des Cours*, The Hague, 1925.

Spiropulos, Jean. "L'Abus de droit du vote par un membre du Conseil de Securité," *Revue du droit international héllenique*, 1948.

Schlochauer, Hans. "Die Theorie des abus de droit im Völkerrecht," *Zeitschrift für Völkerrecht*, 1932–1933.

6. State Territory

Andrassy, Juraj. "Les relations internationales de voisinage," *Recueil des Court*, The Hague, 1951.

Barsegov, Iu. G. *Teritorija v mezdunarodnom prave*, Moscow, 1958.

Schoenborn, Walther. "La Nature juridique du territoire," *Recueil des cours*, The Hague, 1929.

Sursalov, V. M. "Ob objekte medzunarodnogo prava," *Sovetskoe gosudarstvo i pravo*, 1957.

Luard, Evan, ed., The International Regulation of Frontier Disputes, New York, 1970.

Jenks, Wilfred. *Space Law*, London, 1965.

McDougal, Laswell, Vlašić. *Law and Public Order in Space*, New Haven, 1963.

Nikolajevic, Borko, "Outer space as New Field of Law," *International Review of International Law*, 1960.

Pepin, Eugène. "Le droit aerien," *Recueil des Cours*, The Hague, 1947.

Vlašić, Ivan. edit., *Explorations in Aerospace Law*, Montreal, 1968.

Baxter, Richard. *The Law of International Waterways*, Cambridge, 1964.

Bourquin, Maurice. "L'Organisation internationale des voies de communications," *Recueil des Cours*, The Hague, 1924.

Durdenevski, V. N. *Dunajskaja problema*, Moscow, 1947.

Imbert, Louis J. "Le regime juridique actuel du Danube," *Revue générale de droit international public*, 1951.

Siegfried, André. "Les canaux internationaux et les grandes routes maritimes mondiales," *Recueil des Cours*, The Hague, 1949.

Višinski, A. J. "Dunavska konferencija i nekatori voprosi meždunarodnogo prava," *Sovetskoe gosudarstvo i pravo,* 1948.

Winiarski, Bohdan. "Principes generaux du droit fluviale international," *Recueil des Cours,* The Hague, 1933.

Buzan, Barry. *Seabed Politics,* New York, 1976.

Colombos, Constantine John. *Le droit international de la mer,* Paris, 1952.

Gidel, Gilbert C. *Le droit international de la mer, I, II, III,* Paris, 1930–1934.

Green, Leslie C. "The Continental Shelf," *Courent Legal Problems,* 1951.

Matesco, N. *Vers un nouveau droit international de la mer* Paris, 1950.

Mouton, Martinus Willem. *The Continental Shelf,* 1950.

Oda, Shigeru. *The International Law of the Ocean Development,* Leiden, 1972.

Selak, Charles B. "Recent Developments in High Seas Fisheries Jurisdiction," *American Journal of International Law,* 1950.

Scelle, Georges. *Plateau continental et droit international public,* 1955.

Yepes, J. M. F. "Les nouvelles tendences du droit international de la mer et droit international americain," *Revue générale de droit international public,* 1956.

Brüel, Erik. *International Straits, I, II,* London, 1947.

Strohl, Mitchell P. *The International Law of Bays,* The Hague, 1963.

Tchirkovitch, Stevan. "La Question de la Convention de Montreux concernant le regime des detroits turcs, Bosphore et Dardanelles," *Revue générale de droit international public,* 1952.

Reid, Helen Dwight. "Les servitudes internationales," *Recueil des Cours,* The Hague, 1933.

7. Responsibility of States

Berlia, Georges. "De la responsabilité internationale de l'état," *La Technique et les principes du droit public,* II, Paris, 1950.

Cohn, G. "La Theorie de la responsabilité internationale," *Recueil des Cours,* The Hague, 1939.

Eusthatiades, Constantin. *La responsabilité internationale de l'état pour les actes des organes judiciaires et le probleme du deni de justice en droit internationale,* Paris, 1936.

—————— , "Les sujets du droit international et la responsabilité internationale, Nouvelles tendences," *Recueil des Cours,* The Hague, 1953.

Garcia-Amador, Francisco V. "State Responsibility in the Light of the New Trends of International Law," *American Journal of International Law,* 1955.

Merle, Marcel. *Le procès de Nöremberg et la chatiment des criminels de guerre,* Paris, 1949.

Chapter Two: International Organizations

1. Introduction: International Congresses and Diplomatic Conferences

Eles, Georges T. *Le Principe de l'Unanimité dans le Société des Nations et les exceptions à ce principe,* Paris, 1935.

Fenwick, Charles. "Unanimity Rule in Inter-American Conference," *American Journal of International Law,* 1948.

Hoffmann, Stanley. "Deux Directoires des grandes Puissances au XX siècle," *Revue générale de Droit International Public,* 1954.

Koo, Wellington. *Voting Procedures in International Political Organisation,* New York, 1947.

Kunz, Josef. "The Bogota Charter and the Organisation of American States," *American Journal of International Law,* 1948.

Lapradelle, Alfred de. "La Conférence de la Paix," *Revue générale de Droit International Public,* 1899.

Padirac, Raoul. *L'egalité des etats et l'organisation internationale,* Paris, 1953.

Prélot, Marcel. "Le droit des assemblées internationales," *Recueil des Cours,* The Hague, 1961.

Scelle, Georges. *L'Evolution des Conférences internationales,* UNESCO, Bulletin international des Sciences Sociales, 1953.

Streit, Georges. "Les Grandes puissances dans le Droit international," *La Revue de Droit international et de Législation comparée,* 1900.

2. Antecedents and the League of Nations

Andrassy, Juraj. *La souveraineté et la Société des Nations,* Paris, 1938.

Depuis, Charles. "Les antécédents de la Société des Nations," *Recueil des Cours,* 1937.

Goodrich, Leland. "From League of Nations to the United Nations," *International Organisation,* 1947.

Hoffmann, Stanley. *Organisations internationales et pouvoirs politiques des Etats,* Paris, 1954.

Radojkovich, Milos. *La Révision des Traités et le Pacte de la Société des Nations,* Paris, 1930.

Scelle, Georges. *Le Pacte des Nations et sa liaison avec le traité de paix,* Paris, 1919.

Walters, Francis Paul. *A History of the League of Nations, I, II,* 1952.

Zimmern, Sir Alfred Eckhard. *The League of Nations and the Rule of Law, 1918–1935,* 1936.

3. Creation of the United Nations Organization

Documents of the United Nations Conference on International Organisation, (UNESCO), I–XV, 1945.

Klafkowski, Alfons. *L'Accord de Potsdam*, Warsaw, 1964.

Krilov, S. B. *Materijali k istoriji OUN*, t. I, Moscow, 1949. Materials of the United Nations History,

Pan, Stephen C. Y. "Legal Aspects of the Yalta Agreement," *American Journal of International Law*, 1952.

Chaumont, Charles. *Les Organisations internationales*, Paris, 1955.

Engel, S. "The Charter of the United Nations," *Year Book of World Affairs*, 1953.

Feller, Abraham Howard. *United Nations and World Community*, Boston, 1952.

Goodrich, Leland Matthew and Hambro, Edvard. *Charter of the United Nations*, London, 1949.

Janković, Branimir. "Verfahren zur Revision der Satzung der Vereinten Nationen," *Jahrbuch für Internationales Recht*, 1956.

Kelsen, Hans. *The Law of the United Nations*, London, 1951.

Schlochauer, Hans. "Quelques aspects de la révision de la Charte des Nations Unies," *Revue générale de droit international public*, 1961.

Schwelb, Egon. "Amendments to Articles 23, 27 and 61 of the Charter of the United Nations," *American Journal of International Law*, 1965.

Verdross, Alfred von. "Idées directrices de l'Organisation des Nations Unies," *Recueil des Cours*, The Hague, 1953.

Wright, Quincy. "The Jural Personality of the United Nations," *American Journal of International Law*, 1949.

5. Membership

Berlia, Georges. "Admission, d'un Etat aux Nations Unies," *Revue Générale de droit international public*, 1949.

Hsueh, ____ . *L'Organisation des Nations Unies et les Etats non members*, Paris, 1953.

Kelsen, Hans. "Du droit de se retirer de l'ONU," *Revue Générale de droit international public*, 1948.

Livingstone, Frances. "Withdrawal from the United Nations, - Indonesia," *International and Comparative Law Quarterly*, 1965.

Unni, A. C. C. "Indonesia's Withdrawal from the United Nations," *Indian Journal of International Law*, 1965.

6. Organs

Tung, Lin William. *International Organization under the United Nations,* New York, 1969.

7. The United Nations General Assembly

Barbier, ____ . *Le Comité de Décolonisation des Nations Unies,* Paris, 1974.

Brugiere, Pierre F. *Les pouvoirs de L'Assemblée générale des Nations Unies en matière politique et de sécurité,* Paris, 1955.

Johnson, D. H. N. "The Effect of Resolution of the General Assembly of the United Nations," *British Yearbook of International Law,* 1955/56.

Haviland, Henry Field. *The Political Role of the General Assembly,* New York, 1951.

8. The Security Council

Arechaga, Eduardo Jiménez de. *Voting and the Handling of Dispute in the Security Council,* New York, 1950.

Brugière, P. F. "La règle de l'unanimité des membres permanents au Conseil de Sécurité," *Droit de veto,* Paris, 1952.

Chassèriaux, Georges. *Le veto en droit international,* Paris, 1948.

Day, George. *Le droit de veto dans l'ONU,* Paris, 1952.

Koo, Wellington. *Voting Procedures in International Political Organisation,* New York, 1947.

Lacharière, R. "L'Accord des grandes puissances dans la Charte des Nations Unies," *Annales Universitatis Saraviensis,* 1952.

Preux, Jean de. *Le droit de veto dans la Charte des Nations Unies,* Paris, 1949.

Rudzinski, Alexander W. "The So-called Double Veto," *American Journal of International Law,* 1951.

Salomon, André. *L'ONU et la Paix,* Paris, 1948.

9. The Economic and Social Council

Aleksandrowicz, Charles Henry. *International Economic Organizations,* New York, 1953.

Fortman, ____ . "The United Nations and the Underdeveloped Areas," *The United Nations Ten Years Legal Progress,* The Hague, 1956.

Padelford, Norman J. "Politics and the Future of the Economic and Social Council," *International Organisation,* 1961.

10. The Trusteeship Council

Bailey, Sydney D. "The Future Composition of the Trusteeship," *International organisation,* 1959.

Beauté, Jean. *Le Droit de Pétitions dans les Territoires sous Tutelle,* Paris, 1963.

Štein, Dj. *Sistema meždunarodni opeki,* Moscow, 1948.

Vedovato, Giuseppe. "Les Accords de tutelle," *Recueil des Cours,* The Hague, 1950.

11. The Secretariat

Goodrich, Leland. "The Political Role of the Secretary-General," *International Organisation,* 1962.

Bastid, Suzanne. "Le Statut juridique des fonctionnaires de l'ONU," *The United Nations Ten Years Legal Progress,* The Hague, 1956.

Cohen, Maxwell. "The United Nations Secretariat," *American Journal of International Law,* 1955.

Jankovič, Branimir, "The Concept of Troika in International Law," *The Harvard International Law Journal,* 1962.

Langrod, Georges S. "Problème du Sécrétariat international," *Revue générale de droit international public,* 1957.

Siotis, Jean. *Essai sur le Sécrétariat international,* Genève, 1963.

Swift, Richard N. "Personnel Problems and the United Nations Secretariat," *International Organisation,* 1957.

Virally, Michel. "Le Rôle de Secrétaire Général des Nations Unies," *Annuaire français de droit international,* 1958.

12. Specialized Agencies

Alexandrowicz, Charles Henry. *International Economic Organisation,* 1953.

Blagoev, Borislav. "La Yugoslavie et l' Organisation internationale de Travail," *Yugoslav Review of International Law,* 1956.

Pollaczek, Gustav. "The United Nations and Specialized Agencies," *American Journal of International Law,* 1946.

Saba, Hanna. "L' activité quasi-legislative des institutions specialisées des Nations Unies," *Recueil des Cours,* The Hague, 1964.

Sulkowski, Joseph. "Competence of the International Labor Organisation under the UN System," *American Journal of International Law,* 1951.

13. Regional Arrangements and Agencies

Yepes, J. M. "La Conférence Panaméricaine de Bogota et la droit international américain," *Revue générale de droit international public,* 1949.

14. Other International Organizations

Stošić, Borko. *Les Organisations non gouvernementales et les Nations Unies,* Geneva, 1964.

White, Lyman Aymard C. "Les organisations non gouvernementales et leurs relations avec les Nations Unies," *Revue générale de droit international public,* 1952.

Chapter Three: Man as a Subject of International Law

1. Introduction

Cassin, René. "La Declaration universelle et la mise en oevre des droits de l'homme," *Recueil des Cours,* The Hague, 1951.

Jevremović, Brana. "Consideration sur l'unité des droit de l'homme politiques et civils et economiques et sociaux dans la pratique Yougoslave," *Yugoslav Review of International Law,* 1956.

Lauterpacht, Hersh. *International Law and Human Rights,* London, 1950.

McDougal-Bebr. "Human Rights in the United Nations," *American Journal of International Law,* 1964.

Milenkovíc, Slobodan. *Unutrašnja nadležnost država i medjunerodna zaštita ljudskih prava,* Belgrade, 1974.

Moskowitz, Moses. *The Politics and Dynamics of Human Rights,* New York, 1968.

Norgaard, ____ . *The Position of the Individual in International Law,* Copenhagen, 1962.

Mirkine-Guetzevitch, Boris. "L'ONU et doctrine moderne des droits de l'homme," *Revue générale de droit international public,* 1952.

Sohn, Louis B. and Buergenthal, Thomas. *International Protection of Human Rights,* New York, 1973.

2. Fundamental Human rights

Aroneanu, Eugène. *Le Crime contre l'humanité,* Paris, 1961.

Božović, Aleksandra. "Some Tendencies in the Develpment of the Right of Self-determination," *Yugoslav Review of International Law,* 1958.

Drost, Pieter Nicolaas. *The Crime of State,* Leyden, 1959.

Heuven Goedhart, G. J. van. "The Problem of Refugees," *Recueil des Cours,* The Hague, 1953.

Koziebrodzki, ____ . *Le Droit d'Asile,* Leyden, 1962.

Luard, David Evan Trant, ed. *The International Protection of Human Rights,* London, 1967.

Morgenstern, Felice. "The Right of Asylum," *The British Yearbook of International Law,* 1949.

Thirkovitch, Stevan. "La règle de non-discrimination et la protection des minorités," *Revue générale de droit international public,* 1951.
Woetzel, Robert K. *The Nuremberg Trials in International Law,* London, 1960.

3. Regional Universal Protection

Modinos, Polys. "La Convention européenne des droits de l'homme," *Revue générale de droit international public,* 1956.
Schwelb, Egon. "On the Operation of the European Convention on Human Rights," *International Organisation,* 1964.
Vasak, Karel. *La Convention Européenne des droits de l'homme,* Paris, 1964.
Weil, Gordon Lee. *The European Convention on Human Rights, Background, Development and Respects,* Leyden, 1963.

PART II — Legal Regulation of International Relations

1. Introduction

Genet, R. *Traité de diplomatie et de droit diplomatique, I, II, III,* Paris, 1930–1932.
Dillard, Hardy C. "Some aspects of law and diplomacy," *Recueil des Cours,* The Hague, 1957.
Diplomatic Vocabulary, Moscow, 1948.
Jessup, Philip. "Parliamentary Diplomacy; An Examination of the Legal Quality of the Rules of Procedure of Organs of the United Nations," *Recueil des Cours,* The Hague, 1956.
Naggiar, _____ . "Diplomatie, ancienne et nouvelle," *Revue d'histoire diplomatique,* 1952.
Nicolson, Harold. *Diplomatie,* Neuchâtel, 1948.
Szilassy, J. de. *Manuel pratique de la diplomatie moderne,* Paris, 1925.

2. Chief of State

Djordjević, Jovan. "La Constitution de la Yougoslavie et le droit international," *Yugoslav Review of International Law,* 1956.
_____ . *Introduction in Constitutional Law,* 1966.
Wolther, _____ . *Das Staatshaupt in den Republiken,* 1907.

3. Government and the Minister of Foreign Affairs

Castberg, F. "Le Conflit du Groenland," *Revue générale de droit international et de legislation comparée,* III, serie, t., V.

Tilley and Gaselec. *The Foreign Office,* 1933.

Kraus, ____ . *Der auswärtige Dienst des Deutschen Reiches,* 1931.

4. Diplomatic Representatives

Berlia, Georges. "Contribution a l'étude de la nature de la protection diplomatique," *Annuaire français de droit international,* 1957.

Cahier, Philippe. *La droit diplomatique contemporain,* Geneva, 1964.

Chesney, "Diplomatic and Consular Immunity," *American Journal of International Law,* 1957.

Colliard, C. ____ . "La Convention de Vienne sur les relations diplomatiques," *Annuaire français de droit international,* 1961.

Deener, David R. "Some Problems of the Law of Diplomatic Immunity," *American Journal of International Law,* 1956.

Genet, R. *Traité de diplomatie et de droit diplomatique I, II, III,* Paris, 1930–1932.

Geršić, Gliša. *Contemporary Diplomatic and Consular Law,* Belgrade, 1898.

Hurst, Sir Cecil. "Les immunités diplomatiques," *Recueil des Cours,* The Hague, 1926, N. 12.

Rousseau, Charles. "Agents diplomatiques et consuls," *Revue générale de droit international public,* 1958.

Satow, Sir Ernest Mason. *A Guide to Diplomatic Practice,* 1932.

Tunkin, Grigorij. "Questions of Diplomatic Law on Session of the Commission for International Law," *Sovetskoe gosudarstvo i pravo,* 1957.

Wolgast, Ernst. "La diplomatie te ses fonctions," *Recueil des Cours,* The Hague, 1937, N. 60.

5. International Officials

Bogdanov, O. V. "Immunities of Officials of International Organization in Contemporary International Law," *Sovetskoe gosudarstvo i pravo,* 1956.

Hill, William Martin. *Immunities and Privileges of International Officials,* Washington, 1947.

Kunz, Josef. "Privileges and Immunities of International Organisations," *American Journal of International Law,* 1947.

Perrin, M. "Les privilèges et immunités des représentants des Etats auprès des organisations internationales," *Revue générale de droit international public,* 1956.

Chapter Two: International Acts

Part One: Unilateral Legal Acts

Brüel, Erik. "La protestation en droit international," *Revue de droit international,* 1932.

Garner, James W. "The International Binding Force of Unilateral Oral Declaration," *American Journal of International Law,* 1933.

Pflüger, Heinz. *Die Einseitigen Rechtsgeschäfte im Völkerrecht,* 1936.

Rödiger, ____. *Notifikation, Wörterbuch des Völkerrechts,* Band II.

Rousseau, Charles. *Principes généraux du droit international public,* t. I. Paris, 1944.

Schlochauer, Hans Jürgen. *Wörterbuch des Völkerrechts,* 1960, 1961, 1962.

Suy, Eric. *Les actes juridiques unilatéraux en droit international public,* 1962.

6. Conculs

Heyking, Alfons. "La théorie et la partique des services consulaires," *Recueil des Cours,* The Hague, 1930. n. 34.

Libera, Kazimierz. *Prawo konsularne,* Warsaw, 1952.

Lee, Luke T. "Consular Status under Unrecognized Regimes," *British Year Book of International Law,* Oxford, 1955/1956.

Turack, Daniel C. *The Passport in International Law,* Toronto, 1972.

Part Two: International Treaties

1. Introduction

Arechaga, Eduardo Jiménez D. de. "Treaty Stimulations in Favor of Third States," *American Journal of International Law,* 1956.

Ballreich, ____. "Völkerrechteiche Verträge zu Lasten Dritter," Max-Planck-Institut für ausländiches Recht und Völkerecht, Heidelberg, Heft 29, 1954.

Brandon, Michael. "Analysis of the Terms 'Treaty' and 'Agreement' for Purposes of Registration under Art. 102 the UN Charter," *American Journal of International Law,* 1953.

Genet, R. "Le Problème de la clause 'Rebus sic stantibus,' " *Revue Générale de droit international public,* 1930.

Heyde, ____. *Interpretation of Treaties,* 1909.

Hoijer, Olof. *Les traités internationaux,* Paris, 1958.

Lachs, Manfred. "Le développement et fonctions des traités multilatéraux," *Recueil des Cours,* The Hague, N. 92, 1957.

Milovanowisch, Milovan. *Les traités de garantie au XIX-ème sièle,* Paris, 1901.

McNair, Arnold Duncan. *The Law of treaties,* Oxford, 1961.

Pereterski, _____ . "Meaning of International Treaties Towards Third States," *Sovetskoe gosudarstvo i pravo,* 1957.

Radojković, Miloš. *La révision des traités et la Pacte de la Société des Nations,* Paris, 1930.

Rosenne, Shabtai. "United Nations Treaty Practice," *Recueil des Cours,* The Hague, No. 86, 1954.

Satow, Sir Ernest Mason. *Guide to Diplomatic Practice,* 1957.

Siorat, Lucien. *Le problèm des lacunes en droit international,* Paris, 1959.

Suršalov, V. M. "Juridical Content of the Principle *PACTA SUNT SERVANDA* and Its Realisation in International Relations," *Sovetski ežgodnik meždunarodnog prava,* 1959.

Tomšić, Ivan. *La réconstruction du droit international en matière des traités,* 1931.

Vellas, Pierre. *Contribution à l'étude des obligations à la charge des tiers en droit international public,* Paris, 1950.

Vischer, C. de. "Methodologische Fragen bei der objektiven Ankupfung im Internationalen Vertragsrecht," *Annuaire Suisse de Droit International,* 1956.

2. Treaty Making Power

Blix, Hans. *Treaty Making Power,* London, 1960.

Huber, J. *Le droit de conclure des traités,* Paris, 1951.

Pallieri, Comte Giorgio Balladore. "La formation des traités dans la pratique internationale contemporaine," *Recueil des Cours,* The Hague, 1949.

Parry, Clive. "Treaty Making Power of the United Nations," *Recueil des Cours,* The Hague, 1956.

Schneider, Johannes Wilhelmus. *Treaty Making Power of International Organisations,* Geneva, 1959.

Zemaneck, Karl. *Das Vertragsrecht des internationalen Organizationen,* Wien, 1957.

3. Origin of Treaty

Blix, Hans. "The Requirement Ratification," *British Yearbook of International Law,* 1953.

Brandon, Michael. "Analysis of the Terms, 'Treaty' and 'Agreement' for Purposes of Registration under art. 102 of the UN Charter," *American Journal of International Law,* 1953.

_____ . "The Validity of Non Registered Treaties," *British Yearbook of International Law,* 1952.

_____ . *Treaty Making Power,* London, 1960.

Fitzmaurice, G. G. "Do Treaties Need Ratification?," *British Yearbook of International Law,* 1934.

Jessup, Philip. "Modernization of Law of International Contractual Agreements," *American Journal of International Law,* 1947.

Liang, Yuen-Li. "The Use of the Term, 'Acceptance' in the Treaty Practice of United Nations," *American Journal of International Law,* 1950.

Lukachuk, I. L. *Parties in International Treaties,* Moscow, 1966.

Rosenne, Shabtai. "United Nations Treaty Practice," *Recueil des Cours,* The Hague, 1959.

Schneider, Johannes Wilhelmus. *Treaty-making Power of International Organizations,* Geneva, 1959.

Weinstein, ____ . "Exchanges of Notes," *British Yearbook of International Law,* 1952.

4. Observance, Application and Interpretation of Treaties

Fenwick, Charles. "Reservations to Multilateral Treaties," *American Journal of International Law,* 1952.

Hambro, E. "The Interpretation of Multilateral Treaties by the International Court of Justice," *Grotius Society,* 1953.

Liang, Yuen-Li. "Colonial Clauses and Federal Clauses in United Nations Multilateral Instruments," *American Journal of International Law,* 1950.

Sur, Serge. *L' Interpretation en droit international public,* Paris, 1974.

Visscher, Charles de. *Problèmes d'interprétation judiciare en droit international public,* 1963.

5. Effect of Treaties and the Principle

Kelsen, Hans. "Traités internationaux à la charge d'Etats tiers," *Mélanges Mahaim,* 1935.

Roxbourgh, Ronald Francis. *International Conventions and Third States,* London, 1917.

6. Fulfilment of Treaties

Berthoud, ____ . *Le contrôle internationale de l'exécution des conventions collectives,* Geneva, 1946.

7. Amendment of Treaties

Blix, Hans. "The Rule of Unanimity in the Revision of Treaties," *International and Comparative Law Quarterly,* 1956.

Hoyt, Edwin Chase. *The Unanimity Rule in the Revision of Treaties,* 1959.

Radojković, Miloš. *La révision des traités et la Pacte de la Société des Nations,* Paris, 1930.

Scelle, Georges. *Théorie juridique de la révision des traités,* Paris, 1936.

8. Termination and Suspension of Treaties

Anzilotti, D. "La clause Rebus sic stantibus," *Revue générale de droit international,* 1930.

Garner, J. W. "The Doctrine of *Rebus sic stantibus* and the Termination of Treaties," *American Journal of International Law,* 1927.

Giraud, ____ . "Modification et termination des traités collectifs," *Annuaire de l'institut de droit international,* 1961.

Hill, William Martin. *The Doctrine* REBUS SIC STANTIBUS *in International Law,* 1934.

McNair, Arnold Duncan. "La terminaison des et la dissolution des traités," *Recueil des Cours,* The Hague, 1928.

Simeonoff, ____ . "La Clause Rebus sic stantibus," *Revue de droit international,* 1949.

Tobin, Harold James. *The Termination of Multipartite Treaties,* New York, 1933.

9. Effect of War on International Treaties

Dennis, William C. "Effect of War on Treaties," *American Journal of International Law,* 1929.

Lesser, ____ . "International Law - Treaty Provisions Dealing with the Status of Prewar Bilateral Treaties," *Michigan Law Review,* 1953.

McNair, Arnold Duncan. "Les Effets de la Guerre sur les Traités," *Recueil des Cours,* The Hague, 1937.

Ränk, ____ . *Einwirkung des Krieges auf die nichtpolitischen Staatsverträge,* Uppsala, 1942.

Webber, ____ . "Effects of War on Contracts," *Grotius Society,* 1947.

Wolf, ____ . *The Problem of Prewar Contracts in Peace Treaties,* London, 1946.

10. State Succession and International Treaties

Bartoš, Milan. "Les nouveaux Etats et les Traités internationaux," *Yugoslav Review of International Law,* 1962.

Jenks, Wilfred C. "State Succession in Respect of Law Making Treaties," *British Yearbook of International Law,* 1952.

O'Connell, Daniel Patrick. *The Law of State Succession,* Cambridge, 1956.

Muralt, ____ . *The Problem of State Succession with Regard to Treaties,* The Hague, 1954.

Chapter Three: Peaceful Settlement of Disputes and the Safeguarding of Peace

1. Introduction

Bilfinger, ____ ."Vom politischen und nichtpolitischen Recht in organisatorischen Kollektivvertragen," *Zeitschrift für ausländisches öffentliches Recht und Völkerrecht,* 1951.

Bulajić, ____ . "World Peace Through Law," *Yugoslav Review of International Law,* 1962.

Janovski, ____ . *Peaceful Means of Settlement of International Disputes,* Taškent, 1957.

Kiss, ____ . "Convention europeenne pour le reglement pacifique des differends," *Annuaire français de droit international,* 1957.

Stone, Julius. *Legal Controls of International Conflict,* New York, 1954.

Šurmazanašvili, ____ . "Peaceful Settlement of International Disputes," *Sovetskoe gosudarstvo i pravo,* 1962.

Račić, Obrad. "Peaceful settlement of Disputes," *Annuary of the Institute for International Politics and Economie,* Belgrade, 1963.

Vaucher, Marius. *Le probleme de la justiciabilité et de la non justiciabilité en droit international des differends,* Paris, 1951.

Part One: Means of Peaceful Settlement of Disputes

1. Negotiations

2. Inquiry

Andrassy, Yuraj. *International Judiciary,* Zagreb, 1948.

3. Mediation

Jackson, ____ . "Mediation and Conciliation in International Law," *International Social Science Bulletin,* 1958.

4. Conciliation

Efremoff, Jean. "L'Organization de la concilation comme moyen de prevenir les guerres," *Recueil des Cours,* The Hague, 1937.

Rolin, H. "L'heure de la conciliation comme mode de reglement pacifique de litiges," *Annuaire Europeen,* The Hague, 1957.

Markovitsch, ____ . *Les traités de conciliation et d'arbitrage de la Yougoslavie,* Paris, 1932.

Schücking, ____ . *Das Völkerrechtliche Institut der Vermittlung,* 1923.

5. Arbitration

Carlston, Kenneth Smith. *The Process of International Arbitration,* 1946.

François, J. P. A. "La Cour pèrmanente d'arbitrage, son origine, sa jurisprudence et son avenir," *Recueil des Cours,* The Hague, 1955.

Guyomar, ____ . "L'arbitrage concernant les rapports entre Etats et particuliers," *Annuaire français de droit international,* 1953.

Schachter, Oscar. "The Enforcement of International Juridical and Artibral Decisions," *The American Journal of International Law,* 1960.

Novakovic, ____ . *Les compromis et les arbitrages internationaux du XII au XV siècle,* Paris, 1905.

Stoykovitch, ____ . *L'autorite de la sentence arbitrale en droit international,* 1924.

6. The International Court of Justice

Bastid, Susanne. "La Jurisprudence de la Cour internationale," *Recueil des Cours,* The Hague, 1951.

Borisov, ____ . "U.N. International Court in 1955." *Sovetskoe gosudarstvo i pravo,* 1956.

Briggs, Herbert W. "Reservations to the Acceptance of Compulsory Jurisdiction of the International Court of Justice," *Recueil des Cours,* The Hague, 1958.

Fitzmaurice, G. G. "The Law and Procedure of the International Court of Justice," *British Year Book of International Law,* 1955/56.

Hambro, Edvard Isak. *The Case Law of the International Court,* Leyden, 1952.

Kerno, Ivan S. "L'Organisation des Nations Unies et la Cour de Justice Internationale," *Recueil des Cours,* The Hague, 1951.

Lauterpacht, Hersh. *The Development of International Law by the International Court,* London, 1958.

Negulesco, Démètre. "L'evolution de la procedure des avis consultatif de la Cour permanente de justice," *Recueil des Cours,* 1938.

Sirat, Charles. "Le President de la Cour internationale de Justice," *Revue générale de droit international public,* 1958.

Sörensen, Max. "The International Court of Justice: Its Role in Contemporary International Relations," *International Organisation,* 1960.

Stone, Julius. "The International Court and World Crisis," *International Conciliation,* 1962.

Schwarzenberger, George. *International Law as applied by International Courts and Tribunals,* London, 1949.

Part Two: Maintenance of Peace

1. Maintenance of Peace Under the UN Charter

Andrassy, Juraj. "Uniting for Peace," *American Journal of International Law,* 1956.

Bowett, Derek. "Collective Self-Defence Under the Charter of the United Nations," *British Year Book of International Law,* 1955/56.

Cavaré, Louis. "Les sanctions dans le cadre de l'O.N.U.," *Recueil des Cours,* The Hague, 1952.

Goodrich, Leland Matthew and Simons, Anne P. *The United Nations and the Maintenance of International Peace and Security,* Washington, 1955.

Kelsen, Hans. "Problems of Collective Security," *Annuaire de l'association des auditeurs de l'academie de droit international de la Haye,* 1958.

2. Procedure for the Peaceful Settlement of Disputes Under the Auspices of the United Nations

Arechaga, Eduardo Jiménez de. "Le traitement des differends internationaux par le Conseil de Securite," *Recueil des Cours,* The Hague, 1954.

Kerley, Ernest. "The Power of Investigations of the United Nations Security Council," *The American Journal of International Law,,* 1961.

Schachter, Oscar. "The Quasi-Judicial Role of the Security Council and the General Assembly," *The American Journal of International Law,* 1964.

Vallat, Francis Aimé. "The Competence of the United Nations General Assembly," *Recueil des Cours,* The Hague, 1959.

3. Procedure for the Maintenance of Peace

Komarnicki, Waclaw. "La definition de l'agresseur dans le droit international moderne," *Recueil des Cours*, The Hague, 1949.

Ninčić, ____ . "The problem of Collective Measures," *Yugoslav Review of International Law*, 1956.

Pereterski, ____ . "Concept of Guaranties in International Law," *Sovetskoe gosudarstvo i pravo*, 1956.

Semenov, ____ . "Some Problems of the Use of Armed Forces of the UN," *Sovetski ežegodnjik meždunarodnogo prava*, 1964–1965.

Sohn, Louis B. "Authority of the United Nations to Establish and Maintain a Permanent United Nations Force," *American Journal of International Law*, 1958.

Wehberg, Hans. "L'interdiction du recours à la force," *Recueil des Cours*, The Hague, 1951.

Žourek, Jaroslav. "La definition de l'agression et le droit international," *Recueil des Cours*, The Hague, 1957.

Chapter Four: International Conflicts

1. Compulsive Means of Settlement of International Disputes

Castren, Erik Johannes Sakari. *The Present Law of War and Neutrality*, 1954.

Delbez, Louis. *La notion de guerre*, 1953.

Green, Leslie C. "Armed Conflict, War and Self-Defence," *Archiv des Völkerrecht*, 1957.

Jessup, Philip. "Political and Humanitarian Approaches to Limitation of Warfare," *American Journal of International Law*, 1957.

Kotzsch, Lothar. *The Concept of War in Contemporary History and International Law*, 1956.

Yokota, ____ . "War as an International Crime," *Festschrift Spiropoulos*, 1957.

2. Sources of the Law of War

Constantopoulos, D. S. "Les rasions de la crise du droit de la guerre," *Jahrbuch für internationales Recht*, 1956.

Genet, R. *Precis de droit maritime pour le temps de guerre*, 1937.

Huber, Max. "Quelques considerations sur une revision eventuelle des Conventions de la Haye rélatives à la guerre," *Revue internationale de la Croix - Rouge*, 1955.

Krylov, Sergei Borisovitch. "Les nations principales du droit de guerre," *Recueil des Cours*, The Hague, 1947.

Kunz, Josef L. "La crise et les transformations du droit des gens," *Recueil des Cours*, The Hague, 1955.

_____ . "The Law of War," *American Journal of International Law*, 1956.

Marin Luna, Miguel A. "The Evolution and Present Status of the Law of War," *Recueil des Cours*, 1957.

Rolin, Henri. *Le droit moderne de la guerre, I, II, III*, 1920–1921.

Sandiford, Roberto. "Evolution du droit de la guere maritime et aerienne," *Recueil des Cours*, 1939.

Spajingt, ____ . *Air Power and War Rights*, 1947.

Stone, Julius. *Legal Controls of International Conflict*, New York, 1954.

3. Commencement of Hostilities

Aroneau, ____ . "Le conflit israelo-egyptien et la justice internationale," *Revue de droit international de science diplomatiques et politiques*, 1957.

Asbeck, ____ . *Das Ultimatum im modernen Kriegsrecht*, 1933.

McNair, Sir Arnold Duncan. *Legal Effects of War*, 1948.

4. The Region of War

5. Armed Forces

6. Parties to a Conflict

Siotis, ____ . *Le droit de la guerre et les conflits armes d'un caractère non-international*, Paris, 1958.

Schmid, ____ . *Die völkerrechtliche Stellung der Partisanen im Kriege*, Zürich, 1956.

7. Recognition of the National Liberation Army of the Peoples of Yugoslavia as a Belligerent

8. The Protecting Power

Janner, ____ . *La puissance protectrice en droit international, d'apres les experiences faites par la Suisse pendant la Seconde guerre mondiale*, Basel, 1948.

Siordet, ____ . *Le problème du contrôle*, Geneva, 1952.

Franklin, William McHenry. *Protections of Foreign Interests,* Washington, 1947.

9. Restraints in Warfare

Charpentier, ____ . *L'humanisation de la guerre aerienne,* 1938.

Kosović, ____ . "Consideration on the Necessity of Review of the International Law Concerning the War," *Yugoslav Review of International Law,* 1956.

Röhrig, ____ . *Die Ziele selbständiger Luftangriffe,* 1938.

Sloutzky, N. "Le bombardement aerien des objectivs militaires," *Revue générale de droit international public,* 1957.

10. Relations Between Parties to a Conflict

Stone, Julius. *Legal Controls of International Conflict,* New York, 1954.

11. Protected Persons in a Military Conflict

Andrassy, Juraj. "L'Individu en droit international humanitaire," *Festschrift Spiropoulos,* 1957.

Castren, Eric. "La protection juridique de la population civile dans la guerre moderne," *Revue générale de droit international public,* 1955.

Coursier, ____ . "Le Comité international de la Croix - Rouge et la protection des populations civiles en temps de guerre," *Annuaire de l'association des auditeurs de l'academie de droit international de la Haye,* 1958.

_____ . "Definition d'un droit humanitaire," *Annuaire français de droit international,* 1955.

Huber, Max. "Le droit des gens et l'humanite," *Revue internationale de la Croix - Rouge,* 1952.

Ivanović, Djoko. "Des mesures propres à garantir l'observation des Conventions de Geneve relatives à la protection des victimes de la guerre," *Yugoslav Review of International Law,* 1958.

Pictet, Jean S. "La Croix-Rouge et les Conventions de Geneve," *Recueil des Cours,* The Hague, 1950.

12. Military Occupation

Lemkin, ____ . *Axis Rule in Occupied Europe,* 1944.

Novaković, ____ . *L'occupation austro-bulgare en Serbie,* 1918.

13. Neutrality

Boye, Thorvald. "Quelques aspects du developpement des regles de la neutralite," *Recueil des Cours,* The Hague, 1938.

Jessup, Philip and Deak, Francis. *Neutrality, I, II, III, IV.,* 1935–1939.

Komarnicky, Titus. "The Place of Neutrality in the Modern System of International Law," *Recueil des Cours,* The Hague, 1952.

Kunz, Josef L. *Kriegsrecht und Neutralitätsrecht,* 1935.

Politis, Nicolas Socrate. *La neutralité et la paix,* 1935.

Waldkirch. "Militärische Rechte und Pflichten des neutralen Staates im Luftkriege, unter besonderer Berücksichtigung der Schweiz 1939–1945," *Jahrbuch für internationales Recht,* 1955.

14. The End of War

Selected Bibliography

Andrassy, Andraj. *Medjunarodno pravo.* Zagreb, 1971.
Anzilotti, Dionisio. *Cours de droit international.* Paris, 1929.
Avramov, Smilja. *Medjunarodno javno pravo.* Belgrade, 1963.
Annual Digest and Reports of Public International Law. Annuaire de la Commission de Droit International, 1950–1966.

Bartoš, Milan. *Medjunarodno javno pravo.* Belgrade, 1951.
_____ . *Medjunarodno javno pravo,* I, II, III. Belgrade 1954, 1956, 1958.
Berezowski, Cezary. *Mjedzynarodowe prawo publiczne.* Warsaw, 1953.
Blagojević, Borislav. *Medjunarodno privatno pravo.* Belgrade, 1950.
Bluntschli, Johann Kaspar. *Das moderne Völkerrecht der zivilisierten Staaten.* Nordlingen, 1978.
_____ . *Le droit international codifié.* Paris, 1886.
Brierly, James Leslie. *The Law of Nations.* Oxford, 1950.
Briggs, Herbert Whittaker. *The Law of Nations: Cases, Documents and Notes.* New York, 1952.

Cavare, Louis. *Traité de droit international public positif,* I, II. Paris, 1951.
Chaumont, Charles. *Les Organisations internationales,* fasc. I, II. Paris, 1955.
Colliard, Claude Albert. *Droit international et histoire diplomatique.* Paris, 1950.

Dahm, Georg. *Völkerrecht,* I, II. 1958, 1961.
Depuy, René-Jean. *International Law.* UNESCO, Paris, 1967.
Delbez, Louis. *Manuel de droit international public.* Paris, 1948.
Durdenevski-Krilov (ed.). *Meždunarodnoe pravo.* Moscow, 1947.

Fauchille, Paul. *Traité de droit international public.* Paris, 1921, 1922, 1925, 1926.
Fenwick, Charles Gheguiere. *Cases on International Law.* 1935.
_____ . *International Law.* New York, 1948.
Funk-Brentano and Sorel. *Medjunarodno javno pravo.* Belgrade, 1893.

Gavranov-Stojkovic. *Medjunarodni odnosi i spoljna politika Jugoslavije.* Belgrade, 1972
Geamanu, Grigore. *Dreptul international contemporain.* Bucharest, 1965.
Green, Leslie C. *International Law Through the Cases.* London, 1951.
Guggenheim, Paul. *Traité de droit international public.* Geneva, 1953.

Hackworth, Green Haywood. *Digest of International Law,* I–VIII. 1940–1944.
Hambro, Edvard Isak. *The Case Law of the International Court.* Leyden, 1952.
Harris, D. J. *Cases and Materials on International Law.* London, 1979.
Hold-Ferneck, H. *Lehrbuch des Völkerrechts.* Leipzig, 1930.
Hudson, Manley O. *International Legislation,* I–IX. Washington, 1931–1951.
Hyde, Charles Cheney. *International Law,* I, II, III. Boston, 1951.

Jessup, Philip. *A Modern Law of Nations.* New York, 1956.

Kelsen, Hans. *Principles of International Law.* New York, 1952.
Korovin, Evgenii Aleksandrovich. *Mezdunarodnoe pravo.* Moscow, 1951.
Kozevnikov, F. I. *Ucebnoe posobie po mezdunarodnomu publicnomu pravu.* Moscow, 1947.
——————. ed. *Kurs mezdunarodnogo prava,* I, II, III. Moscow, 1967.

La Pradelle, Paul. *Cours de droit international public.* Aix-en-Provence, 1954.
La Pradelle, Paul and Niboyet, ____ . *Repertoire de droit International,* I–X. 1929–1934.
Le Fir, Luj. *Medjunarodno javno pravo.* Belgrade, 1934.
Le Fir and Chklaver. *Recueil des Textes de droit international.* Paris, 1934.
Liszt, Franz von. *Das Völkerrecht.* Berlin, 1925.
Lorimer, James. *Principés de droit international.* Brussels, 1885.

McDougal, Myres S. *Studies in World Public Order.* New York, 1960.
Magarasevic, Aleksandar. *Osnovi medjunarodnog prava.* Novi Sad, 1965.
Martens, Fedor Fedorovich. *Traité de droit international,* I–III. Paris, 1881, 1886, 1887.
Moore, John Bassett. *A Digest of International Law,* I–X. Washington, 1906.

Novakovic, Milata. *Osnovi medjunarodnog javnog prava,* I, II. Belgrade, 1936, 1938.
Nys, Ernest. *Le droit international,* I–III. Brussels, 1904, 1906.

Oppenheim , Lassa Francis Lawrence and Lauterpacht, E. *International Law,* I.II. London, 1952.

Pavithran, A. K. *Substance of Public International Law.* Madras, 1965.

Pradier-Fodéré, Paul Louis Ernest. *Traité de droit international public et americain, I–VI. Paris, 1885, 1887, 1888, 1891, 1894, 1897.*

Racic, Obrad. *Medjunarodne organizacije.* Belgrade.

Radojkovic, Milos. *Medjunarodno javno pravo.* Belgrade, 1957.

Redslob, Robert. *Les principés du droit des gens moderne.* Paris, 1937.

_____ . *Traite de Droit des Gens.* Paris, 1950.

Rousseau, Charles. *Droit international public.* Paris, 1953.

Sauer, Ernst Friedrich. *Grundlehre des Völkerrechts.* Cologne-Berlin, 1955.

Scelle, Georges. *Manuel de droit international public.* Paris, 1948.

_____ . *Précis de droit des gens, I, II.* Paris, 1934.

Schwarzenberger, George. *A Manual of International Law.* London, 1950.

_____ . *International Law as Applied by International Courts and Tribunals, I.* London, 1949.

Sibert, Marcel, *Traité de droit international public, I, II.* Paris, 1951.

Sohn, Louis B. *Cases and Materials on United Nations Law.* Brooklyn, 1956.

Sorensen, Max. *Manual of Public International Law.* 1968.

Spiropoulos, Jean. *Theorie générale du droit international.* Paris, 1930.

Strupp, Karl. *Documents pour servir a l'Histoire de droit des gens, I–V.* 1923.

_____ . Elements de droit international public universel, europèen et americain. Paris, 1927.

_____ . *Grundzüge des positiven Völkerrechts.* Bonn, 1928.

Tunkin, Grigorij. *Voprosi teorii meduzjnarodnoga pravo.* Moscow,

Twiss, Sir Travers. *Le droit des gens ou des national considerées communautées politiques independantes, I, II.* Paris, 1887, 1899.

Ullmann, Emanuel. *Völkerrecht.* Tübingen, 1908.

United Nations. *Recueil des Traites.*

_____ .*Repertoire de la Pratique suivie par les Organes des Nations Unies, I–V.* New York, 1955, 1956.

Vaifel, ____ . *Le droit des gens ou principes de la loi naturelle, I–III.* Paris, 1956.

Verdross, Alfred von. *Völkerrecht.* Wien, 1955.

Visscher, Charles de. *Theories et réalités en droit international public.* Paris, 1953.

Waldkirch, Edvard Otto von. *Das Völkerrecht in seinen Grundzügen darge stellt.* Bales, 1926.

Wengler, Wilhelm. *Völkerrecht,* I, II. Berlin, 1964.

Westlake, John. *Traité de droit international.* London, 1924.

Wheaton, Henry. *Elements du droit international,* I, II. Leipzig, 1874.

Index